VISUAL
METHODOLOGIES

For Giorgio and Lydia, again

VISUAL
METHODOLOGIES
An Introduction to Researching with Visual Materials

4TH EDITION

GILLIAN ROSE

Los Angeles | London | New Delhi
Singapore | Washington DC | Melbourne

Los Angeles | London | New Delhi
Singapore | Washington DC | Melbourne

SAGE Publications Ltd
1 Oliver's Yard
55 City Road
London EC1Y 1SP

SAGE Publications Inc.
2455 Teller Road
Thousand Oaks, California 91320

SAGE Publications India Pvt Ltd
B 1/I 1 Mohan Cooperative Industrial Area
Mathura Road
New Delhi 110 044

SAGE Publications Asia-Pacific Pte Ltd
3 Church Street
#10-04 Samsung Hub
Singapore 049483

Editor: Robert Rojek
Editorial assistant: Matthew Oldfield
Production editor: Katherine Haw
Copyeditor: Catja Pafort
Indexer: Judith Lavender
Marketing manager: Michael Ainsley
Cover design: Wendy Scott
Typeset by: C&M Digitals (P) Ltd, Chennai, India
Printed and bound in Great Britain by
Ashford Colour Press Ltd

MIX
Paper from
responsible sources
FSC
www.fsc.org   FSC® C011748

This edition first published 2016

First edition published 2001, reprinted in 2003, 2005
and 2006.
Second edition published 2006, reprinted 2006, 2007,
2008, 2010 and 2011.
Third edition published 2011, reprinted 2011, 2012, 2014
and 2015.

Library of Congress Control Number: 2015948265

British Library Cataloguing in Publication data

A catalogue record for this book is available from
the British Library

ISBN 978-1-4739-4889-1
ISBN 978-1-4739-4890-7 (pbk)

Gillian Rose has provided a welcome overview of the state of the field. *Visual Methodologies* succeeds both as an introductory text, certain to be widely adopted in the classroom, and as a sophisticated refresher course for those who have followed the rapid maturation of this remarkable interdisciplinary discourse. Added material on the latest advances in digital technology brings this latest edition to the cutting edge of visual culture studies.
Martin Jay, Ehrman Professor, University of California, Berkeley

Visual Methodologies is an indispensable resource for anyone working with visual materials. It offers practical guidance and expert theoretical orientation on how to approach, think about, and interpret visual culture, ranging from archival photography and documentary film to websites and social media. An important aspect of this book is the attention paid to audiences and viewing publics, as well as to the ethical demands of visual research. In this new edition, Gillian Rose brings the book fully up to date with contemporary developments in media arts and digital culture, and explores the new possibilities for visual research made possible by developments in software and data analytics. Whether you are new to studying visual culture or a seasoned expert seeking to refine your approach, *Visual Methodologies* has you covered.
Christoph Lindner, Professor of Media and Culture, University of Amsterdam

Visual Methodologies is an indispensable book for teaching and understanding methods in visual culture. Clear, comprehensive, and lucid, it makes accessible the how, why, and what of different methodological approaches in ways that elucidate paths to better research and argument. The constantly changing terrain of visual culture today makes many demands on scholarly and theoretical approaches, and this fourth edition does not disappoint, with updated concepts and an explanation of digital methods. As an introduction of methods in cultural studies, communication, and visual culture research, this book is unparalleled. It is essential reading for anyone writing an MA thesis of doctoral dissertation.
Marita Sturken, Professor of Media, Culture and Communication, New York University

Visual Methodologies is an essential book for all students, researchers and academics interested in visual culture. The book has always had an interdisciplinary research, making it an adaptable, meaningful text. With this new edition, the application of *Visual Methodologies* is made even more vital given its coverage of digital technologies and our expanded engagement with the image through complex and nuanced visualization of everything online. This extends not only our daily perception of the visual, but creates new ground through which to understand ourselves and our relationship to others. *Visual Methodologies* treats the emergence of this with passion, providing a theoretical and methodological framework that is accessible, engaging and exciting.
Adrienne Evans, Principal Lecturer in Media and Communication, Coventry University

Through its previous editions *Visual Methodologies* has undoubtedly become a profoundly influential text. Through a series of telling and careful revisions it has been significantly updated in response to changing visual cultures. This edition refreshes and reinvigorates what was already a lively, revealing and vital text. Not least, this updated edition responds directly to changes in digital cultures and the new possibilities of visual engagement and communication. It is the ideal guide to teaching and researching with visual methods.

David Beer, Reader in Sociology, University of York

Gillian Rose has done it again. This indispensable guide to visual methodologies improves with each edition. Extensively updated and revised, there is a new emphasis here on the circulation of images through varied technologies and the potential for digital methods to reveal patterns in the movements, translations and social value of such images. The reader comes away not only with practical knowledge for designing research questions and methods, but crucially with an enhanced understanding of the theoretical foundations and ethical considerations which underpin the most valuable and insightful visual analyses. This is not simply a 'how to' methods book.

Katy Parry, Lecturer in Media and Communication, University of Leeds

For the last 15 years, Rose's *Visual Methodologies* has been an exceptionally influential and invaluable text for those wishing to engage with visual research methods, with each new edition evolving and building upon the strengths of the previous. This fourth edition is no exception. With an expanded coverage of new media, Rose's revised work encompasses a comprehensive and detailed overview of imaginative approaches and engagements with visual materials that are readily accessible for undergraduate and postgraduate researchers. Moreover, this new edition effectively addresses many of those pressing questions often asked by student researchers, not only in terms of the practical aspects of using critical visual methods, but also in relation to the dissemination of research through visual techniques. In short, this fourth edition represents a welcome expansion of an already definitive introductory text on critical visual methods.

James Robinson, Lecturer in Cultural Geography, Queen's University Belfast

Gillian Rose's *Visual Methodologies* remains the authoritative introductory text on the methods of visual research. Conveying the richness and excitement of visual culture research, Rose expertly navigates across a range of methodologies, explaining in detail their particular usefulness and limitations through practical examples. For anyone already familiar with *Visual Methodologies*, this fourth edition offers a significant reworking of previous content. This includes a discussion of digital methods for online imagery and expansion of digital media examples, the production and use of images for research dissemination and, most significantly, the inclusion of the cite of circulation within the framework that Rose presents for the analysis of visual culture.

As such, Rose demonstrates the evolving nature of visual research and its methods, and reminds us of the passion involved in its study. It is a must buy for students and scholars alike.
Julie Doyle, Reader in Media and Communication, University of Brighton

One and half decades after its first edition, *Visual Methodologies* continues to position itself as key reading for anyone who is looking for a solid, accessible and systematic introduction to the increasingly popular but complex domain of image analysis and visual culture research. Gillian Rose deserves much praise for her sustained and highly successful efforts to keep this core text in critical visual analysis as fresh and relevant as ever. This fourth edition includes discussions about the newest visual and digital technologies and their interrelated practices. But the author has also thoroughly revisited and refined the book's overall structure to better guide the uninitiated reader through this kaleidoscopic and somewhat confused area of study.
Luc Pauwels, Professor of Visual Research Methods, University of Antwerp

Clear, comprehensive, theoretically informed, and now fully updated and revised, *Visual Methodologies* is an excellent guide to the rapidly growing field of visual research.
Theo van Leeuwen, Emeritus Professor, University of Technology, Sydney

There is simply no better resource or inspiration for conducting, analyzing, and disseminating visual research than Gillian Rose's *Visual Methodologies*. Her theoretical clarity about visual culture and power relations is seamlessly woven into her discussion and evaluation of a wide range of research methods. The breadth, depth, and detail of the exemplary research upon which she draws to elucidate the different approaches increases with each revised volume, and the 4th Edition is no exception. Rose has given us a comprehensive, wise, and rigorous guide for doing visual research that will invigorate the field and its practitioners.
Wendy Luttrell, Professor of Urban Education, Graduate Center, City University of New York

CONTENTS

FIGURES AND TABLES

Figures

Tables

ABOUT THE AUTHOR

Gillian Rose is Professor of Cultural Geography at The Open University. Her current research interests lie within the field of contemporary visual culture and visual research methodologies. She is interested in ordinary, everyday ways of seeing and the effects of that seeing in domestic as well as urban public spaces. One long-term project has been examining family photos as visual objects that circulate between a range of different practices in the global visual economy – *Doing Family Photography: The Domestic, The Public and The Politics of Sentiment* was published by Ashgate in 2010. Another is her ongoing work on the intersection of digital technologies and the visualisation of cities. The longest project of all, though, has been *Visual Methodologies*.

Gillian blogs at visualmethodculture.wordpress.com and tweets @ProfGillian. Her Open University webpage is http://www.open.ac.uk/people/gr334.

ACKNOWLEDGEMENTS

This book is based on a course I taught at the Graduate School for the Social Sciences, Edinburgh University, in 1996, 1997 and 1998. The first edition benefited from useful and pleasurable discussions in Edinburgh about matters visual and interpretative with Sue Smith, Charlie Withers and, especially, Mark Dorian; this fourth edition is indebted to conversations with many colleagues at The Open University and elsewhere. Richard Rogers generously read a draft of Chapter 11 and suggested some additions. Robert Rojek has been a great editor throughout.

PREFACE: INTRODUCING THE FOURTH EDITION

This fourth edition of *Visual Methodologies* contains some significant differences from its predecessor.

As with its third edition, several of these changes have been driven by the development of digital technologies. The range of digital media it discusses has expanded to include Twitter and Instagram. The chapter on content analysis now includes a discussion of 'cultural analytics', which is a term used to describe the analysis, by software, of huge numbers of online images. There are two new chapters. The first is on 'digital methods' in relation to online images; while this chapter is more speculative than substantive, it points to a significant area in which visual methods will develop in the next few years. The second is a chapter on making images as a way of disseminating the results of a research project, and it discusses data visualisations, photo-essays, films and interactive documentaries. The book's framework for discussing contemporary visual culture and the methods for interpreting has also changed. It is now based on four sites, not three: the site of the production of images, the image itself, its circulation and its audiencing. Adding the site of circulation seemed necessary in order to assess how different methods address the mobility of digital images across many kinds of social media and image-sharing platforms and devices. I hope all these changes will continue to help social researchers both explore and use images in creative ways.

Gillian Rose

Cambridge, July 2015

AN INTRODUCTION TO VISUAL METHODOLOGIES

The first edition of this book was written mostly during 1999; this fourth edition has been prepared fifteen years later. The need to engage critically with visual culture – both historical and contemporary – seems no less pressing now than it was when the book was first being written, and many scholars continue to make their own significant contributions to the field (Beer, 2013; Casid and D'souza, 2014; Cubitt, 2014; Grace, 2014; Hartley, 2012; Howells and Negreiros, 2012; Jenkins et al., 2013; Joselit, 2012; Manghani, 2013; Manovich, 2013; Rettberg, 2014). The number of guides to possible methods of interpreting visual culture has increased too (Banks and Ruby, 2011; Bates, 2014; Bell, Warren, and Schroeder, 2014; Gaimster, 2011; Hughes, 2012; Jordanova, 2012; Mannay, 2016; Margolis and Pauwels, 2011; Pink, 2012; Reavey, 2011; Tinkler, 2012); there is also now a journal called *Visual Methodologies*. But this book remains unique in the breadth of its attempt to discuss and evaluate systematically a wide range of methods for doing research with visual materials. It is addressed to the undergraduate student who has either found some intriguing visual materials to work with, or who wants to make some to work with, or who is excited by the visual culture literature and wants to do a research project that engages with some of its arguments.

The first chapter of this book remains an overview of different theoretical approaches to understanding visual culture. These theoretical debates are diverse and often complex. They can also be rather abstract. In contrast, a particular concern of mine is to encourage the grounding of interpretations of visual materials in careful empirical research of the social circumstances in which they are embedded (Rose, 2012). This is not because there is some essential truth lurking in each image, awaiting discovery (although we will encounter the latter claim in some of the early chapters of this book). As Stuart Hall says:

> It is worth emphasising that there is no single or 'correct' answer to the question, 'What does this image mean?' or 'What is this ad saying?' Since there is no law which can guarantee that things will have 'one, true meaning', or that meanings won't change over time, work in this area is bound to be interpretative – a debate between, not who is 'right' and who is 'wrong', but between equally plausible, though sometimes competing and contesting, meanings and interpretations. The best way to 'settle' such contested readings is to look again at the concrete example and try to justify one's 'reading' in detail in relation to the actual practices and forms of signification used, and what meanings they seem to you to be producing. (Hall, 1997a: 9)

Interpreting images is just that: interpretation. But my own preference – which is itself a theoretical position – is for understanding visual images as embedded in the social world and only comprehensible when that embedding is taken into account. As Hall suggests, though, it is still important to justify your interpretation, whatever theoretical stance you prefer. To do that you will need to have an explicit methodology, and this book will help you develop one.

The book does not offer a neutral account of the different methods available for interpreting visual materials, though. There are significant differences between various theories of the visual. In the first chapter, I agree with those scholars who argue that the interpretation of visual images must address the social effects of images: effects that images can achieve by being both meaningful and affective. That position has certain implications for the way in which I subsequently assess the various methods the book discusses. For example, while quantitative methods can be deployed in relation to these sorts of issues (as Chapter 5 will suggest), nonetheless the emphasis on meaning, significance and affect in Chapter 1's overview suggests that qualitative methods are more appropriate. Indeed, every chapter here except Chapter 5 and Chapter 11 explores qualitative methodologies. More broadly, Chapter 1 also makes some specific suggestions about why it is important to consider visual images carefully, why it is important to be critical about visual images, and why it is important to reflect on that critique. These three issues are developed in Chapter 1 into three criteria for what I term a 'critical visual methodology'. By 'critical' I mean an approach that thinks about the visual in terms of the cultural significance, social practices and power relations in which it is embedded; and this means thinking about the power relations that produce, are articulated through, and can be challenged by ways of seeing and imaging. Those criteria then provide the means by which the various methods in this book are evaluated. Using these criteria, for each method I ask: How useful is it in achieving a critical methodology for visual images? Chapter 2 elaborates a more practical framework for approaching images in this way.

Chapters 4 through to 12 each discuss one method that can be used to interpret visual materials, and the sorts of visual materials each chapter draws on to explore that method is dictated by what best exemplifies the method's procedures, strengths and weaknesses. So while the book covers a wide range of visual materials – listed in Table 3.1 in Chapter 3 – there are also plenty that this book does not discuss. There are no discussions of maps, film posters, arts-based visual methods, graphic novels, medical imaging or diagrams, for example. What the book does do, though, is discuss each method in some depth.

Chapters 4 through to 11 all focus on methods that work with found images; that is, images that already exist, and which you can explore as part of some sort of research project. However, Chapter 12 focuses in more detail on another approach to researching with visual images, which is those methods that involve making visual images as a way of answering a research question. Such visual research methods have exploded in popularity over the past decade, and are now found across a great many disciplines, being put to use to answer a vast range of research questions that very often have come out quite right in your photography, you can digitally manipulate it on your computer. At New York's Empire State Building, the queues are longer for the virtual reality New York Ride than for the lifts to the observation platforms. Alternatively, you could save yourself the trouble by catching the entire New York skyline, rendered in attractive pastel colours, at the New York, New York resort in Las Vegas. This virtual city will shortly be joined by Paris Las Vegas, imitating the already carefully manipulated image of the city of light. (Mirzoeff, 1998: 1)

This is what Jean Baudrillard (1988) some time ago dubbed the simulacrum. Baudrillard argued that in postmodernity it is no longer possible to make a distinction between the real and the unreal; images have become detached from any certain relation to a real world with the result that we now live in a scopic regime dominated by simulations, or **simulacra**.

simulacra

The development of digital **new media** has a special place in these discussions (Gane and Beer, 2008). While computing has a long history – the 'Analytical Engine' which Charles Babbage began designing in 1833 has some claim to be the first computer – many commentators argue that the emergence of a wide range of digital production, storage and communication devices over the past twenty years has significantly changed visual culture. They argue not only that these inventions account in large part for the pervasiveness of visual images in Western societies now – because they make images so easy to make and share – but also that the nature of digital images is changing contemporary visualities. This claim is built on the difference between **analogue** images and digital images, and in particular on the difference between the technologies underlying the production of an image (see Figure 1.1). Analogue images are created through technologies that have a one-to-one correspondence to what they are recording. Photography is an obvious example: an analogue photograph is created by light falling onto chemicals which react to that light to produce a visual pattern. Whether we are looking at an image of a leaf made by leaving that leaf on a sheet of light-sensitive paper in the sunshine, or at a famous photograph, like Figure 2.2, taken with a relatively complex single lens reflex camera, they are both analogue photographs because both have a direct, physical relationship to a continuous pattern of light generated by objects.

new media

analogue

Digital images, on the other hand, have no one-to-one correspondence with what they show. This is so for at least two reasons. First, the images produced with a digital camera are made by sampling patterns of light, because in a digital camera light falls on discrete light-sensitive cells. There is thus 'a minute gap between samples which the digital recording can never fill' (Cubitt, 2006). Secondly, that pattern of light is converted

digital

Amplitude

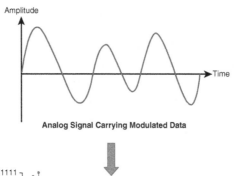

Time

Analog Signal Carrying Modulated Data

FIGURE 1.1A
Diagram showing
the difference
between digital
and analogue
signals

11111111
11111110

00000001
00000000

PCM Encoded Signal

FIGURE 1.1B
Image of Barack
Obama from a
website protesting
at his decision to
extend the cut-off
date for analogue
television

FIGURE 1.1C
Image from the
(now defunct)
website
getdigitaltelevision.
com

FIGURE 1.1   These three images are very different representations of the difference
between analogue and digital technologies. They were all found on the web in 2010

into binary digital code by the digital camera's software, and that binary code is then itself converted into different kinds of output. Of course, most cameras use a combination of hardware and software to convert the code back into an image to be viewed on a camera or computer or phone screen, but this is a programmed process rather than an inevitable consequence of using the light-sensitive technology embedded in a digital camera. In fact, since the pattern of light generated by what is being pictured has become computer code, that code can be used to produce all sorts of different things. As Sean Cubitt notes:

> from the standpoint of the computer, any input will always appear as mathematical, and any data can be output in any format. Effectively, an audio input can be output as a video image, as text, as a 3D model, as an instruction set for a manufacturing process, or another digital format that can be attached to the computer. (2006: 250)

The same image file can thus be materialised in many different forms, which may well invite different ways of seeing it: as a billboard; on a website; in a smartphone app. Moreover, digital images can also be edited very easily. It is this mutability of the digital image that for many scholars is its defining quality.

For some, the difference between analogue and digital images is profound. David Rodowick (2007), for example, has argued that images made with digital cameras should not be called photographs. For him, the chemical process that creates analogue photographs gives them a unique quality which digital images do not and cannot have, such that 'one feels or intuits in digital images that the qualitative expression of duration found in photography and film is missing or sharply reduced' (2007: 118). In this sense, he argues that analogue photography is a specific medium, with particular visual qualities immanent in its analogue technology.

1.1.2 Materiality and affect

Indeed, for some time now in the literature on visual culture, there has been an emphasis on the **materiality** of the media used to make and carry visual images, inspired by a range of theorists, including Bruno Latour and Friedrich Kittler. In this work, the specific effects of a material object – a printed analogue photograph, for example – are understood through ontological claims about its inherent nature (Packer and Crofts Wiley, 2012). There are different inflections to this claim. Sometimes the emphasis is on the way that a specific technology – the analogue camera, say – has a direct effect on the nature of the image it produces. This is the argument made by Rodowick (2007), and has also been argued at length by Kittler (1999).

materiality

affordances   Other authors suggest that the material qualities of technologies offer a limited number of possibilities – or **affordances** – for how they can be used, but that humans can choose between those possibilities. Sean Cubitt's (2014) recent history of visual technologies takes this position, as does Fernando Rubio (2012) in a study of work by the American artist Robert Smithson called *Spiral Jetty* (see Figure 1.2). Rubio suggests that, in fact, it wasn't only Smithson who made *Spiral Jetty*: so too did the rocks and rubble that form *Spiral Jetty*, the water of the lake it extends into, the ground pressure, the dumper trucks that carried the rocks ... the physical properties of all of these were active partners in Smithson's creative process, allowing him to do some of the things he wanted but preventing him from doing others. Rubio thus argues more generally that 'artistic production is a form of practice that emerges and unfolds from a material engagement within the world' (Rubio, 2012: 147; see also Rubio and Silva, 2013).

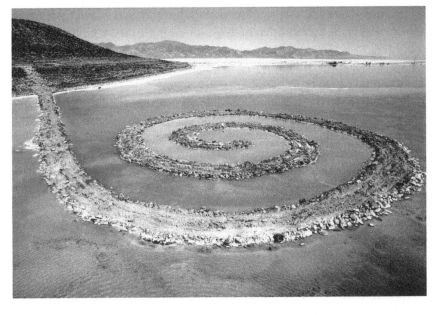

FIGURE 1.2
Robert
Smithson's
Spiral Jetty,
built in 1970
into the Great
Salt Lake, Utah
© Estate of
Robert Smithson/
DACS, London/
VAGA, New York
2015

The last couple of decades have in fact seen extended bodies of work emerge that explore the agency of material objects and the particularities of digital media, and often both at the same time. Both these bodies of work have questioned the utility of the notion of representation. At the end of the twentieth century, and inspired both by the work of philosophers such as Gilles Deleuze and of information theorists such as Claude Shannon and Warren Weaver, as well as by the growth in digital media (visual and otherwise), a number of scholars began to argue for a different understanding, not just of particular types of images like digital photographs, but of contemporary visual culture itself. For Katherine Hayles (1999), the proliferation of digital technologies invites a different way of thinking about how we are human, no less; indeed, she argues we are becoming **posthuman** because of the increasingly intense flows of information occurring now between humans, animals and machines. She sees these flows as 'a co-evolving and densely interconnected complex system' (Hayles, 2006: 165; Thrift, 2008), the scale and intensity of which has been immeasurably enhanced by development of high-speed computers and the Internet. Rodowick (2001) argues that these flows – in the extent and intensity of their dispersal, and in their ability to constantly reform coded information from one output to another – demand a specifically Deleuzian response, and it is this that challenges the usefulness of the concept of representation. This is because, according to Ambrose (2007), Deleuze's

posthuman

> creative ontology of becoming ceaselessly strives to go beyond mere surface fixities associated with the 'actual' (for example the existing conditions of current culture and society) in the effort to assemble a conceptual discourse capable of conveying pre-individual impersonal forces, energies, fluxes, flows and sensations that actual socio-historical situations occlude, reify and domesticate into rational orders, conceptual systems and clichéd patterns of representation and intellegibility (2007: 118).

These 'pre-individual impersonal forces, energies, fluxes, flows and sensations' are termed **affect** in Deleuzian work, and this approach has had a significant impact on how some scholars theorise visual culture, in relation to both digital and analogue images. While some theorists equally interested in the energies and sensations of digital images draw more on phenomenological philosophies than on Deleuze, this broad concern with the experiential has produced two particularly significant effects for theorising images.

affect

First, the affective emphasis on embodiment rejects the distinction between vision and visuality so central to the cultural turn. Vision is as much corporeal as cultural in this work. Mark Hansen's (2004) discussion of digital art, for example, claims that the human body becomes especially important in relation to digital images, and argues for 'the refunctionalization of the body as the processor of information' (Hansen, 2004: 23). Indeed, bodies in this kind of work are understood as highly sensitive, sensorimotor information processors in constant, energetic relation with other human and nonhuman information processors. In affective work there is thus an emphasis on 'a dynamism immanent to bodily matter and matter generally' (Clough, 2008: 1).

Secondly, the posthuman is not a person engaging with the world by interpreting and exchanging meanings (the figure evoked by Stuart Hall at the very beginning of this chapter). Understanding the posthuman in this sort of work does not involve the exploration of meaning, but rather the perceptual, the experiential and the sensory. Indeed, geographer Nigel Thrift (2008) has for some time been describing this sort of theory as 'addressing the nonrepresentational'. Nonrepresentational work is interested in articulating the perceptual, bodily and sensory experience created in encounters with specific materials (Beugnet and Ezra, 2009). As Laura Marks says, 'to appreciate the materiality of our media pulls us away from a symbolic understanding and toward a shared physical existence' (Marks, 2002: xii). Marks (2000, 2002) is a leading exponent of this affective approach to visual imagery. Like Hansen (2004), her arguments draw on both affective and phenomenological philosophical traditions. She describes watching artists' analogue videos, for example, as 'an intercorporeal relationship', suggesting that the video is as much a body as she is (Marks, 2002: xix). Her aim is not to interpret what the videos mean, but to find richness and vitality in the images; hence she says that there is 'no need to interpret, only to unfold, to increase the surface area of experience' (Marks, 2002: x).

For all their theoretical differences, however, it could be argued that theories of both representation and affect have one thing in common: a commitment to a close engagement with specific images. Whether carefully unpacking layers of representational references, or sensitively responding to corporeal affects, all the scholars discussed so far take a very attentive stance towards their materials. An important, emerging methodological question, however, is whether such an attentive stance by visual culture scholars is sustainable, at least in relation to the very large numbers of images that are now to be found on various online social media sites and elsewhere. The numbers are mind-boggling, and given current growth trends, always underestimated – in late 2014, 60 million photographs were uploaded to Instagram, 350 million onto Facebook, and 400 million onto Snapchat every day, while a hundred hours of video were uploaded to YouTube every minute; and on a much smaller but still massive scale, museums and galleries around the world are digitising their entire collections and making them available online. This is the visual culture equivalent of the 'big data' currently preoccupying much of the social sciences. If visual culture scholars are to grasp what's going on in these huge image collections, it is now often claimed that close, attentive reading alone is unlikely to be effective. Where would you start, and how would you ever finish? Some scholars – in the digital humanities as well as the social sciences – are therefore arguing that new methods are needed, methods which use software to analyse these huge numbers of images. Such methods might be the digital equivalents of existing methods, and Chapter 5 will discuss a digitised version of content analysis. Others, though, will use the uniquely digital affordances of softwares to create what Richard Rogers (2013) argues are 'natively digital methods', as Chapter 11 in this book will discuss.

is to differentiate between the social effects of those different visions. All these arguments make clear the necessity of understanding what social relations produce, and are reproduced by, what forms of visuality, and Section 1.2 explores this argument more fully.

1.1.5 Visual research methods

Before moving on, though, this chapter needs to pause and remark on one specific example of the increasing ubiquity of visual images in Western culture. In the grand scheme of things, it is a rather small aspect of contemporary visual culture, but it is particularly pertinent to this book's discussion of research methods. It is the increasing use of research methods in the social sciences that use visual materials of some kind, sometimes to explore questions about visuality, but more often as a means of exploring an aspect of social life: attitudes to illness, for example (Frith and Harcourt, 2007), or feelings about living in an informal settlement (Lombard, 2013). The use of images by social scientists has, in fact, a long history. Both anthropology and human geography have used visual images as research tools for as long as they have been established as academic disciplines: mostly photographs, diagrams and film in the case of anthropology (Banks and Ruby, 2011; Pink, 2013), and photos, maps and diagrams in the case of geography. Visual sociology is a more recent development; although the earliest sociological journals carried photographs for a short period before the First World War, it was not until the 1960s that a book by an anthropologist encouraged some sociologists to pick up their cameras again (Collier, 1967). Recent years, however, have seen a proliferation of visual methodologies being used across the social sciences (see for example: Banks, 2008; Bell, Warren, and Schroeder, 2014; Emmison et al., 2012; Gaimster, 2011; Hamilton, 2006; Hughes, 2012; Knowles and Sweetman, 2004a; Margolis and Pauwels, 2011; Pink, 2012, 2013, 2015; Pole, 2004; Prosser, 1998; Reavey, 2011; Spencer, 2011; Stanczak, 2007; Theron et al., 2011; Thomson, 2008; Tinkler, 2012).

These **visual research methods** can use already-existing images, from the mass media for example; or images can be made by the researcher; or they can be made by the people being researched. Sometimes the images are treated as research data that does not, or should not, be reproduced when research results are written up; sometimes, in contrast, it is argued that images are the only way the results should be conveyed, and there are now social science scholars who

visual research
methods

have films, websites and photo-essays, as well as books and journal articles, as an integral part of their academic work. To date, many of these visual research methods use film and photography; but as digital methods are being developed, software-generated visualisations are also emerging as ways of presenting and interpreting data. Oddly, little of this work engages explicitly with the sorts of debates that this chapter has thus far been summarising, although it is certainly possible to detect parallels between discussions about contemporary visual culture and the various ways in which social scientists have used images (Rose, 2014). Some social scientists approach images as representational, for example, while others focus more on their affective qualities. And many social science researchers working with images are concerned about the sorts of questions raised by Haraway's account of visuality: debates about how images are part of the power relations between researcher and researched are framed as a discussion about research ethics. This book addresses two of the most commonly used types of visual research methods in Chapter 12. Chapter 13 discusses using or making images as a way of disseminating research findings, while the ethics of doing visual research is discussed in Chapter 14.

So far, this chapter has given you an overview of what I see as the key aspects of the literatures currently exploring the visual. What I now want to do is to explain how the structure of this book draws on elements of those literatures to make sense of the proliferation of both images and ways to study them in recent years.

1.2 Understanding the Social Effects of Visual Materials

Visual culture critics have concentrated their energies on critically examining the effects of visual images already out there in the world, already part of visual culture, and Chapters 4 to 11 of this book discuss a range of methods for understanding such 'found' images. As I have already suggested, theorists of the cultural turn, with their emphasis on representation, have now been joined by theorists more concerned with the affective (other reviews can be found in Barnard, 2001; Evans and Hall, 1999; Heywood and Sandywell, 2012; Howells and Negreiros, 2012; Manghani, Piper, and Simons, 2006; Manghani, 2013; Mirzoeff, 2009; Rampley, 2005). Each of these bodies of work draws on a range of different theorists and philosophers, and each has its own internal debates and disagreements; moreover, the work of some philosophers and theorists is used to make arguments for both representation and non-representation. This diversity obviously makes generalising about studies of visuality a difficult task. Nevertheless, I am going to suggest that there are five aspects of the recent literature that engage with visual culture which I think are valuable for thinking about the social effects of images.

1.2.1 Visualising social difference

The first point I take from the literature on 'visual culture' is its concern for the way in which images visualise (or render invisible) social difference. As Fyfe and Law (1988: 1) say, 'a depiction is never just an illustration ... it is the site for the construction and depiction of social difference.' One of the central aims of 'the cultural turn' in the social sciences was to argue that social categories are not natural but instead are constructed. These constructions can take visual form, a point that has been made most forcefully by feminist and postcolonial writers who have studied the ways femininity and blackness have been visualised. An example would be Tanner Higgin's (2009) discussion of the massively multiplayer online role-playing game (MMORPG) *World of Warcraft*. Tanner's topic is the representation of race in *World of Warcraft* and he approaches it by noting not only that the characters in most computer and video games are white, but also that 'black and brown bodies, although increasingly more visible within the medium, are seemingly inescapably objectified as hypermasculine variations of the gangsta or sports player tropes' (Higgin, 2009: 3). He then explores various reasons for the 'commonsense notion that Blacks are not heroes, paladins, or mages' and what he sees as the consequent lack of black bodies in *World of Warcraft* (Higgin, 2009: 6). He notes that the game itself gives players white avatars by default, and that black skin choices are very limited; he discusses the importance of whiteness to the literary genre of high fantasy that games like *World of Warcraft* are related to; and he suggests that

> when one sees a race called 'human' within a MMORPG and it is westernized as well as White with different shades of color for diversity (but nothing too Black), a powerful assertion is made. This assertion is that humanity will only be understood within the fantasy world if it is primarily coded White. The player base has affirmed this understanding by choosing largely White human avatars in order to match the discursive framework set up by these racial logics. (Higgin, 2009: 11; see also Nakamura 2002, 2008, 2009, 2014)

Higgin concludes that, 'because video games both model and shape culture, there is a growing danger and anxiety that some games are functioning as stewards of White masculine hegemony' (2009: 3).

Hence Fyfe and Law's general prescription for a critical approach to the ways images can picture social power relations:

> To understand a visualisation is thus to enquire into its provenance and into the social work that it does. It is to note its principles of inclusion and exclusion, to detect the roles that it makes available, to understand the way in which they are distributed, and to decode the hierarchies and differences that it naturalises. (Fyfe and Law, 1988: 1)

Looking carefully at images, then, entails, among other things, thinking about how they offer very particular visions of social categories such as class, gender, race, sexuality, able-bodiedness and so on.

1.2.2 How images are looked at

Secondly, writers on visual culture, among others, are concerned not only with how images look, but also with how they are looked at. This is a key point made by Maria Sturken and Lisa Cartwright's (2009) book on visual culture, which they title *Practices of Looking*. They argue that what is important about images is not simply the image itself, but how it is seen by particular spectators who look in particular ways. Sturken and Cartwright (2009) take their inspiration on this point in part from an influential book written in 1972 by John Berger, called *Ways of Seeing*. Berger's argument there is important because he makes clear that images of social difference work not simply by what they show but also by the *way of seeing* that they invite. He uses the expression **ways of seeing** to refer to the fact that 'we never look just at one thing; we are always looking at the relation between things and ourselves' (Berger 1972: 9). His best-known example is that of the genre of female nude painting in Western art. He reproduces many examples of that genre (see Figure 1.4), pointing out as he does so the particular ways they represent women: as unclothed, as vain, as passive, as sexually alluring, as a spectacle to be assessed.

ways of seeing

Berger insists though on who it is that does the assessing, who this kind of image was meant to allure:

> In the average European oil painting of the nude, the principal protagonist is never painted. He is the spectator in front of the painting and he is presumed to be a man. Everything is addressed to him. Everything must appear to be the result of his being there. It is for him that the figures have assumed their nudity. (Berger, 1972: 54)

Thus for Berger, understanding this particular genre of painting means understanding not only its representation of femininity, but its construction of masculinity too. And these representations are in their turn understood as part of a wider cultural construction of gendered difference. To quote Berger again:

> One might simplify this by saying: *men act* and *women appear*. Men look at women. Women watch themselves being looked at. This determines not only most relations between women and men but

also the relation of women to themselves. The surveyor of woman in herself is male: the surveyed female. Thus she turns herself into an object – and most particularly an object of vision: a sight. (Berger, 1972: 47, emphasis in original)

While later critics would want to modify aspects of Berger's argument – most obviously by noting that he assumes heterosexuality in his discussion of masculinity and femininity – many critics would concur with his general understanding of the connection between image and spectator. Images work by producing effects every time they are looked at.

Much of this work in visual culture argues that the particular 'audiences' (this might not always be the appropriate word) of an image will bring their own interpretations to bear on its meaning and effect. Not all audiences will be able or willing to respond to the way of seeing invited by a particular image and its particular practices of display (Chapter 10 will discuss this in more detail). Taking an image seriously, then, also involves thinking about how it positions you, its viewer, in relation to it.

She is not naked as she is.
She is naked as the spectator sees her.

Often – as with the favourite subject of Susannah and the Elders – this is the actual theme of the picture. We join the Elders to spy on Susannah taking her bath. She looks back at us looking at her.

In another version of the subject by Tintoretto, Susannah is looking at herself in a mirror. Thus she joins the spectators of herself.

The mirror was often used as a symbol of the vanity of woman. The moralizing, however, was mostly hypocritical.

You painted a naked woman because you enjoyed looking at her, you put a mirror in her hand and you called the painting *Vanity*, thus morally condemning the woman whose nakedness you had depicted for your own pleasure.
     The real function of the mirror was otherwise. It was to make the woman connive in treating herself as, first and foremost, a sight.

     The Judgement of Paris was another theme with the same inwritten idea of a man or men looking at naked women.

FIGURE 1.4   Double-page spread from John Berger's *Ways of Seeing* (Penguin Books 1972: 50–1)
© John Berger

1.2.3 Differentiating visual cultures

Thirdly, there is the emphasis in the very term 'visual culture' on the embeddedness of visual images in a wider culture. Now, 'culture', as Raymond Williams (1976) famously noted, is one of the two or three most complicated words in the English language. It has many connotations. Most pertinent to this discussion is the meaning it began to be given in various anthropological books written towards the end of the nineteenth century. In this usage, culture meant something like 'a whole way of life', and even from the brief discussion in this chapter so far you can see that some current writers are using the term 'visual culture' in just this broad sense. Indeed, one of the first uses of the term 'visual culture', by Svetlana Alpers (1983: xxv), was precisely to emphasise the importance of visual images of all kinds to many aspects of seventeenth century Dutch society. In this sort of work, it is argued that a particular, historically specific visuality was central to a particular, ocularcentric culture. In using the notion of culture in this broad sense, however, certain analytical questions may become difficult to ask. In particular, culture as a whole way of life can slip rather easily into a notion of culture as simply a whole, and the issues of differences within that culture – and its connections to other cultures – can become obscured. This is certainly evident in the recent debates generated by cartoons showing the prophet Muhammad, when 'the West' and 'Islam' were sometimes mistakenly described as separate and monolithic 'cultures' or 'civilisations'.

In order to be able to deal with questions of social difference and the power relations that sustain them, then, a notion of culture is required that can also address questions of social difference, social relations and social power. One means of keeping these sorts of differentiations in the field of visual culture in analytical focus is to think carefully about just who is able to see what and how, where and with what effects. Indeed, W.J.T. Mitchell (1994: 420) argues that this is precisely the question that a concern for representation poses: 'Who or what represents what to whom with what, and where and why?' Berger's (1972) work is in some ways exemplary here. An image will depend on a certain way of seeing for its effects, as he argued in relation to female nude painting. But this effect is always embedded in particular cultural practices that are far more specific than 'a way of life'. So Berger talks about the ways in which nude paintings were commissioned and then displayed by their owners in his discussion of the way of seeing which they express. Describing a seventeenth century English example of the genre, he writes:

> Nominally it might be a Venus and Cupid. In fact it is a portrait of one of the king's mistresses, Nell Gwynne ... [Her] nakedness is not, however, an expression of her own feelings; it is a sign of her submission to the owner's feelings or demands. (The owner of both the woman and the painting.) The painting, when the king showed it to others, demonstrated this submission and his guests envied him. (Berger, 1972: 52)

It was through this kind of use, with its specific audience and their established way of interpretation, that this type of painting achieved its effects. The seeing of an image thus always takes place in a particular social context that mediates its impact. It also always takes place in a specific location with its own particular practices. That location may be a king's chamber, a Hollywood cinema studio, an avant-garde art gallery, an archive, a sitting room, a street. These different locations all have their own economies, their own disciplines, their own rules for how their particular sort of spectator should behave, including whether and how they should look, and all these affect how a particular image is seen (Rose, 2012). These specificities of practice are crucial in understanding how an image has certain effects, particularly when the 'same' image, circulating digitally, can appear in very different kinds of places.

1.2.4 The circulation of images

The way in which so many images now circulate online leads to the fourth element which I think can be usefully drawn out of current work on visual culture. Visual objects have always circulated between different places: from the artist's studio to the king's picture gallery; from a child's birthday party to a photo developing lab to a photo frame on a mantelpiece (Rose, 2010); from a makeshift studio in Mumbai to an archive in London. And ever since the invention of technologies of mass reproduction, images of visual objects have also been made and circulated. The German Marxist cultural critic Walter Benjamin wrote about this in the 1930s, exploring what he thought were the effects of photographing art objects so that most people came to 'see' such objects through photos of them rather than through directly experiencing them (Benjamin, 1973). There have therefore always been important questions to ask about how images circulate in the visual economy, why, and with what effects. Those questions remain necessary to pose to the massive numbers of images that are now 'shared' on various social networking sites (Beer, 2013). As Chapters 5 and 11 will discuss in more detail, online sharing is no less complex than any other kind. The processes of circulation are therefore the fourth aspect of work on visual culture that is important to consider when thinking about the social effects of images.

1.2.5 The agency of images

Finally, there is an insistence that images themselves have their own agency. In the words of Carol Armstrong (1996: 28), for example, an image is 'at least potentially a site of resistance and recalcitrance, of the irreducibly particular, and of the subversively strange and pleasurable', while Christopher Pinney (2004: 8) suggests that the important question is 'not how images "look", but what they can "do"'. An image has its own materiality, if you like, and in the search for an image's meaning it is therefore important not to claim that it merely reflects meanings made elsewhere – in newspapers, for example, or gallery catalogues. It is certainly true that visual images very often work in conjunction with other kinds of representations. It is very unusual, for example, to encounter a visual image unaccompanied by any text at all, whether spoken or written (Armstrong, 1998; Wollen, 1970: 118); even the most abstract painting in a gallery will have a written label on the wall giving certain information about its making, and in

certain sorts of galleries there will be a sheet of paper giving a price too,
and these make a difference to how spectators will see that painting.

image/text   W.J.T. Mitchell (1994) coined the term **image/text** as a way of emphasising the interrelation of images and written texts. So although virtually all
visual images are mixed in this way – they always make sense in relation
to other things, including written texts and very often other images – they
are not reducible to the meanings carried by those other things. The colours of an oil painting, for example, or the visible decay of video tape
(Marks, 2002), or the blurriness of a badly made Internet meme, will all
carry their own peculiar kinds of visual resistance, recalcitrance, argument, particularity, banality, strangeness or pleasure.

Thus I take five major points from current debates about visual culture
as important for understanding how images work: an image may have its
own visual effects; these effects, through the ways of seeing mobilised by
the image, are crucial in the production and reproduction of visions of
social difference; but these effects always intersect with the social context
of viewing, with how the image is circulated, and with the visualities
spectators bring to their viewing.

1.3 Three Criteria for a Critical Visual Methodology

Given this general approach to understanding the importance of images,
I can now elaborate on what I think is necessary for a 'critical approach'
to interpreting found visual images. A critical approach to visual culture:

- *takes images seriously*. I argue here that it is necessary to look very carefully at visual images, and it is necessary to do so because they are not
  entirely reducible to their context. Visual images have their own effects.
- *thinks about the social conditions and effects of images and their
  modes of distribution*. The cultural practices that create and circulate
  images both depend on and produce social inclusions and exclusions,
  and a critical account needs to address both those practices and their
  cultural meanings and effects.
- *considers your own way of looking at images*. This is not an explicit
  concern in many studies of visual culture. However, if, as Section 1.2
  just argued, ways of seeing are historically, geographically, culturally and socially specific, and if watching your favourite movie on
  a DVD for the umpteenth time at home with a group of mates is not
  the same as studying it for a research project, then – as Mieke Bal
  (1996, 2003; Bal and Bryson 2001) for one has consistently argued –
  it is necessary to reflect on how you as a critic of visual images

are looking. As Haraway (1991: 190) says, by thinking carefully about where we see from, 'we might become answerable for what we learn how to see'. Haraway also comments that this is not a straightforward task (see also Rogoff, 1998; Rose, 1997). Several of the chapters will return to this issue of reflexivity in order to examine what it might entail further, and Chapter 14 will discuss the related issue of the ethics of using images in your research.

The aim of this book is to give you some practical guidance on how to do these things; but I hope it is already clear from this introduction that this is not simply a technical question of method. There are also important analytical debates going on about visualities. In this book, I use these particular criteria for a critical visual methodology to evaluate both theoretical arguments and the methods discussed in all the chapters, including visual research methods.

Having very briefly sketched a critical approach to images that I find useful to work with and which will structure this book's accounts of various methods, the next chapter starts more explicitly to address the question of methodology.

Summary

Visual imagery is never innocent; it is always constructed through various practices, technologies and knowledges. A critical approach to visual images is therefore needed: one that thinks about the agency of the image, considers the social practices and effects of its circulation and viewing, and reflects on the specificity of that viewing by various audiences, including the academic critic.

Further Reading

Stuart Hall, in his essay 'The Work of Representation' (1997b), offers a very clear discussion of the debates about culture, representation and power. A collection of some of the key texts that have contributed towards the field of visual culture has been put together by Jessica Evans and Stuart Hall as *Visual Culture: The Reader* (1999). *The Handbook of Visual Culture* is a very useful collection of essays on different aspects of visual culture, with a substantial introduction by its editors (Heywood and Sandywell, 2012). The collection of essays edited by Diarmuid Costello and Jonathan Vickery called *Art: Key Contemporary Thinkers* (2007) contains some very useful essays on a range of philosophers and theorists, including Adorno, Barthes, Baudrillard, Bourdieu, Deleuze, Foucault, Mitchell and Pollock. And for some provocations on the difference that digital technologies may make to cultural analysis, take a look at John Hartley's book *Digital Futures for Cultural and Media Studies* (2012).

2

TOWARDS A CRITICAL VISUAL METHODOLOGY

As should be evident from the previous chapter, the theoretical sources that have produced the recent interest in visual culture and visual research methods are philosophically, theoretically and conceptually diverse. This chapter will try to acknowledge some of that diversity, while also developing a framework for exploring the almost equally diverse range of methods that scholars working with visual materials can use. The framework developed is based on thinking about visual materials in terms of four sites: the site of *production*, which is where an image is made; the site of the *image* itself, which is its visual content; the site(s) of its *circulation*, which is where it travels; and the site where the image encounters its spectators or users, or what this book will call its *audiencing*. This chapter examines those sites in some depth, and explains how they can be used to make sense of theories of visual culture and of the methods used to engage with it. It has five sections:

1. The first discusses the four sites in a little more detail.
2. The second looks at ways of understanding the site of the production of visual materials.
3. The third looks at approaches to the visual materials themselves.
4. The fourth explores ways of understanding how visual materials circulate.
5. And the fifth examines the sites where visual materials are audienced.

2.1 Introducing the Four Sites of a Critical Visual Methodology: Production, the Image Itself, its Circulation and its Audiencing

sites
production
image
circulation

Interpretations of visual images broadly concur that there are four **sites** at which the meanings of an image are made: the site(s) of the **production** of an image, the site of the **image** itself, the site(s) of its **circulation**, and the methods being deployed in relation to specific sorts of visual materials are less easy to understand, however. For example, audience studies, also discussed in Chapter 10, have focused almost entirely on the audiencing of television programmes and videos. Why? Chapter 10 offers one or two reasons, but none of them is completely satisfying. I can not see any compelling reason that explains why television should have dominated audience studies to the extent that it has; indeed, examining the interpretative work done by audiences of films or glossy magazines or museum exhibits would seem to be just as valid, given the theoretical arguments underpinning audience studies.

Even when there do seem to be good reasons why a method is applied to one sort of visual material rather than another, though, it is important to think carefully before deciding that you too will apply the same method to the same sorts of materials. It may be that approaching the same visual images from a different methodological direction will yield much more interesting results. Each chapter points out in its opening section what other methods have been applied to the sorts of visual materials explored in its main examples.

Bearing those caveats in mind, Table 3.2 lists the methods discussed in this book and the sorts of images to which they have been most often applied. If you already have some images you want to work with, find them (or something like them) in this list, see what methods have been used to interpret them, and start with the chapters on those methods. Again, that doesn't mean you have to use those methods – but they will most likely provide a starting point for thinking methodologically.

TABLE 3.2   A summary of the methods and visual materials discussed in each chapter

	method	visual materials
Chapter 4	compositional interpretation	fine art paintings (and video games and films)
Chapter 5	content analysis cultural analytics	any sort of images but in large numbers: newspapers, magazines, selfies
Chapter 6	semiology and social semiotics	advertising (and fine art and films)
Chapter 7	psychoanalysis	films (and the mass media)
Chapter 8	discourse analysis I	a wide range of still images, including book illustrations, maps, photographs, paintings and cartoons
Chapter 9	discourse analysis II	institutions that display visual images and objects, for example museums and art galleries
Chapter 10	ethnographic methods	television audiences
Chapter 11	digital methods	digital objects like tweets and Instagram photos
Chapter 12	visual research methods	photography, video, collage, maps and drawing

It is obvious from Table 3.2 that, to repeat a point made in the Preface, there are many sorts of visual objects that this book does not examine. Again, this can only serve as encouragement to sever any automatic link between a method and an image. A method should be used for its interpretative possibilities, not because of conventional ways of using it.

3.3 Why You Should Also Read Books Other Than this One

If you want to interpret visual materials successfully, there are at least two other sorts of reading you need to be doing.

First, you will have to engage with the theoretical arguments underpinning the method you eventually choose. Methods do not work in isolation; they depend on understandings of how meaning is made, and you will need to appreciate those understandings in order to make the method work well.

Secondly, there is another sort of preparation that is needed, regardless of theoretical starting point, methodological implications or visual materials. All of these methods require some sorts of contextual knowledge about the imagery you are interested in. It is always important to know something about all aspects of the image you want to research; even if the audience is your main analytical focus, it is often useful to know something about the production of the image too. So before you utilise any of the methods the following chapters discuss, look at the bibliographies at the end of the book to help you find some background material, and use the other resources at your disposal too: libraries, databases, reading lists and so on. Search for what others have written on the medium in which you are interested and on the genres you think are relevant to the images you are concerned with. If you have an 'artist' of some kind as the producer of your images, look for what has been written by or about them.

To get you started, each chapter here concludes with some recommended extra reading about the method discussed; and at the end of the book there are lists of reading about specific kinds of visual materials.

3.4 How Each Chapter Works

In terms of using this book, each chapter shares a similar structure:

- The very beginning of each chapter tells you what key examples are discussed by the chapter.
- The chapter proper then opens with a more or less brief introduction to the method and its theoretical context.
- The theoretical context is then elaborated in more detail.
- The method is described – particular aspects of some methods are given special attention in some chapters, for example reflexivity or locating images.
- Throughout each chapter, there are boxes that ask you to focus on trying out specific parts of the method, and boxes that discuss some of the method's complexities. Key terms – both conceptual and technical – are highlighted in bold.
- Each chapter's final section is an assessment of its method's strengths and weaknesses in relation to the critical visual methodology developed in Chapter 1.

paintings. The 'good eye' pays attention to what it sees as high art, and refuses to be either methodologically or theoretically explicit. It thus functions as a kind of visual **connoisseurship**:

connoisseurship

> Connoisseurship involves the acquisition of extensive first-hand experience of works of art with the aim, first, of attributing works to artists and schools, identifying styles and establishing sources and influences, and second, of judging their quality and hence their place in a canon. (Fernie, 1995: 330)

Developing the 'good eye' of an art connoisseur requires much of a certain kind of what the previous chapter described as 'contextual information'. Specifically, you need a lot of knowledge about particular painters, about the kinds of painting they did, about the sorts of visual imagery they were looking at and being inspired by. All this is then used by the 'good eye' to assess paintings for their 'quality'. Thus compositional interpretation claims to look at images for 'what they are', rather than for, say, what they do or how they were or are used. The 'good eye' therefore looks mostly at the site of an *image itself* in order to understand its significance, and pays most (although not exclusive) attention to its *compositional* modality.

As this is an approach long-established in art history, it is most often used in relation to one of the sorts of objects that art historians have traditionally studied – paintings. However, as many accounts of art history as an academic discipline make clear (see for example Costello and Vickery, 2007; Pooke and Newall, 2007), this is by no means the only approach to understanding art images: indeed, many art historians rather disparage connoisseurship as a method. As a method for developing a critical visual methodology along the lines sketched in Chapters 1 and 2, compositional interpretation has its limitations. Visual images do not exist in a vacuum, and looking at them for 'what they are' neglects the ways in which they are produced and interpreted through particular social practices. Bryson makes this clear when he adds two qualifications to his comments quoted above about the power of the painting. First, he says, 'my ability to recognise an image ... is ... an ability which presupposes competence within the social, that is socially constructed, codes of recognition' (Bryson, 1991: 65). Secondly, 'the social formation isn't ... something which supervenes or appropriates or utilizes the image so to speak *after* it has been made; rather, painting ... unfolds from within the social formation from the beginning' (Bryson, 1991: 66). In its focus on the image itself, compositional interpretation neglects both socially specific ways of seeing and the visual representation of the social; hence the fact that very few academic art historians use it unaccompanied by methods discussed elsewhere in this book, such as semiotics, psychoanalysis or discourse analysis. Moreover, compositional interpretation does not reflect on its own practices. This chapter will therefore be able to pay little attention to these two aspects of a critical visual methodology.

However, precisely because it is not especially concerned with questions of representation, compositional interpretation – of a kind – does seem to be the method of choice for some of those theorists of visual culture concerned to emphasise the affective and the nonrepresentational. Deleuze himself gave extensive attention to cinema, and developed a rich vocabulary for understanding its spatial, visual and temporal structures. Deleuzian methodologies for understanding film are thoroughly discussed elsewhere – for example, by Ronald Bogue (2003) and Patricia Pisters (2003) among others – and this chapter will not repeat that work. However, those scholars of visual culture who are interested in the embodied experiencing of digital art, like Mark Hansen (2004), or art video (whether digital or analogue), like Laura Marks, do seem to use an approach similar to compositional interpretation. Recall Laura Marks's (2002: x) claim from Chapter 1, for example, that there is 'no need to interpret, only to unfold, to increase the surface area of experience'. Elements of compositional interpretation provide one way to increase the experiential, embodied response to visual images, because the method entails close attention to all aspects of the image itself; it is one way in which 'sense experience can be learned and cultivated' (Marks, 2000: 23). This chapter will thus suggest that compositional interpretation is the method of choice for the more phenomenologically inclined visual culture critic.

This chapter will use as its main example of compositional interpretation a review written by Adrian Searle of an exhibition of self-portraits by Rembrandt van Rijn, a Dutch painter who was born in 1606 and died in 1669. Searle's review is reprinted here, with two of its five illustrations. Read it now; I will return to it throughout this chapter in order to discuss specific aspects of compositional interpretation as a method.

'I can think of no room of paintings in the world so moving'

Adrian Searle is astounded by Rembrandt's self-portraits

It is night in the National Gallery. The lights are off. The machines that sniff the humidity and check the temperature are quietly ticking over, the alarm system is primed. The guards make their rounds, and outside in Trafalgar Square the clubbers are waiting for the night bus home. From tomorrow morning the queues will be forming for the exhibition 'Rembrandt By Himself', which brings together almost all of Rembrandt's self-portraits, the paintings, etchings and drawings he made of himself over the entirety of his artistic career. But for now I imagine Rembrandt's self-portraits, looking out into the twilit empty rooms in the Sainsbury Wing. I know they're there.

I think of his ghost, with what Picasso called 'that elephant's eye of his', that bulbous nose and the head with its curls spilling from under a mob cap, a turban, a plumed beret, a helmet. Rembrandt young, porcine and adenoidal; Rembrandt old as the painter-king. Rembrandt grimacing open-mouthed into a mirror as he draws on an etching-plate. Rembrandt dressed as an Oriental Potentate, Rembrandt in a cloak and Rembrandt as a beggar. I think of his multiple selves looking out into the dark, painting himself as though he were already a figure from history ...

Looking at late Rembrandt, we think we can tell how it is to be old, to have been old then, in 1669, prematurely aged at 63. What we are looking at is an old man with old skin in an old painting with a cracked and sallow surface, Rembrandt in the soft yellowing light, the last bright highlights in his eyes. It is almost impossible to look at Rembrandt's paintings of himself without regarding them as the artist's meditations on mortality, as a dialogue with himself conducted with a heart-breaking truthfulness and candour. That is how we are accustomed to read these self-portraits, as we look into their painted space, now three-and-a-half centuries old. We think we are looking at the painter as much as the paintings, seeing the man himself in his own self-image, and in the brushwork that created it. The paint molten, distressed, frank, concentrated, cursory, darkened, yellowed, translucent and papery. The painted surface at times as worn and slovenly as an old man's table, as though the painting itself were evidence of human fortitude and endurance. The catalogue essays can't dispel this view, but they set Rembrandt's self-portraiture within a context that tempers our projected existential feelings about it. It is odd, isn't it, that Rembrandt painted himself so often in clothing from the dressing-up box of the previous century – a rag-bag property-box of costumes, outlandish headgear, brocades and cloaks – and yet that he should also be a painter whose timelessness and contemporaneity continues to strike us so forcibly ...

But what scholarship cannot do, finally, is to dispel the disquiet Rembrandt's paintings arouse, the sense that Rembrandt was both unrepeatable and inescapable as a painter of himself. He painted and drew with a candour – at least, we suppose it was candour – about what was happening to his appearance as he got older. Perhaps he saw himself as

FIGURE 4.1
Self Portrait, 1629 (oil on panel) by Rembrandt Harmenszoon van Rijn (1606–69)
© Isabella Stewart Gardner Museum, Boston, MA, USA/The Bridgeman Images

FIGURE 4.2
Self Portrait,
aged 51, 1657
by Rembrandt
Harmenszoon
van Rijn
(1606–69)
© National
Galleries Scotland

a 'type', no less than his paintings were 'types', and saw his own face as a vessel of universal characteristics – melancholia and black bile marking his like a map ...

Later, he tries on all manner of costumes, and grows in stature and solidity with every one. He paints the spots on this cheek and that inescapable great nose. He goes on to paint himself in all his guises, but he ends up painting himself, both with a sort of grandeur, and with what we can only see as humility.

'Rembrandt By Himself' is undoubtedly going to be a blockbuster, although it is a much smaller show than Monet at the Royal Academy, with only 30 painted self-portraits by the artist – over some of which, the question of attribution still hangs – as well as his numerous etchings of himself, in numerous states, and works by Rembrandt's pupils, and paintings which might be seen as precursors to the artist's works, such as the National's 'Portrait Of A Man', by Titian, assumed by some to be Titian himself.

Apart from the two self-portraits by Carel Fabritius, Rembrandt's most talented pupil (who was accidentally blown up when a gunpowder factory exploded in Delft), most of these works are unnecessary to the show. They are makeweights. But there's nothing to truly argue with here. I can think of no other room of paintings in the world at this moment (apart from the room of Goya's black paintings in the Prado) so moving and disquieting as the central gallery of the Rembrandt show, containing the self-portraits of the last half of his career. Standing in this room I realised that you can't review Rembrandt. Rembrandt reviews you.

Extracted from 'Here's looking at me', *The Guardian*, 8 June 1999, page 12 of arts supplement

Compositional interpretation is also a useful method because it does offer a way of looking very carefully at the content, form and experiencing of images; and the successful deployment of many of the other methods discussed in this book – methods centrally concerned with questions of representation that I think are more appropriate for a critical visual methodology – nonetheless rely, initially, on the detailed scrutiny of the image itself. As well as art paintings, then, this chapter offers an approach to moving images – film – and takes a few glances at video-games. It will occasionally draw on writers whose work has in many ways distanced itself from more traditional art history approaches, but who still offer useful methodological pointers.

The chapter has four sections:

1. The first is this introduction.
2. The second looks at how compositional interpretation considers the technologies and the production of images.
3. The third looks at how compositional interpretation approaches the site of the image itself.
4. And the final section assesses compositional interpretation as a method for a critical visual methodology.

4.2 Compositional Interpretation: Technologies and the Production of the Image

Despite its lack of methodological explicitness, then, compositional interpretation is a very particular way of looking at images. It focuses most strongly on the image itself, and although it pays most attention to its compositionality, it also pays some attention to its *production*. As Joshua Taylor (1957: 70) notes, the only reason for paying much attention to the technologies of an image's production is 'when a knowledge of the technique helps in describing the particular characteristics of the work'.

In art connoisseurship, a note is usually made of aspects of the *social* modality of its production: who commissioned it, why, who painted it, and what then happened to it before it ended up in its current location. The various owners and locations of a painting are known as its **provenance**, and discovering the provenance of an image **provenance** will reveal the sites of its circulation. However, connoisseurship is more concerned to explore the *compositional* modality of its production, when it identifies the influence of other artists in a particular work, for example.

Usually, attention is focused mostly on the *technological* modality of the making of an image. As the discussion of technologies in Chapter 2 noted, it can be important to know with what material and technique an image is made, because this can affect the impact an image has.

Taylor (1957) provides some very useful discussions of the various technologies that have been used to produce visual images. He explores the particular qualities of both certain media – drawing, paintings, graphic arts, sculpture and architecture – and the different ways in which these can be deployed. His discussion of painting, for example, examines the techniques of fresco, watercolour, tempera, oil, encaustic and collage. James Monaco (2009) examines the various technologies of moving images in similar detail, and Chapters 1 and 2 have already discussed at some length the debates about the difference between images produced by analogue technologies and those produced by digital technologies.

focus

Where does Searle's essay refer to the effect of the use of oil paints on Rembrandt's portraits? What effects does his description of the oils have?

functionality

A more specific issue in relation to many kinds of digital imagery is what Michael Nitsche (2008) calls their **functionality**. Nitsche is discussing computer games, and describes functionality as 'the interactive access and underlying rules determining what the player can do in the game space and what the space can do to adjust that' (Nitsche, 2008: 7). Functionality is defined by the rules built into a computer game by the designer and programmer, and they clearly shape what the game looks and feels like to a significant degree. Finding out what these rules are could be an important part of the compositional interpretation of a computer game. Another component of computer games emphasised by Nitsche is **structure**. For Nitsche (2008: 7), the structure of a computer game is given by 'the events a player causes, triggers, and encounters inside a videogame space'. While the structure is in part a consequence of how the player plays the game, it is also an effect of the rules embedded in the game's software at production stage. Computer game structure can only be investigated by playing the game repeatedly; and indeed, most scholars of computer games also seem to be keen players.

structure

4.3 Compositional Interpretation:
The Compositionality of the Image Itself

Compositional interpretation pays most attention to the compositionality of the image itself. This section breaks down the compositionality seen by the 'good eye' into a number of components. This is a schematic device, however, since in practice few of these components are completely distinct from each other. Indeed, the notion of **composition** refers to all these elements in combination.

composition

4.3.1 Content

When looking at an image for itself, a starting point could be its content. What does the image actually show? This might seem a very obvious question not worth spending much time on, and for some images it will indeed be a very simple question. For others, though, it will not. Sometimes this difficulty will arise from the formal complexity of the image. For example, some viewers of the Doisneau photograph reproduced as Figure 2.2 need a bit of time to work out that the photographer is inside the gallery looking out into the street. Moreover, some images picture particular religious, historical, mythological, moral or literary themes or events, as Acton (2008) discusses (Section 8.3.2 will explore a method – iconography – whose aim is to decode the conventionalised visual symbols used to refer to such themes and events). Take some time to be sure about what you think an image is showing; this may lead you to consider its genre. A painting with a nude as its main subject refers to the genre of female nude painting that John Berger (1972) discusses (see Figure 1.4); and Chapter 2 discussed the parts of Robert Doisneau's photograph reproduced in Figure 2.2 that suggest it has a relation to the genres of documentary and street photography. The 'portrait' is also a particular genre of painting.

For other sorts of image, there is a different kind of difficulty in working out what the image actually shows. I am thinking of moving images. Most critics of film analyse films using a DVD so they can play, replay, pause and review all parts of the film to develop their analysis. Computer games, though, pose a different challenge. The structure of many computer games is such that the number of possible images in any one game is immense. There are the rules and definitions that guide each element, but also the rules and definitions that guide all the possible interactions between elements, so that 'any movement at any point and any specific interaction at that point change the [game's] condition … Any small change in a pattern might be the difference between glorious victory and miserable failure and will trigger a different move of the opponent' (Nitsche, 2008: 20). As Nitsche (2008: 19) explains, it is because of these complexities that such games have to be played in order to be interpreted. However, a research project on computer game imagery still needs to analyse specific parts of a game. There seem to be two possibilities here, both of which involve sampling images as you play. One strategy is to sample still images:

- William Sims Bainbridge (2010), for example, calculates he spent over 2,300 hours in the *World of Warcraft* in 2007 and 2008. He created seventeen characters, had two accounts and two computers; and captured around 22,000 screenshots from his computer screens as he played (Bainbridge, 2010: 18). He says he took screenshots because they recorded both the visual image on the screen and the talk between the players; he does not comment on exactly when and why he took specific shots, however. He then created a folder for each of his characters and put the relevant screenshots there, later arranging them by topic and analysing them (although he says nothing about that analysis stage either).

The other strategy for sampling constantly changing computer games is to make clips:

- Alan Brooksby (2008) was interested in the representation of 'health' in computer games and assumed that players' avatars would best show this. He thus decided to play each of ten games for two hours and then, two hours in, he videoed 15 minutes of play on his computer screen. The resultant ten, 15-minute clips of play were what he analysed.

Different ways of sampling make different assumptions about what is important to analyse in a computer game. Both of these examples assume that it is the images that are most important in a computer game, not its structure or functionality. Chapter 5 has something more to say about the implications of different kinds of sampling strategies.

4.3.2 Colour

Colour is another crucial component of an image's compositionality. Taylor (1957) offers three ways of describing the colours of a painting:

hue
- *hue*. This refers to the actual colours in a painting. Thus the dominant hues used in the Rembrandt portraits reproduced for Searle's review are browns, blues, and orange-tinted yellow.

saturation
- *saturation*. Saturation refers to the purity of a colour in relation to its appearance in the colour spectrum. Thus saturation is high if a colour is used in a vivid form of its hue, and low if it is nearly neutral. The blue and yellow colours in the review's illustrations are low, but the browns are high: rich and intense.

value
- *value*. This refers to the lightness or darkness of a colour. If a colour is in its near-white form, then its value is high; if in its near-black

form, its value is low. The browns, blacks and some of the blues in the illustrations have low value: they are all dark. But other blues, and yellows, seem to have quite high value.

These terms can describe the colours used in a painting, or any other kind of visual image. But it is also necessary to describe the effects of the colours in an image. Colour can be used to *stress* certain elements of an image, for example. The yellows in particular in the illustrations to Searle's essay seem to have quite high value, because they are often where the light falls in the painting; but of course since these are portraits, the high value of the face colours serves to draw our attention to the point of portrait paintings, the face.

There is also the question of how *harmonious* the colour combination of a painting is. There have been many theories about what colours combine most harmoniously with each other, and John Gage (1993) offers a very full account of the different ways in which colour has been understood 'from antiquity to abstraction', as the subtitle of his book says. For our purposes here, however, it is sufficient to consider whether the colours of a painting rely on contrasts or on the blending of similar value, saturation or hue. The Rembrandt illustrations appear very harmonious since they have a limited range of colours that blend into each other; even the blue is a muted contrast to the brown since, like the browns, it is mostly of low saturation. Gunther Kress and Theo van Leeuwen (2006: 228–35) also suggest that the combination of hues, values and saturations of an image affect how realistic audiences will imagine that image to be. If the colours look the same as a colour photograph of the same subject would, then our sense of its realism is heightened, they suggest.

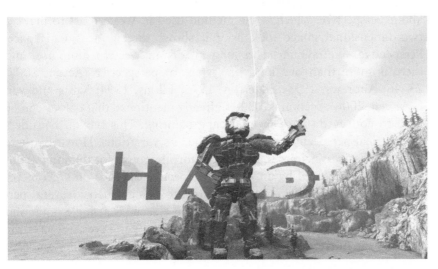

FIGURE 4.3
Screenshot from the computer game *Halo: Reach* (2010), showing atmospheric perspective. This is also an example of remediation, as the computer game is copying a convention first developed in Western landscape painting

Colour can also work to suggest an effect of distance in a painting, or other image, especially in landscape paintings. In that genre, the hues used often become more bluish as a means of suggesting the way a landscape recedes. This is known as **atmospheric perspective** (see Figure 4.3).

atmospheric perspective

4.3.3 Spatial organisation

All images organise their space in some way, and there are two related aspects of this organisation to consider – the organisation of space 'within' an image, and the way the spatial organisation of an image offers a particular viewing position to its spectator. This offer is part of an image's way of seeing.

This subsection's discussion begins with a consideration of the spatial organisation of still images.

First, think about the spatial organisation within a still image (Acton [2008: 1–76] has a useful discussion of this). Take a look at the three-dimensional *forms* of an image. How are these arranged in relation to each other? Are some forms connected in some way to others by vectors, while others are left isolated? How? What about the *lines* of the forms and their connections? Which directions do they follow? Are they fluid curves or jagged fragments? What sort of *rhythm* do they have: static or dynamic? What are the effects of these things? Kress and van Leeuwen (2006: 79–87) have an interesting discussion of images such as diagrams, flow charts and maps that explores how their elements are conventionally structured in relation to each other.

Then consider the space in which these forms are placed. Think about width, depth, interval and distance. Is this space simple, or complicated? In answering this question, it is important to understand something about perspective, which is the method used in Western art to make a two-dimensional image look as if it shows three-dimensional space. Perspective, like colour, has a long history in Western discourse, and there is more than one kind of system of perspective (Acton, 2008: 29–46; Andrews, 1995; Edgerton, 1975; Elkins, 1994; Kress and van Leeuwen, 2006). Section 4.3.2 has already mentioned that colour can be used to convey distance in landscape painting. This section considers **geometrical perspective**, and this too has its variations. However, there are some basic principles that provide starting points for thinking about the space represented by an image. Perspective depends on a geometry of rays of vision, and your eye is central to this geometry (several perspective systems assume that the viewer of a scene is a single point and thus that you have only one eye). The level of your eye is always the same as the horizon of a painting. It is also the level at which the rays

geometrical perspective

eye level - - - - -

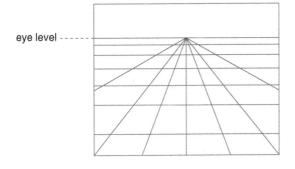

eye level - - - - -

FIGURE 4.4
Geometrical
perspective:
Eye levels

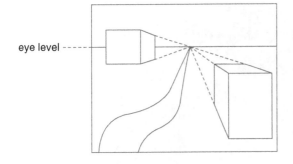

eye level - - - - -

FIGURE 4.5
Geometrical
perspective:
Distance

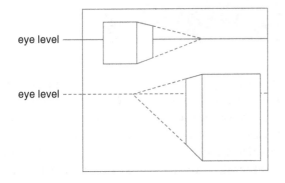

eye level ————

eye level - - - - -

FIGURE 4.6
Geometrical
perspective:
Multiple
vanishing
points

of vision converge at what is called the vanishing point. Figure 4.4 shows what difference your eye level makes to the representation of a paved area if you were sitting, first, on the ground and then on a high wall, according to this kind of perspective. Now let's see what happens if some basic building blocks appear in this scene, one close to us and one further apart (Figure 4.5). Finally, Figure 4.6 shows what happens if there are two different eye levels and two different vanishing points in an image of blocks.

Paintings can have different effects depending on their manipulation of this kind of perspective. In relation to Figure 4.6, for example, since one eye is assumed to be normal in this geometrical system, the space constructed with two eye levels seems strange and incoherent. Other paintings try to shift the spectator's point of view through their use of perspective. For example, using a very low eye level might represent the way a child sees the world, and Pollock (1988: 65) suggests that Mary Cassatt painted some of her canvases with this effect in mind (see Figure 4.7). Or a low eye level might suggest that the painting was made to be seen from below, and this is the case with, for example, Masaccio's crucifixion (Figure 4.8), painted in about 1427 as a fresco on the wall of the church of Santa Maria Novella in Florence, where the congregation would sit beneath it (Edgerton, 1975).

FIGURE 4.7
Little Girl in a Blue Armchair, 1878 by Mary Cassatt

Perspective thus provides a means of representing three-dimensional space on a two-dimensional surface. It dominated Western painting for centuries, from its first explication in the fifteenth century to its rejection by some painters in the early twentieth. Although now it is only one means among many of organising its space, it can provide a benchmark for thinking about the representation of space in any particular image.

focus

How do the Rembrandt portraits use geometrical perspective? Do we look down on the painted figure, or up to him?

A useful way to explore these aspects of the spatial organisation within an image is to try to draw a summary diagram of the image you are looking at (see Taylor [1957] and Kress and van Leeuwen [2006: 135, 137] for some examples). Look for lines that show the edges of things; extend them, and see where and how they intersect. The Rembrandt illustrations reproduced here are perhaps too simple in terms of their spatial organisation to make this a worthwhile exercise; but you might try making a simplified version of the painting reproduced as Figure 8.1, which is a marriage portrait of Giovanni Arnolfini and Giovanna Cenami, painted in 1434 by Jan van Eyck. Try extending the lines of the floorboards, the windowsill and the bedstead, for example. James Elkins (1991) has explored the use of perspective in this painting through just such a diagram of its converging and diverging lines. Compare his to yours.

FIGURE 4.8 *Crucifixion* (fresco), 1427, by Masaccio

This discussion of perspective brings us to the second aspect of the spatial organisation of an image that it is necessary to consider. This is the way in which the picture also offers a particular position to its viewers. We have already seen this process at work in our discussion of the Doisneau photograph in Chapter 2. The elements 'inside' that photo are arranged in such a way that they construct a particular viewing position 'outside' the photo (and this makes the distinction between 'inside' and 'outside' difficult to sustain). The Doisneau photograph aligns the spectator with the look of the man. Michael Ann Holly (1996) has argued that it is this positioning of the viewer that is most important when thinking about how visual images have their own effects. She calls the **logic of figuration** position offered to a viewer by an image its **logic of figuration**. In relation to the painting in Figure 4.7, for example, we can say that its logic of figuration places us low down in the painted room, inviting us to adopt a child's point of view. In asking 'what the work of art does for us' (Holly, 1996: xiv), Holly argues that it is the spatial and temporal organisation of a painting which structures its effects most profoundly; 'legislated and predicted by the spatial and temporal organisation of the visual field: we stand where the works tell us to stand and we see what they choose to reveal', she says (Holly, 1996: 9). Kress and van Leeuwen (2006: 114–49) talk in similar terms about the ways images can be seen as designing the position of the viewer through, in part at least, their spatial organisation.

Kress and van Leeuwen (2006: 124–49) also explore the effects of the spatial organisation of visual images on the position of the viewer. They examine the effects of geometrical perspective in some detail. They suggest, for example, that the *angle* between the spectator and what is pictured produces particular effects, with frontal angles engaging the viewer more with what is pictured than oblique angles. They also explore the effects of apparent differences in *height* between the spectator of an image and what is pictured: if the viewer is positioned by the image's perspective to look down on it, Kress and van Leeuwen (2006: 140–8) argue, they are given some sort of power over its subject matter; if they look up to it, then they are positioned as in some way inferior to it; and if they look at it at the same level, then a relationship of equality between spectator and pictured is suggested. They also look at other aspects of the spatial organisation of images, with *distance*, for example, suggesting that pictures of people in close-up usually offer a relation of intimacy between the person pictured and the spectator (Kress and van Leeuwen, 2006: 124–9). Searle assumes this in his discussion of the Rembrandt portraits. However, an exception to this latter claim suggests that these sorts of generalisations must always be carefully examined in relation to specific images: think for example of the use of police mugshots in newspaper reports of crimes, where the close-up format of the mugshot suggests precisely a big difference between the person pictured – the criminal – and the person looking – the innocent newspaper reader. In this case too, though, the spatial organisation of the composition is a crucial element of the relationship between an image and its audiences.

Mieke Bal (1991: 158–60), on the other hand, advocates concentrating less on the *spatial* organisation of an image, and more on the *visual* organisation of looks and gazes in her notion of the **focalisers** of an image. She points out that all paintings have a range of viewers: addressed, implied and represented. Each focalises – or looks – in their own way (see also Kress and van Leeuwen, 2006: 116–24). They look in a particular way, at specific things. The relations of looks between them – who can see what and how – can tell us much about how the image works to catch our gaze. This is in part how the discussion of the site of the image itself in Chapter 2 approached the photograph by Robert Doisneau reproduced as Figure 2.2. If an external focaliser – a spectator – can look in the same way at the same things as a focaliser in the picture, then the spectator's identification with the image will be strong, says Bal. Nitsche (2008) explores this point in relation to a couple of computer games.

focalisers

FIGURE 4.9
Screenshot from the computer game *Prince of Persia: The Forgotten Sands* (2010), showing how its external focalisation is very close to that of the Prince
Courtesy of *The Escapist* Magazine

In the game *Prince of Persia: The Sands of Time*, the Prince is both the hero and the narrator, and the game's structure follows the events he remembers; as a result, the events and some camera positions are controlled by the game rather than by the player in order to align the player with the Prince (Figure 4.9). In contrast, the strategy computer game *Age of Mythology* gives players an aerial view of the battlefield and the ability to instantly reposition as events unfold (Figure 4.10). These different external focalisations produce two very different effects. Bal's logic suggests that a player would be more caught up in *Prince of Persia* than *Age of Mythology* because they are focalising with the Prince; Kress and van Leeuwen, however, might counter that the power offered by the aerial view is more seductive and enjoyable.

FIGURE 4.10
Screenshot from the computer game *Age of Mythology* (2002), demonstrating that its external focalisation is a point of view not shared by any of the game's character

focus

What position are we offered by the logic of figuration and the focalisers of the Rembrandt portraits? What account does Searle give of this position? Through their use of geometrical perspective, the Rembrandt portraits position us as looking at the same level as the painter; we neither look down onto his image nor up at it. In that spatial sense we are at the same level as him. And we look at him in the way that he seems to be looking at us – directly.

Searle develops this sense of directness and equality between the artist's self-image and our view of it in particular ways. Searle says that these are paintings done by a man in dialogue with himself; we as spectators are now in the place of the mirror that Rembrandt must have used to make these pictures of himself. But he also suggests that Rembrandt's face is 'a vessel of universal characteristics' that he painted with 'candour'; the artist's honesty, his directness in confronting his own image and now us, mean that his portraits touch us now in 'moving and disquieting' ways. Indeed, such is the strength of Rembrandt's gaze, Searle eventually claims that he is reviewing us, not the other way round.

Thus Searle glosses aspects of the spatial organisation and focalisation of these portraits in specific ways. He gives a particular meaning to them. He suggests that they are an expression not only of Rembrandt's qualities – his honesty – but also of ours, since in looking at his portraits we are forced to confront the fact that we too will age and die. Rembrandt's honesty in confronting his ageing makes us honest and face ours. Thus he claims the portraits' power depends on showing the commonalities between us in the late twentieth century and Rembrandt in the seventeenth.

The spatial organisation of an image is not innocent. It has effects and it produces a specific relation between image and spectator. (These are not uncontroversial claims, however; Chapter 10 in particular will emphasise that particular spectators may not take up the position offered to them by an image.)

The spatial organisation of film and video requires further descriptive terminology. James Monaco (2009: 91–249) offers a detailed vocabulary for describing both spatial and temporal organisation of moving images, and this chapter draws heavily on his very useful discussion. The spatial organisation of a film is called its **mise-en-scène**. A mise-en-scène   mise-en-scène
is a result of decisions about what to shoot and how to shoot it. Monaco (2009: 205) suggests that what is shot involves looking at how the film frame is used, and that how it is shot concerns the structure of the shots themselves.

There are three aspects of the framing of film scenes that Monaco (2009) calls attention to. The first of these is the **screen ratio**. The   screen ratio
screen ratio is the ratio between the height of the projected image and its width: that is, the screen ratio describes the shape of the screen. In classic Hollywood movies – those made in the Hollywood studio system of the 1930s, 1940s and 1950s – the screen ratio was 1:33:1. Monaco (2009: 206) suggests that this proportion facilitated directors and audiences focusing on faces and dialogue. In the 1950s, the arrival

of widescreen, with screen ratios of 2:33:1 or more, was parallelled by more landscape shots, location shooting and action movies. The second aspect of framing, according to Monaco (2009), is how the **screen frame** works. If the action is filmed in such a way that the space beyond the screen frame is important, then the screen frame is *open*. Open screen frames are often used in horror and thriller films, where the suspense builds because the audience knows or suspects someone or something is lurking outside the screen frame, outside what we or the film's characters can actually see. If, on the other hand, the scene makes no reference to the space beyond its own frame, the screen frame is *closed*. A closed screen frame can be used to suggest a particular mood or emotion. For example, in Steven Soderbergh's film *Ocean's Eleven* one of the characters is making money in LA teaching poker to film stars. There is a long scene early in the film of one of his lessons, and the confined space of its closed screen frame manages to imply how restrictive and boring the character finds his work. Finally, Monaco (2009: 210–12) discusses the **screen planes**. There are three of these, and they intersect. The *frame plane* is how forms are distributed across the screen; the *geographical plane* is how forms are distributed in three-dimensional space; and the *depth plane* is how the apparent depth of the images is perceived.

*[margin: screen frame]*

[margin: screen planes]

Also in relation to the frame, Monaco (2009) points out that a frame can contain **multiple images** if it is split, or images can be shown as **superimpositions**, through techniques such as double exposure. Sometimes this is done as a sort of visual in-joke (as when the film *The Incredible Hulk* uses multiple images to reference the original source of the Hulk story, which was a comic). Sometimes it is done to make a connection between different characters: *Ocean's Eleven* does this, when, after the first few minutes of the film has introduced us to one main character, a wipe to the right stops half-way across the screen (the next section explains wipes), revealing the second main character eating a burger; for a moment their two images are seen side-by-side, before a second wipe to the right obscures the first character and takes us into the second character's story and how the two meet to work together again.

[margin: multiple images superimpositions]

The second aspect of moving images' mise-en-scène is their shots. **Shot distance** refers to how much of a figure is shown by a particular shot, and a shot can be an *extreme long shot* (where the figure is in the far distance), a *long shot*, or a *full, three-quarters, medium, head and shoulders* or *close-up* shot. Monaco (2009: 221–3) tentatively suggests some of the effects that frequent use of one or other of these sorts of shots might produce in a particular film. The repeated use of close-ups, for example, may produce a sense of claustrophobic intensity, while

[margin: shot distance]

long shots may imply alienation and emptiness. However, as Monaco himself comments, these sorts of generalisations about the effects of the spatial organisation of images always need to be assessed carefully in relation to specific images.

The **focus** of shots is also important. *Deep focus* is when the foreground, middle ground and background of a shot – all of the frame's geographical plane – are in focus. *Shallow focus* is when one of these grounds is more in focus than others. Shallow focus is sometimes used to direct attention to a particular character or event in a scene; for example, in *Ocean's Eleven*, again, there is a dialogue scene between the two main characters in which the focus repeatedly shifts from one to the other as they talk with each other. Focus can also be *sharp* or *soft*. Monaco comments that certain kinds of focusing may have particular effects. Soft focus may be used to create a romantic or nostalgic feel to a scene, for example. But again, the precise effects of a particular kind of focus may not correspond to these sorts of generalisations. **focus**

The **angle** of shots also needs to be considered. The angle of *approach*, for example: is it square or oblique? The angle of *elevation* matters too: it can be overhead (looking right down onto the scene), high-angle, eye-level or low-angle (looking up at the scene). The shot may also *roll*, which is when the horizon of the image changes its angle, although Monaco notes that this is rare, since it disrupts the union between camera and audience that cinema especially very often tries to maintain. **angle**

The **point of view** adopted by shots is also crucial to a film's effects. The camera may adopt the point of view of a particular character, for example, and in Chapter 7 we will see what use Hitchcock made of this device in his film *Vertigo*. The *reverse-angle* shot is a particular case of the camera adopting characters' points of view. It is very often used to show a conversation between two people: one is seen talking or listening from approximately the other's viewpoint as the other listens or talks. An example of this technique was the conversation between villain (Robert De Niro) and cop (Al Pacino) in Michael Mann's *Heat*: their conversational confrontation in the movie was shot entirely with reverse angles so the viewer never saw the two men in the same frame together, an indication of the divisions between them perhaps. The camera may also adopt what Monaco (2009: 234) calls the '*third person*' shot, in which 'the camera often seems to take on a character of its own, separate from those of the characters'. In classic Hollywood movies, the opening point of view is very often a particular sort of this third person shot. It is an *establishing* shot, which works to give the audience the information they need about place, time and character before the narrative begins. **point of view**

Finally, Monaco offers a number of terms that refer to the way that the camera itself moves in film images. The camera can revolve while remaining stationary, or it can physically move. There are three kinds of shots possible when the camera revolves: the **pan**, when the camera moves along a horizontal axis, perhaps along the horizon of a landscape; the **tilt**, when it moves along a vertical axis, perhaps moving from the head to the feet of a character; and the **roll**, which has already been noted. When the camera itself moves, the shot is a **tracking shot** if the line it follows is horizontal, and a **crane shot** if the line it follows is vertical. An example of a tracking shot mentioned by Monaco (2009: 237) is the opening shot of Robert Altman's film *The Player*. This is a very long tracking shot which is also an establishing shot, as it moves through the lot of a Hollywood studio introducing location and characters to the audience. Finally, there is the **zoom shot**, which is similar to a tracking shot but is made by a stationary camera. In a zoom shot, the figure in a scene remains the same size while the surroundings appear to be moving through changes in size.

pan

tilt
roll
tracking shot
crane shot

zoom shot

Finally, there is a connection to be made here to the discussion in Chapter 1 about a distinctively digital form of visual spatial organisation. Recall Thomas Elsaesser's claim that a 'new default value of digital vision' is emerging (2013: 240) that is evident in many different visual genres. His particular example is the recent resurgence in 3D cinema. Elsaesser acknowledges that it is difficult to feel totally immersed in a 3D space while also sitting in a cinema seat, though, and Nitsche (2008) argues that the spatial organisation of computer games is different from other sorts of digital and non-digital moving images, including film, precisely because it encourages a more 'immersive' sense of space. Nitsche (2008) suggests that this is because the spatiality of computer games are not created 'as foregrounded spectacles based on visual cues such as perspective and parallax but as presented spaces that are assigned an architectural quality' (Nitsche, 2008: 3), which do offer greater feelings of immersion to players than can films, even 3D films (see also Ash, 2015).

4.3.4 The montage of film

montage

Montage is another term related to the composition of moving images, and refers to the temporal organisation of a film. If a film's mise-en-scène is a result of decisions about what to shoot and how to shoot it, according to Monaco (2009: 239) its montage is how those shots are put together; that is, how they are presented. Another term for montage is **editing**. As Monaco (2009) comments, the vocabulary for describing different montage techniques is much less well developed than that which can be used to describe frames and shots. (A quite distinct aspect

editing

of the temporal organisation of a film is its narrative; describing its **narrative structure** can also be an important way of interpreting a film.)

    In classic Hollywood cinema, and in many of its commercial products today, the principle behind montage is the maintenance of an impression of both narrative flow and spatial coherence. The kind of editing used to achieve this is known as **continuity cutting**. Shots are edited in order to allow the clear development of the story and to maintain a realistic representation of the spaces which the narrative occupies. There are many ways in which this is done, and as audiences of films we take many of them for granted. Establishing shots and reverse angles, for example, are seen as realistic ways of showing place and characters. Editing techniques like *jump cuts*, for example, when two completely unrelated images are spliced together, were rare in classic Hollywood cinema, because we do not perceive the world like that (although as Monaco [2009] comments, many of the techniques we see as representing realistically how we see the world bear little resemblance to how we do actually look).

    The jump cut is one sort of connection, or **cut**, that can be made between shots. It is an example of an *unmarked cut*, where one image ends and another starts. Other sorts of connections are the *fade*, where an image fades to black, the *dissolve*, which superimposes a fade in over a fade out, the *iris*, in which the image is reduced in size by an encroaching border circle, and the *wipe*, mentioned in the previous section, where one image removes another. *Ocean's Eleven* has a striking dissolve cut too, which fades out of focus (not to black) on a bunch of red balloons being sold in a street in Las Vegas and fades in again to the same bunch of balloons being carried through a casino. The *rhythm* of cuts, determined by how long each shot is held, may also be important in considering a film's effects. Jose Arroyo (2000) comments on the effects of a certain rhythm of cuts in the first *Mission: Impossible* film, in a scene where our hero is suspended by wires from the ceiling of a high-security room, attempting to steal a computer disk; as he hangs, a bead of sweat drops from him onto the pressure-sensitive floor. This is filmed in a series of short, sharp cuts, to build suspense, interspersed with longer slow-motion shots as the sweat drop falls. Arroyo (2000: 25) says that 'the combined effect [of these shots] is sublime. The slow motion fixes our gaze with awe; the quick cuts rush us headlong into terror.' Indeed, Monaco comments that a series of progressively shorter scenes is a technique often used to accumulate tension as a narrative climax develops. Monaco (2009: 244–6) also spends some time on the complicated schema for describing montage developed by Christian Metz (1975), a rare example of an attempt to formulate a typology for all montage possibilities, and rather elaborate as a result.

Margin notes:

narrative structure

continuity cutting

cut

focus

Steven Soderbergh's film *Ocean's Eleven* is a slick Hollywood thriller, superbly shot and edited to maintain the flow of its story, which follows a group of conmen as they attempt to steal millions of dollars from the vault of a Las Vegas casino. (The soundtrack is also crucial to its flow and style [see Monaco, 2009: 235–9].)

Watch *Ocean's Eleven* on DVD. Choose a chapter at random and describe it using the vocabulary presented here.

You will have found that describing all the shots and edits of even a small part of a film is very time-consuming. This raises an interesting question for the compositional interpretation of moving images, which Section 4.3.1 rather glossed over: how do you choose which shots and edits to discuss when you are describing the film?

4.3.5 Sound

Sound is also crucial to many moving images, especially movies. Monaco (2009: 235–9) suggests that there are three types of sound: *environmental*, *speech* and *music*. Environmental sounds are noise effects, whether 'real' or artificial, and they can be crucial to a movie's expressive content. The music soundtrack of a movie is also fundamental to its effect. A final example from *Ocean's Eleven* makes this point. The opening scene has one of the main characters, Danny Ocean, in prison, facing his parole board. When asked what he intends to do if he is given parole, he doesn't answer; instead, the soundtrack music begins that will accompany the gang through their con, clearly suggesting that Danny has planned the con already and it is what he will do if released.

Monaco (2009: 238) also suggests three overlapping ways in which the relation between the sound and the image of a film can be considered. The *source* of the sound can be in or out of the frame. *Parallel* sound is sound that is actual, synchronous with and related to the image. In contrast, *contrapuntal* sound is commentative, asynchronous and opposes the image.

4.3.6 Light

The light shown in both still and moving images is clearly related to both its colours and its spaces. What *type* of light an image shows – candlelight, daylight, electric light – will clearly affect the saturation and value of its hues and the illusion that geometrical perspective realistically represents three-dimensional space can be enhanced or called into question by the use of light *sources*. The apparent realism of *The Arnolfini Portrait* (see Figure 8.1) is increased, for example, by the dominant source of light coming from the window and the way all the shadows in the painting are consistent with this. Light can also be used to *highlight* certain elements of a painting, as we have seen in the case of the Rembrandt portraits. Light is also central to creating the mood or atmosphere of an image, which takes this part of the chapter to its final subsection.

4.3.7 Expressive content

The 'mood' or 'atmosphere' of an image is both difficult to explain, often, and also crucial to compositional interpretation as a method. An important part of compositional interpretation is the evocation in writing of the 'feel' of an image, or what, after Taylor, I will call its **expressive content**. Taylor (1957: 43–4) describes an image's expressive content as 'the combined effect of subject matter and visual form'. Separate consideration of expressive content is necessary because breaking an image into its component parts – spatial organisation, montage, colour, content, light and so on – does not necessarily capture the look of an image. Instead, what may be needed is some imaginative writing that tries to evoke its affective characteristics. As an example, here is the art historian Erwin Panofsky writing about the Arnolfini portrait reproduced as Figure 8.1:

> In a comfortably furnished interior, suffused with a warm, dim light, Giovanni Arnolfini and his wife are standing represented in full-length ... The husband gingerly holds the lady's right hand in his left while raising his right in a gesture of solemn affirmation. Rather stiffly posed and standing as far apart as the action permits, they do not look at each other yet seem to be united by a mysterious bond ... (1953: 201–2)

Panofsky uses terms like 'comfortably', 'gingerly' and 'solemn' which would be difficult to produce relying solely on the list of concerns this chapter has offered, yet they seem necessary elements in any account of this painting.

The notion of expressive content is important in many discussions of film and computer games too; indeed, Jesper Juul (2010: 45) argues that attractive expressive content is fundamental to successful computer games. Nitsche (2008: 7) uses the term 'presentation' to refer to the expressive content of computer games, while Juul (2010) uses the term

expressive content

juiciness   **juiciness.** In his discussion of juiciness, Juul distinguishes between hardcore games – which require high levels of time, skill and commitment,
and are usually played on computers or game consoles – and casual
games, which are short, interruptible, easy to learn and often played on
mobile phones. He suggests that in hardcore games, the sensory and
visceral feelings provoked tend to be focused on events happening
within the game (Figure 4.11). Casual computer games, on the other
hand, tend to make their expressive appeal directly to the player, giving
them an immediate and pleasurable experience (Figure 4.12).

The work of scholars interested in the embodied and sensory experiencing of images also depends on conveying their sensory engagement with an image. Marks (2002: xii), for example, describes her approach to visual images as mimetic, in that she wants to get 'close enough to the other thing to become it'. Her task is then to convey how that closeness makes her feel in her critical writing: 'I search the image for a trace of the originary, physical event. The image is connective tissue ... I want it to reveal to me a continuity I had not foreseen, and in turn reveal that to you' (Marks, 2002: x). Laura Marks (2002: xxii) describes this kind of criticism as a 'radical **formalism**', which pays such close attention to the form – or composition – of an image that it goes beyond representation and towards 'a trace of an originary event'. Marks also describes her approach as **haptic,** a term also used by Hansen (2004: 12) to emphasise the way bodies can be experienced in new ways through such close encounters with images. Hansen's (2004) discussion of new media is based entirely on his encounters with various artworks and his philosophical convictions; in his writing, his own embodied experiences become the content of these works. After visiting an exhibition with work by the art collective Mongrel, for example, Hansen (2004: 151) says, 'As I now reflect on the experience, I can see more clearly still how the play between image, voice, and the spatialized data field was instrumental to the affective impact of the work'. *His* experience becomes '*the* experience', and that experience allows him to describe and explain the affective impact of Mongrel's work.

Can paying so much attention to the experiencing of an image be congruent with a critical visual methodology concerned with the social effects of imagery? Paying close attention to images can seem very much like the traditional form of connoisseurship, in which an informed and sensitive individual pronounces on the meaning or value of an art image. This similarity is not helped, according to Patricia Ticineto Clough (2008), by Hansen's insistence in particular on the body being the centre of his critical practice. Because, of course, when using compositional interpretation to get close to an image, 'the' body is not some generic body, but the specific body of the critic. While Marks (2002) does reflect on how her own sensory perceptions are specific to herself, there is no sign of such reflexivity in Hansen's work.

formalism

haptic

Return to Searle's review one more time. The expressive content of the Rembrandt portraits is central to his discussion of them. Pick out the moments in his text when he evokes it.

Searle's efforts to articulate the expressive content of the Rembrandt self-portraits are interesting because they explicitly reject (or marginalise) other ways of relating to the paintings. He suggests that both the gallery and the catalogue are somewhat irrelevant next to the extraordinary effects of the portraits. This tactic is typical of the connoisseurship central to the 'good eye'. Only the 'quality' of the paintings matters; everything else – all the other sorts of interpretative apparatus brought to bear on them – is insignificant.

But of course Searle, too, is bringing an interpretative apparatus to bear on the portraits; the 'good eye' is itself an interpretative technique. This apparatus assumes that only the paintings are important, to begin with. But his discussion of them also draws on at least two other assumptions regarding great art. One is that it is produced by something called **genius**: a marvellously gifted individual who can rise above the specificities of his circumstances to touch what are apparently the fundamental concerns of human life (see Battersby [1994] for a critique of the notion of genius, particularly the way it is a masculinised category). And the other is that art – **Art** – can speak directly to this humanity in everyone.

genius

Art

Victor Burgin summarises this understanding of Art and genius thus:

> *Art* is an activity characteristic of humanity since the dawn of civilisation. In any epoch the *Artist*, by virtue of special gifts, expresses that which is finest in humanity ... the visual artist achieves this through modes of understanding and expression which are 'purely visual' ... This special characteristic of art necessarily makes it an autonomous sphere of activity, completely separate from the everyday world of social and political life. The autonomous nature of visual art means that questions asked of it may only be properly put, and answered, in its own terms – all other forms of interrogation are irrelevant. (1986: 30, emphasis in original)

Hence Searle's assertion that galleries and catalogues are irrelevant in relation to the Rembrandt portraits; because these portraits are Art, only his, and our, humanity matters. In this view, art is seen as cross-cultural, with universal appeal. In the introduction to their book on *Visual Culture* (1994), Norman Bryson, Michael Ann Holly and Keith Moxey make clear the difference between approaches to visual images that depend on this notion of Art, and the approach to visual images that the contributors to their book adopt:

> Instead of seeking to promote and sustain the value of 'great' art by limiting discussion to the circumstances of the work's production and to speculation about the extraordinary impulses that may

have characterized the intentions of its makers, these contributors examine the work performed by the image in the life of culture ... Instead of applying a Kantian aesthetic, according to which value is an intrinsic characteristic of the work of art, one capable of being perceived by all human beings regardless of their location in time and place – a recognition that depends only on one's status as a human being – these writers betray an awareness that the aesthetic value of a work depends on the prevailing cultural conditions. They invest the work with value by means of their appreciation of its meaning both in the cultural horizon of its production and its reception. (Bryson et al., 1994: xvi)

Thus, while the connoisseurship usually accompanying the exercise of 'the good eye' denies the cultural specificity of Art, the notion of visual culture addresses that specificity directly.

Thus the expressive content of an image is always necessary to consider. However, Chapter 2 suggested that not all visual culture critics agree on its significance, and it may be important that your reaction to it does not obscure other, possibly more important issues concerning the meaning of the image.

4.4 Compositional Interpretation: An Assessment

Compositional interpretation offers ways of describing the content, colour, spatial organisation, mise-en-scène, montage, light and expressive content of various kinds of still and moving images. This is very useful as a first stage of getting to grips with an image that is new to you, and it remains useful as a way of describing the visual impact of an image. In its concern for the spatial organisation of an image, moreover, compositional interpretation may also begin to say something about an image's possible effects on a spectator.

However, in relation to the criteria for a critical visual methodology spelled out in Chapter 1, compositional interpretation has many shortcomings. While the interest of art historians in the provenance of artworks may direct some attention to the circulation of an image, the method in general does not encourage discussion of the production of an image (other than of its technological or compositional modalities), nor of how it might be used, understood and interpreted by various viewers. Thus compositional interpretation can end up relying on notions of connoisseurship, or genius, or Art, for example, as Searle's essay does, that simply cannot get to grips with the concerns of the previous chapter about the specificities of particular visualities. And with its unproblematised concern for visual images 'as they are', compositional interpretation does not allow for reflexive consideration of the particularity of any interpretation. Seltzer (2009: 109) makes this point in relation to 'the current affective turn in academic criticism', which can produce what he rather witheringly calls 'sensibility criticism'. Indeed, compositional interpretation's implicit reliance on the heightened sensitivity of the critic to the expressive content of images can be 'ultimately egocentric and narcissistic' (Boothroyd, 2009: 339). Compositional interpretation thus needs to be combined with other methodologies in order to address these latter sorts of issues. In his discussion of film, for example, Monaco (2009) also uses terms drawn from semiology (see Chapter 6) to explore how films carry meanings.

Summary: Compositional Interpretation

- *associated with*:
  Compositional interpretation can (and should) be used in relation to any sort of image, but its roots lie in a certain tradition of art history, and it continues to be used on its own most often in relation to paintings.

- *sites and modalities*:
  Compositional interpretation pays some attention to the production of images, especially their technologies, but is mostly concerned with the image itself in its compositional modality.

- *key terms*:
  According to compositional analysis, some of the key components of a still image are its content, colour, spatial organisation, light and expressive content. Moving images can be described in terms of their mise-en-scène, montage and functionality.

- *strengths and weaknesses for a critical visual methodology*:
  This method demands careful attention to the image, which is crucial for any discussion of images. A disadvantage of this method is its uninterest in the social practices of visual imagery.

Further Reading

Joshua Taylor's *Learning to Look* (1957) is very useful for still art images, while James Monaco's *How to Read a Film* (2009) is excellent for approaching film, television and video images (and also covers far more ground than just compositional interpretation).

 COMPANION WEBSITE

Visit **https://study.sagepub.com/rose4e** for:

- **Links to a range of podcasts by art historians**, many using compositional interpretation to explore different kinds of fine art from contemporary to medieval.
- **An interactive online exercise** based on a painting by the Italian Renaissance artist Titian, which gives you a chance to practise making your own interpretation guided by the art historian Catherine Belsey.

5

CONTENT ANALYSIS AND CULTURAL ANALYTICS

FINDING PATTERNS IN WHAT YOU SEE

key example: a book by Catherine Lutz and Jane Collins which analyses nearly six hundred of the photographs published in the magazine *National Geographic* between 1950 and 1986.

Other examples discussed in less detail in the chapter include. studies of computer games and Instagram photographs.

5.1 Content Analysis and Cultural Analytics: An Introduction

This chapter discusses two methods for analysing large numbers of images.

The first of these is content analysis. Content analysis is a method of analysing visual images that was originally developed to interpret written and spoken texts. In one way, content analysis stands in sharp contrast to the method examined in the previous chapter. Whereas compositional interpretation is methodologically silent, relying instead on that elusive thing called 'the good eye', content analysis is methodologically explicit. Indeed, it is based on a number of rules and procedures that must be rigorously followed for the analysis of images or texts to be reliable (on its terms); these concern the selecting, coding and quantitative analysis of large numbers of images. It was first developed as a research method in the interwar period by social scientists wanting to analyse the journalism of the emerging mass media, and was given a further boost during the Second World War, when its methods were elaborated in order to detect implicit messages in German domestic radio broadcasts (Krippendorff, 2013) – hence its explicit quantitative methodology, through which, it was claimed, analysis would be rigorous, reliable and objective.

mass media   Content analysis's close attention to the **mass media** – television, newspapers and radio – occurred not only because it was seen as a way of generating objective data about these new phenomena, however, but also because it was a method that could address the sheer scale of those media. The reach of the mass media in the interwar period was unprecedented; they were broadcast or sold to thousands if not millions of people every day of the week, every month of the year. If it was important to understand what 'the newspapers' were saying, or what 'the radio news' was broadcasting, an analysis based on looking at a few issues of a paper, or listening to a few programmes, was clearly at risk of being unrepresentative. Appropriate methods of analysis had to reflect the scale at which the mass media operated, it was argued, and similar arguments are now made in relation to the vast numbers of digital images on the Internet (Burgess and Green, 2009; Hartley, 2012; Manovich and Douglass, 2011; this argument will be addressed again in Chapter 11).

Indeed, a version of content analysis has recently been developed by Lev Manovich which harnesses the processing power of computers in order to analyse tens of thousands of digital images, including social media images. He calls this method *cultural analytics*. Cultural analytics is an 'automatic computer-based method to describe large numbers of cultural objects quantitatively' (Manovich and Douglass, 2011: 325), and it is part of a larger shift towards the use of computational methods in the digital humanities (Hall, 2013).

In various forms, then, content analysis remains an important visual research method, because it can deal with large amounts of data. However, the congruence between mass or social media and content analysis or cultural analytics is by no means inevitable; there are many other methods for interpreting mass media texts and images other than content analysis. Many of these other methods are qualitative rather than quantitative. Semiology, for example, which this book discusses in Chapter 6, has been used in relation to the photographs and advertisements carried by newspapers and magazines; so too has the type of discourse analysis discussed in Chapter 8. The mass media have also been examined from the perspectives of their audiences, as Chapter 10 discusses at some length. Content analysis, then, is just one option to consider if you are working with mass or social media images. Conversely, content analysis can be applied to materials other than those found in mass or social media; cultural analytics has been used on paintings and manga comics, for example.

While it is true that the software programmes of cultural analytics can analyse very large numbers of images, the practicalities of accessing and storing images at such a scale are significant and this chapter assumes that most of its readers will be able to work with a few hundred images at most. Its key example is therefore a content analysis of nearly 600 of the photographs printed in the magazine *National Geographic* over nearly three decades, by Catherine Lutz and Jane Collins (1993).

Lutz and Collins (1993) use content analysis as a useful way of dealing manually with relatively large numbers of images. Their defence of content analysis also suggests that content analysis can be useful for the visual critical methodology outlined in Chapter 1 of this book:

> Although at first blush it might appear counterproductive to reduce the rich material in any photograph to a small number of codes, quantification does not preclude or substitute for qualitative analysis of the pictures. It does allow, however, discovery of patterns that are too subtle to be visible on casual inspection and protection against an unconscious search through the magazine for only those which confirm one's initial sense of what the photos say or do. (Lutz and Collins, 1993: 89)

This passage is worth expanding on, particularly as it also underpins the justification for cultural analytics. First, Lutz and Collins are suggesting that content analysis can reveal empirical results that might otherwise be overwhelmed by the sheer bulk of material under analysis, and Manovich and Douglass (2011) also argue that cultural analytics can reveal patterns that would not be visible to lone researchers exploring a handful of images.

Secondly, Lutz and Collins are insisting that content analysis can include qualitative interpretation. Content analysis and qualitative methods are not mutually exclusive. Some discussions of content analysis argue, on the contrary, that its definition of 'reliable' equates reliability with quantitative methods of analysis (Ball and Smith, 1992; Neuendorf, 2002; Slater 1998). However, as Krippendorff (2013) makes clear in his discussion of content analysis, content analysis also involves various qualitative procedures. Instead of focusing on the question of quantification, Krippendorf's definition of content analysis emphasises two different aspects of the method: replicability and validity (these terms will be defined in Sections 5.2.2 and 5.2.3 respectively). In line with the broad approach to visual images outlined in Chapter 1, he insists that content analysis is a way of understanding the symbolic qualities of texts, by which he means the way that elements of a text always refer to the wider cultural context of which they are a part. Content analysis aims to analyse those references in any one group of texts in a replicable and valid manner.

And finally, Lutz and Collins also suggest that content analysis prevents a certain sort of 'bias'. Cultural analytics, as a type of content analysis, makes the same claim: it is a method for analysing images that does not rely on pre-existing interpretative categories. Content analysts are therefore concerned to avoid searching through images in order only to confirm what they think they already know about them. They suggest that this danger can be avoided by following the rules of content analysis, which force a researcher to be methodologically explicit rather than rely unknowingly on 'unconscious' strategies. Being so up-front about your research procedures is a sort of reflexive research strategy, then. Their argument thus coincides at this point with the third criterion for a critical visual methodology that Chapter 1 outlined: the need to be as methodologically explicit as possible in order to make your own way of seeing as evident as possible.

Content analysis and its variations do have some weaknesses in the sorts of interpretative work they can do with visual images, however. There are aspects of visual imagery which they are not well equipped to address. They focus almost exclusively on the *compositional* modality of the site of the *image* itself. They therefore have very little to say about the production, circulation or the audiencing of images, and the uninterest in audiences has perhaps been the most persistent criticism of this method. In this sense, they are paradoxically very much like compositional interpretation, which has little to say about the audiencing, circulation and production sites of meaning-making either. Some critics also argue that neither content analysis nor cultural analytics are capable of dealing with the cultural significance of images (Hall, 2013). This latter criticism, it seems to me, depends on how successfully the links between the content of the images undergoing content analysis and their broader cultural context are made. If those links are tenuous, then this final criticism is also valid.

This chapter examines content analysis in four sections:

1. The first is this introduction.
2. The second explores the key stages in a content analysis.
3. The third briefly summarises the key stages of the cultural analytics process.
4. And the fourth section assesses the usefulness of the kinds of evidence it produces, using the criteria for a critical visual methodology outlined in Chapter 1.

5.2 Four Steps to Content Analysis

The method of content analysis – and its variations, like cultural analytics – is based on counting the frequency of certain visual elements in a clearly defined population of images, and then analysing those frequencies. For content analysis, each aspect of this process has certain requirements in order to achieve replicable and valid results.

5.2.1 Finding your images

As with any other method, the images chosen for a content analysis must be appropriate to the question being asked. Take computer games, for example. These games are constituted by the images on the screen, of course, but also, it might be argued, by the image on their box, by their advertisements and by their websites. Which content is most relevant to addressing your research questions? The previous chapter mentioned Alan Brooksby's (2008) study of the representation of 'health' in computer games, and his decision to analyse 15 minutes of play in each of ten games. He chose to record those 15 minutes after playing each game for two hours. Another study of computer games was concerned with their representation of female bodies; this one collected the bestselling games across nine major platforms, and took screenshots of all the female characters to analyse (Martins et al., 2009). For Miranda Burgess and her colleagues (Burgess et al., 2007), though, analysing computer games by using images from the game itself assumes that the most significant content of a computer game is seen when a game is played. Their study was concerned with how gender and violence are represented by computer games, and especially with how such representations might impact upon young children. Young children may never get to play *Halo* or *Grand Theft Auto* – but they might see the boxes of those games lying around in their home. So Burgess and her team decided to analyse the covers of computer games, not the games themselves, downloading the images of 225 computer game box covers from a popular online store (Burgess et al., 2007: 422).

Lutz and Collins describe their research question thus:

> Our interest was, and is, in the making and consuming of images of the non-Western world, a topic raising volatile issues of power, race, and history. We wanted to know what popular education tells Americans about who 'non-Westerners' are, what they want, and what our relationship is to them. (Lutz and Collins, 1993: xii)

Given that research question, they then explain why they chose *National Geographic* as an appropriate source of images:

> After much consideration, we turned to the examination of *National Geographic* photographs as one of the most culturally valued and potent media vehicles shaping American understandings of, and responses to, the world outside the United States. (Lutz and Collins, 1993: xii)

They point out that *National Geographic* is the third most popular magazine subscribed to in the USA; each issue is read by an estimated 37 million people worldwide. They also note that in its reliance on photography, it reflects the importance of the visual construction of social difference in contemporary Western societies (see Figure 5.1).

Unlike many other of the methods this book will discuss, however, content analysis places further strictures on the use of images. To begin with, content analysis must address all the images relevant to the research question. This raises questions for content analysts about the *representativeness* of the available data. If, for example, you are interested in tracing the increasing acceptability of facial hair on bourgeois men in the nineteenth century, you may decide that the most appropriate source of images for assessing this acceptability are the popular magazines that those men would have been reading. If, however, you find that a 20-year run of the best-selling of those

FIGURE 5.1
*Adiokrou
Queen*, an
image from
*National
Geographic*
magazine
© Carol
Beckwith and
Angela Fisher/
photokunst

magazines is missing from the archive you have access to, you face a serious problem in using content analysis: your analysis cannot be representative since your set of relevant images is incomplete.

Many content analyses rely on some sort of sampling procedure in order to make their dataset manageable. Sampling in content analysis is subject to the same concerns it would be in any quantitative study. It should be both *representative* and *significant*. There are a number of sampling strategies described in Krippendorff (2013). They include:

- *random*: Number each image from 1 onwards, and use a random number generator to pick out a significant number of images to analyse.
- *stratified*: Sample from subgroups that already exist in the dataset, choosing your image from within each subgroup again by using a clear sampling strategy.
- *systematic*: Select every third or tenth or *n*th image. Be careful that the interval you are using between images does not coincide with a cyclical pattern in your source material, otherwise your sample will not be representative. For example, in a study of weekday newspaper advertisements, choosing every fifth paper might mean that every paper in your sample contains the weekly motoring page, which might mean that your sample will contain a disproportionate number of adverts for cars.
- *cluster*: Choose groups at random and sample from them only.

Which sampling method – or which combination of methods – you choose will depend on the implications of your research question. If you wanted to sample the full range of television programmes in order to explore how often people with disabilities were given air-time, for example, you might use a stratified sampling procedure which involves stratifying a whole year's programming into week-days and time slots and then randomly selecting one programme for each time slot out of the 52 possibilities.

focus

If you were interested in the representation of Edinburgh in contemporary picture postcards, a random sample would be an appropriate sampling strategy. But this raises some interesting questions about how you access a representative random sample of that sort of imagery. How would you do that?

Would you go into every shop in Edinburgh's main tourist street – the Royal Mile – and buy five cards at random, and if so, how? Would you contact all the postcard manufacturers and ask them to send you copies or catalogues of their current postcards, and select from there?

Think about what you want your postcards to be representative of. While the latter method would be more representative of current postcard production, the former would be more representative of the cards most often on sale.

There are no hard-and-fast rules for deciding what size your sample should be. Sample size depends in part on the amount of variation among all the relevant images. If there is absolutely no variation, a sample of one will be representative. If though there are a whole range of extreme variations, the sample size must be large enough to contain examples of those extremes. There are also practical considerations, however, in considering sample size. The sample should not be so large that it overwhelms the resources you have available for analysing it. In their study of *National Geographic*, Lutz and Collins chose one photo at random from each of the 594 articles on non-Western people published between 1950 and 1986 (Lutz and Collins, 1993: 88). This was a stratified sampling procedure, since they were choosing an image from subgroups, in this case the groups of photos contained in each article; and it also produced a manageable number of photos that they and their two research assistants could analyse.

5.2.2 Devising your categories for coding

Having selected a sample of images to work with, the next stage is to
devise a set of categories for coding the images. 'Coding' means attaching a set of descriptive labels (or 'categories') to the images. This is a
crucial stage. As Slater (1998: 236) notes, much of the rigour of classic
content analysis relies on the structure of categories used in the coding
process, because the categories should be apparently objective in a number of ways and therefore only describe what is 'really' there in the text
or image. More recent users of content analysis like Lutz and Collins
(1993) develop their categories in relation to their theoretical concerns
so that their categories are immediately more obviously interpretative.
This is one of their tactics that allows them to make their claim that
content analysis and qualitative analysis are not mutually exclusive.

codes   The coding categories ('**codes**') used must have a number of characteristics regardless of their putative status as descriptive or interpretative,
however. They must be:

- *exhaustive*: Every aspect of the images with which the research is
  concerned must be covered by one category.
- *exclusive*: Categories must not overlap.
- *enlightening*: As Slater (1998: 236) says, the categories must produce 'a
  breakdown of imagery that will be analytically interesting and coherent'.

Achieving a list of coding categories that satisfies these criteria is
extremely difficult. When faced with a large number of images, their
sheer richness is likely to be overwhelming. For advertisements or TV
programmes, the written or spoken text will also need coding, and so
too may background music. As Lutz and Collins (1993: 89) say, the
process of reducing the rich material in any photograph to a series of
codes is just that: a reduction in which much will be lost. The key
point to remember, though, is that the images must be reduced to a
number of component parts that can be labelled in a way that has
some analytical significance. That is, the codes used must depend on a
theorised connection between the image and the broader cultural context in which its meaning is made. 'Theorised', because making this
connection entails drawing on a theoretical and empirical understanding of the images under consideration. Thus the connection between
text, context and code requires careful thought, and it is on the integ-
valid   rity of this link that the codes can be judged **valid** (Krippendorff, 2013:
129). A starting point is the research question driving the content

analysis. What coding categories does that suggest? Some may be obvious. For more, though, it is necessary to return to the wider theoretical and empirical literature from which the research question has been formulated. Are there arguments there that suggest other codes? This return to the broader context of the research question will hopefully ensure that the categories eventually decided upon are 'enlightening'. Further codes might suggest themselves from the familiarity you already have with this particular set of images. Does anything strike you as interesting, unusual or unexpected about them that might bear further analysis?

The coding categories developed by Lutz and Collins (1993: 285) depend on a particular theoretical literature about 'power, race, and history'. Each of the 598 photographs in their sample was coded for:

1. world location
2. unit of article organization (region, nation-state, ethnic group, other)
3. number of photographs including Westerners in an article
4. smiling in a photograph
5. gender of adults depicted
6. age of those depicted
7. aggressive activity or military personnel or weapons shown
8. activity level of main foreground figures
9. activity type of main foreground figures
10. camera gaze of main person photographed
11. surroundings of people photographed
12. ritual focus
13. group size
14. Westerners in photograph
15. urban versus rural setting
16. wealth indicators in photograph
17. skin colour
18. dress style ('Western' or local)
19. male nudity
20. female nudity
21. technological type present (simple handmade tools, machinery)
22. vantage (point from which camera perceives main figures).

focus

Think about these categories. Are they exhaustive? Are they exclusive?

Lutz and Collins (1993) are fairly clear about the connection between these coding categories and their initial research question. Their question is formulated by drawing on a large body of work that examines how the West has seen and pictured people in the non-Western world. Some of the key texts they cite include Sarah Graham-Brown's (1988) book on photographs of women taken by European travellers in the Near East, Sander Gilman's (1985) study of racial stereotypes, Elizabeth Edwards' (1992) edited collection on anthropologists' uses of photography in the nineteenth century, and Christopher Lyman's (1982) work on photographs of native American peoples. Drawing on this body of work, they argue that, in very broad terms, Westerners have represented non-Western peoples as everything that the West is not. (Hence their use of the term 'non-Western'.) This structure of representation is complex; it draws on a wide range of discourses and varies both historically and geographically, and Lutz and Collins address various aspects of this complexity in their book. However, to take one example of how their codes connect to this understanding of certain parts and peoples of the world as the opposite of the West, much of the literature they draw on suggests that, historically, non-Western peoples have been represented by Westerners as 'natural'. The West sees itself as technologically advanced but therefore also alienated from nature; thus non-Westerners are represented as technologically less advanced and as closer to nature. Non-Westerners are thus often pictured as using little or so-called primitive technologies, for example, being more spiritual, more in tune with the environment and their bodies, wearing fewer clothes. These analyses inform a number of Lutz and Collins's codes: 12 (ritual focus), 15 (urban versus rural setting), 19 and 20 (male and female nudity) and 21 (technological type present). Given the way their codes flow from a wider set of ideas about power and representation, it is clear that many of their codes are likely to be enlightening, and so it proves. For example, they point out that *National Geographic* represents non-Western people as either natural or as modern, but very rarely as both. It is as if non-Westerners can only be the opposite of, or the same as, the West.

As well as being enlightening, though, exhaustiveness and exclusivity must also be considered when coding categories are being formulated. The only way to ensure that the categories fulfil these latter two requirements is to try them out on the images. Putting the initial categories to use in a trial run on a few of your sample images will almost certainly reveal overlaps between categories and relevant elements of images not covered by categories. The categories must be revised and tried again until they are exhaustive and exclusive. Oddly, the list of codes used by Lutz and Collins (1993), at least as it is reproduced in their book, do not seem to fulfil these other requirements of content analysis coding. There seem to me to be some instances of overlap, for example. Thus 'surroundings of people photographed' seems to overlap with 'urban versus rural setting'; and perhaps 'ritual focus' overlaps with 'dress style', since ritual would only be seen as such (on the theoretical arguments that Lutz and Collins draw on) if it was in local dress.

discussion

The coding categories used by Lutz and Collins are quite elaborate. However, there might be research questions that could be answered with much more simple coding categories. Rebekah Willett (2009) was interested in what people videoed with their cameraphones, for example. She interviewed ten research participants, who also gave her 177 videos to examine, which she categorised into just four groups: 'personal documentary', 'non-personal documentary' and 'public performance', those not fitting a category simply being classed as 'other'. While her discussion includes specific examples from each of these categories, even her simple scheme nonetheless helps her to convincingly characterise such videos as records of fleeting, emotional, dynamic moments that help build both memories and social relationships.

The codes discussed so far also all relate to the content of the image itself. However, you may wish to code other aspects of the image, depending on your research question.

A study of YouTube by Jean Burgess and Joshua Green (2009), for example, was keen to get a sense of just how much of YouTube was generated by ordinary folk uploading their own video efforts, and how much was generated by large – or even small – media corporations. This was part of their interest in how YouTube fits into the broader landscape of media change. So three of the codes they used on their sample 4,320 videos were 'user-generated' (ordinary folk), 'traditional' (media corporations) and 'uncertain'. These codes referred to *who* was doing the uploading onto YouTube and not *what* they were uploading; thus an illegal copy of a *Simpsons* episode uploaded by a fan counted as 'user-generated', while an episode uploaded by Fox (the corporation who produce *The Simpsons*) counted as 'traditional'. (Chapter 11 will return to this study, as it is also an example of digital methods.)

And one more point about coding: as Chapter 1 noted, images very rarely appear on their own. This is especially true of images in the mass media. These are almost always accompanied by text, voice or music, which can radically alter the meaning of the image. If you were undertaking an analysis of the photographs in a print newspaper, you need to consider whether it is important to code the captions of photos, the headlines of the piece the photo illustrates, the full article, or all of them.

The codes of a content analysis therefore do not have to refer only to the visual content of an image.

5.2.3 Coding the images

My queries about the Lutz and Collins categories raise the issue that content analysis tries to obviate, which is that different coders might interpret what seem to be the same codes in different ways. In order to avoid this possibility, according to content analysis, the coding categories must be completely unambiguous. They must be so clearly defined that different researchers at different times using the same categories would code the images in exactly the same **replicable** way. This, it is claimed, makes the coding process **replicable**. A content analysis should take various steps to ensure this replicability. Codes must be defined as fully as possible and a pilot study should ensure that two different coders using the same codes produce the same results from the same set of images. If they do not, the codes must be refined so that they do. Further tests of coder reliability may also take place during the research process, as Philip Bell (2001) discusses at some length. Lutz and Collins (1993: 88) say that the photographs in their study were coded independently by two coders, with 86 per cent agreement between them after the final codes had been agreed. The disagreements were resolved by discussion, they say. Their categories must therefore have been defined much more fully than the list they reproduce in their book.

Then the coding proper begins. The application of any set of coding categories must be careful and systematic. Each image must be carefully examined and all the relevant codes attached to it. This process is both tedious and extremely important. It needs a great deal of attention, otherwise the danger of 'unconscious' lapses looms, but it can also be rather boring.

Practically, there are different ways to record your coding. You might do it manually, with an index card for each image on which you note the codes you think are relevant to it (perhaps in some abbreviated form), or you might be able to create a dedicated database or set up a computer spreadsheet to record this information. The advantage of the latter methods is that they will make subsequent quantitative analysis easier, especially if you want to do more than just count up totals (see next section).

5.2.4 Analysing the results

The sample of images is now coded. Each image has a number of codes attached to it. The next stage is to count them, in order to produce a quantitative account of their content. Cultural analytics software will do this for you, and present the results in a variety of ways.

Otherwise, the simplest way to count the codes is to produce frequency counts, which can be absolute or relative (the latter expressed as a percentage of the total number of images, for example). If you are using a spreadsheet, producing frequency counts is very easy; make sure that you don't count everything simply for the sake of it, though. Choose the important frequencies only, deciding which are important by referring to the broader theoretical and empirical framework with which you are working.

A common use of frequencies is to compare them with some other value, and Kimberley Neuendorf (2002: 167–90) offers a useful guide to a range of ways of doing this. A comparison can be made across time, for example, in a graph. Lutz and Collins (1993: 40) do this for their code 3 (number of photographs including Westerners in an article). (This code too seems rather odd: their codes were apparently applied to one photograph randomly chosen per article, but this code refers not to a photograph but to the article.) This shows a striking decrease in the number of times Westerners were shown in *National Geographic* photographs after the mid-1960s (see Figure 5.2).

In making sense of this drop, Lutz and Collins again turn to their contextual understanding of *National Geographic*. They suggest that, unlike some other photo-magazines, *National Geographic* consistently avoids presenting images of conflict. Yet the 1960s were a period of conflict both in the USA and elsewhere, and of conflict moreover focusing on precisely the issues of 'race, power, and history'. Both the civil rights movement in the USA and anti-colonial struggles elsewhere in the world, particularly in Vietnam, made the relations between West and non-West, black and white, especially troubled. *National Geographic* responded by removing pictures that showed West and non-West, black and white, in contact. Thus the illusion of social harmony could be preserved. Lutz and Collins (1993: 120) also compare frequency counts across space using bar charts, pointing out that the distribution of *National Geographic* articles does not follow the distribution of world population, but rather the geopolitical interests of the USA (see Figure 5.3).

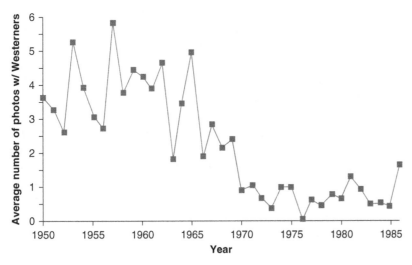

FIGURE 5.2
Average number of *National Geographic* photographs with Westerners in non-Western settings per article, 1950–86 (Lutz and Collins, 1993: 40)
© University of Chicago Press

FIGURE 5.3
Regional
population
compared to
*National
Geographic*
articles
published
on Latin
America,
Africa and
the Middle
East, as
percentage
of total,
1950–86 (Lutz
and Collins,
1993: 121)
© University of
Chicago Press

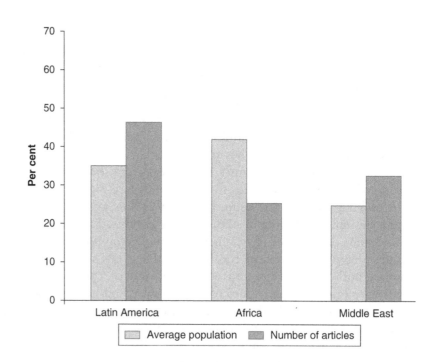

A more sophisticated analysis can be developed by exploring the relations between different coding categories. This can be done qualitatively and quantitatively. Quantitative measures of possible relationships between categories include associations, cross-tabulations and correlations between two variables, and multivariate analyses between more. Krippendorff (2013) offers guidance here. The study of computer game box covers (Burgess et al., 2007), for example, tests a number of correlations between representations of gender and violence and in the process develops a rich account of this sort of image: 'Males were almost five times more likely to be portrayed as the primary character (N = 140) than the females (N = 30) (c^2 = 69.88, df = 1, p <.0001)' (2007: 424–5); 'Physical objectification of females occurred on 47.4% (N = 35) of the covers and ... for males, physical objectification occurred in 13.5% (N = 21) of the covers' (2007: 425); 'Female characters were significantly more likely to be portrayed as busty/super-busty than their male counterparts were to be portrayed as muscular/super-muscular (z = 4.568, p <.0001). 49% of the females were portrayed as either busty (N = 19) or super-busty (N = 32), while 25.7% of the male characters were portrayed as muscular (N = 37) or super-muscular (N = 61)' (2007: 426); 'Covers were almost four times more likely to portray males as violent (65%, 102/156) than females

(38%, 28/74), z = 3.937,p <.01' (2007: 426). From this, the conclusion is drawn 'that, in spite of their less frequent representation, female characters were dramatically more likely to be negatively portrayed. This negativity ranged from their relative lack of action to their physical portrayal' (Burgess et al., 2007: 427).

Lutz and Collins use quantitative correlations at certain points in their book. They note, for example, that 'ritual tends to be depicted in color (c^2 = 3.008, df = 1, p =.083)' (Lutz and Collins, 1993: 94). The correlation between colour and ritual suggests that these are exotic people living spectacular lives; as they say, 'color is the vehicle of spectacle' (Lutz and Collins, 1993: 94). But they mostly seem to rely on qualitative interpretations of the relations between their categories. They say that from their content analysis of *National Geographic*, four overarching themes emerged. These were the depiction of third world people as exotic, idealised, naturalised and sexualised. Now, none of these themes appears directly in the list of coding categories deployed by Lutz and Collins. Instead, they were reached by amalgamating some of those codes on the basis of the theoretical and empirical literature their study was drawing on. Thus 'idealised' was formed from a number of codes: 'smiling in a photo', 'group size', 'aggressive activity ...' and 'wealth indicators'. Given the number of smiling portraits, the prevalence of pictures of small groups, the rarity of pictures of aggression, and the dominance of pictures of work and middle-class social groups, Lutz and Collins conclude that third world people are presented as 'idealised': 'gentle natives and wars without brutalized bodies' (Lutz and Collins, 1993: 98). Thus non-Westerners are not shown as ill or very poor or hungry: instead they are given the qualities that the North American *National Geographic* would like to see: happy, not too badly off, hard-working, content. In this way, Lutz and Collins elaborate the symbolic meanings carried by *National Geographic*.

Thus content analysis is a technique the results of which need interpreting through an understanding of how the codes in an image connect to the wider context within which that image makes sense. To do that requires not just quantitative skills but also qualitative ones. Even an advocate of quantitative, computerised content analysis like Robert Weber (1990: 69) has to acknowledge that 'time, effort, skill, and art are required to produce results, interpretations, and explanations that are valid and theoretically interesting'.

5.3 Doing Cultural Analytics

This section offers a brief account of the principles underlying a cultural analytics research project.

First, you must gather the images you want to analyse: these must be in digital format. Advocates of cultural analytics say that one of its strengths is that, given it is an automated process, it is in fact possible to analyse every single image in a relevant population no matter how large, as long as they are accessible digitally. Sampling is therefore not necessary.

discussion

If you are interested in analysing the images that appear on webpages, or on YouTube, or on social media, accessing those images is not always straightforward (Lewis et al., 2013). For example, there are various free software packages that will automatically scrape those images from their websites and download them to your computer; but if they only scrape the images you will not be able to analyse captions, comments and other surrounding text. Some platforms, like Facebook, do not allow images to be downloaded; and there are also copyright and ownership issues to consider. Chapter 11 discusses accessing social media images in more depth.

Once you have collated your images, you process them using software that can be downloaded from the Software Studies Initiative website: the software will extract various features from each image. Automated visual pattern recognition like this is an area to which both academic and commercial researchers are devoting a lot of energy right now, given how important images currently are to both social life and online shopping. What can currently be identified using such software includes grey tones, colours, the curvature and orientation of lines, brightness, texture, composition, and combinations of these, and this is what underpins the smile detection software in digital cameras and the face recognition software in desktop photoediting applications. The aspects of an image that can be identified in this kind of analysis are totally dependent on what the software can recognise in the image file. Thus while a software package might very effectively identify the colours of dresses in a collection of online images, currently it would have much greater difficulty in consistently identifying 'dress style' because a 'style' is a combination of very many different elements. The *validity* of its cultural analytics' coding, then, is currently less sophisticated than manual content analysis can be.

The next stage of the cultural analytics process is that more software will then create visualisations of the results of the data extraction process carried out on your images. Cultural analytics has a distinct approach to analysing its results: it visualises

New York

San Francisco

FIGURE 5.4   The Phototrails project: New York and San Francisco as pictured by 50,000 Instagram photos, organised by hue mean (radius) and brightness mean (perimeter), http://phototrails.net/

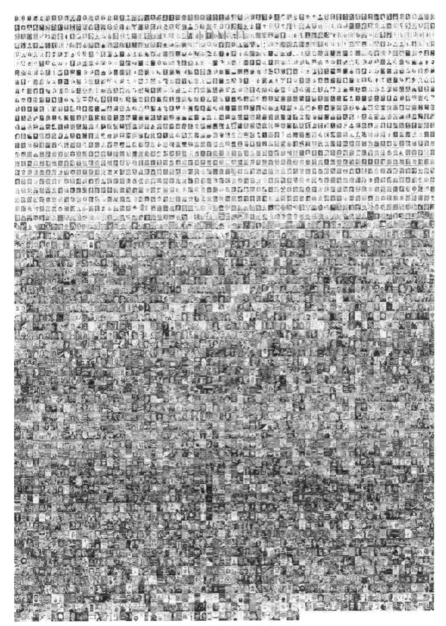

FIGURE 5.5
The 4535
covers of *Time*
magazine
published
between 1923
and 2009, with
the magazine's
red borders
removed,
https://www.
flickr.com/
photos/
culturevis/sets/
7215762252
5012841
Source: Software
Studies Initiative

them, often compiling tiny thumbnails of each image into various kinds of collages (see Figure 5.4). These are often striking images in their own right but, as with any content analysis, their significance needs elaborating by careful contextualisation and explanation. Figure 5.5 effectively forces us to ask what a city looks like now, in the age of social media photography, I think, whereas the cultural significance of the data in Figure 5.5 is less clear to me.

discussion

Figures 5.2, 5.3 and 5.4 all show the results of content analyses in visual form. Representing these forms of analysis visually is often more striking for a reader than a list of numbers. Indeed, one of the interesting things about cultural analytics is its experiments in presenting its data. Chapter 13 will discuss data visualisation in more detail.

5.4 Content Analysis and Cultural Analytics: An Assessment

Content analysis offers a clear method for engaging systematically with large numbers of images. And it is not simply a quantitative method; clearly, every stage of content analysis, from formulating the research question, to selecting images, to developing coding categories, to interpreting the results, entails decisions about meaning and significance. Ball and Smith (1992) and Bell (2001) both suggest that content analysis is pretty much useless for understanding the cultural meaning of the visual components it analyses, and Hall (2013) suggests slightly more tentatively that the same might apply to cultural analytics. But the main case study explored in this chapter disputes this claim, I think. The analysis offered by Lutz and Collins (1993) suggests that, especially if the coding of images is carefully formulated, content analysis can indeed be used to interpret the cultural meaning of images. So too does the study by Yukari Seko (2013) on images of self-harm on Flickr (which also has a very clear description of the content analysis undertaken).

However, to the extent that content analysis and cultural analytics do indeed depend on quantitative analysis, some difficult questions about their usefulness for a critical visual methodology remain. First, it is important to remember that numbers do not translate easily into significance. There is a tendency in content analysis and cultural analytics to assume that if something occurs very often, it is more important than something that occurs rarely. As Weber (1990: 72) and Ball and Smith (1992) note, this is not necessarily the case. Something that is kept out of the picture may nonetheless be extremely significant to its meaning. I am not making the point here that there is a single reality that visual images only selectively represent. Rather, I mean to suggest that certain representations of what is visible depend on other things being constructed as their invisible opposite; and content analysis is incapable of addressing these invisibilised others.

Moreover, content analysis does not discriminate between occurrences of a code: that is, it cannot discriminate between an aspect of an image that exemplifies a code perfectly, and one that is only a weak example of it. Thus simple frequencies may be problematic to interpret. A further problem arises when the difficulty that content analysis has in handling the context of its coded image components is considered. Content analysis breaks an image into parts and has no way of handling any interconnections that may exist between its parts, other than by statistical correlation. These are probably not the best ways to understand how images work. Lutz and Collins (1993) demonstrate this when they turn not to statistical tests but to theoretical accounts to pull together some of their codes into overarching themes that form the basis of their analysis of the *National Geographic* photographs.

There is also another problem produced by the fragmentation of an image when it undergoes coding, which is the inability of content analysis to articulate what compositional interpretation would call the expressive content of an image. It is very hard to evoke the mood or the affect of an image through codes. Cultural analytics arguably fares rather better on this point, though, because its montages retain the original image and – as Figure 5.4 shows – its visualisations can show quite striking colour effects.

Finally, there are the broader issues in analysing visual images that content analysis cannot address. Content analysis focuses on the image itself. But there are the three other sites at which an image's meanings are made: the site of its production, the site of its circulation, and the site of its audiencing. Neither content analysis nor cultural analytics have much purchase on these sites.

Lutz and Collins (1993) acknowledge this limitation and try to overcome it by using other research methods to access the way meaning is made at two of these other sites. At the site of *National Geographic* production, they conducted interviews with the magazine's photographers and editors, to gain an understanding of the social and compositional modalities of production. As for the site of audiencing, as section 5.2.3 pointed out, in its concern for coder replicability, content analysis assumes that different viewers can see the same image in the same way; while in the case of cultural analytics, the human coder is replaced by a piece of software. Neither method has any interest in audience creativity. So to explore the site of *National Geographic* audiencing, Lutz and Collins conducted group interviews with *National Geographic* readers in which they discussed particular photographs. What they found was that at each site the meanings given to the photographs varied.

Nor does content analysis address the circulation of images between different sites. Are *National Geographic*'s images seen differently in different places, as well as by different readers? And there is a more serious absence in the analyses of images from social media sites like Instagram in cultural analytics, I think. Take another look at Figure 5.4, which shows montages of 50,000 photos of New York and San Francisco, uploaded onto Instagram and visualised by their saturation and hue. The visualisations offered in this project's collages are zoomable – that is, online, it is possible to zoom into their component images and then zoom back out again to the overall pattern. This zoomability occludes a key aspect of their organisation by

Instagram, though, which is precisely their integration into social networks. Instagram is a highly complex series of networks algorithmically shaped by 'likes' and 'followings', location and privacy settings. The circulation of Instagram images therefore follows certain patterns, which cultural analytics does not show (although see Salah et al. [2013] for an attempt). While it reveals some things, then, cultural analytics does not thus far seem able to address the complex circulations of social media imagery.

Further issues are raised if we recall the claim, made on behalf of both cultural analytics and content analysis, that their discovery of patterns and trends is somehow objective. This removes any need on the part of researchers to be reflexive in any way other than by reporting their method in detail; any other form of reflexivity is not part of these methods because they assume that they are objective. But what does that suggest about the other meaning-makers, like the ones Lutz and Collins interviewed, for example? That their interpretations are more unconscious? Less valid? Lutz and Collins (1993) deny that they are implying this. But their defence of content analysis leaves that lingering impression nonetheless.

Summary: Content Analysis

- *associated with*:
  Content analysis is used to analyse large numbers of images. Most typically it is used in relation to mass media images found in newspapers and magazines, or on television and on social media platforms.

- *sites and modalities*:
  Content analysis focuses most on the image itself in its compositional modality.

- *key terms*:
  Key terms for content analysis are validity and replicability, in relation to the development and use of coding categories.

- *strengths and weaknesses as a critical visual methodology*:
  Content analysis provides clear guidelines for dealing with large numbers of images consistently and systematically. But it has no way of dealing with those sites at which the meanings of images are made other than that of the image itself. Nor, apart from its methodological explicitness, does it demand reflexivity on the part of the researcher.

Further Reading

For a clear discussion of content analysis, consult Neuendorf's *The Content Analysis Guidebook* (2002). Gary Hall (2013) offers a sympathetic but critical account of cultural analytics which makes several points that are relevant to content analysis more generally.

COMPANION WEBSITE

Visit **https://study.sagepub.com/rose4e** for:

- **Links to online tutorials** that say more about how to undertake content analyses, and to **the Global Media Monitoring Project**, which uses content analysis to conduct surveys of the gender balance in the media globally.
- **Links to the Software Studies Initiative**, the main home of cultural analytics, headed by Lev Manovich. The Software Studies Initiative site has all sorts of examples and resources – including free software – that will enable you to conduct your own cultural analytical study.
- **Exercises** where you can practise both content analysis – particularly coding both what images show and what they do not – and cultural analytics.

6

SEMIOLOGY: LAYING BARE THE PREJUDICES

BENEATH THE SMOOTH SURFACE OF THE VISIBLE

key examples: the chapter looks at several studies applying semiological approaches to advertisements and advertising, including Judith Williamson's classic *Decoding Advertisements*.

The chapter also briefly looks at applying semiology to the design of brand-name shops.

6.1 Semiology: An Introduction

This chapter examines an approach to visual images which has been much more prominent than either compositional interpretation or content analysis in the development of the debates about the visual that were briefly reviewed in Chapter 1. This method is semiology (sometimes also called social semiotics). Its prominence is due in part to the fact that semiology confronts the question of how images make meanings head on. It is not simply descriptive, as compositional interpretation appears to be; nor does it rely on quantitative estimations of significance, as content analysis at some level has to. Instead, semiology offers a very full box of analytical tools for taking an image apart and tracing how it works in relation to broader systems of meaning. Semiology is also influential as an approach to interpreting the materials of visual culture because it draws upon the work of several major theorists whose impact on the social sciences since the 1960s has been immense. Judith Williamson's (1978) classic semiological study *Decoding Advertisements*, for example, cites Althusser, Barthes, Benjamin, Berger, Brecht, Foucault, Freud, Gramsci, Lacan, Levi-Strauss, Marx and Saussure at the end of her book, and this is a roll-call of many of the twentieth century's most important critical writers.

Semiology is thus embedded in a rich and complex series of ideas whose implications are still bearing valuable fruit: a significant recent development, for example, is social semiotics (Hodge and Kress, 1988; Jewitt, 2009; Kress, 2010; van Leeuwen, 2005). The most important tool in any semiological box is the 'sign': semiology means 'the study of signs'. As art historians Mieke Bal and Norman Bryson (1991: 174) say in their defence of semiology, 'Human culture is made up of signs, each of which stands for something other than itself, and the people inhabiting culture busy themselves making sense of those signs.' This position is quite close to that of Stuart Hall, quoted at the beginning of this book's opening chapter, and semiologists of various kinds have made key contributions to the critique of representation. In particular, semiology has an elaborate analytical vocabulary for describing how signs make sense. A semiological analysis entails the deployment of a highly refined set of concepts that produce detailed accounts of the exact ways the meanings of an image are produced through that image.

Semiology offers a certain kind of analytical precision, then. As was noted in the previous chapter, so too does content analysis. And, again like content analysis, a certain sort of semiology claims to be a scientific approach to the analysis of meaning. Content analysis is said to be a science because it is quantitative, replicable and valid. These are not the grounds on which some advocates of semiology as a science claim semiology as a science, however. Semiologists depend on a definition of science that contrasts scientific knowledge with **ideology** (this distinc- **ideology** tion is usually elaborated with reference to the Marxist theorist Louis Althusser). Ideology is knowledge that is constructed in such a way as to legitimate unequal social power relations; science, instead, is knowledge that reveals those inequalities. This use of the term 'ideology' is evidence of the formative influence of Marxism on semiology. Marx and Engels famously claimed in *The German Ideology* that 'the ideas of the ruling class are in every age the ruling ideas', and here are Robert Hodge and Gunther Kress defining ideology in the introduction to their book *Social Semiotics*:

> In contemporary capitalist societies as in most other social forma-tions there are inequalities in the distribution of power and other goods. As a result there are divisions in the social fabric between rulers and ruled, exploiters and exploited: such societies exhibit characteristic structures of domination. In order to sustain these structures of domination the dominant groups attempt to represent the world in forms that reflect their own interests, the interests of their power. (Hodge and Kress, 1988: 3)

Ideology is those representations that reflect the interests of power. In particular, ideology works to legitimate social inequalities. Semiology, then, is centrally concerned with the social effects of meaning; hence

Margaret Iversen's (1986: 84) description of semiology as 'laying bare the prejudices beneath the smooth surface of the beautiful'.

Williamson (1978) argued that one of the most influential ideological forms in contemporary capitalist societies is advertising. She claimed that advertisements are ubiquitous and thus appear autonomous. Robert Goldman agrees: 'Ads saturate our lives,' he says, and he goes on, 'yet, because ads are so pervasive and our reading of them so routine, we tend to take for granted the deep social assumptions embedded in advertisements: we do not ordinarily recognise them as a sphere of ideology' (Goldman, 1992: 1; see also Goldman and Papson, 2011). Both Williamson and Goldman choose to use semiology as a method that can help them penetrate the apparent autonomy and reality of adverts, in order to reveal their ideological status. This chapter follows Williamson's early example and also explores semiology as a method for critical visual analysis in relation to advertising. However, it is important to note that many other methods can be used to analyse advertisements; and since all forms of semiology are concerned with the making of meaning, semiology is an approach that can be applied to all kinds of visual materials (Bignell, 2002).

Writing in the 1970s, and influenced by the work of Althusser, Willliamson (1978) claimed that her critique of the ideology of advertising was itself non-ideological; rather, it was (Althusserian) science. Many semiologists writing more recently, however, are much more circumspect than Williamson in claiming that their knowledges are objectively true. Hodge and Kress (1988) suggest that any knowledge that sanctions a particular form of social organisation must be described as ideological. Thus knowledge that legitimates the social position of dominant groups is ideological; but so too are those knowledges of other possibilities for social organisation that are held by dominated groups. To capture this 'double and contradictory' notion of ideology, they prefer to use the term 'ideological complex': 'a functionally related set of contradictory versions of the world, coercively imposed by one social group on another on behalf of its own distinctive interests or subversively offered by another social group in attempts at resistance in its own interests' (Hodge and Kress, 1988: 3).

The implication of this argument is that the critical goals of semiology are just as ideological as the adverts or whatever are being critiqued; the difference between them is in the social effects of the knowledges each depends on, not its truth status. Bal and Bryson (1991) offer another version of this argument, simply pointing out that since all knowledge depends on signs, all knowledge is vulnerable to semiological reinterpretation, including that of the semiologists themselves. Elsewhere Bal (1996) has described this as a process of 'double exposure'. When a critic writes about, let's say, a video, not only is the video interpreted and exposed to interpretation; the interpretation is also on display, exposing the critic's ideas to interpretation by others. As she says, there are 'intricacies between ... academic subjectivity and the subject matter it purports to analyse' (Bal, 1996: 7). Bal therefore acknowledges the importance of the third criterion outlined in Chapter 1 for a critical visual methodology, and tries to be reflexive about her own viewing practices. This reflexivity is not ubiquitous among semiologists, however: although Williamson (1978) offers a personal account in the preface to her book of why she was interested in writing about adverts, *Decoding Advertisements* is not reflexive in the way that Bal (1996) advocates.

Williamson's (1978) early account of ideology in advertising focuses on class relations in both their 'real' and 'ideological' forms. In her book, though, she also recognises the centrality of gender to how adverts are constructed; and another development in more recent semiological studies is the way in which the construction of many forms of social difference are explored: class, gender, race, able-bodiedness and so on. Semiology assumes that these constructions of social difference are articulated through the working of signs in images themselves. Many semiological studies therefore tend to concentrate on the *image itself* as the most important site of its meaning. Its focus on signs means that semiology always pays very careful attention to the *compositional* modality of that site; but its concern for the social effects of an image's meaning mean that some attention is also paid to the *social* modality of that site. However, a significant number of semiologists prefer to emphasise what this book is calling the social modality at other sites. Bal and Bryson (1991: 184), for example, emphasise above all the site of an image's *audiencing*, arguing that semiology 'is centrally concerned with reception', and **social semiotics** emphasises what this book is calling the social modality at all sites of meaning-making. As Theo van Leeuwen says:

> In social semiotics the focus [has] changed from the 'sign' to the way people use semiotic 'resources' both to produce communicative artefacts and events and to interpret them – which is also a form of semiotic production – in the context of specific social situations and practices. (2005: xi)

Section 6.3 of this chapter will consider what Hodge and Kress (1988: 1) call 'mainstream' semiology, mostly using examples drawn from magazine advertising, while social semiotics will be explored in Section 6.4.

This introduction is suggesting, then, that semiological approaches can fulfil the criteria for a critical visual methodology that were outlined in the first chapter of this book. They offer a range of tools for looking at images carefully; they are centrally concerned with the ways in which social difference is created; and at least some of their practitioners advocate a reflexivity in their deployment. However, as an approach semiology also has its drawbacks. Semiology of whatever stripe is conceptually elaborate. Each semiological term carries substantial theoretical baggage, and mainstream semiology and social semiotics have both developed their own, quite distinct analytical vocabularies (for a recent example developed in relation to photojournalism, see Caple [2013]).

social semiotics

This terminological precision accounts for the analytical precision of semiology. It also accounts, however, for a certain density of terminology that is not always easy for the novice to grasp. Don Slater (1998) offers another criticism: that for all its analytical richness, semiology does not offer a clear method for its application. This chapter therefore focuses more on suggesting some ways to do semiology than on elaborating its theoretical implications. The chapter has five sections:

1. The first is this introduction.
2. The second examines how to choose images for a semiological study.
3. The third discusses mainstream semiology, especially its various discussions of the sign;
4. The fourth explores social semiotics.
5. And the final section assesses the strengths and weaknesses of semiology as a critical visual methodology.

6.2 Choosing Images for a Semiological Study

Semiological studies require extensive knowledge of the type of image the case studies will examine. Judith Williamson (1978: 9) tells her readers that she arrived at the University of California at Berkeley to take a course on popular culture in the mid-1970s with 'a bulging file of advertisements collected over many years' that eventually provided the illustrations for her book. Goldman (1992: 2) says he was 'watching ads for over decade' before writing his book, and in a more recent study looking at how advertisements picture the 'landscapes of capital', he notes that his analysis is based on 2,400 TV ads that were digitised, coded and transcribed, but says no more about his methods (Goldman and Papson, 2011). None of these authors suggests they had a rigorous sampling procedure, as a content analyst would; and nor do they say how they chose which of these many adverts to discuss in detail as examples in their books.

This uninterest in justifying the selection of images to be analysed is shared by social semiotics too (Kress, 2010; van Leeuwen, 2005). There are two reasons for this, I think. The first is that semiologists of any sort seem to choose their images on the basis of how conceptually interesting they are; they select images that will make their point well. The second is that all kinds of semiology are concerned to analyse processes of meaning-making that are socially significant. Mainstream semiology chooses to look at advertisements, for example, because they are core to the ideologies structuring contemporary society; social semiotics has undertaken many studies of classrooms of different kinds, again focusing on a key location in the reproduction and contestation of contemporary ideologies. There is no concern among semiologists to find images that are statistically representative of a wider set of images, for example, as there is in content analysis. Thus semiology very often takes the form of detailed case studies of relatively few images, and the case study stands or falls on its analytical integrity and interest rather than on its applicability to a wide range of material.

discussion

When Judith Williamson worked on *Decoding Advertisements* during the 1970s, the location of advertisements was fairly straightforward. The vast majority were found in the mass media – in newspapers, magazines, television and radio – and on bill-boards. Advertising has changed, to an extent, over the past three decades though, and three of these changes have implications for locating adverts to analyse (Leiss et al., 2005).

First, new kinds of advertising can now be found across the Internet. Many advertising campaigns build their own websites, rely on webpages to carry their TV adverts, and even commission short films for viewing on videosharing sites like YouTube. And some new kinds of adverts have emerged that are unique to that medium – in particular, the 'banner ad' that sits atop many a webpage (Bermejo, 2009; Spurgeon, 2008). These sorts of advertisements often animate their text as well as their visuals, which emphasises the need to consider both text and image in the analysis of found visual materials, but also, as Carey Jewitt (2005: 321) points out, blurs the very distinction between text and image.

Secondly, many Internet adverts are no longer designed to appeal to the large and fairly diverse audiences of mass media; instead they are often designed to appeal to very specific audiences. This is because large sites like Google, Amazon and Facebook gather information about your use of their site, and then put what they think are appropriate adverts on the pages you see when you log in to your account. Belinda Barnet (2009) describes this as **idiomedia**:

> We have entered an era of content-based filtering across millions of Web feeds, of on-demand video transcoding, behavioural metrics and user pro-filing. Increasingly, digital content is produced on demand based on your current location; it is shaped by your social network and what they are recommending; it is predicted based on your personal Google search his-tory or what you've been writing about in your webmail account. (2009: 94)

Think about the implications this has for an analysis of adverts on large, popu-lar websites like Google or Amazon. How would you access adverts directed at people who search for very different things from you on Google, or who order very different sorts of things from you on Amazon?

Thirdly, what counts as an advert is not always as obvious as it once was. This is largely a consequence of the increasing importance of brands (Arvidsson, 2006; Lury, 2004). A **brand** is the name of a company *and* the values and feel-ings attached to that name. From the 1970s onwards, the commercial importance of those values has increased dramatically; indeed, for some com-panies the brand accounts for 30 per cent of their earnings. 'Originally brands had referred to producers,' says Adam Arvidsson (2005: 243–4):

> They had generally served as a trademark or a 'maker's mark' that worked to guarantee quality or to give the potentially anonymous

idiomedia

brand

mass-produced commodity an identity by linking it to an identifiable (if often entirely fictional) producer or inventor or a particular physical place. Now the brand, or the 'brand image', began to refer instead to the significance that commodities acquired in the minds of consumers. (Arvidsson, 2005: 244)

Advertising, of the sort examined by Williamson (1978), remains an important part of giving commodities and brands that significance. But now, so too are many other sorts of activities (Leiss et al., 2005): sponsorship of major sporting or cultural events (Figure 6.1), for example, product placements in movies and video games, logos on freebies, events (think of the celebrations that accompany the opening of a new Apple store or the launch of a new version of a popular video game like *Call of Duty*), celebrities as 'product ambassadors', and websites that offer all sorts of activities like games or discussion boards. None of these things aim at selling anything specific, but instead work to give a brand a certain set of values or a certain emotional association (Johnson, 2008: 207). The pervasiveness of brands can make deciding what is an advert and what is not rather difficult.

Try exploring the website of a major brand like Chanel or Nike or Lego, and see how easy it is to distinguish its 'adverts' from its other content.

So if you are interested in exploring how advertisements represent social differences, you might need to think carefully about how you are defining adverts and advertising and thus where you should look to gather your data for analysis. You might want to consider not only what the advert itself is representing, but also what values it is associating with its brand and what other strategies are being used to make that association. And finally, you might need to think about what your adverts are assuming about, and inviting from, their audiences. The chapter will return again to these questions in later focus boxes.

6.3 The Sign and its Meaning-Making Processes in Mainstream Semiology

This section explores how 'mainstream' semiology works. As the first section of this chapter noted, mainstream semiology tends to focus on the site of the image itself. This section echoes that focus by working with a selection of adverts, mostly from magazines of various kinds. However, it is important to remember both that advertisements can be analysed using many other methods, and that semiology as a method can be used with many other kinds of visual (and other) materials.

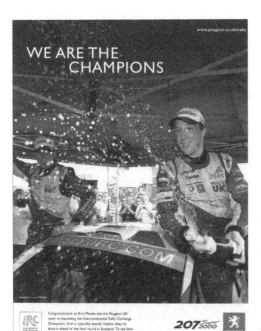

WE ARE THE
CHAMPIONS

FIGURE 6.1 The car manufacturer Peugeot put this advertisement into the male-oriented film magazine *Empire* in January 2010, hoping the glamour of a sporting triumph would accrue to their brand; note the link to their corporate website

© Peugeot

6.3.1 What is a sign?

The 'sign' is the most fundamental unit of mainstream semiology. Semiological understanding of the sign depends in part on the work of Ferdinand de Saussure, and in particular on his *Course on General Linguistics*. Saussure wanted to develop a systematic understanding of how language works, and he argued that the **sign** was the basic unit of language. The sign consists of two parts, which are only distinguishable at the analytical level; in practice they are always integrated into each other. The first part of the sign is the **signified**. The signified is a concept or an object, let's say 'a very young human unable to walk or talk'. The second part of the sign is the **signifier**. The signifier is a sound or an image that is attached to a signified; in this case, the word 'baby'. The point that Saussure made with this distinction between signifier and signified, and which semiological analysis depends upon, is that there is no necessary relationship between a particular signifier and its signified. We can see this if we think of the way in which different languages use different words for the same signified: 'baby' in English is 'bimbo' or 'bimba' in Italian, for example. Moreover, the same signifier can have different meanings; 'baby' can also be a term of endearment between adults, for example, and in English 'bimbo' does not refer to babies at all but is a term that stereotypes certain kinds of adult women. Whatever stability attaches to a particular relationship between a signifier and signified does not depend on an inherent connection between them, then. Instead, Saussure argued that it depends upon the difference between that particular sign and many others. Thus one meaning of 'baby' in English depends for its significance not on a necessary relation between the word 'baby' and 'very young humans unable to walk or talk', but rather on the difference between the sign 'baby' and other signs such as

sign

signified

signifier

'toddler', 'child', 'kid', 'teenager', 'adolescent', 'adult' and so on. The actual
referent　object in the world that the sign is related to is called the sign's **referent**.

The distinction between signifier and signified is crucial to semiology,
because it makes the relation between meanings (signifieds) and signifiers not
inherent but rather conventional, and it can therefore be problematised.
Because 'a sign is always thing-plus-meaning' (Williamson, 1978: 17), the
connection between a certain signifier and a certain signified can be questioned; and the relations between signs and their signifieds can also be
explored. In relation to advertisements, semiologists look at the way that
signified meanings are transferred between the ad's signifiers. The elaborate
technical vocabulary of semiology is aimed at clarifying the different ways in
which signifiers and signifieds are attached to (and detached from) each other.

FIGURE 6.2
Advertisement
for the Alfa
Romeo
Giulietta, with
the actor Uma
Thurman
© Alfa Romeo

The first stage of a semiological analysis, then, is to identify the basic building blocks of an image: its signs. Bal and Bryson (1991: 193–4) point out that it is often quite difficult to differentiate between visual signs, because frequently there are no clear boundaries between different parts of an image. However, once certain elements of an image have been at least tentatively identified as its signs, their meanings can be explored.

discussion

Celebrities are often used in advertisements in the hope that some of the celebrity's qualities will become associated with a brand (a strategy which can backfire if the celebrity misbehaves, of course). The website CarsUK (2010) described the connection they make between the Alfa Romeo car and Uma Thurman in this ad:

> What was needed was someone who wasn't cute, but so sexy you'd walk over hot coals just for the chance to play. Someone who wasn't safe and predictable, but fascinating and more than a little dangerous. Someone who wouldn't bend to your will at the drop of a hat, but fight you all the way. Someone who's a very sexy challenge. Just like a good Alfa. So Alfa got Uma Thurman. She may not be Italian but she fits the bill better than anyone we can think of. (CarsUK, 2010)

They link the particular characteristics of Thurman – sexy but dangerous (after her role in the *Kill Bill* films) – to the qualities they associate with Alfa Romeo as a brand.

Gillian Dyer's book *Advertising as Communication* (1982) points out that the photographs of many adverts depend on signs of humans that symbolise particular qualities to their audience. These qualities – these signifieds – are shifted in the advertisement from the human signifiers and onto the product the advert is trying to sell. She has a useful checklist for exploring what signs of humans might symbolise (Dyer, 1982: 96–104):

- *representations of bodies*:
  - *age*. What is the age of the figures in the photograph meant to convey? Innocence? Wisdom? Senility?
  - *gender*. Dyer argued in 1982 that adverts still very often rely on stereotyped images of masculinity and femininity. Men are active and rational, women are passive and emotional; men go out into the world, women are more associated with the domestic. This is less true now, but gendered differences are still crucial to advertising, as Figure 6.2 suggests.
  - *race*. Again, adverts often depend on stereotypes. To what extent does an advert do this (Johnson, 2008)? Or does it normalise whiteness by making it invisible (see Dyer, 1997)?

- o *hair*. Women's hair is often used to signify seductive beauty or narcissism.
- o *body*. Which bodies are fat (and therefore often represented as undesirable and unattractive) and which are thin? Are we shown whole bodies, or does the photo show only parts of bodies (women's bodies are often treated in this way in cosmetic ads)?
- o *size*. Adverts often indicate what is more important by making it big.
- o *looks*. Again, adverts often trade on conventional notions of male and female beauty. Susan Bordo's book *Unbearable Weight* (1993) is an excellent discussion of, among other things, how adverts picture bodies in ways that depend on cultural constructions of race, gender and beauty.

- *representations of manner*

  - o *expression*. Who is shown as happy, haughty, sad and so on? What facial and other expressions are used to convey this?
  - o *eye contact*. Who is looking at whom (including you) and how? Are those looks submissive, coy, confrontational?
  - o *pose*. Who is standing and who is prone? What does that convey about their social position?

- *representations of activity*

  - o *touch*. Who is touching what, with what effects?
  - o *body movement*. Who is active and who passive?
  - o *positional communication*. What is the spatial arrangement of the figures? Who is positioned as superior and who inferior? Who is intimate with whom and how? Hodge and Kress (1988: 52–63) have a useful discussion of positional communication.

- *props and settings*

  - o *props*. Objects in adverts can be used in a way unique to a particular advert, but many ads rely on objects that have particular cultural significance. For example, spectacles often connote intelligence; golden light indicates tranquillity, and so on.
  - o *settings*. Settings range from the apparently 'normal' to the supposedly 'exotic', and can also seem to be fantasies. What effects does its setting have on an advert?

Dyer's list provides a good way of specifying in some detail how a visual image of humans produces certain signifieds. However, this kind of interpretation clearly requires the kind of extensive knowledge of images of culturally specific social difference and social relations.

focus

Look at the advertisement reproduced in Figures 6.3, 6.4 and 6.5. What do the various human figures signify?

FIGURE 6.3   T-shirt advertisement for the Italian newspaper *il Manifesto*. This image was first created in the early 1990s and still appears on banners and flags at political protests in Italy

6.3.2 Ways of describing signs

There is some debate about how useful Saussure's legacy is to semiology beyond this fundamental understanding of the structure of signs. Bal and Bryson (1991) and Hodge and Kress (1988) both argue that Saussure had rather a static notion of how signs work and was uninterested in how meanings change and are changed in use. Other writers wonder whether a theory based on language can deal with the particularities of the visual (Iversen, 1986: 85; see also Armstrong, 1996; Hall, 1980: 132). Many semiologists, therefore, while acknowledging the importance of Saussure's

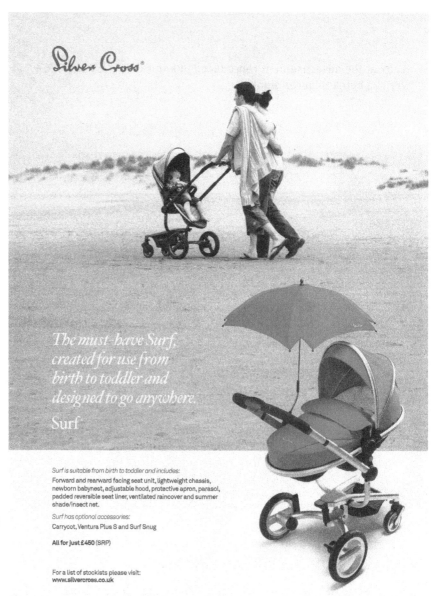

FIGURE 6.4
Advertisement
for a Silver
Cross
pushchair
© Silver Cross
(UK) Ltd

discussion of the sign, prefer to turn to the work of the American philo-sopher Charles Sanders Pierce (see also Wollen, 1970: 120). This is because 'Pierce's richer typology of signs enables us to consider how dif-ferent modes of signification work, while Saussure's model can only tell us how systems of arbitrary signs operate' (Iversen, 1986: 85).

Pierce's work is complex, but its usefulness is often taken to be his suggestion that there were three kinds of signs, differentiated by

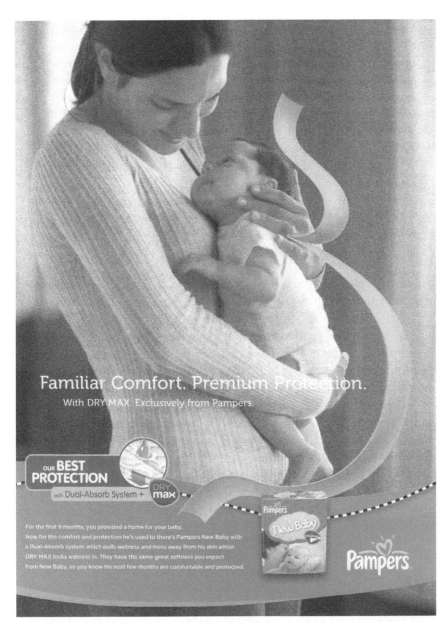

the way in which the relation between the signifier and signified is
understood:

- *icon.* In iconic signs, the signifier represents the signified by app-   **icon**
  arently having a likeness to it. This type of sign is often very
  important in visual images, especially photographic ones. Thus a
  photograph of a baby is an iconic sign of that baby. Diagrams are

also iconic signs, since they show the relations between the parts of their object.

index
- *index*. In indexical signs, there is an inherent relationship between the signified and signifier. 'Inherent' is often culturally specific, so a current example familiar to Western readers might be the way that a schematic picture of a baby soother is often used to denote a room in public places where there are baby-changing facilities.

symbol
- *symbol*. Symbolic signs have a conventionalised but clearly arbitrary relation between signifier and signified. Thus pictures of babies are often used to represent notions of 'the future', as in a t-shirt produced by the Italian communist newspaper *il Manifesto* (see Figure 6.3). This shows a sleeping baby with a raised fist, and the text 'la rivoluzione non russa' ('the revolution isn't snoring/sleeping' but also 'not the Russian revolution').

Since signs work in relation to other signs, it might also be useful to distinguish between two further kinds of signs, paradigmatic and syntagmatic. **Syntagmatic signs** gain their meaning from the signs that

syntagmatic signs
surround them in a still image, or come before or after them in sequence in a moving image. Syntagmatic signs are often very important for semiologies of film, since film is a sequence of signs. Thus certain signs in a film may gain extra meaning because they have occurred in a previous scene (for a discussion of semiology in relation to film specifically,

paradigmatic signs
see Monaco, 2009: 170–91). **Paradigmatic signs** gain their meaning from a contrast with all other possible signs; thus the baby in the t-shirt in Figure 6.3 is a paradigmatic sign because we understand that sign as a baby by deciding that it is not a toddler, an adolescent or an adult.

Signs are complex and can be doing several things at once; so you may have to describe the same sign using several of the terms discussed in this section.

focus

Study the advertisements reproduced up to this point in the chapter, using the terms introduced so far in this section.

What are the photographs' signs? What do each of the photograph's signs signify? In doing this, are they indexical, iconic or symbolic? Are there syntagmatic signs? What about the text? What signifieds does it evoke? Given the signifieds attached to the visual signifiers, what qualities are viewers of these ads meant to associate with the product?

There are other ways of describing signs. Signs can be distinguished depending on how symbolic they are. Signs can be **denotive**, that is, describing something: a baby, a soother. Roland Barthes (1977) suggests that signs that work at the denotive level are fairly easy to decode. We can look at a picture of a baby and see that it is a baby and not a toddler or an adult, for example. A related term is **diegesis**. Diegesis is the sum of the denotive meanings of an image. My description of the t-shirt reproduced as Figure 6.3 as showing 'a sleeping baby with a raised fist, and the text "La rivoluzione non russa"' is a diegesis of that image. The term is often used in film studies to offer a relatively straight-forward account of a film, before a more complex analysis begins. However, although denotive signs at one level may be easy to understand, at another they may have so many potential meanings that a viewer may be confused. A card showing a baby, for example, could be a birth announcement, or an advert for baby cream or cot blankets, or just a cute card. It is often the text that provides what Barthes (1977: 38–41) called **anchorage**. It allows the reader to choose between what could be a confusing number of possible denotive meanings of a card showing a baby. Text in adverts often works as anchorage. In other media, however (television is an example), the text is much more important in relation to the image; they are complementary, and in this case Barthes (1977: 38–41) described the written or spoken text as having a **relay-function**.

But signs can also be **connotive**. Connotive signs carry a range of higher-level meanings. For example, that t-shirt uses a picture of a baby as a connotive sign, because this baby connotes the future when the revolution will happen. Connotive signs themselves can be divided into two kinds:

- *metonymic*. This kind of sign is something associated with something else, which then represents that something else. Thus in the t-shirt example, babies are associated with notions of the future, and the baby is thus also a metonymic sign.
- *synecdochal*. This sign is either a part of something standing in for a whole, or a whole representing a part. Thus the city of Paris is often represented by a picture of one part of it, the Eiffel Tower: the image of the tower is a synecdochal sign of Paris as a whole.

Again, it is important to stress that any one sign may be working in one or more of these ways.

Thus semiology offers a detailed vocabulary for specifying what par-ticular signs are doing.

denotive

diegesis

anchorage

relay-function
connotive

metonymic

synecdochal

discussion

At this point, it is appropriate to mention an interpretative debate among semiologists over the status of signs in photographic images. It is relevant first of all because it has implications for interpreting (some sorts of) photographic images; it suggest that the vocabulary developed in this section may not fully address the impact of photographic imagery on its viewers. Secondly, it is relevant because it parallels the debate in visual culture studies mentioned in Section 2.3, which is that too much analysis refuses to engage with the 'awe at the power of a ... visual experience' (Holly in Cheetham et al., 2005: 88). And finally, in a chapter looking at a lot of adverts, it is relevant to how advertising has changed historically.

Photography is often thought of as picturing reality, as Section 2.2 noted. Unlike any other visual technology, there is a sense in which the camera is an instrument that records what was in front of its lens when the shutter snapped; and although photographic images can be framed and filtered and cropped, and can subsequently be manipulated in all sorts of ways and put to all sorts of uses, they nevertheless always retain a visual trace of what was there when the picture was made. (It is important to note here that both digital and analogue photographs have that trace between light and image – though it occurs in different media, possibly with different consquences, as Chapters 1 and 2 suggested – and that both digital and analogue photos can be manipulated.) Paradoxically, the writer who has made this claim most persuasively – and most movingly – is Roland Barthes, who has also contributed hugely to semiological studies. In his book *Camera Lucida*, which is prompted by Barthes's search for a photograph of his mother, Barthes suggests that:

> It is as if the Photograph always carries its referent with itself, both affected by the same amorous or funereal immobility, at the very heart of the moving world; they are glued together, limb by limb, like the condemned man and the corpse in certain tortures. (1982: 5–6)

studium

punctum

The referent is there in photographic images in ways it is not in other sorts of visual imagery, Barthes argues. And as a result, he suggests that photographs can be interpreted in two ways. First, there is the level of the **studium**, which is a culturally informed reading of the image, one that interprets the signs of the photographs. But he says that some photographs produce a different response, which is a second kind of reading, by containing what he called a **punctum**. A *punctum* is unintentional and ungeneralisable; it is a sensitive point in an image which pricks, bruises, disturbs a particular viewer out of their usual viewing habits. And he went so far as to suggest that 'while the *studium* is ultimately always coded, the *punctum* is not' (Barthes, 1982: 51). That is, there are points in some photographs that escape signifiers and shock the viewer with their 'intractable reality' (Barthes, 1982: 119). And while shock is not something that most adverts aim to achieve, it is the case that recent advertising is relying more and more, not only on the transfer of meaning between signs, but also on the evocation of a feeling or a mood attached to a brand that is difficult to analyse using semiological terminology.

Other semiologists disagree with Barthes's claim that parts of some photographs are beyond signification, however (e.g. Hall, 1980: 131–2). They argue that photographs are always understood through the meanings that are articulated through them, and that no photograph can escape this process even partially. John Tagg (1988), for example, insists that the signifieds of photographic signs always have signifiers, and Section 8.1 will return to his argument. Even in indexical signs, where the signifier represents the signified by having a physical relation to it, these semiologists insist that this likeness is culturally established, not inherent. As Iversen (1986: 92) says, iconic signs have 'a reception as a reflection of the real'. That is, they are seen like that; they are not actually like that.

Photography thus raises some specific questions in relation to semiology, and these have methodological implications. Is the analytical language of signs adequate to the task of elucidating the impact of photographs? Or is some notion necessary, like the *punctum*, or the 'feel' of an image, or its 'expressive content', which lies beyond the field of its meaning? This is a question relevant to a lot of contemporary advertising, which seems to rely as much on the affective impact of striking imagery as it does on conveying meaning. The watch in Figure 6.6, for example, is a diving watch and the ad plays with signs of water in its colour and images of bubbles; but the huge size of the watch seems to me also to emphasise the physical qualities of the object itself.

FIGURE 6.6   Advertisement for a Chanel watch. This advertisement was originally a double-page magazine spread and emphasises the visceral look and feel of the watch as an object
© Chanel

6.3.3 Signs in relation to each other

To reiterate a point already made in passing, the distinction between signifier and signified can help us understand the structure of advertisements. Semiologists argue that adverts work by transferring (or trying to transfer) visual and textual signifieds onto their product. Thus the signs in an ad's image and writing usually signify notions of taste, luxury, health, happiness and so on, and adverts attempt to shift the signifiers from the signs in the image and text to their own product. This section explores this process of meaning-transference in advertising images more fully.

One of the most productive aspects of Williamson's (1978) analysis of images is precisely the way she shows how adverts work by shifting signifieds from one signifier to another. Indeed, she suggests that this is crucial to how adverts work. The signifieds attached to certain signs in adverts get transferred to other signifiers. This process is at work in all the adverts reproduced in this chapter. Williamson suggests that the transfers are often made so persuasively that certain objects become the **objective correlates** of certain qualities: certain objects become taken for granted as having certain qualities. Alfa Romeo cars are sexy; Chanel products are gorgeous.

objective
correlates

Williamson (1978: 20–4) discusses some of the formal mechanisms used by adverts that facilitate this transfer of meaning between objects, humans and qualities in an image. She suggests that the spatial composition of the advert is important – what is put next to what, how certain elements are framed. Goldman (1992) concurs, and he notes that most adverts have the same basic visual structure (Goldman, 1992: 39–40). First, they have a photographic image; secondly, they have what Goldman (1992: 61–84) calls a **mortise**, which is an image of the product framed in some way; thirdly, they have text in the form of headlines, captions and copy; and, finally, they use graphic framing devices to make certain visual links between these components. (However, as Goldman [1992: 70] himself notes, the mortise box may not literally appear in the advert.) Williamson (1978) suggests that one of the most subtle ways in which signifieds are transferred by images is in their use of colour. The use of similar colours in different signs in an advert work to connect those signs and to effect a transfer of their signifieds. These transfers can be between the product and an object, the product and the world, or the product and a person; or the whole world might be retinted in the product's colours. Colour is how the advert in Figure 6.2 transfers the qualities associated with Uma Thurman to the Alfa Romeo car: the red of her lipstick is repeated in the red of the car lights and the Alfa Romeo logo, with almost everything else black or grey.

mortise

The transfers of meaning within an image – which operate between and within both text and image – can be very complex. Goldman (1992: 77) suggests that one way to begin to unravel that complexity is to map the transfers. He offers an example of this technique in which he reduces an advert to its basic spatial organisation by sketching its compositional structure (see Section 4.3.3 for another example of this technique); he then annotates that sketch to show the advert's signs, signifieds and how they are transferred. Figures 6.7a and 6.7b do this on the Alfa Romeo advertisement. Goldman suggests this is rather a schematic and crude way to represent a process as complex and fluid as the advert's meaning-making, and in this he is correct. But it is also a useful way to begin to think carefully about the relationships between signs in an advert.

focus

How do the adverts in Figures 6.4 and 6.5 work to transfer signifieds between signifiers? Try mapping these exchanges of meaning using Goldman's suggestions: sketch the structure of the adverts, label each sign, and draw links to show the transfers of meaning between signs.

FIGURE 6.7A   This is how I initially divided the advert in Figure 6.2 into four signs

FIGURE 6.7B   This shows how I then thought meanings are transferred between those signs

FIGURE 6.7   Note how the second diagram works with much smaller elements of the advertisement than the first. This is certainly not the only way to analyse this advert, though. How do the fonts work, for example? What is the effect of the diagonal red line behind the car, apart from its colour linking the car to the star?

Williamson (1978) also shows how the relationship between the signs in different adverts has meaningful effects. In her book she compares two perfume adverts from the 1970s, one of which used an older, French actress and the other a young American actress. She shows how the adverts work, not only by the movement of meaning within each advert, but also on the contrast between two adverts. Figures 6.8 and 6.9 show a contemporary example of the same process. In Figure 6.8, a Dior perfume is given certain qualities by association with actor Jude Law: a slightly formal Englishness, perhaps. In Figure 6.9, another perfume is given a very different character by its association with the US TV star Josh Holloway. However, in doing this the two adverts are also distinguishing their products from each other. As Williamson notes, this is part of the ideological effect of advertising. She points out that actually (scientifically), there is very little difference between the products that advertisers aim to sell, so advertisers have to create difference. Thus two perfumes are sold not only in terms of what they apparently are (English, smart) but also in terms of what they apparently are not (American, rough).

FIGURE 6.8
Advertisement
for Dior
perfume with
British film star
Jude Law
© Dior

In relation to the connections between adverts, Williamson's argument has some methodological implications which she does not spell out. It suggests that in order to analyse one image, or a few, it is necessary to look at the images they are constructed in contrast to, or in relation to. But how are these other images to be identified? Williamson offers no guidance on this point, other than implying that, since adverts have to create difference between basically the same products, it is to other ads for the same sort of product that the semiologist should look; hence her example comparing two perfume adverts. However, there are a number of other issues to bear in mind. First, both adverts use celebrities to promote products, and in this sense, the two ads here are actually quite similar. So the criteria of 'similarity' and 'difference' in the relations between ads may need to be carefully considered. Secondly, the self-referentiality of much contemporary advertising might mean that comparing adverts selling similar products may be too restrictive to pick up on an ad's resonances. Thirdly, the meanings of adverts may also be established less in relation to other (dis)similar ads and more in relation to whatever other texts and images surround them in their place of display, and indeed elsewhere. This is a consideration ignored by many mainstream semiologists of advertising. Mieke Bal (1996: 117–28), though, offers an interesting interpretation of a visual image which argues that the context of its display is crucial to the meanings it accrues to its viewers (and more particu-

FIGURE 6.9   Advertisement for Davidoff perfume with US TV star Josh Holloway
© Davidoff

larly to her as its viewer: an example of her reflexivity). Her example is a painting by Caravaggio hanging in the Gemäldegalerie Berlin–Dahlem, and she suggests that both the surrounding paintings and the captions on the wall of the gallery, as well as the knowledges and feelings she brings to the painting, affect what it means to her.

If images gain meanings not only from their own signs then, but also from their relation with the signs of other images, it is necessary to consider what sort of relation to other images is most important for the images you are considering. Is it a relation based on 'content'? Or on a shared location of display? Or on explicit cross-referencing? Reaching this decision will help to clarify what other images you need to examine in relation to the ones of your case study. Even so, you will need to develop a broad knowledge of other images in order to be able to identify those that are in a relevant relation to the ones that constitute your case study.

6.3.4 Signs and codes, referent systems, and mythologies

Section 6.3.2 noted that certain sorts of signs – indexical, symbolic and connotive especially – refer to wider systems of meaning. These 'wider systems' can be characterised in a number of ways. They have been called 'codes' by Stuart Hall (1980), 'referent systems' by Williamson (1978), and 'mythologies' by Barthes (1973). Each of these terms means something rather different, and each has somewhat different methodological implications.

A code is a set of conventionalised ways of making meaning that are specific to particular groups of people. In the context of making television news programmes, for example, Stuart Hall (1980: 136) comments on what he calls the 'professional code' that is mobilised in the work of producers, editors, lighting and camera technicians, newscasters and so on. This professional code guides such things as 'the particular choice of presentational occasions and formats, the selection of personnel, the choice of images, the staging of debates'. It has a 'techno-practical nature' according to Hall because it operates with 'such apparently neutral-technical questions as visual quality, news and presentational values, televisual quality, "professionalism" and so on' (Hall, 1980: 136). The makers of adverts have their professional codes too, which results in the frequent occurrence of the visual structures described by Goldman (1992) as photographic image, text, mortise and graphics (see also Dyer, 1982: 135; Myers, 1983). Adverts depend on other sorts of codes as well. Crucially, they depend on the codes held by the particular group of consumers their makers want to sell their product to (hence the use of focus groups by advertising agencies to find out what those codes are). Thus the perfume advert in Figure 6.8 depends for its effectiveness on its audience 'knowing' that Jude Law is English and stylish; he has to be already encoded as such for the advert to be able to transfer those signifiers from him to the perfume.

Codes can be researched in a number of ways. Goldman (1992), for example, seems to use a very informal (and implicit) kind of content analysis of the adverts to reach his fourfold characterisation of advertising's visual code. Catherine Lutz and Jane Collins (1993), in their study of the photographs used in *National Geographic* that was examined in the previous chapter, supplemented their content analysis with interviews with the editors, writers and photographers at the magazine, in order to explore the codes they mobilised to make the publication look the way it does.

As Hall (1980) makes clear, codes allow the semiologist access to the wider ideologies at work in a society. 'At the connotive level, we must refer, *through* the codes, to the orders of social life, of economic and political power and of ideology', because codes 'contract relations for the sign with the wider universe of ideologies in a society' (Hall, 1980: 134). Thus Jude Law and Josh Holloway are both encoded as sexy, and that code is a particular expression of the ideology that male film stars should be physically attractive. Hall (1980) describes such ideologies as **dominant codes** 'metacodes' or '**dominant codes**'. Williamson (1978), on the other hand, **referent systems** describes something similar as **referent systems**. Williamson (1978) says that there are three major referent systems on which the signs of adverts depend – Nature, Magic and Time. Referent systems, like dominant codes, are knowledges that exist prior to advertising and that structure not only adverts but many other cultural and social forms. Thus of the referent system of Nature she says, 'Nature is the primary referent of a culture' (Williamson, 1978: 103). However, Williamson characterises referent systems in a more rigid way than Hall does dominant codes. Following the work of the structuralist anthropologist Claude Levi-Strauss, Williamson argues that referent systems are organised in binary terms. Hodge and Kress (1988: 30) refer to this structure as 'an abstract elemental binary principle, with infinite particular forms produced by this principle applied repeatedly to the material basis of the code'. Thus Nature, says Williamson (1978: 103–37), is in adverts represented in only two ways: it is either 'raw' or 'cooked' (that is, transformed by culture). Many adverts suggest that their products improve nature, and picture this with images of 'cooked' nature. Many ads use images of 'science' to suggest that their products can order, investigate or overcome nature (again, in Williamson's terms, cooking it), and many others use images of 'raw' nature to confer apparently natural qualities onto their products, such as perfectibility, danger and obviousness (see Figure 6.10). Thus Nature is for Williamson a referent system that underlies many of the particular signs and codes of adverts.

Using Willamson's notion of referent systems depends on a broader understanding of culture that is more likely to come from social theory than from empirical investigation. Indeed, William Leiss and his colleagues (2005: 165) find Williamson's referent systems just too huge to shed much light on adverts specifically. They imply that analyses of ads would be better based on some sort of 'middling level' structures of meaning, like 'fashion' or 'domesticity'.

Barthes's notion of **mythology** is different again. Barthes (1973: 117)   *mythology*
says that 'myth is not defined by the object of its message, but by the way in which it utters this message: there are formal limits to myth, there are no "substantial" ones'. That is, whereas Williamson's referent systems are substantive – her discussion of Nature, for example, is about how Nature is pictured in adverts – Barthes instead argues that mythology is defined by its form, not its content. Myth, he suggested, is a 'second-order semiological system' (1973: 123). By this he meant that myth builds upon denotive signs. Denotive signs consist of a signifier and a signified but they are fairly easy to understand, and Barthes suggests this is the first-order semiological system. The denotive sign, however, becomes a signifier at the second, or mythological, level of meaning. At this second level of meaning, this signifier is then accompanied by its own signified. And these second-level signifieds and signifiers then form second-level signs. In order to avoid confusion, Barthes adopted a clear terminology

FIGURE 6.10 Advertisement showing the positive values associated with nature. This is an advert for allergy relief medication. Although the product is not itself natural, it is related to nature through its green packaging and the green graphics, both of which link the product visually to the photograph. As well as the visual relation to nature, a number of social identities are represented in the photo by the figures 'having fun', their clothing, and what they are pictured doing: Are there audiences that might challenge those identities? *Hello* magazine, 31 May 2010

for these different elements of signs (see Figure 6.11). He called the sign at the first level, 'meaning'; when it is referred to as the signifier of a mythical sign, he called it 'form'. The signified is the concept. And the second level of sign – at the level of myth – he called 'signification'.

'In myth', Barthes (1973: 127) writes, 'the meaning is already complete, it postulates a kind of knowledge, a past, a memory, a comparative order of facts, ideas, decisions.' Barthes elaborates what he means by this through an example: 'I am at the barber's, and a copy of *Paris-Match* is offered to me. On the cover, a young Negro in a French uniform is saluting, with his eyes uplifted, probably fixed on the fold of the tricolour' (Barthes, 1973: 125). This is the meaning of the image (at the denotive level). He suggests that the image contains a kind of richness at this level (remember Barthes's claim that the photograph carries its referent with it in ways other forms of visual imagery do not); the black boy 'appears as a rich, fully experienced, spontaneous, *indisputable* image' (Barthes, 1973: 128, emphasis in original). When this meaning becomes form, however, this richness is almost lost. 'When it becomes form, the meaning leaves contingency behind; it empties itself, it becomes impoverished, history evaporates' (Barthes, 1973: 127). The meaning is put at a distance, and what fills the gap is signification. In this case, signification produces the notion that 'France is a great Empire, that all her sons, without any colour discrimination, faithfully serve under her flag, and that there is no better answer to the detractors of an alleged colonialism than the zeal shown by this Negro in serving his so-called oppressors' (Barthes, 1973: 125). The contingency and the history of the meaning becomes remote, and instead a myth inserts itself as a non-historical truth. Myth makes us forget that things were and are made; instead, it naturalises the way things are. Myth is thus a form of ideology. French imperialism is the drive behind this myth, says Barthes, and this image presents it as natural. But the myth is believable precisely because form does not entirely replace meaning. 'The meaning will be for the form like an instantaneous reserve of history, a tamed richness, which it is possible to call and dismiss in a sort of rapid alternation' (Barthes, 1973: 127); the meaning both hides and sustains the form.

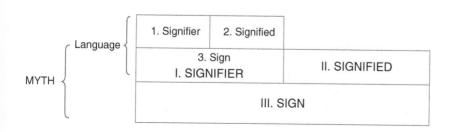

FIGURE 6.11
Diagram showing the structure of myth, from Roland Barthes's book *Mythologies* (1973)

As with dominant codes and referent systems, then, the interpretation of mythologies requires a broad understanding of a culture's dynamics.

6.3.5 Slippery signs

This section has explored some of the various ways in which mainstream semiology understands how signs make meanings. Not all these approaches are completely compatible; however, they do share certain characteristics. Above all, they emphasise the relationality of signs: what one sign means depends on its relations with others. As Bal and Bryson (1991: 177) note, this makes the analysis of signs difficult because it is hard to know where to break into that relationality: 'Meaning [arises] exactly from the movement from one sign or signifier to the next, in a *perpetuum mobile* where there could be found neither a starting point for semiosis, nor a concluding moment in which semiosis terminated and the meaning of signs fully "arrived".' In semiology there is no stable point that can provide an entrance into the meaning-making process; all meanings are relational not only within the image but also in relation to other images and to broader dominant codes, referent systems and mythologies. Any point of entry will be artificial and arbitrary, then. But, providing this is borne in mind, this section has suggested a number of steps through which, faced with an image, a semiological analysis might be initiated. In summary, these are:

- Decide what the signs are.
- Decide what they signify 'in themselves'.
- Think about how they relate to other signs 'in themselves' (here the vocabulary of Section 6.3.2 is useful, and making a diagram of the movement of signifieds between the signifiers of an image may also help).
- Then explore their connections (and the connections of the connections) to wider systems of meaning, from codes to ideologies.
- And finally return to the signs via their codes to explore the precise articulation of ideology and mythology.

6.3.6 Mainstream semiology and the decoding of adverts

The meanings of signs are, therefore, extraordinarily complex. This complexity means that their meanings are multiple, and this multiplicity

polysemy   is referred to as **polysemy**. A sign is polysemic when it has more than one meaning. How is it then that Williamson (1978), for example, can speak of an advert as having a powerful meaning that positions its viewers in a specific imaginary social place? Is polysemy limited in some way? Williamson argues it is. This subsection explores how semiology argues that most images most of the time produce what Hall calls the **preferred meaning**.

preferred meaning

> Any ... sign is potentially transformable into more than one connotive configuration. Polysemy, however, must not be confused with pluralism ... Any society/culture tends, with varying degrees of closure, to impose its classifications of the social and cultural and political world. These constitute a *dominant cultural order*, though it is neither univocal nor uncontested ... The different areas of social life appeared to be mapped out into discursive domains, hierarchically organised into dominant or preferred meanings. (Hall, 1980: 134)

These preferred meanings (or ideologies) become **preferred readings** when they are interpreted by audiences in ways that retain 'the institutional/political/ideological order imprinted on them' (Hall, 1980: 134).

preferred readings

In its discussion of mainstream semiological approaches to advertising, this chapter has so far argued that the fundamental process through which adverts make meaning is by transferring signifieds between signs. But this elides a crucial part of Williamson's (1978) arguments. Adverts do not effect this transfer by themselves. The source of the movement of signifieds is not the advert itself, says Williamson, but the viewer of the advert. It is the viewer who makes sense of the advert, not the advert itself. Indeed, without a viewer to decode the advert, it would be, literally, meaningless. 'All signs depend for their signifying process on the existence of specific, concrete receivers, people *for* whom and in whose systems of belief, they have a meaning' (Williamson, 1978: 40). It is in this sense that Bal and Bryson argue that semiology is centrally concerned with the reception of images by audiences: 'Semiotic analysis of visual art does not set out in the first place to produce interpretations of works of art, but rather to investigate how works of art are intelligible to those who view them, the processes by which viewers make sense of what they see' (Bal and Bryson, 1991: 184).

Williamson (1978) elaborates this argument in a way that has particular methodological implications; she develops an analysis of how adverts encourage their viewers to produce preferred readings. Her analysis proceeds by exploring the stages of a viewer's encounter with an ad. First, she says, the viewer creates the meaning of a product by making links between signs. Then, the viewer gives meaning to him- or herself from the product; we believe we will get 'familiar comfort' and 'premium protection' by buying a specific brand of nappy. Thirdly, we become created by the advert, in a process Williamson calls, after Althusser, **appellation**. The advert hails us, 'hey you', often quite directly, and thus incorporates us into its signifying world:

appellation

> Every ad assumes a particular spectator; it projects out into the space in front of it an imaginary person composed in terms of the relationship between the elements in the ad. You move into this space as you look at the ad, and in doing so 'become' the spectator, you feel that the 'hey you' *'really did'* apply to you in particular. (Williamson, 1978: 50–1)

Williamson suggests a number of ways in which advertisements pull a spectator into their signifying effects:

- The *spatial organisation* of an image offers a particular position to its spectators. For example, Chapter 2 explored how a photograph by Robert Doisneau projects out into the space in front of it a spectator composed in terms of the relationship between the elements of the photograph.
- Adverts contain or imply *visual absences* that the viewer is invited to fill.
- The *written text* draws us in (many commentaries on Alfa Romeo's campaign for the Giulietta note that the phrase 'such stuff as dreams are made on' is from Shakespeare).
- Many adverts rely on textual and visual *puns* or puzzles, which make us stop and look at them in order to work out 'what's going on'. Ads can show incongruity, or use no words at all, again to attract our attention and involvement.
- *calligraphy*. This is when the product is transformed into a word. The word then becomes a referent of a real object, the product.

Thus Williamson focuses on the compositional modality of the adverts themselves in her understanding of how they produce preferred meanings.

Finally, she suggests that we create ourselves in the advertisement itself. At this point in her argument she turns to certain ideas from psychoanalysis – including the imaginary – in order to explore the dynamics of precisely how we imagine adverts mirror our self. These arguments will be explored in the following chapter.

discussion

How can mainstream semiology help us to interpret other kinds of visual materials?

As this chapter has noted more than once, semiological methods can be used on many different cultural texts. Let's try thinking about how they can help to make sense of a particular sort of building: a shop. Actually, this example is related to some of the discussion in this chapter about brands, because the shop I'm asking you to think about is an Apple store. You may well have visited one. If you haven't, browse through Apple's store locator on its website, or google 'apple store images' and take a look.

The design of Apple stores is pretty similar regardless of where the shop is located; although some have more striking frontages than others, most look more or less the same once you are inside. This design is part of the Apple brand. This brand is created in large part through a range of different kinds of adverts – magazine ads, TV ads and billboards, as well as product placements, say – but it is also created by the design of its website and how its stores look. The stores are particularly key, because as well as a visual style they can offer potential customers an 'experience'. Back in 1999, Joseph Pine and James Gilmore wrote a book discussing 'the experience economy', arguing that what created the character of a brand and what helped potential customers to identify with it was, in part, the 'feel' of the brand's shops. When you shop at the store of a major brand now, the idea is that you are buying not just a product with a specific functionality but also a whole experience that you like.

Apple's brand depends a lot for its distinctiveness on the importance of 'good design' to its products, and its stores are also very carefully designed. In March 2015 there were over 450 Apple stores worldwide (deAgonia, 2015), and they look very similar. The front of the shop uses lots of glazing if it can (the New York store entrance is a huge glass box, with the actual store located underground) and the Apple logo is always prominent. The shop floor is open; you can see it all as you walk in. There are a few large, pale wooden tables with Apple products on them, and wide table-shelves along the side of the shop with more laptops and iPhones and iPods. The walls are mostly empty of objects, apart from a few shelves at the back somewhere carrying boxes of hardware, software and accessories; instead, there are large back-lit light boxes incorporated into the top third of the walls, looking a bit like screens, emphasising the services available instore and showing specific products, with the images and text sharing Apple adverts' style. The floors are dark grey stone and the rest of the walls are grey like the aluminium Apple uses for many of its computers.

So, how does mainstream semiology help us to get to grips with what this store means? Work through the five steps listed at the end of Section 6.3.5 in relation to the stores. Try to identify the signs in the store, then think about what they signify. Think about how meanings are transferred between signs both within the store and to other things outside it. And consider what sort of ideologies are at work as a result.

This is a complex task, but here are a few starting points. Do the maple tables and stone floors signify 'nature', for example? And are they therefore attempts to invoke the natural amidst all the high-tech gadgets? What about the light grey colour of both Apple computers and the shop walls? That colour, with its associations with cool and elegant design, is clearly a symbolic sign too. It is also a paradigmatic sign, in that it distinguishes Apple products from all its competitors who offer multicolour laptops. The dazzling images on the walls, and the way in which the store focuses so much on the products it sells as individual physical objects, lined up under careful spotlighting, perhaps suggests a degree of commodity fetishism.

What other meaning-making happens in an Apple store? Are there important aspects of the store that these questions generated by mainstream semiology do not address?

6.4 Making Meaning Socially: Social Semiotics

As the previous subsection noted, Judith Williamson (1978) explores how adverts work to produce their viewers in particular ways. Even though she says it is the viewers doing the work, nonetheless her argument implies that adverts are themselves powerful in the sense that they produce certain kinds of ways of seeing through their visual and verbal organisation and connotations. Other semiologists, however, have paid much more attention to the ways in which the meanings of signs are made socially. Indeed, this is the core focus of social semiotics. Hodge and Kress (1988) argue that mainstream semiology stresses 'system and product' (which is certainly true of Williamson's work, for example), whereas they prefer to emphasise 'speakers and writers or other participants in semiotic activity as connecting and inter*acting* in a variety of ways in concrete social contexts' (Hodge and Kress 1988: 1; see also Jewitt and Oyama, 2001; Jewitt, 2014a). As this implies, social semiotic theory is built by drawing on detailed accounts of people making meaning in social settings.

This immediately addresses a problem that might have occurred to you if you did stop to think about how mainstream semiology can be used to analyse a shop like an Apple store: mainstream semiology does not focus attention on the ways in which the people working or shopping in an Apple store interpret the significations of the store's physical design. In the case of the Apple store, this is particularly apparent because, as one group of observers remarks, the design of an Apple store creates 'an uncluttered shrine to objects *that invite play*' (Washor et al., 2009: 60; emphasis in original). Apple stores contribute to the Apple brand not only because of the semiology of their material signs, but also because of what people are invited to do there and, indeed, what actually happens there. When you visit an Apple store, you can play with the gadgets with no pressure to buy; you can get informal advice or more specific technical support from knowledge-able but also relaxed workers in their bright t-shirts; and it all feels fun, helpful and cool. Social semioticians would argue that these interactions, both between people and between people and objects like iPads and laptops, are also key to understanding how meaning is made in an Apple store. And being semiologists, they would also point out that such interactions build up yet further the impact of the Apple brand, which means Apple sells more products and makes more profits.

How does social semiotics focus on social interaction in relation to signs? Social semiotics, as this chapter noted in its opening section, is concerned with signs but also, crucially, with what it calls **semiotic resources**. Semiotic resources are:

> signifiers, observable actions and objects that have been drawn into the domain of social communication and that have a *theoretical* semiotic potential constituted by all their past uses and all their potential uses and an *actual* semiotic potential constituted by those past uses that are known to and considered relevant by the users of the resource, and by such potential uses as might be uncovered by the users on the basis of their specific needs and interests. (van Leeuwen, 2005: 4, emphasis in original)

semiotic resources

A significant part of social semiotics is devoted to exploring the theoretical semiotic potential of particular kinds of semiotic resources: what kinds of meanings could potentially be made by what particular resources. Chapter 4 mentioned Kress and van Leeuwen's (2006) exploration of the grammar of visual design, for example, and in particular their discussion of the importance of spatial organisation to an image's meaning. But it is the *actual* semiotic potential of a semiotic resource that is the main focus of social semioticians. For Kress (2010), the semiotic potential of signifiers, actions and objects is drawn upon by people when we communicate with each other. That is, the semiotic potential of signifiers, actions and objects is utilised both when we produce meanings – when we create something as some sort of attempt to communicate something – and also when we receive meanings – when we interpret the meaning-making of others. Social semiotics focuses on this complex process of communication by exploring specific examples of what Kress calls the **design** of meaning – when humans in specific situations make particular kinds of meaning in the context of particular communicative

design

acts (Gee, 2013). Social semioticians bring the detailed analysis so typical of mainstream semiology to bear on specific actual examples of real-world social communication.

First, their emphasis is usually on the social context in which semiotic work is taking place; that is, particular examples of meaning being made in order that communication happens. To return to magazine advertisements for a moment, a social semiotician would not consider a folder of those adverts torn from magazines to be an adequate basis for making claims about how those adverts have effects, for example. Rather, they would explore how the adverts are part of a communication process or event. It is more likely, I think, that a social semiotician would examine the process of looking at magazines in a specific context: doctors' waiting rooms, say, by people waiting more or less patiently, and more or less anxiously, for their appointment, and surrounded by talk, furniture, toys and other people, as well as many other sorts of communicative images on the waiting room's noticeboard, for example, or on its TV screen (McCarthy, 2001). That is, the meaning made by an advert would be inflected not only by how the reader looked at the advert, but also by the context in which that looking takes place.

Secondly, the emphasis in social semiotics is on the wide range of modes in which meaning is made. 'Mode' here means something like the medium of the communicative act in question, though modes tend to be described very broadly in this work. Kress (2010: 79), for example, lists key modes as:

- image
- writing
- layout
- music
- gesture
- speech
- moving image
- soundtrack
- 3D objects.

multimodality

Crucially, most communication involves more than one mode; hence social semiotics emphasises the **multimodality** of semiotic design (and social semiotics is sometimes called multimodal research). This is another important reminder that nothing is ever just visual, and that all visual images are accompanied by other kinds of semiotic resources that are integral to their meaning.

discussion

Multimodal research is now a well-established research method in its own right, and Carey Jewitt (2014a) offers a useful summary of its theoretical assumptions and core concepts. It has developed from the work of Gunther Kress in particular and his work on understanding how young people learn in classroom situations. The essays collected together by Margit Böck and Norbert Pachler (2013) explore different aspects of his work.

Thirdly, social semiologists emphasise that both the production of specific semiotic resources and modes, and the way that they are interpreted by people, are shaped by social processes. They are shaped by a number of conventions in terms of how meaning is organised. Van Leeuwen (2005) argues that there are three of these:

- *discourse*. Discourses are frameworks for making meanings. They are plural, have histories, and are enacted in various ways. (Chapters 8 and 9 here explore discourse at greater length.)
- *genre*. A group of texts that share certain characteristics and follow certain rules. (Chapter 2 in this book used genre in just this sense.)
- *style*. A style is a particular manner of writing, speaking and doing. For example, street photography (discussed in Chapter 2) could be seen as a particular style of documentary photography.

Van Leeuwen (2005) breaks each of these three terms down further, to offer sub-categories of genre and style, for example, and also explores how rhythm, composition, information linking and dialogue hold the three together in specific texts and communicative events. He does this through a series of fine-grained readings of specific examples of meaning-making, including newspaper cartoons, magazine graphics, logos, school students' concept maps, fine art paintings and photographs, dresses and a printer cartridge package. Kress (2010), meanwhile, ranges from school textbooks to car park signs to a website homepage. This emphasises how semiological methods can be used with a very wide range of materials; but it also shows how social semiotics shares mainstream semiology's concern to focus very carefully on the specific components of meaning-making.

Finally, the circumstances in which semiotic resources are used are also shaped by established practices:

> Such uses take place in a social context, and this context may either have rules or best practices that regulate how specific semiotic resources can be used, or leave the users relatively free in their use of the resource. (van Leeuwen, 2005: 4)

discussion

The kind of social semiotic – or multimodal – analysis discussed by van Leeuwen (2005) and Kress (2010) is often applied to visual materials as they are being used in particular situations. This can be done in different ways.

Jewitt's (2005) discussion of the multimodality of multimedia resources designed to teach English and science to secondary school students analyses a CD-ROM of a novel and an interactive science CD, and explores how their text and their still and animated visuals are designed to convey specific meanings: about the characters in the novel, for example, or about the relationships between solids, liquids and gases. To understand how students actually used the CDs, she studied the students' projects and was able to show that they used similar devices to organise text and image in their own work.

However, social semioticians also often turn to another kind of method to generate data: video. They often use video recorders to film people engaging with visual (and other) materials, in ordinary situations like classrooms or museums. The video recording is then used to observe in very close detail how meaning is designed: in particular, attention is paid to interactions between and among objects (which might include visual materials of various kinds) and people, including both voice and bodily movement. Videorecording naturally occurring social situations is a specific visual research method, and there are a range of ways in which the data it produces can be analysed – not just social semiotics. This is discussed in detail by Hubert Knoblauch (2009) and by Christian Heath, Jon Hindmarsh and Paul Luff (Heath et al., 2009; Hindmarsh et al., 2010). Chapter 12 here will also refer to it.

The use of semiotic resources is heavily shaped by the established meanings of those resources; as Kress (2010: 74) says, 'makers of signs … live in a world shaped by the histories of the work of their societies; the results of that work are available to them as the resources of their culture.' Hodge and Kress emphasise the shaping of semiotic design work by **logonomic system**   describing what they called the **logonomic system**:

A logonomic system is a set of rules prescribing the conditions for production and reception of meanings; which specify who can claim to initiate (produce, communicate) or know (receive, understand) meanings about what topics under what circumstances and with what modalities (how, when, why). Logonomic systems prescribe **production**   social semiotic behaviours at points of production and reception, **regimes**   so that we can distinguish between **production regimes** (rules con- **reception regimes**   straining production) and **reception regimes** (rules constraining reception). A logonomic system is itself a set of messages, part of an ideological complex but serving to make it unambiguous in practice … The logonomic rules are specifically taught and policed by concrete social agents (parents, teachers, employers) coercing concrete individuals in specific situations by processes which are in principle open to study and analysis ... Logonomic systems cannot be invisible or obscure, or they would not work. (Hodge and Kress, 1988: 4)

Now, while there are a number of emphases on the way in which the design of semiotic resources is shaped and structured in social semiotics, it is important to note that there is never any assumption that any act of semiotic design is necessarily successful, in the sense that the same meaning is shared by both the producer and the interpreter of semiotic resources. Hodge and Kress (1988), for example, point out that different social groups (however defined) encode the world in very different ways and may thus interpret visual images in very different ways. Their example is an advert for cigarettes that has been covered with graffiti by an anti-smoking organisation. Bal and Bryson (1991) make the same point in their discussion of visual art. They suggest that there is probably always resistance to dominant scopic regimes, which might 'range from polite parody to outright defacement, from the clandestine inversion of existing rules of viewing to the invention of wholly new sets of rules, from subtle violations of propriety to blank refusal to play the game' (Bal and Bryson, 1991: 187) – quite apart from the private languages of looking that are evoked, for example, by Barthes's notion of the *punctum* (Bal and Bryson, 1991: 187). Figure 6.12 shows an outright parody of a certain kind of advertisement for men's perfume.

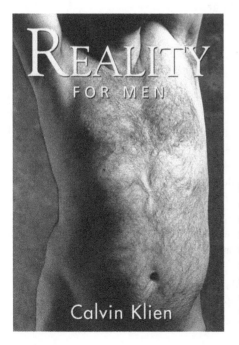

FIGURE 6.12
A challenge to current forms of advertising men's perfume, created by the campaigners at Adbusters
© Christopher Turner

Interestingly, though, in his book on social semiotics published in 2010, Gunther Kress explicitly shifts his analytical terms, in relation to the making of meaning, away from those he used working with Robert Hodge in their 1988 book. In the newer book, Kress suggests that the notion that there is a logonomic system produced by powerful actors, against which marginalised others will protest, is now a rather outdated model of social meaning-making. He argues that both the increasing individualism and the rhetoric of choice associated with neo-liberalism, as well as the participatory possibilities of the Web, have significantly altered the 'forms, processes and possibilities of communication' over the past two or three decades (Kress, 2010: 21). In some ways, his argument echoes that of Henry Jenkins (2008) on convergence culture, which Chapter 2 discussed. Like Jenkins, Kress argues that hierarchical structures and institutions of communication are increasingly participatory in their processes and thus 'flatter' in their distribution of power; both cultural and technological shifts are permitting young people in particular to begin 'acting in their own interests in the domain of their "own" culture and in their own cultural/semiotic production. The best examples here are "user-created content" and the new genres, forms and sites of dissemination such as blogs, wikis, YouTube and Myspace' (Kress, 2010: 21). For Kress, this means that accounts of meaning-making must focus on specific instances of design (analysed using the tools of social semiotics) and must be embedded in quite particular accounts of social relations, practices and institutions as they are made and remade through rich and complex acts of multimodal communication.

Clearly, social semioticians are interested in social difference and power relations. But how do they reflect on their own work? Well, there is little overt navel-gazing; nor is there a strong sense of provisionality in the analyses of specific situations. In this, social semioticians and mainstream sociologists are alike.

6.5 Semiology: An Assessment

Despite the doubts voiced by some about the appropriateness of using semiological approaches to interpret visual images, it seems that semiology (in both its mainstream and social semiotic versions) can nonetheless be a very productive way of thinking about visual meaning. Semiological approaches demand detailed analysis of images. Their reliance on case studies and their elaborate analytical terminology create careful and precise accounts of how the meanings of particular images are made. Moreover, all semiology is centrally concerned with the construction of social difference through signs. The focus on ideology, ideological complexes and dominant codes, and logonomic systems and genres, and the recognition of resistance to (as well as creation of) all of those, mean that any semiological approach cannot avoid considering the social effects of meaning.

> Sign-events occur in specific circumstances and according to a finite number of culturally valid, conventional, yet not unalterable rules ... The selection of those rules and their combination leads to specific interpretative behaviour. That behaviour is socially

framed, and any semiotic view that is to be socially relevant will have to deal with this framing, precisely on the grounds of the fundamental polysemy of meaning and the subsequent possibility of dissemination. In the end, there is no way around considerations of power, inside and outside the academy. (Bal and Bryson, 1991: 208)

As Bal and Bryson's last sentence indicates, semiology can also imply the need for academic accounts of signs to reflect on their own meaning-making tactics (although, as I have noted, not many semiologists seem to follow through on that).

Thus it would seem that semiology fulfills all the criteria for a critical visual methodology outlined in Chapter 1. It takes images seriously, providing a number of tools for understanding exactly how a particular image is structured. It considers the social conditions and effects of images, both in terms of how an image itself may have its own effects and how the logonomic system shapes its production and reception. And it is able to acknowledge that semiologists are themselves working with signs, codes and referent systems and are thus imbricated in nothing more, though certainly nothing less, than another series of transfers of meaning in which a particular image participates. This allows a certain reflexivity.

However, semiology also has some methodological drawbacks. First, mainstream semiology's preference for detailed readings of individual images raises questions about the representativeness and replicability of its analyses. This is a doubt Leiss and colleagues (2005: 166) have about Williamson's work. They are unclear about how or why Williamson chose the adverts she works with; are they representative of adverts in general? And would someone else using those same adverts have come to the same conclusions about them? Similarly, stimulating as the eclectic range of materials worked with by van Leeuwen (2005) is, there is no discussion of why these examples in particular were chosen, nor whether a different choice would have affected the theoretical framework being elaborated. Both semiologists would presumably respond that these questions are not important since they are not using their visual and other materials as the basis of a general theory that could critique how all semiosis works; neither was trying to offer empirical generalisations about semiology or social semiotics. Instead, the illustrations in their books are just that – illustrations of particular processes of meaning-making – and the important part of the books is their conceptual analysis.

Another criticism often faced by semiology is its elaborate theoretical terminology. Ball and Smith (1992), Wells (1992), Chandler (2007) and Leiss et al. (2005: 165) all voice concern that semiology, in all its guises, tends to invent new terminology for its own sake, and from my experience of writing this chapter, I tend to agree. Often these terms are useful; they have particular meanings that are clearly defined, and refer to processes that are not easily described otherwise (this latter point is crucial). These sorts of neologisms are thus worth persevering with, no matter how clumsy their use might feel initially. However, sometimes new terms are confusing or unnecessary, and they may be used to give a veneer of sophistication to something that is actually not particularly interesting. As Leiss et al. (2005: 165) remark, in unskilled hands this can lead to an obscurantist text that does 'little more than state the obvious in a complex and often pretentious manner'. This sort of use of jargon should be avoided. If a simpler term will do, use the simpler term.

The use of a somewhat elaborate terminology leads to another issue that needs some thought when semiology is deployed as a method – reflexivity. I have commented, mostly in relation to the work of Mieke Bal, that semiology is capable of acknowledging its own interpretative practices. I would term such an acknowledgement 'reflexive'. However, there is also a strong anti-reflexive strain in certain sorts of semiology, particularly those that claim to delve beneath surface appearances to reveal the true meaning of images. Thus Goldman (1992: 36), at the end of his first chapter, which argues that adverts embody three key aspects of commodity form, says that 'the triumph of the commodity form is that we do not recognise its presence at all'. This statement immediately invites the question, 'Who is this "we"?' It clearly excludes Goldman, since he has just spent 36 pages describing the commodity form in detail. So does 'we' refer to the rest of us poor dupes who don't know our Marx (and Goldman) well enough? What makes Goldman so insightful? How can he see these adverts differently to recognise their commodification of product and viewer? Goldman positions himself here as the one who sees and knows. He does not even clarify his methodology as a way of grounding his claims. This kind of non-reflexivity, I think, cannot be part of a critical visual methodology. Social semioticians, on the other hand, at least do offer very detailed accounts of how they are producing their interpretations of communication events, even if they still refuse to address explicitly Bal's double exposure.

Another omission in much mainstream semiological work is the empirical exploration of polysemy and logonomic systems. Mainstream semiology is very ready to admit to polysemy and to the contestation as well as to the transfer and circulation of meaning in theory, but there are still very few mainstream semiological studies that really get to grips with diverse ways of seeing (Chandler, 2007). Social semiotics and multimodal research are much better at this task.

Slater (1983) has addressed the uninterest in polysemy in mainstream semiology as an approach and suggests that it is not a coincidence: putting to one side the efforts of social semioticians, semiology is simply not concerned with the social practices, institutions and relations within which visual images are produced and interpreted. He blames this on the structuralist tradition within which much semiology was situated when he was writing, which, he says, 'takes as assumed, as given, precisely what needs to be explained: the relations and practices within which discourses are formed and operated' (Slater, 1983: 258). This is certainly the case with Williamson's work. She does not explain how she decided that there were only three referent systems underpinning adverts, for example, nor how she decided that Nature, Magic and Time were the three. It seems that this was a theoretical decision that then informed her reading of the adverts. Nor does she pay any attention to the social institutions producing adverts, or consider how different audiences might react to adverts differently or even simply not 'get' them (Myers, 1983; Wells, 1992). For example, the watch in Figure 6.6 is advertised in the USA using the surfer Laird Hamilton, but only in the USA because only there is it likely that the association between his picture and a diving watch will work. Williamson (1978) does not talk about adverts that fail because their signifieds are not recognised; her focus on 'the image itself' produces what Slater (1983: 258) calls a 'radically internal analysis of signification' which cannot address these sorts of issues. This is perhaps the most telling criticism of semiology, and one that social semiotics is responding to by filling the semiological toolbox with yet more concepts.

Finally, a question for all the varieties of semiology discussed in this chapter: Is the semiological focus on meaning-making adequate to the character of contemporary advertising? Advertisers are increasingly aiming for an emotive response from their target audience (Malefyt, 2010). Many adverts now are about associating a particular 'feel' to a brand or product, rather than specific meanings, often by using the particular digital visual aesthetic described by Lev Manovich (2013) and discussed in Chapter 1 (see also Figure 6.6). Whether semiology of whatever variety is able to analyse the visual aspects of such non-representational strategies is still an open question. As Chapter 1 pointed out, there is increasing interest among some scholars of visual culture precisely in the experiential and affective qualities of visual images. If semiology has little to say about this in relation to advertising, it may not be the most appropriate method to interpret the affective elements of other visual materials either.

Summary: Semiology

- *associated with*:
  Semiology, in its various forms, has been extremely influential across the whole range of disciplines currently interested in visual culture. Its approach has therefore been applied to many sorts of visual materials. Given its theoretical provenance, it is used as a form of critique of those materials.

- *sites and modalities*:
  Mainstream semiology focuses on the site of the image and its compositional and social modalities. Social semiotics focuses more on the site of audiencing, in its compositional and social modalities.

- *key terms*:
  The sign is the key term of semiology, which consists of a signifier and a signified; these are semiotic resources, which are often multimodal. The referent is what a sign refers to in the real world. The transfer of a sign's signifieds is structured through codes, which in turn give onto dominant codes. Codes and dominant codes encourage preferred readings of images by viewers.

- *strengths and weakness for a critical visual methodology*:
  This method provides a precise and rich vocabulary for understanding how the structure of images produces cultural meaning. It permits reflexivity. It does not, however, demand reflexivity; its terminology can be difficult to understand, and in some versions it remains uninterested in how different viewers interpret images differently. It also has difficulty addressing the affective.

Further Reading

On semiology in general, David Chandler's *Semiotics: The Basics* (2007) does what it says on the tin (to quote an old advertising slogan); it is a good introduction to mainstream semiology. As a classic text on semiology, Roland Barthes's *Mythologies* (1973) is still worth looking at; it consists mostly of short essays, each concerned with elements of post-war French culture, but the last section on 'Myth Today' is a more analytical account of Barthes's approach. The emergence of social semiotics in recent years has been signalled by three very helpful volumes: Gunther Kress's *Multimodality* (2010) is especially useful, with clearly explained analyses and lots of examples, but Theo van Leeuwen's *Introducing Social Semiotics* (2005) and *The Routledge Handbook of Multimodal Analysis* (Jewitt, 2014b) are also valuable resources.

 COMPANION WEBSITE

Visit **https://study.sagepub.com/rose4e** for:

- **Links to a range of online videos** that discuss the theory of semiotics in more detail.
- **Further resources on advertising**, from the history of advertising to the **Landscapes of Capital website**, put together by Robert Goldman and Steven Papson, which hosts all of the TV advertisements that they analysed for their book of the same name.
- **An exercise** on semiological analysis and how the signs of an image link to wider cultural discourses.

7

PSYCHOANALYSIS

VISUAL CULTURE, VISUAL PLEASURE, VISUAL DISRUPTION

key examples: feminist psychoanalytic criticism of three films directed by Alfred Hitchcock: *Rebecca* (released in 1940), *Rear Window* (1954) and *Vertigo* (1958).

The chapter also looks at how psychoanalysis has been used by some scholars to understand recent news coverage of violent conflict in the mass media.

7.1 Psychoanalysis and Visuality: An Introduction

Psychoanalysis consists of a range of theories that deal most centrally with human subjectivity, sexuality and the unconscious. Many of its key concepts were developed, and often then revised, by Sigmund Freud (1856–1939). Later writers have then taken his ideas and reworked them again, so psychoanalysis is now a very large and diverse body of work. This chapter cannot hope to cover all aspects of psychoanalysis; even more than other chapters in this book, this will be a very selective account. One element of its selectivity is that it will focus on those parts of psychoanalysis that address the visual. However, the visual is actually very important to psychoanalysis. Freud suggested that **scopophilia** – pleasure in looking – was one of the basic drives with which all (sighted) children are born, and the visual is especially important in the work of the psychoanalyst Jacques Lacan (1901–1981). Lacan, building on various claims of Freud, argues that certain moments of seeing, and particular visualities, are central to how subjectivities and sexualities are formed. For this reason, his work has become quite prominent in some approaches to visual culture.

    Another aspect of this chapter's selective approach to psychoanalysis is the key example it uses to explore how psychoanalysis can be used to

scopophilia

interpret visual materials. The chapter focuses on a number of feminist authors who are using psychoanalysis, often in its Lacanian guise, to understand how the visual is imbricated in the production of sexual difference in Hollywood films. They pay close attention to these visual images, and they are centrally concerned with their social effects: the ways they produce particular spectating positions that are differentially sexualised and empowered. In this way their use of psychoanalysis conforms to the first two criteria for a critical visual methodology that the first chapter of this book outlined. As for the third criterion – reflexivity – the assumptions made by psycho-analysis about subjectivity raise some interesting questions in relation to reflexivity, and this chapter will explore these in Section 7.8.

Psychoanalysis often takes the form of a therapeutic practice, with an individual talking to their analyst over a long period of time, hoping to find rest from some sort of psychic pain or blockage. However, the psychoanalytic skills brought to bear on the analysis of an individual are not those used in relation to visual culture. Psychoanalysis is not used to analyse the personality of the person producing a particular image, although this can be done; Freud himself wrote an essay on Leonardo da Vinci, for example. Those writers using psychoanalysis, like so many others currently addressing issues of visual culture, are not interested in the producer of images as an individual. Instead, psychoanalytic concepts are used to interpret aspects of visual images and, in particular, their effects on spectators. Psychoanalysis does not have a strict code of methodological conduct like content analysis, nor does it operate on the 'tool-box' model as the previous chapter suggested semiology does. Rather, many psychoanalytic critics often work with just one or two psychoanalytic concepts, exploring their articulation – or rearticulation – through a particular image.

This close theoretical and empirical focus has consequences in relation to an important point raised in the introductory comments to this book, and rather underplayed by the methods discussed in previous chapters: that there is no absolute right or wrong way to interpret a visual image. Different psychoanalytic concepts brought to bear on the same image can produce very different interpretations of that image. The case study discussed by this chapter makes the possibility of different interpretations of the same image clear: it is an examination of diverse feminist viewings of some of the films of Alfred Hitchcock. After beginning his filmmaking in Britain, Hitchcock moved to Hollywood in the late 1930s and then directed many films which, as Tania Modleski (1988) observes, continue to fascinate their audiences – audiences that include feminist critics, some of whom have claimed the films for feminism while others have rejected them as irredeemably misogynist. Three films in particular have been the focus of feminist debate – *Rebecca* (1940), *Rear Window* (1954) and *Vertigo* (1958) – and this chapter will focus on them too.

Film has proved particularly amenable to psychoanalytic interpretation. From the mid-1970s and throughout the 1980s, the journal *Screen* carried many essays exploring particular films in relation to psychoanalytic ideas. Cinema is an especially powerful visual medium because a film can create a total world for its audience. Films manipulate the visual, the spatial and the temporal and, as Laura Mulvey (1989: 25) says, by 'playing on the tension between film as controlling the dimension of time (editing, narrative) and film as controlling the dimension of space (changes in distance, editing), cinematic codes create a gaze, a world and an object'. In particular, film is a powerful means of structuring looking, both the looks between the film's protagonists but also the looks between its protagonists and its spectators. Since psychoanalysis in its Freudian and Lacanian forms argues that visuality is central to subjectivity, it follows that film can address our sense of self very powerfully – and that psychoanalysis can offer some powerful readings of films.

However, it is also the case that films can be interpreted using many other visual methodologies. James Monaco (2009: 178) for example argues that semiology is the best method for interpreting films because, he says, films communicate meaning and semiology has the best tools for analysing visual meaning-making. It is also the case that psychoanalysis can be applied to media other than film. To demonstrate this, this chapter will also look briefly at a body of work that puts psychoanalytic concepts to work in relation to the mass media, and in particular to how the mass media reports conflict in the news, especially war and terrorist attacks. These writers find psychoanalytic terms useful partly because, as Andrew Hill (2009) and Jennifer Good (2015) argue, events like 9/11 and the subsequent so-called 'War on Terror' are intensely visual, screened as they constantly are on computers and television sets and mobile devices (see Figure 7.1). These media critics also argue that, in order to understand the power of these images, a theory is needed which can show that audiences are drawn into particular relationships with the news images they are seeing, thus creating certain kinds of subjectivities for those audiences. Feminist psychoanalytic film critics have of course also been particularly concerned with the same problematic: they want to understand how, by visualising masculinity and femininity in ways that disempower women, films position their audiences in specific, gendered terms. Psychoanalysis directly addresses the co-constitution of images and subjectivities.

You might hear about it again and again on the T.V. or radio or read about it in the newspaper.

FIGURE 7.1 Page from a colouring book for young children, prepared by the US Federal Emergency Management Agency to help young children prepare and cope with disasters

Source: The Crisis Response Team of Freeborn County

discussion

The popularity of psychoanalysis among film scholars has declined in recent years, and at the same time many critics have been finding the work of the French philosopher Gilles Deleuze particularly helpful for approaching film. As Chapter 1 suggested, Deleuze is a major theorist of the affective, and has also written about cinema (Deleuze, 2005). There are already several excellent introductions to Deleuzian film analysis, and this book will not repeat them (see for example Bogue, 2003; Buchanan and MacCormack, 2008; Colman, 2011; Coleman and Ringrose, 2013; Marrati, 2008; Pisters, 2003; Rizzo, 2012; Rodowick, 1997, 2010; Rushton, 2009).

Yet psychoanalysis is, as I have already noted, a very diverse field. There are differences between Freud and Lacan; and, for example, between Lacan and one exponent of his ideas in relation to film that this chapter does not discuss, Slavoj Žižek (see for example Žižek, 2010). Moreover, the relationship between feminism and psychoanalysis has always been an uneasy one, for reasons the next section will explain, and this has meant that psychoanalytic terms have not always been used by feminist film critics in strict accordance with their definitions by Freud or Lacan either. And of course, like any theory, psychoanalysis is more effective at addressing some aspects of the visual than others. There are issues that psychoanalysis is not concerned to address but that certain images may insist upon, and this chapter will conclude by exploring these absences in psychoanalytic theory.

To expand on these comments, this chapter has nine sections:

1. The first is this introduction.
2. The second examines some of the founding assumptions of psychoanalysis's understanding of subjectivity, sexuality and the unconscious.
3. The third explores psychoanalytic arguments about how sexual difference is articulated visually, particularly in terms of the castration complex and the mirror stage.
4. The fourth also explores psychoanalytic arguments about how sexual difference is articulated visually, this time using the concepts of the fetish and masquerade.
5. The fifth examines other, more fallible ways of seeing, by exploring the Lacanian Gaze.
6. The sixth looks at ideas about fantasy.
7. The seventh examines 'queer looking'.
8. The eighth discusses how psychoanalytic approaches deal with reflexivity.
9. And the final section assesses psychoanalytic approaches as candidates for a critical visual methodology.

7.2 A Longer Introduction to Psychoanalysis and Visuality: Subjectivity, Sexuality and the Unconscious

To say that psychoanalysis deals with subjectivity, sexuality and the unconscious provides a starting point for introducing the ways that psychoanalysis contributes to discussions about the visual. These three terms have implications for how psychoanalysis conceptualises both the viewer of an image and the image itself, and these two sites – that of the *image itself* and its *audiencing* – are the two sites of meaning production that psychoanalysis examines. Discussion here will begin with their implications for understanding the audience of an image.

To begin with, the use of the term **subjectivity** to refer to a viewer's characteristics – rather than, say, identity – has a number of consequences for psychoanalytic approaches. First, 'subjectivity' entails the acknowledgement that individuals are indeed *subjective*: that we make sense of ourselves and our worlds through a whole range of complex and often non-rational ways of understanding. We feel, we dream, we fantasise, we take pleasure and are repulsed, we can be ambivalent and contradictory, panic-stricken and in love; and we can react to things in ways that feel beyond words. Psychoanalysis addresses these sorts of emotional states (and indeed would argue that rationality too is often secretly dependent on these other non-rational states of mind). In relation to the visual, this means psychoanalysis often focuses on the emotional effects of visual images, on the way that the impact of an image may be 'immediate and powerful even when its precise meaning remains, as it were, vague, suspended – numinous' (Hall, 1999: 311).

But the notion of subjectivity in this context has further implications. In particular – and this is what distinguishes psychoanalytic approaches from others that engage with the emotional – psychoanalysis argues that understanding emotional reactions to, let's say, visual images requires the recognition that not all of those reactions are working at a wholly conscious level. Some reactions may be coming from the **unconscious**. Freud's elaboration of the unconscious is sometimes seen as the founding moment of psychoanalysis. Put simply, the unconscious is created when a very young child's drives and instincts start to be disciplined by cultural rules and values. The child is forced to repress the culturally forbidden aspects of those drives and instincts, and their repression produces the unconscious. The unconscious is thus a forbidden zone in two senses: it is forbidden because the conscious mind cannot access it; and it is forbidden because it is full of outlawed drives and energies and

subjectivity

unconscious

logics. But Freud insisted that it nevertheless has its effects on our conscious selves. Sometimes the boundary between the conscious and the unconscious leaks, and the unconscious finds indirect expression in things like gestures, slips of the tongue (which the speaker does not notice), dreams and so on. Thus because of the unconscious, subjectivity, in psychoanalytic terms, is never fully conscious, coherent or complete. We can never fully know ourselves, according to psychoanalysis, because the unconscious remains beyond self-consciousness; and our conscious selves are always likely to be infiltrated by excursions from the unconscious. As Jacqueline Rose (1986: 3) says, 'The unconscious is the only defence against a language frozen into pure, fixed or institutionalised meaning, and ... in its capacity to unsettle the subject, is a break against the intolerable limits of common sense.' Psychoanalysis does not therefore concur with the modernist notion that to see is to know; indeed, Lacan (1977: 93) has commented that 'in this matter of the visible, everything is a trap'. Instead, the notion of the unconscious focuses attention on the uncertainties of subjectivity and on the uncertainties of seeing; psychoanalysis is especially interested in visual confusions, blindspots and mistakes.

There are two more implications of this particular understanding of subjectivity that need to be addressed before this chapter explores some of the more detailed methodological implications of psychoanalysis. As well as focusing on the subjective and the unconscious, psychoanalysis emphasises that subjectivity is also always *subject to* certain disciplines. This should be clear from the previous discussion of the unconscious: the unconscious is formed by the disciplines of a culture, by its particular pattern of interdicts and permissions. Subjectivity is thus culturally as well as psychically constructed, and this process of subjection continues throughout our lives. We are made as subjects through disciplines, taboos and prohibitions. And in the sorts of psychoanalysis influenced by Lacan, visuality is one of those disciplines. We learn to see in particular ways, and this is a process that is reiterated every time we look. Thus visualities and visual images are given a kind of agency by psychoanalysis, because our immersion in a certain kind of visuality and our encounters with certain kinds of visual images tutor us into particular kinds of subjectivity. Thus psychoanalytic approaches, while centrally concerned with the psychic processes of subjectivity and visuality, also address the *social modality* of these processes by considering their cultural constitution. (However, as Section 7.8 will explore, not all critics are happy with the way in which psychoanalysis deals with cultural processes.)

Psychoanalysis, then, has a dual emphasis: on the one hand, it examines the constant disciplining of subjectivity; on the other hand, it stresses the instabilities of the unconscious which always threaten those disciplines with disruption. Finally and concomitant with this, psychoanalytic approaches also emphasise that subjectivity is always *in process*. Never fully achieved, subjectivity must constantly be reiterated through its engagements with various structures of meaning, including visual images. As Griselda Pollock (1992: 10) says, 'Visual representation is analysed ... in terms of its continuing necessity as a site for the perpetual cultural process of shaping and working the subject, conceptualized as precarious and unfixed.'

As a consequence of this particular theorisation of subjectivity, psychoanalysis under-stands the process of audiencing in a specific way. The viewer of an image is understood as bringing a certain subjectivity to bear on an image. But, as the previous two para-graphs have also been suggesting, that subjectivity is imbricated in the images it sees. It is formed through specific visualities, and these visualities are constructed through repeated encounters with images that invite specific ways of seeing. Psychoanalysis is therefore also concerned with the effects of visual images on spectators and pays careful attention to images themselves, especially their *compositional modality*. Stuart Hall summarises this understanding of the relation between image and audience thus:

> The articulation between viewer and viewed is ... conceptualized in this body of work ... as an internal relation. Indeed, the two points in the circuit of articula-tion privileged here – the viewer and viewed – are seen as mutually constitutive. The subject is, in part, formed subjectively through what and how it 'sees', how its 'field of vision' is constructed. In the same way, what is seen – the image and its meaning – is understood not as eternally fixed, but relative to and implicated in the positions and schemas of interpretation which are brought to bear upon it. Visual discourses already have possible positions of interpretation (from which they 'make sense') embedded in them, and the subjects bring their own subjective desires and capacities to the 'text' which enable them to take up positions of iden-tification in relation to its meaning. (1999: 310)

This understanding of the mutual constitution of visual images and spectators often encourages psychoanalytic accounts to take the form of case studies of particular visual images and the precise ways in which they subject the spectator. Even longer studies of a particular genre of film, for example, tend to depend on careful viewings of indi-vidual movies in order to develop an argument in relation to the genre as a whole.

In their emphasis on the image itself in its compositional modality as a site of mean-ing production, psychoanalytic approaches are similar to the previous three methods already discussed in this book. The differences between psychoanalysis, compositional interpretation and content analysis, however, should already be clear. Unlike com-positional interpretation, psychoanalysis has an explicit interpretative framework. Content analysis, meanwhile, assumes the rational, scientific researcher who can be fully explicit about their methods; Lutz and Collins (1993: 89) in their study of *National Geographic* magazine, remember, advocated content analysis precisely as a means of 'protection against an unconscious search through the magazine for only those which confirm one's initial sense of what the photos say or do'. Psychoanalysis suggests that such a fully rational procedure (and researcher) is an impossible fantasy. Semiology, on the other hand, does have some connection to psychoanalysis. Indeed, Bal and Bryson (1991), in their discussion of semiology, suggest that psychoanalysis is simply a particular type of semiology; they suggest that it offers a way of interpret-ing the signs of an image not in relation to particular referent systems, dominant codes or mythologies, but rather in relation to the unconscious and its dynamics.

One area where psychoanalysis and semiology do differ, though, is the specific things that a psychoanalytic approach picks out.

According to Bal and Bryson (1991: 197), psychoanalysis is 'a search-light theory, allowing specific features [of an image] to be illuminated, sometimes explained but primarily read, by means of psychoanalytic concepts'. Again, the key concepts in psychoanalytic accounts of the compositional modality of an image are concepts that offer particular understandings of subjectivity, sexuality and the unconscious. Images are interpreted in terms of their subjective effects; and one of the subjections that psychoanalysis has most to say about is that of **sexuality**. Psychoanalysis is centrally concerned with the process through which sexual difference is established and (often precariously) maintained. Freud elaborated what he termed the **castration complex** to explain the differentiation of babies into boys and girls. Freud assumes that all humans begin life in an undifferentiated relationship with their mother. He locates the break from the mother and the beginning of subjectivity with the intervention of the father. (Heterosexual) masculinity is constituted by the boy-child feeling threatened by the father with castration if he does not give up his closeness to the mother (a threat made effective by the sight of the mother's genitalia as apparently lacking); (heterosexual) femininity, in ways less convincingly theorised by Freud, is produced by girl-children seeing themselves as lacking – as already castrated – and transferring their attachment from the mother to the father. (More will be said about the castration complex in Section 7.3.1.) It is this disciplining process, resolved by the Oedipus complex, that represses the child's profound drives and desires and thus produces the unconscious.

The psychoanalytic discussion of sexuality is extremely complicated and often hotly debated. Many feminists reject psychoanalysis outright because they see Freud's account as naturalising the inferiority of girls or women by affirming them as lacking on biological grounds. Many queer theorists reject psychoanalysis on the grounds that it assumes that heterosexuality established through the castration complex is the norm and that homosexuality is a deviation from it. And many black feminists reject psychoanalysis as a colonising theory that simply erases race as an analytical and political category (see for example Iginla, 1992). However, many feminists and theorists of sexual orientations and race continue to struggle with psychoanalysis, for all its difficulties, because they see it as the only productive theory of sexuality that can speak of its complexity, its disciplines and its disruptions. In one of the first sustained explorations of the usefulness of Freudian psychoanalysis for feminism, Juliet Mitchell (1974: xv), for example, insisted that 'psychoanalysis is not a recommendation *for* a patriarchal society, but an analysis *of* one'. And that is the spirit in which the authors featured

(margin notes)
sexuality

castration
complex

in this chapter will approach psychoanalysis too: as offering some helpful tools for analysing aspects of the intersection of subjectivity and visuality.

The potential relevance of psychoanalysis to critical studies of visual culture is also demonstrated by a number of scholars who have deployed a broadly psycho-analytic approach to the mass media's coverage of violent events like the attacks on the World Trade Center in New York in September 2001, and the wars in Iraq and Afghanistan. Writers like Jennifer Good (2015), Andrew Hill (2009), Nicholas Mirzoeff (2005), Thomas Stubblefield (2015) and Slavoj Žižek (2002) have all writ-ten books that draw in more or less detail on psychoanalytic ideas to understand how the media's audiences – and especially the viewers of its images – are positioned in specific ways by the media's coverage of such events. None of the writers just mentioned pays much attention to the sexual politics of the media's coverage, but many feminists have written at length on the way in which sexualised positions were indeed invoked in the media's visual, spoken and written coverage of 9/11 and its aftermaths (see for example Dowler, 2002; Hyndman, 2003; Rose, 2009; *Signs,* 2002; Tickner, 2002; Young, 2003). None of these feminist accounts uses psycho-analytic concepts explicitly, but all are concerned to trace the masculinisation of the US and its allies as powerful and omnipotent, and the feminisation of what were positioned as its enemies as weak and lacking. Iris Marion Young (2003), moreover, in her reflection on what she calls the US 'security state', argues that the Bush administration, in its representation by a compliant mass media, spoke and pictured itself as a strongly masculine state that was defending and protecting a weak, vul-nerable and passive citizenry, which was thus placed in a feminised position. For Young (2003: 2), this organisation of the visual field into a masculine state and feminine citizens created a 'logic of gendered meanings and images [which] helps organize the way people interpret events and circumstances, along with the posi-tions and possibilities for action within them' (Young, 2003: 2; see also Rose, 2009). Like psychoanalytic critics, then, Young is also interested in how the media's repre-sentations positioned its audiences in particular ways. The following sections elaborate both psychoanalytic feminist approaches to film and, in less detail, some aspects of psychoanalytic accounts of the mass media.

7.3 How is Sexual Difference Visual 1: Watching Movies with Laura Mulvey

One of the first – and still one of the most important – essays of psychoanalytic feminist film criticism is called 'Visual Pleasure and Narrative Cinema'; it was published by Laura Mulvey in *Screen* in 1975 (Mulvey, 1989: 14–26). By 'narrative cinema', Mulvey means mainstream Hollywood cinema. She cites a number of examples and pays some attention to two films directed by Alfred Hitchcock, *Vertigo* (1958) and *Rear Window* (1954).

visual pleasure   The use of the term 'visual pleasure' in Mulvey's title immediately suggests that she is concerned with the subjective effect of narrative cinema. This is a subjectivity culturally constructed, though: 'This paper intends to use psychoanalysis to discover where and how the fascination of film is reinforced by pre-existing patterns of fascination already at work within the individual subject and the social formations that have moulded him' (Mulvey, 1989: 14). Thus Mulvey is exploring the mutual constitution of the psychic and the social. As a feminist, though, Mulvey assumes that the most important of the social formations shaping the subject is patriarchy. She is thus concerned with the disciplining of subjectivity into a particular form of sexual difference. Mulvey is also exploring the mutual constitution of the movie and spectator. She does that by examining the visual, spatial and temporal construction of narrative cinema, and seeing how this affects both the representation of men and women in the movies and the gendering of the spectator. Thus Mulvey's essay addresses many of the key themes of feminist psychoanalytic film criticism. It does so by drawing on two psychoanalytic concepts – the castration complex and the mirror stage – in order to understand the visual articulation of subjectivity, sexual difference and the unconscious in particular ways.

7.3.1 The castration complex and visual pleasure

Mulvey's account depends on the notion of the castration complex, so, although Section 7.2 briefly outlined Freud's discussion, it is pertinent to say a little more about that complex now. The previous section noted that Freud's account of the castration complex makes the assumption that all humans begin life in an undifferentiated relationship with their mother. However, this is only the first, and least problematic, of a number of assumptions in Freud's argument. Another, and much more problematic assumption, is that all babies feel that to have a penis is normal. Thus when the father intervenes to break up the closeness of that primary relationship, the threat of castration feels real; the baby is threatened with the loss of something important. This notion that the penis is not simply a piece of anatomy but also something meaningful is

phallus   emphasised by the concept of the **phallus**. Reference to the phallus rather than the penis is meant to indicate 'not that anatomical difference *is* sexual difference … but that anatomical difference comes to *figure* sexual difference, that is, it becomes the sole representative of what that difference is allowed to be' (J. Rose, 1986: 66). In the castration complex, the father asserts that the mother is 'his', and the threat that forces the boy to give up his closeness to his mother (in exchange for himself becoming a man and having 'his own' other woman in the future) is that he sees his mother as not having a penis. And here a third assumption in Freud's account comes into play: that when the boy sees his mother's genitalia, he sees them not simply as different from his, but as lacking. This assumption only works, however, if what Freud is talking about here is not simply vision, but visuality. The boy-child must already be seeing through a visuality that asserts that the masculine position is to look and the feminine is to be looked at, and that the feminine is to be seen as lacking.

Mulvey argues precisely that visuality is structured in this gendered way. She claims that 'in a world ordered by sexual imbalance, pleasure in looking has been split between active/male and passive/female. The determining male gaze projects its fantasy onto the female figure, which is styled accordingly' (Mulvey, 1989: 19). Thus sexual difference is understood relationally – visions of femininity depend on the vision of masculinity, and vice versa. As well as this active/male and passive/female distinction, Mulvey argues that the castration complex has impli-cations for images of women in this patriarchal visuality. She says that 'the representation of the female form ... in the last resort ... speaks castration and nothing else' (Mulvey, 1989: 14). Thus Mulvey suggests that women cannot be represented in the movies on their own terms, but only in patriarchal terms, as castrated not-men. The analytical importance given to the (missing) phallus in this sort of account often leads to the use of the term **phallocentrism** rather than patriarchy to describe the way cultural meaning is structured around masculine terms. Thus Mulvey's use of Freud's formulation of the castration complex mobilises a set of ideas about sexual difference not only in relation to subjectivity, but also in relation to visuality.

phallocentrism

Now, it would seem that the sight of women as castrated not-men in the movies would not be very appealing to the movie-goer, and Mulvey has already asserted the pleasurability of the cinema. She resolves this paradox by arguing that cinematic visual pleasure stems precisely from its assuaging of the fear of castration – for men (the role of the female spectator is somewhat problematic in her account, a point to which I will return): 'In the highly developed Hollywood cinema ... the alienated subject, torn in his imaginary memory by a sense of loss, by the terror of potential lack in fantasy, came near to finding a glimpse of satisfaction: through its formal beauty and its play on his own formative obsessions' (Mulvey, 1989: 16). She argues that this is achieved in narrative cinema in two ways (Mulvey, 1989: 21–2). Both these ways involve structuring how the spectator sees images of women in narrative cinema.

discussion

The art historian Linda Nochlin (1989: 138, 142) offers an example of this gendered visuality, reproduced here as Figure 7.2.

On the left is a late nineteenth century soft porn postcard showing a woman offering some fruit to the spectator; she is clearly offering herself for 'picking' too. On the right, Nochlin has constructed an apparently equivalent image with a man offering fruit/himself. Nochlin's point, though, is that of course these are not equivalent images because the visuality that constructs women as objects to be seen does not allow the spectator to make sense of a man being shown in the same terms; the photo of the man is therefore a joke, laughable. Hence we can see that the dominant form of visuality tutors us into finding only women suitable objects for sexual display.

FIGURE 7.2A   A nineteenth century soft porn postcard (Nochlin 1989: 138)

FIGURE 7.2B   An image constructed by feminist critic Linda Nochlin (1989: 142)

voyeurism   The first way she describes as **voyeurism**. Voyeurism is a way of seeing that is active; it distances and objectifies what is looked at. It is controlling and even sadistic, says Mulvey. It is a look that is only given to men by films (whether as characters in the film or as the film's audience).

It deals with castration anxiety by investigating the woman and then punishing or saving her. Mulvey notes how this is typical of how the women in the film noir genre are represented: as threatening but ultimately guilty and weak. The particular ways in which voyeurism is produced by the spatial and visual organisation of a film are various, and some of the tools of compositional interpretation are useful here to describe them (see Chapter 4). What Mulvey looks for is how that relationality between masculinity and femininity is constructed. Particular filmic techniques can include:

- *putting distance between the male and female protagonists of a movie.* In Hitchcock's film *Vertigo*, for example, the retired policeman, Scottie, becomes obsessed with the beautiful woman he has been asked to follow, and the first part of the film shows him trailing her, always keeping his distance to remain hidden from her. In *Rear Window*, photo-journalist Jefferies is immobilised with a broken leg and becomes fascinated with what he sees going on in the apartment opposite his; Mulvey says that his erotic interest in his girlfriend is rekindled only when she enters that other apartment and Jeffries sees her over there, away from him (Figure 7.3).
- *putting distance between the female protagonist of a movie and the movie audience.* In both *Vertigo* and *Rear Window*, the camera often occupies the position of the hero. Thus the audience sees what he sees, and the women in the film (Madeleine/Judy in *Vertigo* and Lisa in *Rear Window*) are distanced from the audience just as they are distanced from him.

The second way that the image of the castrated woman is disavowed by narrative cinema, according to Mulvey, is **fetishistic scopophilia**. This is when the female figure is represented simply as a beautiful object of display (her objectification shows how voyeurism and this kind of fetishism can overlap). Again, this is a mode of representation directed both at the hero of the film and at the male spectator: she is on display for both of them. Her beauty is so overwhelming, often pictured in huge close-ups, so perfect, that the threat of castration is assuaged as she is turned into a reassuring object in an intimate relation to the spectator. Drawing on Mulvey's work, Mary Ann Doane (1982: 76) says that 'the woman's beauty, her very desirability, becomes a function of certain practices of imaging – framing, lighting, camera movement, angle. She is thus … more closely associated with the surface of the image than its illusory depths.' Again, the particular ways in which fetishism is produced by the spatial and visual organisation of a film are various. They can include:

fetishistic scopophilia

- *framing*. The obvious framing device is the use of close-up shots that exclude everything from the viewer's gaze except the body, or parts of the body (often the face) of the female star.
- *lighting*. Doane (1991) describes the way lighting was used in many of Greta Garbo's films to make her face luminous, and so convey a sense of her almost-ethereal, fascinating beauty.
- *camera movement*. Modleski traces the various ways in which the camera shows Madeleine/Judy for the first time in *Rear Window*:

> The camera itself takes over the enunciation ... it first shows Scottie sitting at a bar and then detaches itself from his searching gaze to conduct its own search for the woman through the restaurant. Finally it comes to rest in a long shot of a woman seated ... at a table, with her back to the camera. Romantic music emerges slowly on the soundtrack, and the camera moves slightly forward. It cuts back to Scottie looking and to a point of view shot of Madeleine, who gets up from her chair and walks into a close-up shot of her profile. Only much later will we be able to see her entire face and only at that time will we get to hear her speak. (Modleski, 1988: 91)

This camera movement establishes Madeleine, says Modleski (1988: 92), as the 'mute, only half-seen object of man's romantic quest'.

FIGURE 7.3
Still from Alfred
Hitchcock's film
Rear Window,
1954
Courtesy of
Universal Studios

though, the choice of image is rarely discussed. Feminist critics rarely explain why a specific film has been chosen for analysis, other than because of its inherent usefulness for explicating a relation between the visual and the subjective; and media critics do not explain how they have sampled the very large domain of mass media production.

7.3.3 Mulvey's searchlight

Mulvey focuses on certain aspects of the cinematic image – its spatial organisation, the scale of what it shows, its orchestration of looks both between the actors on the screen and between the audience and the screen, and in particular the gendering of who sees and who is seen in certain ways – in order to characterise a way of cinematic seeing that is both gendered and gendering. The pleasure of these ways of seeing for the audience is then also understood in a particular way, as a denial of the threat of castration.

Mulvey's essay has been enormously influential on feminist film theory and feminist theory more widely. Indeed, notions of a voyeuristic **male gaze** remain extensive in feminist work, and are often used without reference to the specifically psychoanalytic ideas through which Mulvey formulated her arguments. But Mulvey's arguments, though polemical, are nuanced. She suggests that voyeurism and fetishism have quite particular visual, temporal and spatial articulations. These conceptual details are important to remember when utilising psychoanalytic arguments. Psychoanalysis in many ways depends on the details of an image for its interpretative insight; and it is necessary to be similarly attentive to the detail of psychoanalytic concepts.

male gaze

Mulvey's arguments are not without their problems, however. She seems to assume that not only can women only be seen as castrated, women can only see themselves like that too. This is because she assumes that all the members of a cinema audience, whether male or female, are positioned in the same way in relation to the figures on the screen and that all see them in the same way; the implication is that all of a film's spectators are made to be fetishistic and voyeuristic by the visual and spatial structure of the film. In that sense, Mulvey's argument positions all cinema spectators as male. But is she too quick to suggest that women represent castration and nothing else? Or can women be represented differently? Can women also see actively? Moreover, are all men only voyeurs and fetishists when they look at women? Are other ways of seeing possible, less powerful, less pleasurable too perhaps? And what about men who want to look at men, and women who want to look at women, pleasurably? Some of the work on the mass media's coverage of 9/11 and similar events also suggests that the mass media position their readers and viewers as feminine (G. Rose, 2009; Young, 2003). But how might other positions be possible (N. Rose, 2007)?

None of these questions can be addressed in Mulvey's framework. She assumes a powerful, patriarchal and heterosexual narrative cinema, and places her faith for critique and change in avant-garde cinematic practices that refuse the visual and spatial organisation of Hollywood's narrative cinema. However, other feminist critics have been less willing to give up on what are, after all, hugely popular cultural practices like mainstream Hollywood film. They have looked for other psychoanalytic ways of seeing films, and have brought other theoretical terms to bear on them.

7.4 How is Sexual Difference Visual 2: From the Fetish to Masquerade

There are many ways in which psychoanalysis can be used to explore ways of seeing. Many feminists, not surprisingly, have been particularly concerned to see images of femininity that do not 'speak castration and nothing else', for example. Indeed, the notion that femininity can only be represented as lacking – as castrated – has been contested by many feminists, who have turned to other psychoanalytic notions to see femininity in other ways.

One possibility that has been pursued in relation to visual images is to suggest that if women are indeed often represented as smooth surfaces on display for a male gaze, fetishisation might not be the only way to interpret that representation. Perhaps that smooth surface does not hide something horrible, does not conceal a castrated body. Perhaps it hides something else. Or perhaps it is simply that: a surface that hides nothing – **masquerade**   a **masquerade**. This latter possibility was most famously proposed by the psychoanalyst Joan Riviere in an essay first published in 1929 (Riviere, 1986). Riviere's essay took off from her analysis of an academic woman who, after her articulate and professional presentations of her work to her peers, would feel compelled to flirt with the men in her audience. Riviere suggested that this woman saw her success in terms of being successful in a man's world and therefore in a sense, for the duration of her performances, becoming a man. This, though, she knew her mostly male audiences would find very threatening (the only thing more threatening than a castrated woman being a non-castrated one), so after her lectures she would conform to their expectations of female behaviour, and flirt and be charming and non-confrontational. From this Riviere concluded:

> Womanliness could therefore be assumed and worn as a mask, both to hide the possession of masculinity and to avert the reprisals expected if she was found to possess it – much as a thief will turn out his pockets and ask to be searched to prove that he has not stolen the goods. The reader may now ask how I define womanliness or

iridescent, says Lacan. Indeed, given the way it pre-dates and will outlast the subject, in a sense it looks at the subject rather than the subject looking at or through it. 'In the scopic field, the gaze is outside, I am looked at, that is to say, I am a picture … What determines me, at the most profound level, in the visible, is the gaze that is outside' (Lacan, 1977: 106). The consequence of the externality of the Gaze is that when 'I solicit a look, what is profoundly unsatisfying and always missing is that – *You never look at me from the place which I see you*' (Lacan, 1977: 103). Finally, the Gaze fails precisely because it is structured through a screen of signs. Signs, as semiology notes, are substitutes for their referents. As representations, they are different from that to which they refer. For Lacan, the child's entry into culture – into the signs that constitute language, visuality and what he called the Symbolic – is a traumatic separation from intimacy with referents. (Lacan's term for a world of referents before the Symbolic was the **Real**.) Indeed, Lacan **Real** reworked Freud's account of the castration complex to suggest that what that complex deals with is not perceptions of anatomical difference but rather the entry into the Symbolic and the substitution of signs for referents, which all babies – boys and girls – go through. Hence the Gaze, as part of the Symbolic, is also marked by the lack inherent in that substitution.

Lacan uses a painting to emphasise the lack that haunts the Gaze: *The Ambassadors*, painted at the court of Henry VIII in London in 1533 by Hans Holbein (Figure 7.6). The painting shows two men in luxurious dress, surrounded by the instruments of scientific knowledge and artistic expression: they are shown as powerful – socially, artistically and scientifically. But in front of them, at their feet, is a strange oval shape, incomprehensible in terms of the coherent, perspectivally represented space of the rest of the painting. This oval only makes visual sense if the spectator stands to one side of the painting, when it then appears as a skull. It is a reminder of death, a popular device in seventeenth century paintings that otherwise celebrated the richness of life. However, its disruption of the coherent space of the ambassadors and the spectator is a reminder, for Lacan (1977: 88), of 'the subject as annihilated', not only by death, but also by the lack that structures the (visual) Symbolic. Lacanian theory often refers to this lack – 'the void of the Real … a gap in the centre of the symbolic order' (Žižek, 2010: 8) – as the *objet petit a*. **objet petit a**

This definition of the Gaze has some profound implications for Mulvey's argument about sexual difference in the field of vision. As Kaja Silverman (1992: 151) for one notes, 'Since the gaze always emerges for us within the field of vision, and since we ourselves are always being photographed by it even as we look, all binarizations of spectator and spectacle mystify the scopic relations in which we are held.' Hence, since the Gaze looks at everyone, men as well as women are turned into spectacles through it; and since its status as a screen of signs means it is never a complete vision, neither women nor men can attain visual mastery through it.

For feminists like Silverman, this is a much more satisfactory formulation of the dominant scopic regime than Mulvey's analysis of the male gaze. It breaks down the binary distinction between 'woman as image, man as bearer of the look', to suggest that man may be image too and that both men and women may look, but neither and never all-powerfully. For Silverman (1996: 2), this opens the door to what she calls 'an ethics of the field of vision' that might 'make it possible for us to idealize, and, so, to identify with bodies we would otherwise repudiate'. In other words, the Gaze allows a greater range of ways of seeing to become possible, some of which may work against the cultural construction of some visualised identities as inferior.

Some of the methodological implications of working with the Gaze in relation to film are evident in Silverman's (1992) book *Male Subjectivity at the Margins*. Here, she explores what she calls 'deviant masculinities' – those that do not conform to the dominant fiction of phallic masculinity – 'some of which do indeed say "no" to power' (Silverman, 1992: 2). For Silverman, these are masculinities which embrace those qualities that the dominant fiction ascribes to femininity. She thus provides some methodological pointers. She is interested in representations of masculinity that:

- *acknowledge and embrace castration.* Silverman's (1992: 52–121) own example of a film that explores 'the castrations through which the male subject is constituted' (Silverman, 1992: 52) is a 1946 film directed by William Wyler called *The Best Years of Our Lives*. It traces the return home of three soldiers at the end of the Second World War, and according to Silverman (1992: 67), 'Male lack is so fully displayed in that film that even four decades after its original release it remains profoundly disturbing, and at times almost unwatchable.' As just one instance, she notes the way in which the aircraftman who has lost both hands eventually shows his amputated arms to his girlfriend, unable to look at her as he does so. His bodily loss is parallelled by his loss of vision, and it is the female subject who can see this. Modleski (1988) argues strongly that Hitchcock's heroes are also much less secure in their masculinity than Mulvey's argument allows. She points to a number of ways in which the films assert the fragility of masculine subjectivity: in Jeffries' broken leg and his passivity, as opposed to his girlfriend's increasing activity; in Scottie's vertigo, his obsession with Madeleine (which comes close to driving him mad), and his inability to see properly after he thinks he has witnessed her death. (Sarah Hagelin [2008] argues that the Steven Spielberg-directed *Saving Private Ryan* also displays masculine vulnerability in similar ways.)
- *are specular.* Silverman (1992) offers another example from *The Best Years of Our Lives*. Another of the soldiers returning home in uniform and medals is greeted by his wife '*as spectacle* – as a glamorous and heroic image … However, the first time she sees him in civilian clothes she visibly recoils, appalled by his shabby and unfashionable suit' (Silverman, 1992: 77; for more general discussions of spectacularised masculinities in film, see Dyer, 1982; Neale, 1983; Cohan and Hark, 1993).

Mobilising Lacan's notion of the Gaze, then, permits a more complex visuality to be seen than that proposed by Mulvey (1989).

The distinction between the Real and the Symbolic is also central to several psycho-analytic discussions of how the mass media show conflict in their news coverage. Hill (2009: 65) argues that the mutilation and death of the human body in conflict should be understood as Real; yet the Real is also, by definition, something that cannot be part of the cultural signs used by the mass media in its representation of such conflict. This paradox, he argues, produces a number of symptoms in the mass media's images, for example in the photographs of people jumping from the burning World Trade Center. Interpreting both the written texts that accompanied the photographs and the composition of those photographs themselves, Lurie (2006) argues that their viewing is ambivalent. On the one hand, they invite an appalled identification with the falling person that tries to acknowledge the Real of their terrible death. On the other, the photos often integrate the falling body into the architecture of the Twin Towers, thus objectifying the body, aligning it with the Symbolic, and distancing the viewer from it. Although Lurie does not explicitly use the language of the Real and Symbolic in her analysis, she does draw on the related psychoanalytic notions to conclude that in the end these photos 'predicate embodied national strength on difference from rather than vengeful identification with the intolerably vulnerable, trapped, and falling figures' (Lurie, 2006: 50). Another symptom of the Real in the mass media's way of seeing is its haunting by some things that are not quite visible: the mass media's *objet petit a*. Both Hill (2009) and Mirzoeff (2005) have commented on the various almost-but-not-quite things that haunt the newspapers, TV screens and news websites during their coverage of terrorist attacks in particular: terrorist leaders that may or may not be alive; backpackers that in fact were bombers; photographs that were, or perhaps were not, faked; enemies that are both everywhere and impossible to locate; the dead that are never pictured as such (see also Rose, 2010). The Real, then, is a way of thinking about the instabilities of the mass media's way of seeing violent conflict.

7.6 From the Disciplines of Subjection to the Possibilities of Fantasy

Another tactic adopted by some feminist film theorists to explore a wider range of ways of seeing than that allowed by Mulvey's account is to draw on the psychoanalytic understanding of fantasy. In psychoanalytic work, fantasy is not used in the popular sense of something that is quite distinct from 'reality'. Instead, fantasy is seen as something that partly structures a subject's reality.

fantasy   **Fantasy** is located between the conscious and the unconscious; it is where the transactions between these two zones occur (Burgin, 1992). In fantasy – daydreams, for example – the unconscious is given some sort of temporal, spatial and symbolic form by the conscious. Certain lost objects are dreamt about, and they are given a particular spatial arrangement and placed in a particular narrative. Thus fantasy is often described as a kind of staging. This sense of a fantasy being staged is also appropriate because the subject often feels, in part, that they are looking on at the fantasy: they are its audience. A parallel with cinema is immediately obvious, since cinema too stages objects, times and spaces through particular codes of representation for an audience in ways that depend, according to feminist psychoanalytic critics, on fantasies about sexual difference in particular. Elizabeth Cowie (1990: 150) notes, however, that Mulvey for example only allows for one fantasy in cinema: that concerning the masculine fear of castration.

There is another connection too between cinema and fantasy: visual pleasure. Freud suggested that fantasy begins when the infant dreams of lost pleasurable objects – their mother's milk or breast, for example. The pleasure gained from fantasising about lost objects is called **desire**.   **desire**
Cowie (1990: 149) describes fantasy as 'the mise-en-scène of desire, the putting into a scene, a staging, of desire'. These emphases on the spectator's visual pleasure suggest why fantasy has tended to be used to address questions of spectatorship in cinema. Mary Ann Doane's (1987) book about the so-called 'women's films' made by Hollywood in the 1930s and 1940s is called *The Desire to Desire*. Like Mulvey though, Doane does not see narrative cinema allowing women to see films, or be seen in them, in terms other than those set by phallocentric visuality. Thus, in relation to these movies, women can only desire.

Cowie sees Mulvey's and Doane's reliance on the implications of the castration complex as too restrictive in the way it fixes the spectator into a particular, masculinised viewing position. Cowie (1990) instead turns to the notion of fantasy because she thinks it provides a way of loosening that fixity. In that sense, her aims are the same as those feminists who have deployed the masquerade or the Gaze. All want to suggest that even within a phallocentric cultural form like mainstream Hollywood cinema, there are traces of non-dominant ways of seeing, in both the film and in its audience.

Cowie's (1990) key point about fantasy is that the subject need not only be the audience of a fantasy. The subject may also imagine that they participate in the fantasy as well, and in perhaps more than one role. All fantasies, she says, 'present a varying of subject positions so that the subject takes up more than one position and thus is not fixed' (Cowie, 1990: 160). This is because the fantasy consists, not of objects per se, but of their interrelations, their staging. Thus 'the subject is present or presented through the very form of organization, composition, of the scene' (Cowie, 1990: 160); the subject is positioned through the scenic organisation of the fantasy and is therefore part of each object in it. The implications for cinema spectatorship are that audiences may refuse to be positioned in the ways that Mulvey suggested they would be, as men. Instead, men and women in the audience may be positioned while watching a film in ways that correspond to the dynamics of their own fantasies.

Cowie's (1990) essay contains an extended discussion of one of the 'women's films' of the 1940s, *Now, Voyager* (1942), directed by Irving Rapper and starring Bette Davis. She begins by noting what sort of fantasies the film addresses, and she detects these fantasies by looking at three aspects of the film:

- *narrative*. Cowie notes how the story of the film contains a number of wishes for rather conventional kinds of success: erotic success and social success in particular. But the film also presents some more prohibited fantasies. Cowie (1990) argues that fantasies very often do just this, because of their borderline location between the conscious and the repressions of the unconscious. The prohibited desires often centre on the relations between parents and children. Thus in *Now, Voyager*, the Bette Davis character rejects her own domineering mother as head of the household, and mothers in her turn without a male partner.
- *equivalences between characters*. In a discussion of another film, Cowie (1990) suggests another way in which a film may allow multiple entry points for fantasied identifications with several characters. She notes that both narratively (in terms of what they do, especially in relation to other characters) and visually (in terms of how they are seen), a film may suggest that certain characters are equivalent: two characters may be shown as 'fathers' in relation to a family, for example, even though only one 'really' is. Thus spectators may respond to both characters as 'fathers'.
- *visual substitutions*. If fantasies often articulate repressed desires, they must do so seductively in ways that do not invite rejection, says Cowie. And Hollywood movies can achieve this by making visual substitutions: visual moments that repeat themselves but with a difference. Cowie (1990: 178–9) explains this with an example from *Now, Voyager*. Bette Davis's transformation from dowdy daughter to glamorous independent woman (an articulation of both her erotic and social success) is marked by a tilt shot that starts at her legs and ends at her head. The first time, it shows flat shoes, thick stockings, glasses; the second time, beautiful shoes, silk tights, a stunning hat and no glasses. Such visual puns entice the audience into accepting the film's terms, says Cowie.

Cowie's last example is, as she notes, also an example of the masquerade of femininity. But she argues that the subversiveness of the masquerade can only be understood if the fantasies in which it is embedded are also made clear. (Modleski [1986: 129] also notes that the 'elsewhere' central to Irigaray's account of masquerade needs to be specified if its potential for critique is to be fulfilled.) In particular, Cowie (1990: 180) argues that the narrative resolution of *Now, Voyager* – in which Bette Davis agrees to mother the daughter of the married man she spent one night with – is a woman's fantasy of having a child without accepting the (role of the) father. It thus sidesteps the position offered to women in Freud's account of the castration complex.

FIGURE 7.7
Still from Irving
Rapper's film
Now, Voyager,
1942
© Warner Bros

Cowie's discussion of fantasy clearly remains within psychoanalysis. Fantasy, it is argued, still deals with subjectivity, sexuality and the unconscious, with the dynamics of the child's relation to its early carers and of sexual difference. Teresa de Lauretis (1995: 75) insists on this, and warns against 'the optimistically silly notion of an unbounded mobility of identities for the spectator-subject … the film's spectator [cannot] pick and choose any or all of the subject-positions inscribed in the film regardless of gender or sexual difference, to say nothing of other kinds of difference.' However, in its engagement with the repressions of the unconscious, fantasy also allows a greater range of interpretative possibilities in relation to films and their audiences.

focus

Watch *Rebecca* if you can.

What are the fantasies of success (and failure) that structure the film?

How are characters made equivalent? For example, in an early scene the heroine describes to Maxim her close relation to her father, and is shown as childlike as she does so: clumsy, gauche, eating runny eggs. Does Maxim become equated with her father? And if that is the case, is the heroine's struggle to become a 'proper' wife also a struggle to overcome Rebecca as some sort of powerful mother? Modleski (1988) suggests this is the case.

Are there visual substitutions? What are the implications of both Rebecca and the heroine dressing up in the same costume in terms of fantasy, and for whom?

7.7 Queer Looks

Much psychoanalytic feminist film theory (and certainly that of Mulvey) assumes that the structure of gendered differences in visuality and representation is heterosexual: that is, that the important structure is one articulated between masculine and feminine, or male and female. This assumption clearly produces a number of omissions in Mulvey's account, and these have been criticised by gay and lesbian critics. Writers adopting Mulvey's analysis are unlikely to pay much attention to how gay and lesbian characters might be represented in a film, and nor are they likely to consider the possible ways that lesbian and gay movie-goers might see certain scenarios or narratives in particular ways.

Psychoanalysis does have something to say about homosexuality, but this is often to position lesbian and gay sexuality as in some way perverse or deviant. This means that the psychoanalytic concepts that might be useful in focusing on the possibility of gay and lesbian desires in the cinema usually need to be heavily reworked. As Patricia White (1995: 87) says of psychoanalysis, 'lesbianism can not be fully "explained" in its terms'. However, some of that reworking has been done, and one starting point has been the difficult position of little girls in relation to the castration complex.

> Unlike the little boy, who must simply displace his love for the mother to other women and thereby consolidate his identification with the father and all that he represents, the little girl is asked to change her object from mother to father, her disposition from active to passive, and her sexual zone from clitoris to vagina, in order to become woman, post-Oedipal and heterosexual. (White, 1995: 86)

Given the elaborateness of this change, it is not surprising that the little girl might not manage all of it successfully, and might retain her desire for her mother. Freud certainly thought this could and did occur, although he tended to see it as a problem in the path towards 'normal' heterosexual womanhood. Silverman (1988) has picked up on this, however, and, far from seeing it as a 'problem', has suggested that elaborating this desire between mother and daughter could provide a way of inserting desire between women into psychoanalytic accounts of sexuality.

This is a controversial suggestion. Teresa de Lauretis (1994) in particular has criticised it for evoking a general feminine subjectivity and thus erasing the specificity of lesbian desire. For her own part, de Lauretis suggests that what defines lesbian desire is a desire for a lost female body which is actually the subject's own lost body image (de Lauretis, 1994: 231). Sue Thornham (1997: 128) responds in turn that de Lauretis's concern with the particularity of lesbian desire ends up reasserting a fixed boundary between lesbian and heterosexual women, which denies the mobility of desire and fantasy.

These debates are theoretically complex, and this is not the place to attempt their resolution. Their insistence that filmic structures of sexuality, difference and desire are not always heterosexual does, however, offer some further methodological pointers for thinking about visual culture, visual pleasure and visual disruption (and there are parallel debates made by theorists of gay movies and spectators; see, for example, Dyer, 1990). They suggest the need to be alert for narratives, scenes, looks and spaces that do not articulate heterosexual visualities or spatialities.

Modleski (1988) offers an example of this need in her discussion of *Rebecca*. She suggests that there is a strong suggestion in the film that the housekeeper – Mrs Danvers – was sexually attracted to Rebecca. She points to the scene in which Mrs Danvers shows the heroine of *Rebecca* her predecessor's wardrobe and all its beautiful clothes, which Mrs Danvers caresses and strokes. Modleski suggests that this is disruptive of Mulvey's analysis of narrative cinema not only because it is another evocation of the absent Rebecca's powerful and sexual presence, but also because that sexuality is shown to be attractive to women as well as to men.

discussion

Read Modleski's (1988: 43–56) account of *Rebecca*, then Mary Anne Doane's (1987: 123–75), and her later response to Modleski (Doane, 1991: 33–43). Both Doane and Modleski have watched the film carefully and both ground their interpretations in psychoanalytic theory. Modleski argues that Hitchcock's films are ambivalent in their representation of femininity. It is because they show femininity as threatening that they punish their female characters, she says; feminist interpretations, she argues, should therefore focus on that threat. Doane argues that this is an overly optimistic viewing of Hitchcock's oeuvre. She sees the films as fundamentally phallocentric, and insists that, no matter how popular they are, this should not be an excuse for feminists to argue for meanings in them that the films themselves cannot sustain.

Clearly this debate is about more than methodology: it is also about more than abstract theory. It is about the critical effects of different sorts of theory. Modleski demands a kind of viewing of Hitchcock's films that can recover some feminine power for both their characters and their female audiences; Doane argues that these films deny such power and that feminist efforts should be directed at finding new forms of visuality that do give feminine subjectivities power. These are in effect different politics of critique.

7.8 Reflexivity

This chapter has structured its discussion mostly around certain developments in psychoanalytic feminist film criticism since Laura Mulvey's key essay. In many ways, Mulvey's essay has been a point of departure for subsequent critics; they have accepted some of her premises but have sought a less restrictive interpretation of both film and spectatorship. However, there is one thing that later writers share with Mulvey, and that is a certain sort of reflexivity.

In the social sciences, reflexivity is claimed to be unnecessary for work that defines itself as scientific. Thus the practitioners of content analysis and semiology – discussed in Chapters 5 and 6 here – do not engage in reflexivity, since both, for different reasons, claim their work is scientific. However, reflexivity is a crucial aspect of work that participates in the so-called cultural turn. There, reflexivity is an attempt to resist the universalising claims of academic knowledge and to insist that academic knowledge, like all other knowledges, is situated and partial. Reflexivity is thus about the position of the critic, about the effects that this position has on the knowledge that the critic produces, about the relation between the critic and the people or materials they deal with, and about the social effects of the critic's work. Frequently now, it is assumed that before the results of a piece of research can be presented, the author must explain how their social position has affected what they found; a kind of autobiography often precedes the research results.

There are a number of ways in which psychoanalytic approaches are incompatible with this autobiographical reflexivity (for a fuller discussion, see Rose, 1997). To begin with, autobiographical reflexivity implies a full understanding of the researcher's self. It implies that self-knowledge is possible (even if the researcher chooses not to reveal all this knowledge in their reflexive moment). But of course psychoanalysis claims that this is an impossible goal. Full self-knowledge is impossible because a central part of our subjectivity (the unconscious) is not accessible to consciousness. Secondly, psychoanalysis's emphasis of relationality and of subjectivity – the relations between carers and babies, between masculinity and femininity, between movies and their audiences, for example – means that to split an account of 'who I am' from 'what I studied' is also impossible. Who you are depends, in part, on what you study, what you watch, who you talk to. This split is also impossible to sustain because of the psychoanalytic emphasis on the subject in process. Again, who you are also depends on what you relate to. It's a process of mutual constitution, not one of a pre-existing person impacting on other people or images. Moreover, the psychoanalytic account of visual culture also recognises that audiences bring their own ways of knowing to the images they encounter, and the same is true of the audiences for academic work. Thus autobiographical reflexivity may over-emphasise the writer at the expense of the critical agency of their audiences.

So none of the critics whose work I have cited offers any sort of autobiographical account before their interpretation of a movie (although Doane [1991: 1–14] offers an interesting discussion of some of the theoretical and institutional relations within which her work is embedded, and Hill [2009] and Mirzoeff [2005] both briefly locate themselves as viewers of the media that they then analyse). None starts by saying, 'This is who (I think) I am, and this is how that's shaped me as a spectator of this film.' They are, however, theoretically explicit, and, while none of them offers methodological toolkits, it is usually possible to trace quite clearly the methodological implications of their conceptual tools in their work. Their theoretical starting points make clear the particular way of seeing this work invites. The reader can trace the interpretative implications of the theoretical position adopted. This theoretical explicitness has the effect of positioning their work in some way. The frequent use of case studies also often enhances this sense of the particularity of each psychoanalytic study.

However, the positionality of the feminist critics is more strongly marked in another way. Almost all of them say quite clearly that they are writing with political – that is, feminist – aims in mind. Mulvey (1989: 14), for example, begins by saying that in her essay, 'Psychoanalytic theory is ... appropriated here as a political weapon, demonstrating the way in which the unconscious of patriarchal society has structured film form.' Modleski (1988: 121) says her readings are without doubt partial, because she wants to place the evidence in Hitchcock's films of men's guilt in women's hands. And there is Kaja Silverman's (1996) project for an ethics of the field of vision. The reflexivity of this work, then, rests in part on its theoretical explicitness and its reliance on detailed case studies, but mostly on the articulation of its critical aims. It uses its awareness of its status as a particular kind of politics of critique to position itself (as the previous section's discussion of the disagreement between Modleski [1988] and Doane [1987, 1991] implied).

7.9 Psychoanalysis and Visuality: An Assessment

The three criteria for a critical visual methodology outlined in Chapter 1 of this book would seem to be fulfilled by the psychoanalytic work discussed in this chapter. That work pays detailed attention to the images with which it is concerned, whether in the form of case studies of specific images or of a broad domain of imagery. It allows visual images to have their own effects, and these effects are seen as both psychic and social. Discussions of sexual difference, for example, work at both the latter levels: they engage with questions of fantasy but also the cultural coding of masculinity and femininity. The effect of visual images on spectators is a central concern of psychoanalytic approaches too. And there is a certain reflexive effect in their work, even if the explicitly reflexive moments are limited. However, all of these criteria are dealt with by psychoanalytic writers in quite specific ways, which do have some omissions for which psychoanalysis has been criticised. And there are some issues about which psychoanalytic methods have almost nothing to say.

Feminist psychoanalytic approaches to the way visual images produce social difference through their picturing of subjectivity are very much dominated by studies of sexuality. This is hardly surprising, since sexuality was the main concern of both Freud and Lacan. However, sexuality is not the only axis through which social difference and social power relations are articulated: far from it. Psychoanalytic film theory has been criticised for neglecting issues of class and race. As Jane Gaines (1988) points out, at a certain historical period in the United States, men were lynched for looking at women – black men were hanged for looking at white women. Indeed, Gaines (1988) argues that racialised aspects of subjectivity are not just neglected by psychoanalysis, but actively erased from consideration, particularly in generalising accounts of the so-called 'male gaze'. Gaines suggests that the erasure of 'race' from psychoanalytic film theory is produced by the white middle-class norms of family relations that psychoanalysis implicitly assumes; and in her discussion of the film *Mahogany*, starring Diana Ross, she shows that the only men whose gaze at Ross is sanctioned by the film are white. 'Race', she insists, must therefore intersect with sexual difference in accounts of spectatorship, but Gaines (1988) sees psychoanalysis as actively unhelpful in this regard. Lola Young (1996), among others, has nevertheless explored the possibility that psychoanalytic ideas may address issues of racialisation as well as sexuality. She draws on the work of Frantz Fanon (1986) to make this claim. Doane justifies addressing issues of racialisation through psychoanalytic concepts thus:

> For Fanon, a psychoanalytic understanding of racism hinges on a close analysis of the realm of sexuality. This is particularly true of black–white relations since blacks are persistently attributed with a hypersexuality. Why is it sexuality forms a major arena for the articulation of racism? From a psychoanalytic point of view, sexuality is the realm where fear and desire find their most intimate connection, where notions of otherness and the exotic/erotic are often conflated. (Doane, 1991: 217)

Clearly this remains a contested claim, and theorising 'race' through psychoanalytic terms is likely to remain as controversial as theorising gender and sexuality. As for class, there is nothing that I know of in psychoanalytic feminist film criticism that addresses the possible class specificity of certain ways of seeing (but see Pollock

[1994] for a psychoanalytic discussion of this in relation to other visual media). These absences clearly weaken the critical potential of feminist psychoanalytic theory.

The criticism that psychoanalysis pays too little attention to the diversity of ways in which subjectivity is constituted is perhaps less true, though, of those critics of the mass media's news coverage of conflict that this chapter has been discussing. The more explicitly psychoanalytic among them, as has already been implied, have by and large had little to say about the sexual subjectivities evoked by that coverage; however, I think it is fair to say that the many feminist writers who have offered critiques of the gendered subject positions both represented and invited by the mass media have at least been inspired by psychoanalytic ideas, even if they do not wish to use them directly for the reasons just outlined. And all the writers examining how the mass media encourage their audiences to take up specific positions in relation to the 'War on Terror' certainly explore some of the dynamics of race too, as part of their argument that the construction of subjectivity is an important part of the mass media's visualisation of contemporary geopolitics.

Another criticism that applies to all the work discussed in this chapter is that, although psychoanalysis asserts the intersection of the cultural with the psychic, in practice its emphasis is very much on the latter. Evidence of the neglect of the social and cultural in psychoanalytic film and media theory can be found in two places. The first of these is, paradoxically, in its treatment of the audience. While all the writers in this chapter argue that the audience is central to their accounts of the effects of films and mass media images, there has been very little work that tries to explore empirically the workings of specific fantasies, say, for certain spectators constituted by particular mediations of both cultural and psychic dynamics. De Lauretis, for example, is very unusual in her insistence that not all of a fantasy's spectators will get pleasure from it:

> A particular fantasy scenario, regardless of its artistic, formal, or aesthetic, excellence as film representation, is not automatically accessible to every spectator; a film may work as fantasy for some spectators, but not for others … the spectator's own sociopolitical location and psycho-sexual configuration have much to do with whether or not a film can work for her as a scenario of desire, and as what Freud would call a 'visualization' of the subject herself as subject of the fantasy: that is to say, whether the film can engage her spectatorial desire or, literally, whether she can see herself in it. (de Lauretis, 1995: 64)

Because this possibility is rarely acknowledged, let alone investigated, the psychoanalytic claim that the image and its audience are mutually constitutive remains one that is asserted rather than demonstrated. And since it is the image (and its accompanying texts) that are paid most attention in these psychoanalytic accounts, the effect is to suggest that the image positions the audience.

Secondly, the focus in psychoanalytic film theory on the film itself produces a further absence, which is any consideration of the social institutions that produce images and the social contexts in which movies are shown or mass media images viewed, or in which they circulate (Uricchio, 2014), though the work of Guiliana Bruno on cinema (1993, 2002) is an exception here, and Mirzoeff (2005) also touches very lightly on how the media is watched in a specific New York suburb. As the first chapter here suggested, the spaces in which visual images are displayed usually entail quite specific visual practices. How might the social practices of cinema-going intersect with these arguments about cinematic visualities? How might the effects of a news film change between its screening on a home TV screen and its viewing as a YouTube video? I am thinking here not just of things like the size of the screen and so on – which Mulvey for one does mention as part of the visual pleasure of narrative cinema – but of the ways that people watch differently in different places, and how these social practices are disciplined. Psychoanalysis, like the other methods discussed so far in this book, has nothing to say about these questions either, which has motivated Martin Barker (2009: 296) to 'recommend that film theory go to the movies [and] take time to notice that there are other people there, doing all kinds of interesting and unexpected things with what they are watching'. The next two chapters of this book explore an approach which, in contrast, grounds its account of visuality very firmly in social practices and institutions.

Summary: Psychoanalysis and Visuality

- *associated with*:
  Psychoanalysis has most often been used as an approach to interpreting film, but some critics of the mass media have also used some of its concepts.

- *sites and modalities*:
  Psychoanalysis is most concerned with the sites of the image and its audiencing. It is particularly concerned with how aspects of the compositional modality of an image offer particular spectating positions to viewers.

- *key terms*:
  Key terms include subjectivity, sexuality, the unconscious, visual pleasure, fantasy, desire, the Real, the *objet petit a*, and the Symbolic.

- *strengths and weaknesses*:
  Like semiology, psychoanalysis offers a rich and nuanced vocabulary for interpreting the visualisation of sexualised difference, and for speculating about the complicity of audiences with those visualisations. However, kinds of difference other than sexual difference are neglected, and psychoanalysis cannot address the social practices of the display and audiencing of visual images.

Further Reading

An accessible account of the Lacanian Gaze and everyday visuality is a book called *The Power of the Gaze: An Introduction to Visual Literacy* by Janne Seppänen (2006).

COMPANION WEBSITE

Visit **https://study.sagepub.com/rose4e** for:

- **Links to a range of online videos** that discuss the theory of psychoanalysis in more detail, as well as links to clips of the films discussed in the chapter.
- **A link to *A Pervert's Guide to the Cinema***, a film made by the Lacanian cultural critic Slavoj Žižek about Lacanian psychoanalysis and film criticism. This is an interesting opportunity for you to think about what constitutes reflexivity in relation to psychoanalytic approaches to images.

8

DISCOURSE ANALYSIS I
TEXT, INTERTEXTUALITY AND CONTEXT

key example: a wide range of images picturing the East End of London in the 1880s, from maps and fine art paintings to book illustrations and newspaper graphics.

The chapter also discusses using online image banks and archives.

8.1 Discourse and Visual Culture: An Introduction

The previous chapter examined certain psychoanalytic approaches to visual images, and ended with the concerns expressed by some writers that psychoanalysis does not pay enough attention to the social construction of difference. This claim is made on two grounds: first, that psychoanalysis has very little to say about some forms of social difference, such as race and class; and, secondly, that it concentrates on the psychic and visual construction of difference at the expense of considering the social construction and consequences of difference. Very little attention is paid either to the ways of seeing brought to particular images by specific audiences, or to the social institutions and practices through which images are made, circulated and displayed.

One writer whose work is often turned to in order to address some of these absences in psychoanalytic theory is Michel Foucault. For various reasons, Foucault was quite hostile to psychoanalysis, but Foucault's approach does have some compatibilities with that of Freud. Most importantly, perhaps, Foucault's understanding of the subject is in some ways similar to that of psychoanalysis. Like psychoanalytic approaches to the subject, Foucault too considered that human subjects are produced and not simply born. Human subjectivity is constructed through particular processes, he argued, and much of his work consists of detailed historical studies of some of those processes at particular periods in Western history (actually, mostly French history). He wrote books on the emergence of the human sciences in modern Europe, on the development of modern clinical and psychiatric medicine, on the birth of the prison, and on attitudes towards sexuality. In all of these he paid close attention to the ways various practices and institutions defined what it was to be human (and therefore also what it was to be sub-human, abnormal or deviant) in very particular ways. Thus his work has appealed to those writers cited in the previous chapter who are concerned that psychoanalysis, for all its other analytical insights, does not pay enough attention to the social processes through which a range of subjectivities are constituted. Stuart Hall (1996: 7), for example, argues that 'if ideology is effective, it is because it works at *both* "the rudimentary levels of psychic identity and the drives" *and* at the level of the discursive formation and practices which constitute the social field.' Teresa de Lauretis (1994), too, concludes her Freudian account of 'perverse desire' by emphasising the need to connect Foucault and Freud; Freud, she says, provides an account of how the social processes described by Foucault are subjectively articulated. And Kaja Silverman (1992), in the opening pages of her study of *Male Subjectivity at the Margins*, also argues that the work of Foucault and Freud needs to be brought together, although she suggests a rather more complicated relation between the psychic and the social than does de Lauretis.

The notion of **discourse** is central to both Foucault's theoretical arguments and to his methodology. Discourse has a quite specific meaning. It refers to groups of statements that structure the way a thing is thought, and the way we act on the basis of that thinking. In other words, discourse is a particular knowledge about the world which shapes how the world is understood and how things are done in it. Lynda Nead (1988: 4) defines discourse as 'a particular form of language with its own rules and conventions and the institutions within which the discourse is produced and circulated', and she gives medical discourse as an example: 'In this way, it is possible to speak of a medical discourse ... which refers to the special language of medicine, the form of knowledge it produces and the professional institutions and social spaces which it occupies.' Discourse also produces subjects: hence medical discourse produces, among other subject positions, doctors, nurses and patients. Nead suggests that 'art' can also be understood as a discourse, as a specialised form of knowledge. She says that 'the discourse of art in the nineteenth century [consisted of] the concatenation of visual images, the language and structures of criticism, cultural institutions, publics for art and the values and knowledges made possible within and through high culture' (Nead, 1988: 4). (This is very similar to W.J.T. Mitchell's [2005b] definition of a medium, problematised in Section 2.5.) On this understanding, 'art' becomes not certain kinds of visual images but the knowledges, institutions, subjects and practices that work to define certain images as 'art' and others as 'not art'. Discourses are articulated through all sorts of visual and verbal images and texts, specialised or not, and also through the practices that those languages permit. The diversity of forms through which a discourse can be articulated means that **intertextuality** is important to understanding discourse.

discourse

intertextuality

Intertextuality refers to the way that the meanings of any one discursive image or text depend not only on that one text or image, but also on the meanings carried by other images and texts.

It is possible to think of visuality as a sort of discourse too. A specific visuality will make certain things visible in particular ways, and other things unseeable, for example, and subjects will be produced and act within that field of vision. Some of the arguments made by psychoanalytic feminist film critics and discussed in the previous chapter can be recast in these Foucauldian terms. Thus the visuality that, according to Laura Mulvey (1989: 19), makes 'woman as image, man the bearer of the look' could be described as a visual discourse that has effects on the making of masculinity and femininity, men and women. John Berger (1972: 46) points out some of the implications for everyday practice of that discourse: 'A woman must continually watch herself. She is almost continually accompanied by her own image of herself.' This example is also relevant to another Foucauldian term, that of discursive formation.

discursive formation A **discursive formation** is the way meanings are connected together in a particular discourse. Foucault (1972: 37) describes discursive formations as 'systems of dispersion', in that they consist of the relations between parts of a discourse. 'Whenever', he says, 'one can define a regularity (an order, correlations, positions and functionings, transformations), we will say, for the sake of convenience, that we are dealing with a *discursive formation*' (Foucault, 1972: 38). Thus, to continue for a moment to translate psychoanalytic work into Foucauldian terms, Mulvey argues that phallocentric visuality has a structure in which images of women depend on particular forms of masculine seeing. This is a relational argument in that masculinity and femininity depend on each other for their characteristics: woman always signifying castration, and man always enacting voyeuristic and fetishistic ways of seeing. This relation – that correlation and those positions – could be described as a discursive formation.

The Foucauldian understanding of discourse has had a huge impact on studies of visual culture, and both this chapter and the next discuss two somewhat different versions of it, which I call, not very imaginatively, 'discourse analysis I' and 'discourse analysis II'. This chapter's example of 'discourse analysis I' is a body of work that has examined the discursive construction of 'the East End of London' in the 1880s. The focus on the use of discourse analysis I with historical materials is not meant to imply that this method can only be used in historical research, however. Discourse analysis I can be used with many kinds of visual materials, both historical and contemporary. (Indeed, I would argue that a mix of discourse analysis I and semiology, with perhaps a dash of Lacan or Deleuze, seems to constitute the default method of a great deal of cultural and visual studies.) This chapter explores the methodological implications of discourse analysis I in six sections:

1. The first is this introduction.
2. The second is a general introduction to Foucault's work, which makes a distinction between the two kinds of discourse analyses I call 'discourse analysis I' and 'discourse analysis II'.
3. The third discusses finding sources for studies using discourse analysis I.
4. The fourth explores the production and rhetorical organisation of discourse.
5. The fifth discusses discourse analysis I and reflexivity.
6. And the final section assesses discourse analysis I as a critical visual methodology.

8.2 Distinguishing Between Discourse Analysis I and Discourse Analysis II

Foucault was quite clear that discourse was a form of discipline, and this leads us to his concern with power.

8.2.1 Foucault, power and truth

Discourse, Foucault says, is powerful, but it is powerful in a particular way. It is powerful, says Foucault, because it is productive. Discourse disciplines subjects into certain ways of thinking and acting, but this is not simply repressive; it does not impose rules for thought and behaviour on a pre-existing human agent. Instead, human subjects are produced through discourses. Our sense of our self is made through the operation of discourse. So too are objects, relations, places, scenes: discourse produces the world as it understands it.

An important implication of Foucault's account of **power** is that   **power** power is not something imposed from the top of society down onto its oppressed bottom layers. Power is everywhere, since discourse too is everywhere. And there are many discourses, some of which clearly contest the terms of others. Foucault (1979: 95) claimed that 'where there is power, there is resistance ... a multiplicity of points of resistance', and by this he meant that there are many discourses that jostle and compete in their effects. We might define the efforts of feminist film critics like Silverman and de Lauretis, for example, as efforts to develop visual discourses that do not discipline looking in a phallocentric manner, but that produce other (ways of visualising) masculinities and femininities. But certain discourses are nonetheless dominant, and Foucault was particularly concerned in his own work with the emergence of institutions and technologies that were structured through specific, even if complex and contested, discourses. And he suggested that the dominance of certain discourses occurred not only because they were located in socially powerful institutions – those given coercive powers by the state, for example, such as the police, prisons and workhouses – but also because their discourses claimed absolute truth. The construction of claims to **power/knowledge**   truth lies at the heart of the intersection of **power/knowledge**.

> We should admit ... that power produced knowledge (and not simply by encouraging it because it serves power or by applying it because it is useful); that power and knowledge directly imply one another; that there is no power relation without the correlative constitution of a field of knowledge, nor any knowledge that does not presuppose and constitute at the same time power relations. (Foucault, 1977: 27)

Foucault insisted that knowledge and power are imbricated one in the other, not only because all knowledge is discursive and all discourse is saturated with power, but because the most powerful discourses, in terms of the productiveness of their social effects, depend on assumptions and claims that their knowledge is true. The particular grounds on which truth is claimed – and these shift historically – constitute what **regime of truth**   Foucault called a **regime of truth**. Foucault himself, in a series of four essays each on a specific oil painting, was especially interested in the emergence of realistic representation as an aim of Western art, and suggested that painting 'is discursive practice that is embodied in techniques and effects' (Foucault, 1972: 194). Some historians of photography have argued similarly that the 'realism' of the photographic image was produced, not by new photographic technology, but by the use of photographs in a specific regime of truth, so that photographs were seen as evidence of 'what was really there'. This argument will be examined a little more fully in the next chapter.

Foucault's work is radical in many ways. It was adopted with enthusiasm by many working in the social sciences and humanities, but has also been greeted with hostility and even derision by others. His controversial status is in small part explained by his methodological programme (which is perhaps spelled out most clearly in *The Archeology of Knowledge* [1972]; see also Andersen, 2003; Kendall and Wickham, 1999). Foucault refused the premise which forms the basis of all the analytical methods that this book has examined so far.

Content analysis, mainstream semiology and psychoanalysis all assume that analysis needs somehow to delve behind the surface appearance of things in order to discover their real meaning. Content analysis seeks out latent meanings that it claims become evident only from systematic quantitative study; semiology searches for the dominant codes or myths or referent systems that underlie the surface appearance of signs; and psychoanalysis looks for signs of the unconscious as they disrupt the conscious making of meaning. This approach to the interpretation of meaning is widespread in the humanities and social sciences, and subtends many other methods apart from these three. Foucault rejected such 'penetrative' models of interpretation at the level of method, but also at the level of explanation, since he also wanted to avoid explanatory accounts of *why* power works in the way it does. He explicitly rejected the Marxist claim that meaning was determined by the system of production, for example; he was always vague about how discourses connected to other, non-discursive processes such as economic change; and while he acknowledged that power has aims and effects, he never explained these by turning to notions of human or institutional agency. Michele Barrett (1991: 131) says that his notion of causality and dependency is 'polymorphous'. Both methodologically and theoretically, then, Foucault rejected approaches that look behind or underneath things and practices for other processes that would explain them. Instead, as Barrett (1991) makes clear in her account of his work, he focused on the question of *how* power worked. How does it do what it does? How did it do what it did? Certainly his most satisfying works, to me, are his empirical accounts of particular texts and institutions, often focusing on their details, their casual assumptions, their everyday mundane routines, their taken-for-granted architecture, their banalities. It is these detailed descriptions that produce his most startling accounts of how subjects and objects were and are discursively produced.

8.2.2 Developing Foucauldian methods

Elaborating the methods that follow from Foucault's work is not easy, however. As Barrett (1991: 127) notes, his methodological statements are rather vague, and Niels Akerstrom Andersen (2003: 8) comments that he often didn't follow his own prescriptions. More recent discourse analysts can also be rather coy about their methods. Nelson Phillips and Cynthia Hardy (2002: 75) say that methods are 'emergent', for example, while Jonathan Potter (1996: 140) describes discourse analysis as a 'craft skill' and suggests that the only way to learn it is to get on and do it (although in fact these authors do also offer some guidelines; see Phillips and Hardy, 2002: 59–81; Potter and Wetherell, 1987: 158–76). This vagueness, combined with the huge amount of Foucault's work now available – which includes many interviews and pieces of journalism quite apart from his books, lectures and papers – and the fact that, not surprisingly, his ideas changed as his projects shifted, mean that his methodological legacy has been complex and diffuse. (And, to complicate matters further, there is also the 'critical discourse analysis' developed by Fairclough [2010], among others, which owes rather little to Foucault.)

In exploring work that does owe explicit allegiance to Foucauldian arguments, I will use my own terminology. This chapter and the next one will focus on two methodologies which I will call discourse analysis I and discourse analysis II. Both depend on specifically Foucauldian notions of discourse, but each puts Foucault's arguments to work in rather different ways, with rather different effects. I distinguish between them thus:

- *discourse analysis I.* This form of discourse analysis tends to pay rather more attention to the notion of discourse as articulated through various kinds of visual images and verbal texts than it does to the practices entailed by specific discourses. As Rosalind Gill (1996: 141) says, it uses 'discourse' to 'refer to all forms of talk and texts'. It is most concerned with discourse, discursive formations and their productivity.
- *discourse analysis II.* This form of discourse analysis tends to pay more attention to the material practices of institutions than it does to visual images and verbal texts. Its methodology is usually left implicit. It tends to be more explicitly concerned with issues of power, regimes of truth, institutions and technologies.

This distinction is not clear-cut. It is not difficult to find work that examines visual images, verbal texts, institutions and social practices together. However, in terms of current discussions of methodologies in the social sciences, it does seem to me that there is a case to be made for discussing these two methodological emphases separately, since they do produce rather different kinds of research work. Thus this chapter will examine the first type of discourse analysis, and the next chapter will examine the second. For convenience, whenever this chapter mentions discourse analysis, it is referring to what has just been characterised as discourse analysis I, unless the text specifies otherwise.

8.2.3 Discourse analysis I and this chapter's case study

Discourse analysis I is centrally concerned with language. But, as Fran Tonkiss emphasises:

> language is viewed as the topic of research ... Rather than gathering accounts or texts so as to gain access to people's views and attitudes, or to find out what happened at a particular event, the discourse analyst is interested in how people use language to construct their accounts of the social world. (Tonkiss, 1998: 247–8)

Discourse analysis can also be used to explore how images construct specific views of the social world, in which case, to paraphrase Tonkiss, visuality is viewed as the topic of research, and the discourse analyst is interested in how images construct accounts of the social world. This type of discourse analysis therefore pays careful attention to an *image itself* (as well as other sorts of evidence). Since discourses are seen as socially produced rather than created by individuals, this type of discourse analysis is especially concerned with the *social modality* of the image site. In particular, discourse analysis explores how those specific views or accounts are constructed as real or truthful or natural through particular regimes of truth. As Gill (1996: 143) says, 'all discourse is organised to make itself persuasive', and discourse analysis focuses on those strategies of persuasion. It also pays attention to the more socially constituted forms of discursive power, looking at the social construction of difference and authority, for example. Discourse analysis is thus also concerned with the social production and effects of discourses.

This chapter will explore the usefulness of these methodological foci through a case study of the work of several historians who have examined the discursive construction of the East End of London in the 1880s. These historians work with a variety of images and texts in order to examine the way bourgeois commentators produced apparently truthful accounts of this working-class area, and to explore the effects this had on its residents in terms of the various institutional interventions legitimated by that 'truth'. Gareth Stedman Jones (1976: 10–11) points out that in the 1870s and 1880s, most British social thinkers assumed that economic progress would eliminate poverty. The fact that it did not – most blatantly in London's East End, an area with a seasonal and casual labour market and high levels of poverty – was blamed on what were seen as 'the still unregenerate poor: those who had turned their back on progress, or been rejected by it'. Jones continues:

> This group was variously referred to as 'the dangerous class', the casual poor or, most characteristically, 'the residuum' ... In the explanation of the existence of the residuum the subjective psychological defects of individuals bulked even larger than before ... The problem was not structural but moral. The evil to be combated was not poverty but pauperism; pauperism with its attendant vices, drunkenness, improvidence, mendicancy, bad language, filthy habits, gambling, low amusements and ignorance. (1976: 11)

This particular definition of the problem – the truth it assumed – led to specific strategies to combat it: strategies that aimed to alter the morality of the poor rather than their standard of living.

Discourse analysis I thus addresses questions of power/knowledge. Because of this, it fulfils two of the three criteria for a critical visual methodology that were outlined in the first chapter. As a method, discourse analysis pays careful attention to images, and to their social production and effect. Phillips and Hardy (2002) also claim that discourse analytic methods are inherently reflexive. This is a controversial claim, however. Foucault himself, certainly in his early work, was not at all sympathetic to notions of 'reflexivity' as they are currently constituted in the social sciences. He seemed clearly to separate his own practices as an academic from those of the thinkers he was discussing; and, in another parallel with psychoanalytic approaches, in the introduction to *The Archeology of Knowledge* he derided autobiographical efforts at reflexivity: 'Do not ask me who I am and do not ask me to remain the same: leave it to our bureaucrats and our police to see that our papers are in order' (Foucault, 1972: 17). In the section on reflexivity in their book on Foucault, Gavin Kendall and Gary Wickham (1999: 101–9) echo this refusal and say very little about reflexivity as it is currently debated in the social sciences. Phillip and Hardy's assertion that discourse analysis is in fact reflexive depends on their argument that since discourse analysis 'involves a set of assumptions concerning the constructive effects of language' (Phillips and Hardy, 2002: 5), any discourse analysis must implicitly constitute itself as constructed from the effects of language, or risk incoherence. Acknowledging its constructed nature is what constitutes discourse analysis's reflexivity, according to Phillips and Hardy. The final section of this chapter will return to their claim.

8.3 Finding Your Sources for a Discourse Analysis I

Doing a discourse analysis assumes that you are concerned with the discursive production of some kind of authoritative account – and perhaps too about how that account was or is contested – and with the social practices both in which that production is embedded and which it itself produces. Discourses are articulated through a huge range of images, texts and practices, however, and any and all of these are legitimate sources for a discourse analysis. When beginning a piece of discourse analysis, then, it is necessary to think carefully about what sorts of sources you need.

8.3.1 Finding your sources: in general

For most sorts of research questions, some key sources will be immediately obvious, either from your own knowledge or from the work of other researchers. In the work of historians looking at the discursive construction of the East End of London in the 1880s, for example, a number of sources recur (Cowling, 1989; Curtis, 2001; Fishman, 1988; Jones, 1976; Jones, 1989; Keating, 1976; Livesy, 2004; Nead, 1988, 2000; Walkowitz, 1992; Warwick and Willis, 2007). These are: contemporary newspapers, often London ones rather than national ones; contemporary accounts of visits to the East End by journalists, clerics, philanthropists and others, which often take the form of travel diaries and could be published in pamphlet or book form as well as in newspapers; novels and – less often – poems; as well as documents produced by various branches of government such as the Census, reports by local Medical Officers of Health, and other sorts of government reports. Many of these written sources are illustrated with figurative images – often engravings – or with maps or cartoons or other visual images. Almost all of these historians also use photographs of the area, some taken by philanthropic institutions and some by journalists, but the provenance of many of these is now hard to trace. It is important to note the eclecticism of these sources. They are not constrained by notions of genre, for example, or technology.

Even a study concerned to examine just one sort of visual construction relevant to the production of the East End, such as Nead's (1988) study of 'art', uses a wide range of sources, including paintings, engravings and drawings, but also journalism, parliamentary reports and fictional and non-fictional writing.

This eclecticism is demanded by the intertextuality of discourse. As Nicholas Green (1990: 3) says, discourse is 'a coherent pattern of statements across a range of archives and sites'. It suggests that, as well as paying close attention to the site of the image itself, discourse analysis as a method can also track how images, or versions of images – and their truth claims – move among different media and audiences. Discourse analysis can thus also be an effective method for addressing the site of an image's *circulation*.

focus

Suppose you are interested in exploring the ways pregnant women are visualised in contemporary Western culture. What might your initial sources be? Where else might you look for visual images and texts that construct the pregnant female body?

This task raises the question of different, possibly competing discourses that participate in that construction. For example, you may not be familiar with the conventional medical discourse of pregnancy, but this is perhaps the most powerful discourse a pregnant woman encounters as she attends her antenatal appointments. How might you access that particular discourse? And what others might challenge or confirm it? How might you access how some pregnant women construct their sense of bodily self, for example? What about advertising? And are adverts showing pregnant women the only relevant ones? Or is the fact that pregnant women are very rarely visualised in what are called 'women's magazines' also relevant? That is, is the invisibility of pregnant women also an interesting issue to investigate?

In the face of the breadth of source material demanded by discourse analysis I, it is useful to begin by thinking about what sources should be selected as the *starting points* for your own research: the sources that are likely to be particularly productive, or particularly interesting, or 'provide theoretically relevant results' (Phillips and Hardy, 2002: 66). This may mean you draw on sources that others have often used. Or it may mean that you need to locate and access previously unused materials. Or your key sources may already be to hand; perhaps stumbling across them was what started you off on this research in the first place. However, once the more obvious starting points for a discourse analysis have been established, it is important then to *widen* your 'range of archives and sites'. Ways of doing this are diverse. Those initial images and texts may well contain references to other images and texts that you can then track down. Reading what other researchers working on the same or similar topics have said about your area of interest will produce other leads. A discourse analysis may also be able to use verbal material; you may want to conduct interviews yourself, or to record naturally occurring talk (see Potter, 1996; Potter and Wetherell, 1994); and you also need to invest time in the kind of browsing research that leads to serendipitous finds. Some of the most interesting discourse analyses are interesting precisely because they bring together, in convincing ways, material that had previously been seen as quite unrelated.

If this sounds potentially time-consuming – it can be. Indeed, one of the difficulties of the discourse analytic method is knowing where to stop the data collection process. As you begin to find other texts related to the materials you started with, and then more materials related to them in turn, it becomes tricky to know when to stop without making your end points seem arbitrary. Andersen (2003: 13) quotes Foucault's presumably ironic suggestion that 'one ought to read everything, study everything'; but, clearly, reading 'everything' is impossible. What brings the intertextual search to an end, as both Phillips and Hardy (2002: 74) and Tonkiss (1998) note, is the feeling that you have enough material to persuasively explore its intriguing aspects. That is, discourse analysis does not depend on the quantity of material analysed, but its quality. 'What matters', according to Tonkiss (1998: 253), 'is the richness of textual detail, rather than the number of texts analysed'. Thus you may quite legitimately select from all possible sources those that seem particularly interesting to you. As long as you have located some intriguingly complex texts, your discourse analysis can begin.

discussion

Achieving this breadth of source material means spending large amounts of time working your way through lots of different kinds of source material, often in some kind of archive.

Historian Caroline Steedman (2005) describes working in an institutional archive: this might be an impoverished local history museum, or it might be a well-resourced archive like the Harry Ransom Center at the University of Texas, Austin. Her essay includes some valuable practical advice: if you are staying in a hotel to work in an archive, remember to pack something to do in the evenings; take lots of clothes because archives are always cold, to preserve the papers they hold; keep up a rhythm of ordering up materials through the day so you always have something to look at. She also describes some of the feelings that archive work can induce: the physical feel of the materials and dust, the pleasure of discovery, the loneliness, the identifications.

However, in recent years, many archives have begun to put their documents, images and objects into online databases. Harold Short and Marilyn Deegan's (2005) account of working with such digitised archives demonstrates that it is a very different experience from the one described by Steedman. The digital archive is wherever your computer screen is when you go online, which means you can stay at home or in your office, warm and clean, dressed how you want, working when you want.

Some historians have lamented the sort of comfort that online archives afford, suggesting that the true craft of the historian, forged in the archive, is at risk (Hitchcock, 2008). Before dismissing these comments as nothing more than the historian's equivalent of the anthropologist's year of fieldwork – something you have to suffer before you can really claim to be a member of the profession – it is worthwhile pausing and gathering together the scattered comments already made in this book about working with online resources: whether archives or image banks.

Section 3.5 has already pointed out just what rich pickings there are on the Internet for projects interested in visual culture. Online image banks offer historical and contemporary images; they offer images of images in all sorts of media; they offer still and moving images; they offer commercial images, art images and documentary images. As Tim Hitchcock (2008) agrees, in theory such databases make the kind of discourse analysis discussed in this chapter very easy. After all, if you can find some relevant online archives and do a few keyword searches relevant to your topic, bingo! You've got all the source materials you need on your computer screen, apparently. No more dusty archives, no more boring overnight stays in expensive hotels, no more frustrating searches through piles of papers that turn out to be irrelevant to your project.

However, I have already offered a couple of words of caution about this scenario. The first was in section 3.5, which pointed out that online image banks – and online archives more generally – don't give you the same object as the one sitting in the physical archive. They give you digitised versions of those objects. While some aspects of the materiality of images, or documents, is retained when they are digitised, much is also transformed or lost. Size, colour, texture, dust and weight are all shifted or erased when an image is seen on a screen. This loss may or may not matter to your specific project, but you should certainly consider its consequences before relying entirely on digital data.

Secondly, there are issues around how online archives or image banks label and sort their data, so that relying entirely on that apparent time-saver on archive websites – the tempting 'search' box – can create a number of difficulties.

The first is that online archives or image banks' software will search either for the keywords (or 'tags') that have been attached to an image or document by the archivist, or for text within documents. Effective searching thus relies on the database's tags being appropriate for your project, which may or may not be the case. This is particularly the case with images, which are notoriously hard to tag consistently. A second problem is that databases' search engines are driven by software algorithms following rules that are invisible to the user (van Dijck, 2010; Wallace, 2010); if, unbeknownst to you, there is a rule that brings up only the 50 most popular documents or images, you might never see material that could have been crucial to your project. Finally, searching an online archive using key terms means that you need to know what the keywords are that will bring up the documents or images you want. But discourse analysis I assumes that keywords are not what you know before you start, but what you are looking for as you analyse documents. Using keywords to locate materials for a discourse analysis could therefore be putting the cart before the horse. All in all, then, using image bank tags as ready-made codes for interpreting images is not necessarily a good idea.

Finally, a point about the coverage of online image banks and archives: digitising documents is time-consuming and expensive, which means it is only done for specific datasets – those considered particularly important in some way, or those held by organisations who can afford to do it or see a profit in it. You might find that the data you need simply is not available online; or, if it is, it is not affordable. Or you might find it is not in the right format: finding online newspaper archives that show the original page layouts, including images, is not as easy as you might think, for example. Conversely, depending on your topic, you might find yourself overwhelmed with online data.

I am not advocating physical archives over digital ones. Sitting for weeks going through original documents is not without its difficulties either. Physical archives are also sorted and labelled in particular ways, and they too have their gaps; plus you have to get yourself to them, which is not always possible. You should consider the pros and cons of both kinds of archive for your particular research question. What is certainly true is that the questions 'What is it? Who made it? And for what purpose?' are questions to be asked of all archives and image banks, online and not (Steedman, 2005: 23).

8.3.2 Finding your sources: iconography

One method that does offer some clearer guidelines about what sorts of sources are relevant to understanding some kinds of visual image is iconography. Iconography is a method developed by the art historian Erwin Panofsky. Chapter 4 suggested that many art historians rely on having a 'good eye' which focuses almost entirely on how an image looks. Panofsky (1957: 26) distanced himself from this kind of eye by insisting that 'iconography is that branch of the history of art which concerns itself with the subject matter or meaning of works of art, as opposed to their form.' The subject matter or meaning was, for Panofsky, to be established by referring to the understandings of the symbols and signs in a painting that its contemporary audiences would have had. Interpreting those understandings requires a grasp of the historically specific intertextuality on which meaning depends.

Panofsky took care to spell out just how he thought this comparison between different visual images and verbal texts should work. Panofsky (1957) divides visual interpretation into three kinds, to which he gives various names:

1	primary	natural	pre-iconographic
2	secondary	conventional	iconographic
3	intrinsic	symbolic	iconological

The example he uses to explain the differences between these three kinds of images is 'when an acquaintance greets me on the street by lifting his hat' (Panofsky, 1957: 26). He suggests that recognising that he has encountered a 'gentleman' with a 'hat' requires some interpretation, but of an 'elementary and easily understandable' sort (Panofsky, 1957: 26). This is therefore interpretation at the primary or pre-iconographic level. (In methodological terms, this level has some parallels to the close observation demanded by compositional interpretation.) However, 'my realization that the lifting of the hat stands for a greeting belongs in an altogether different realm of interpretation' (Panofsky, 1957: 27). This different realm addresses images that have a specific symbolic resonance; this is the secondary level of interpretation, of a conventional or iconographic image. The third level of interpretation is brought to bear on visual images in order to explore their general cultural significance. Panofsky suggested that, in the case of his acquaintance with the hat, seeing this image in symbolic or iconological terms would mean interpreting the gesture of lifting the hat as a symptom of that man's whole personality and background. The iconological or intrinsic meaning of an image 'is apprehended by ascertaining those underlying principles which reveal the basic attitude of a nation, a period, a class, a religious or philosophical persuasion – qualified by one personality and condensed into one work' (Panofsky, 1957: 30).

As an example of Panofsky's method, we can turn to the portrait painted by Jan van Eyck in 1434 for the marriage of Giovanni Arnolfini, a merchant in Bruges, to Giovanna Cenami, and reproduced in Figure 8.1 (for other accounts of this painting, see Bedaux, 1986; Hall, 1994; Seidel, 1993).

Panofsky (1953: 201–3) offers a detailed iconographic interpretation of this image which depends on his knowledge of the iconography at work in early Netherlandish painting more generally. Thus Panofsky insists that, despite its location in 'a comfortably furnished interior', despite all its signs of worldly wealth (the lamp, mirror, jewellery, clothing), and despite its use of oil paint which, in Berger's (1972) analysis, makes the painting as much of a commodity as the objects it depicts, this is a painting that glorifies the Christian sacrament of marriage. Thus the hand gestures are those of the Catholic marriage ceremony, and the candle, clearly not needed for light since the room is bathed in sunlight from the window, represents the all-seeing Christ. The fruit on the window ledge and chest symbolise the purity of humankind before the Fall. The statue of St Margaret at the top of the tall chairback represents childbirth, and the dog symbolises marital fidelity. Moreover, the colours used by van Eyck also have symbolic meaning. John Gage (1993: 142–3) notes that the colours in the portrait have significance in relation to the ideas of contemporary alchemists about colours and the essential properties of matter. Deep purple and green – the clothes worn by the couple – symbolise fire and water, as does the jewellery hanging next to the mirror in the painting – amber beads and pearls. The painting thus suggest that this is not only a coupling of two people, but a complementary union of two elemental properties which will be harmonious and fertile. Both Panofsky and Gage rely on the notion of intertextuality in order to interpret the meanings this image would have had for its contemporary audiences, although they relate the portrait to different texts: Gage refers to alchemy books while Panofsky compares the portrait to other marriage portraits.

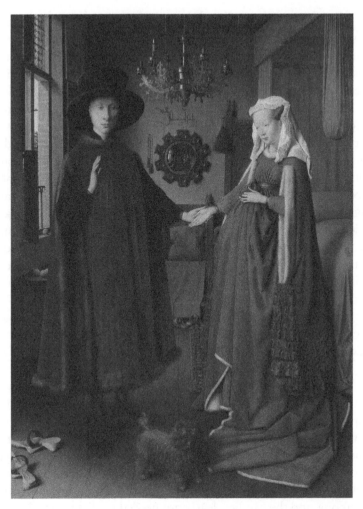

FIGURE 8.1
*The Arnolfini
Portrait*, 1434,
by Jan
van Eyck
© The National
Gallery, London

As an intertextual method, iconography is most often applied to
Western figurative images and to architecture, usually from the sixteenth
to the eighteenth centuries. During that period, compendia of symbols (in
the loose sense of the word) were written for both artists and for
patrons. These explained the meanings of hundreds of visual motifs,
allegories and personifications, and it is these compendia that art historians have consulted to produce iconographic interpretations of specific
images. Iconography needs a thorough grounding in historical context
to be successful, therefore, and Panofsky argued that actually, in order
to understand the possible secondary and intrinsic meanings of an
image, two things were necessary. One was a deep familiarity with the
texts, both visual and written, that the artist producing a particular
piece of work would have been familiar with, and this might need to

extend beyond those published guides to symbolism just mentioned. The second thing was 'synthetic intuition' (Panofsky, 1957: 38), or what other commentators on this method have called common sense. This second quality was important because, while various texts could provide important information and clues about iconographic and iconological meaning, Panofsky (1957) argued that they could never provide full explanations for a particular image, and their relevance thus had to be judged by the critic on the basis of his or her intuition.

There are some aids available for developing this requisite sense of historical context. Roelof van Straten (1994) provides a guide to the compendia of symbols that were used by artists and patrons. Another very helpful publication is the *Encyclopedia of Comparative Iconography* (Roberts, 1998). This two-volume work consists of a number of long, illustrated essays on themes such as Crucifixion, Death, Arms Raised, Money, Whiteness, Pregnancy and Hair/Haircutting (to list some almost at random). Each entry explores the iconography of its theme and lists relevant works of art from various periods. It also suggests other useful reading that can direct you to original sources.

As defined by Panofsky, iconography is not a Foucauldian method. Panofsky (1957: 41) suggested that iconographic analysis could show how the 'essential tendencies of the human mind' were translated into visual themes and concepts, and this reference to the 'essential tendencies of the human mind' is decidedly non-Foucauldian. As we have seen, Foucault insisted that there could be no 'essential tendencies' because human subjectivity is entirely constructed. Iconography has also been seen as close to more structural kinds of semiology, with Panofsky's primary level of interpretation echoed in the notion of denotive signs, and his secondary level in connotive signs (see also van Leeuwen, 2001). However, in their shared concern with intertextuality, there are some parallels between iconography and the sort of discourse analysis under discussion here, and the term 'iconography' is now often used in a loose sense to refer to the kind of approach to images that I am calling discourse analysis I (see, for example, Burke, 2001).

8.3.3 Working with diverse materials: an example

A discourse analytic work that might be described as an 'iconography' in this looser sense is Mary Cowling's (1989) study of 'the representation of type and character in Victorian art'. Cowling's work contributes to an account of the discursive construction of the East End of London in the 1880s too, since she points out that the East Ender was shown by Victorian artists as a particular social type. She argues that Victorian audiences assumed that paintings needed to be read – that their meanings required decoding – and that there were two, related, bodies of knowledge, both understood as scientifically true, that were used especially frequently for decoding images of social difference: physiognomy and phrenology.

> In the Victorian age, physiognomy, or the indication of character through the facial features and forms of the head and body, was all but universally believed in.

The more specific indication of character through the shape of the skull, expounded as a complete system in the form of phrenology, was also widely subscribed to. Whether the human face was looked at with the eyes of the artist, the writer, or even the scientist, belief in physiognomy characterised contemporary attitudes towards it. (Cowling, 1989: 9)

Cowling shows how books like *Physiognomy Made Easy* (c.1880), *Self-Instructor in Phrenology and Physiology* (c. 1886) and *The Study of the Human Face* (1868), among many others, showed faces and heads divided into types that were differentiated in terms of their morality, social position and notions of 'race'. Aspects of heads and faces such as nose profile, forehead slope, chin profile, skull size and lip shape were all presented as clues to the moral standing, social class and 'race' of an individual, and these clues were used too in the work of cartoonists, novelists, scientists and artists. An example of how these shared interpretations of heads and faces were commonplace is given by Cowling (1989: 64–5), and it is also a neat example of her own method (see Figure 8.2). Plate 44 of her book shows a page from the *Self-Instructor in Phrenology and Physiology*. There are two engravings on this page, one of a 'good head' and one of a 'bad head'. Cowling, in her plate 46, compares these to a portrait of J.G. Lockhart, the son-in-law and biographer of Sir Walter Scott, by William Allen in 1876. The 'soaring brow and delicate features' of the latter (Cowling, 1989: 65) are repeated exactly in the *Self-Instructor* as the 'good head', and would have indicated to Victorian audiences that this was a man of high moral probity, high social class, and English origin. Cowling argues that Victorian audiences would have made these same connections and interpretations, as such similar images circulated between different texts. And it is her method to make them too: to trace the relations between different texts in order to identify the meanings their viewers and readers shared.

FIGURE 8.2A 'A good and bad head contrasted', from L.N. Fowler, *Self-Instructor in Phrenology and Physiology*, c.1886 (Cowling, 1989: 64)

FIGURE 8.2B Portrait of J.G. Lockhart by William Allen, engraved by G. Shaw, from J.G. Lockhart, *Life of Sir Walter Scott*, 1871 (Cowling, 1989: 65)

FIGURE 8.3 *The Railway Station*, 1862, by William Powell Frith
Royal Holloway, University of London

Cowling's concern with intertextuality focuses on two particular images, however, one of which is particularly relevant to this discussion, as Cowling (1989: 185–231) argues that it contains several images of East Enders. This is a painting by William Powell Frith, exhibited in 1862 and called *The Railway Station* (Figure 8.3). It is a huge canvas showing the crowd accompanying a train about to leave, and Cowling remarks that it was seen by contemporaries as an image of, and a commentary on, the modern London crowd. That is, its theme was social relations and social difference, and Frith and his audience both used physiognomy and phrenology to make sense of this painting. (It has also been suggested, however, that there is a tension in the painting between such 'types' and the painting's depiction of individuals who would have been recognisable to the contemporary audience; the two men on the right in top hats, for example, were famous detectives [Arscott, 2007].) Having consulted books of physiognomy and phrenology herself, Cowling is able to offer her own key to the painting which notes the kind of social type each figure would have represented to its Victorian audiences (Cowling, 1989: 242–3). Her key includes 'gentleman in reduced circumstances', 'his daughter, off to take up her first position' (as a governess), and 'villainous recruit – vicious type'. Cowling suggests that these latter sorts of images, of the various types from the residuum, would have been seen by contemporary audiences as East Enders. The social differences among Londoners were also understood as geographical differences in this period, and the residuum, certainly by the end of the 1880s, was always located in the East End of the city. Thus images of members of the residuum were also images of East Enders.

Cowling (1989) uses many sorts of texts to make her case for the importance of facial features and head types for understanding Victorian images of social difference, including magazines, anthropology books, novels, paintings and engravings, as well as those books on physiognomy and phrenology. As I have noted, this range of sources is typical of the kind of discourse analysis I am suggesting iconography is related to. Cowling's method is to look for the commonalities, both textual and visual, among these sources, and to establish these by citing the words and images they have in common: thus she quotes extensively from her sources and she also reproduces their images generously (her book has 370 pages of text and 340 plates). This search for recurring themes or visual patterns is also typical of discourse analysis. However, as the rest of this chapter will show, the proponents of discourse analysis also suggest some further methodological tactics for interpreting intertextual meanings.

8.4 Discourse Analysis I: The Production and Rhetorical Organisation of Discourse

Iconography, then, like discourse analysis, depends on intertextuality for its interpretative power. It also depends, though, on what Panofsky called 'common sense', and many discourse analysts also suggest that successful discourse analysis depends less on rigorous procedures and more on other qualities: craft skill, says Potter (1996: 140);

scholarship, according to Gill (1996: 144); 'interpretative sensitivities', in Phillips and Hardy's (2002: 75) words. Nonetheless, there have been some efforts to make the procedures of discourse analysis more explicit, especially in the social sciences. This section explores some of those efforts.

In her discussion of discourse analysis, Tonkiss (1998) suggests that those efforts have been directed in two areas. First, there is the analysis of the structure of the discursive statements. Secondly, there is a concern for the social context of those statements: who is saying them, in what circumstances.

8.4.1 Exploring the rhetorical organisation of discourse

One theme of discourse analysis is the organisation of discourse itself. How, precisely, is a particular discourse structured, and how then does it produce a particular kind of knowledge? In relation to visual images, many studies have been particularly interested in how social difference is constructed, and the previous section briefly discussed one example of this in relation to the East End: Cowling's (1989) study of the intersection between art, physiognomy and phrenology. Another example is Ruth Livesy's (2004) essay on middle-class women who did charity work in London's East End, and how they saw East Enders. Livesy's study is a useful reminder of the complex and often contested nature of discourse, since it begins by remarking that these women disliked physiognomy and phrenology as ways of seeing and understanding people; instead, they drew on a discourse of 'ethical individualism' (Livesy, 2004: 46) which focused on individuals' moral character, and especially their capacity for self-control, thrift, duty and foresight. Hence when they looked at East Enders, they didn't look at the shape of their heads or the character of their faces, but rather looked for signs of cleanliness, sobriety and rectitude in their dress and their houses. Livesy (2004) explores the rhetorical organisation of their discourse to establish this way of seeing; and indeed this kind of discourse analysis is interested in, for example, how a particular discourse describes things (although the power of discourse means that it produces those things it purports to be describing), how it constructs blame and responsibility, how it constructs accountability, and how it categorises and particularises (Potter, 1996).

The first step in this interpretative process is, as Tonkiss (1998) and Gill (1996) both emphasise, to try to forget all preconceptions you might have about the materials you are working with. Although an important part of your preparation for your analysis might have been to study what discourses other scholars have suggested are relevant to your sources (and Sunderland [2004] recommends this), nonetheless, when you approach your materials, try your best to read them and look at them with *fresh* eyes. As Foucault (1972: 25) says, pre-existing categories 'must be held in suspense. They must not be rejected definitively, of course, but the tranquillity with which they are accepted must be disturbed; we must show that they do not come about by themselves, but are always the result of a construction the rules of which must be known and the justifications of which must be scrutinized.' In this way, the material may offer you insights and leads that you would otherwise have missed. For visual images, it may be that the tools of detailed description offered by compositional interpretation have a role to play here, in making you look very carefully at every element of an image, and at their interrelation. Allow this process of reading and looking to take its time. Try to *immerse* yourself in the materials you are dealing with. Read and re-read the texts; look and look again at the images.

Having familiarised yourself with your materials, some slightly more systematic methods might be useful. One is a version of the coding process described in Chapter 5 in connection with content analysis (Phillips and Hardy [2002] recommend a quite rigorous version of this). Familiarity with the sources will allow you to identify *key themes*, which may be keywords, or recurring visual images. (Remember, though, that the most important words and images may not be those that occur most often.) Make a list of these words or images and then go through all your sources, coding the material every time this word or image occurs. Then start to think about connections between and among keywords and key images. According to Foucault, the task is to examine:

> relations between statements (even if the author is unaware of them; even if the statements do not have the same author; even if the authors were unaware of each other's existence); relations between groups of statements thus established (even if these groups do not concern the same, or even adjacent fields; even if they do not possess the same formal level; even if they are not the locus of assignable exchanges); relations between statements and groups of statements and events of a quite different kind (technical, economic, political, social). (Foucault, 1972: 29)

How are particular words or images given specific meanings? Are there meaningful clusters of words and images? What objects do such clusters produce? What associations are established within such clusters? What connections are there between such clusters (Andersen, 2003: 11–12)? Foucault here also suggests the need to consider the broader, non-discursive context of discourse. These sorts of questions address the productivity of discourse in the sense that they focus on its production of meanings and things.

focus

Look at Figures 8.4 to 8.7, all reproduced from Nead's (1988) study.

Consider each one in relation to the key themes identified by Nead: dress, bodily condition, location, looks. In particular, think about how each of those themes can be represented in different ways. Compare this relative flexibility in identifying themes with the coding process demanded by content analysis. Which do you prefer, and why?

Are there other themes that seem to you to be relevant to these images?

FIGURE 8.6
The River, by
Hablot K.
Browne (Phiz);
an illustration
for the novel
*David
Copperfield*
by Charles
Dickens, 1850

FIGURE 8.7
Found Drowned,
1848–50, by
George Frederick
Watts

Nead's (1988) discussion of how 'the prostitute' was discursively constructed through recurring images of bodies and places is exemplary here. Nead accumulates a wide range of visual images of this figure, as well as written accounts, and shows how she was understood by pointing to the limited number of key visual terms used to produce her (see also Gilman, 1990; Walkowitz, 1992). The prostitute worked by exchanging sex for money. She was therefore constructed as a particular sort of moral problem in bourgeois discourses of femininity, and was placed in the residuum. She could be seen as irredeemable or redeemable; prostitutes were portrayed as both evil women and as victims of an evil society. However, as Nead notes, both arguments worked to place her outside 'normal' femininity. This outsider status was signified visually in the way she dressed (provocatively) and the way she looked, especially how she looked boldly at men. Since she was morally deviant, however, she was also pictured as paying the price of her sin. In visual and written narratives of prostitution, she was frequently visualised as losing her looks and her glamorous clothes, and simultaneously moving from the bright lights of the music hall to the dark streets of the East End, and, eventually, down into the dark and murky depths of the River Thames. This last location was often pictured as her final resting place: disease or pregnancy would take their toll, and her inevitable end, according to this discourse, was her suicide by drowning. The final stage of this visual narrative was the verdict passed on her by society. This was usually pictured by representatives of that society looking at the prostitute's dead body. These representatives might be the rivermen who find her, the police-man who inspects the corpse, the passers-by who see it, or the doctor who dissects it; and these are shown either as pitying or condemning. Nead thus identifies sev-eral key visual themes in images of prostitution: dress, bodily condition, location and looks. She shows how these themes could be given different meanings in dif-ferent images or texts – the looks at her dead body could be compassionate or grimly satisfied, for example, depending on whether the prostitute was being con-structed as evil or as a victim – but the basic elements used to represent her were repeated again and again in a wide variety of contexts.

As this coding and interpretation process proceeds, other issues may start to become important to your interpretation – perhaps issues that had not initially occurred to you. Unlike content analysis, this does not mean that you have to halt your analytical process and start again with a revised set of categories. Discourse analysis is much more flexible than that. As new questions occur, prompted by one moment of coding, you can return to your materials with different codes in a second – or third or fourth or twentieth – moment of interpretation. While the Foucauldian framework of discourse analysis is giving you a certain approach to your materials, it is also crucial that you let the details of your materials guide your investigations.

An important part of that framework is how a particular discourse works to per-suade. How does it produce its *effects of truth*? This is another aspect of discourse that your analysis must address. Often this entails focusing on claims to truth, or to scientific certainty, or to the natural way of things. As well as the visual and textual devices used to claim truth, however, it is useful to look for moments at which dis-sent from a discourse is acknowledged (even if implicitly) and dealt with. Search for 'the work that is being done to reconcile conflicting ideas, to cope with contradic-tion or uncertainty, or to counter alternatives' (Tonkiss, 1998: 255), because this work will highlight processes of persuasion that may otherwise be difficult to detect.

An example of an account of the East End of London that claimed to be true because it was scientific was the map of poverty first published by Charles Booth in 1889. Booth used 34 School Board Visitors (the local officials responsible for enfor-cing attendance at school) to survey the income of every household in the East End. He then calculated how many people were living in poverty, and mapped their location

FIGURE 8.8
Detail of
Charles
Booth's
descriptive
map of
London
poverty, from
his *Life and
Labour of the
London Poor*,
1889

(Figure 8.8). The survey was seen as scientific in a number of ways. First, its coverage was more or less complete in terms of the East End's population (456,877 people were included, according to Booth's figures). Secondly, its coverage was seen as complete in terms of its understanding, and here the visual effect of the map was crucial: the map seemed to lay the East End bare to a scientific gaze that penetrated what others described as its darkest recesses. And, thirdly, Booth's survey and the map classified its subjects in ways that were central to contemporary scientific procedures. Booth argued that while over one-third of the residents of the East End were living in poverty, this was mostly due to fecklessness rather than moral depravity; only 2 per cent of the residuum, he argued, fell into that latter category. This sort of moral classification was central to other Victorian sciences, particularly those that constructed racial differences (and it is no coincidence that many journalists compared going into the East End of London with visits to Africa, as did General Booth's *In Darkest England*, published in 1890; see Keating, 1976). Finally, Booth also relied on statistical analyses of his data which gave his arguments scientific authority too; Nead (1988) notes how some arguments about prostitution were legitimated by statistical claims as well. Through these various strategies, then, Booth's map was perceived by (most) contemporaries as scientifically true.

focus

Look at the map in Figure 8.9 and compare it to the extract of Booth's map reproduced in Figure 8.8.

The *Police Illustrated News* was a popular newspaper offering sensational crime stories. Darren Oldridge (2007: 47) discusses the emergence of this sort of newspaper in the late nineteenth century, which 'tried to create interest and sales through focussing on topics such as street crime, prostitution and sexual danger'. Do the maps carry the same claim to truth in both cases? Do they claim different sorts of truth? How?

FIGURE 8.9
Front page of the *Police Illustrated News*, 17 November 1888

Another emphasis in discourse analysis is the *complexity and contradictions* internal to discourses. Discursive formations have structures but that does not necessarily imply that they are logical or coherent. Indeed, part of the power of a specific discursive formation may rest precisely on the multiplicity of different arguments that can be produced in its terms. Potter (1996) uses the term **interpretative repertoire** to address one aspect of this notion of complexity.

interpretative repertoire

> Interpretative repertoires are systematically related sets of terms that are often used with stylistic and grammatical coherence and often organized around one or more central metaphors. They develop historically and make up an important part of the 'common sense' of a culture, although some are specific to institutional domains. (1996: 131)

Potter notes that interpretative repertoires are something like mini-discourses; they tend to be quite specific to particular social situations. The example he cites is a study of how scientists legitimate their own arguments, and the discovery that they use quite different techniques in their published research papers from those used in informal talk. Here, two interpretative repertoires are deployed in different circumstances, but both are part of a complex discourse of scientific truth. An example of a visual interpretative repertoire is offered by Nead (1988: 128–32). She discusses a watercolour by the Pre-Raphaelite painter Dante Gabriel Rosetti. Called *The Gate of Memory* (Figure 8.10), it was painted in 1857 and shows a prostitute standing under an archway staring at a group of children playing. It visualises one of the final verses of a poem by William Bell Scott called 'Maryanne'. But while Scott's poem could describe the degraded body of this woman in some detail, Rosetti's watercolour cannot, says Nead, and this is because 'the prostitute has become the subject of "art" and "art" does not provide space for woman as physically deviant or unpleasurable'

FIGURE 8.10
The Gate of Memory (coloured chalks on paper), 1864, by Dante Charles Gabriel Rossetti (1828–82)
© The Makins Collection/The Bridgeman Art Library

(Nead, 1988: 132). That is, the Victorian discourse of femininity entailed a number of interpretative repertoires, and the repertoire available to artists could only produce certain kinds of images.

An example of the contradictions inherent in discursive formations can be given by placing Jones's (1989) account of the 'cockney' next to other discussions of the construction of East Enders. As we have seen, from the 1880s if not before, the East Ender was constructed as marked, physically and visibly, by moral degeneracy. As Fishman (1988), Jones (1976) and Walkowitz (1992) emphasise, this was a construction that could produce considerable fear among the bourgeois readers of the newspapers, novels, pamphlets and poems through which it was articulated. Walkowitz (1992) and Nead (1988) both emphasise the horror of disease that prostitution might spread, for example (which could involve acknowledging, as it did for campaigners against the Contagious Diseases Act of 1860s, that it was actually men who spread disease, and often bourgeois men visiting working-class prostitutes at that – a good example of the complexity of discourses). Jones (1976) and Fishman (1988) stress the middle-class fear of social unrest that a residuum with no stake in society might create. Hence, through the 1880s and beyond, as a counter to these fears, other images of the East Ender developed. The orderly dock strike of 1889, for example, was seen as evidence that the majority of the poor were decent at heart, and not likely to revolt, and Jones (1989) traces the elaboration of the 'cockney' as the acceptable face of the East End. The cockney was constructed as good-hearted, chirpy, with a resigned sense of humour and a particular style of dress, often a bit flash; they look out for their neighbour and are stoical under conditions of social hardship. Jones argues that the effect of this discourse was to counter imaginatively what was perceived as the threat to society posed by the residuum, by constructing the cockney as different but lovable. Jones (1989) suggests that this vision of the cockney was expressed most unambiguously in music hall songs at the turn of the century, but he also notes that much of the literature at that period 'veered incoherently' between this cockney and the other vision of the residuum East Ender. Thus Jones's work stresses the contradictions within the discursive construction of the East End, through a careful reading of a wide range of materials.

Finally, discourse analysis also involves reading for what is not seen or said. Absences can be as productive as explicit naming; *invisibility* can have just as powerful effects as visibility. Thus Jones (1989) ends his essay on the construction of the 'cockney' by noting that the cockney was always imagined as white, despite the constant presence of large black communities in the East End. The 'cockney' therefore erased racialised difference by making whiteness the taken-for-granted 'race' of the East Ender. As Jones (1989) also notes, however, this erasure did not last beyond the so-called race riots in Notting Hill in the West End of London in 1958. After that, 'race' could not be made invisible so easily, and the cockney fades as a meaningful cultural category.

Discourse analysis thus depends on reading with great care for *detail*. It assumes that the efficacy of discourse often resides in the assumptions it makes about what is true, real or natural, in the contradictions that allow it interpretative flexibility, and in what is not said, and none of these are accessible to superficial reading or viewing. Hence Gill's (1996: 144) emphasis on the scholarship entailed in discourse analysis: 'The analysis of discourse and rhetoric requires the careful reading and interpretation of texts, rigorous scholarship rather than adherence to formal procedures.'

To summarise the strategies for the intepretation of the rhetorical organisation of discourse outlined in this section, then, they include:

- looking at your sources with fresh eyes;
- immersing yourself in your sources;
- identifying key themes in your sources;
- examining their effects of truth;
- paying attention to their complexity and contradictions;
- looking for the invisible as well as the visible;
- paying attention to details.

focus

Consider all the figures reproduced in this chapter. How might you go about finding the social locations of their production and reception? What does 'social location' mean in this sense? Does it mean class, gender, 'race', sexuality and so on? How might an institution be ascribed those characteristics?

8.4.2 Exploring the social production of discourse

As Gill (1996: 142) notes, 'all discourse is occasioned'. All discourse takes place in specific social circumstances, and the authors discussed in this chapter draw two methodological implications for their sort of discourse analysis from this.

The previous section looked at some rhetorical strategies that could visually or verbally assert the truth of a particular discursive claim. However, this is not the only way that certain discourses can become more dominant than others: the *institutional location* of a discourse is also crucial. Foucault, for all his reluctance to ascribe unidirectional causality, insisted on the need to locate the social site from which particular statements are made, and to position the speaker of a statement in terms of their social authority (Foucault, 1972: 50–2). Thus a statement coming from a source endowed with authority (and just how that authority is established may be an important issue to address) is likely to be more productive than one coming from a marginalised social position. The work of the historians examined in this chapter demonstrates this point in a rather paradoxical way. They are forced to rely almost entirely on the images and words of the socially and institutionally powerful in their discussions of the discursive construction of the East End, simply because they are the only visions and words that are now available. The powerful had the resources to make their discourses substantial through books and pictures, and these were the materials then put into libraries and archives. It is therefore extraordinarily difficult now to pick up traces of the discourses about the East End articulated by those who lived there in the 1880s, for example, although Fishman (1988) suggests that some contemporary novelists were the faithful recorders of what they heard there. Thus the social location of a discourse's production is important to consider in relation to its effects.

The second way in which the social context of discourse production matters is in terms of the *audience* assumed by images and texts. The explanation given for the same event may be quite different if the audience for that explanation is different. Or the visual images of the same scene or event may be quite different, in terms of their technology or genre or in other ways, for different audiences. The visual images that surrounded the Jack the Ripper murders in the East End in 1888 are a case in point. Popular newspapers, for example, used sketches and maps to show readers the location of the murders and the victims' faces, as Figure 8.9 demonstrates. This was a kind of realism that might be seen as the visual equivalent of the sensationalistic journalism pioneered in the same decade (Curtis, 2001; Walkowitz, 1992). Other images were used for other audiences, though. Sander Gilman (1990), in his essay on the Ripper murders, notes that police photographs of the victims' mutilated bodies were used by the criminologist Alexandre Lacassagne in his 1889 book on sadism. The apparent veracity of photographs was thought necessary for a scientific text; but only an audience of scientists, too, was considered capable of seeing such images in an objective, scientific way. Notions about audience can thus affect the type of image used.

Thus discourse analysis also entails paying attention to certain aspects of the social context of discourse production. The authors cited in this chapter – Gill, Tonkiss, and Potter and Wetherell – tend to focus on the rhetorical organisation of a discourse's texts and images and on the impact on those texts and images of the social location of their production. This emphasis neglects to explore the social practices and effects of discourse, however, and this indicates the tendency of this sort of discourse analysis to focus more on texts and images than social institutions.

8.5 Discourse Analysis I and Reflexivity

The introduction to this chapter noted that Foucault himself was not sympathetic to certain kinds of reflexivity, particularly those that depended on descriptions of subject positions; for him, such descriptions were the work of the police. However, as Phillips and Hardy (2002) pointed out, from a Foucauldian perspective the social sciences are just as discursive as any other form of knowledge production, and in producing a piece of research you too are participating in their discursive formation. The social sciences are the descendants of those human sciences the truth claims of which Foucault analysed in detail. If you are writing a discourse analysis, then, the

arguments about discourse, power and truth/knowledge must surely be just as pertinent to your work as to the materials you are analysing. Doing a discourse analysis,
then, demands some sort of critical reflection on your own research practice. For, as
Tonkiss (1998: 259) says, 'The discourse analyst seeks to open up statements to challenge, interrogate taken-for-granted meanings, and disturb easy claims to objectivity
in the texts they are reading. It would therefore be inconsistent to contend that the
analyst's own discourse was itself wholly objective, factual or generally true.'
Discourse analysts have a number of ways of addressing this issue.

The first is to think carefully about the rhetorical organisation of a discourse
analysis. How should it be written? Since discourse analyses cannot argue that they
are the only, true analysis of the materials discussed, discourse analysis aims to be
persuasive rather than truthful, and this entails 'a certain modesty in our analytic
claims' (Tonkiss, 1998: 260). According to Phillips and Hardy (2002: 83–5), any discourse analysis should acknowledge that its language is constructing an interpretation
rather than revealing the truth. Different voices, texts and images should pervade the
analysis, they continue (Phillips and Hardy, 2002: 85); you should acknowledge that
you have made choices in what you discuss, emphasising some materials at the
expense of others; and you should open up your own work to other readings and
interpretations, and be aware how your work engages with that of others.

This modesty is what discourse analysis substitutes for more conventional notions
of reflexivity. Clearly, conventional, autobiographical versions of reflexivity are difficult in Foucauldian accounts, for they depend on a notion of human agency that
constructs the author as an autonomous individual who then encounters a part of the
world in their research. Just as this autobiographical form of reflexivity is inconsistent
with psychoanalytic approaches to visual methods, it is equally incompatible with the
Foucauldian notion of a subject constituted through the discourses in which they are
saturated. Another example of a more modest, Foucauldian approach is Kendall and
Wickham's (1999: 101–9) move, in their discussion of reflexivity in relation to
Foucauldian methods, towards discussing whether objects or animals should be given
the same status as knowledge producers as their human researchers. Their answer is
yes. In the visual field, perhaps an equivalent move would be to recognise the power
of visual images that in some way limits that of the researcher. W.J.T. Mitchell (1996)
has addressed this issue in an essay called 'What Do Pictures *Really* Want?' Although
reprimanded by Hal Foster (1996) for a kind of commodity fetishism – and this strategy is also vulnerable to the criticisms of connoisseurship made in Chapter 4 – Mitchell
suggests that the power of images always exceeds our ability to interpret them. He is
perhaps articulating a further form of reflexivity that makes sense for Foucauldian
discourse analyses. There must be others, but all would share that mark of modesty
mentioned by Tonkiss.

However, a complication to this discursive reflexivity arises when the productive
context (rather than the rhetorical organisation) of the analysis is considered. For being
'persuasive' or 'modest' depends on the interpretative context in which the discourse
analysis is produced. And that context is the social sciences. Thus discourse analysis

can end up with a rather conventional list of things to consider when writing up your work. Here are the sorts of things mentioned by Potter (1996: 138–9), Gill (1996: 147) and Tonkiss (1998: 258–60):

- using detailed textual or visual evidence to support your analysis;
- using textual or visual details to support the analysis;
- the coherence the study gives to the discourse examined;
- the coherence of the analysis itself;
- the coherence of the study in relation to previous related research;
- the examination of cases that run counter to the discursive norm established by the analysis, in order to affirm the disruption caused by such deviations.

Clearly, these criteria are unobjectionable in relation to the conventions of the social sciences. However, let us ask Foulcauldian questions of them: What are the effects of these criteria? What do they produce? Well, they aim to produce a certain sort of text: one that locates the plausibility of the discourse analysis in the text alone. The effect of this is to erase (again, we might say) the institutional context in which a discourse analysis is produced. So perhaps another, reflexive strategy to mark the modesty of discourse analysis would be to note explicitly that the institution and its audience are the co-authors of the analysis, and to recognise the claims to interpretative authority that this co-authorship entails.

8.6 Discourse Analysis I: An Assessment

In terms of the critical visual methodology described in Chapter 1, the type of discourse analysis discussed in this chapter has clear strengths. It pays careful attention to images themselves, to the web of intertextuality in which any individual image is embedded, and thus to how images circulate. It is centrally concerned with the production of social difference through visual imagery. It addresses questions of power as they are articulated through visual images themselves. And although reflexivity is a tricky issue for discourse analysis, there are ways in which the authority of the discourse analysis can be both marked (by acknowledging its context of production) and perhaps undermined (by rhetorical strategies of modesty).

There are also some difficulties in the method, however. One of these is knowing where to stop in making intertextual connections, and another related to this is in grounding those connections empirically. Gilman's (1990) essay on Jack the Ripper illustrates the dangers (to me at least) of making so many connections that some start to seem rather tenuous. In order to understand why the murderer was seen by many as Jewish, Gilman cites a huge range of contemporary sources, including: London newspapers; Wedekind's play *Lulu* and Berg's opera of the same name; the psychoanalysts Freud and Fliess; Hogarth the painter; medical texts; Bram Stoker's novel *Dracula*; Hood's poetry, paintings, engravings and posters; the ideas of Hahnemann (the founder of homeopathy); 'Jack's' notes; criminologists Lombroso and Lacassagne; contemporary pornography; contemporary tracts; and novels by Eliot, Proust and Zola. The breadth of scholarship is extraordinary, but I begin to wonder how many of those sources could be said to have produced, even indirectly, the London newspapers' and police's description of the Ripper as Jewish? Some, of course, perhaps many. Maybe all. But Gilman's analysis does not attempt to trace such connections in any grounded way; instead, they are related in his work simply through the category of 'discourse'. In his study, the circulation of images and themes seems to become a free-floating web of meanings unconnected to any social practices. The practical problem posed by this sort of discourse analysis, then – where to stop making intertextual con-nections – can also be an analytical one – how to make the intertextual connections convincingly productive.

Another problem with discourse analysis, for some critics, is its refusal to ascribe causality. As Section 8.1 noted, Foucault's project was in some ways descriptive; he wanted to account for how things happened more than why they happened. This means that discourse analysis too is not always very clear about the relation between discourse and its context. Few guidelines are offered about what that context might be, other than the notions addressed in Section 8.4.2 about the social location of the producers and audiences of specific images or texts. There is also little attempt to outline what the relations between that context and discourse might be, specifically.

Both these problems are connected to the neglected issue in this form of discourse analysis: the social practices of discourse. As this chapter has noted at several points, this kind of discourse analysis is concerned more with images and texts than with the social institutions that produced, archived, displayed or sold them, and the effects of those practices. The next chapter, however, turns to a form of Foucauldian discourse analysis that does address just these issues.

Summary: Discourse Analysis I

- *associated with*:
  The interpretation of wide and eclectic ranges of textual materials, both visual and written.

- *sites and modalities*:
  Discourse analysis is most concerned with the site of the image itself, although reference can be made to the site of production too. It can also address the circulation of images. It is particularly strong at exploring the effects of the compositional and social modalities of images.

- *key terms*:
  Key terms include discourse, discursive formation, power/knowledge and intertextuality.

- *strengths and weaknesses*:
  Discourse analysis I is very effective at looking carefully at images and interpreting their effects, especially in relation to constructions of social difference. It can be less interested in thinking about the practices and institutions through which such constructions are produced, disseminated and lived, however.

Further Reading

Historian Peter Burke (2001) puts a version of iconography to work in his book *Eyewitnesses: The Uses of Images as Historical Evidence*; although he does not refer to Foucault, his exploration of a wide range of images' 'modes of reliability' (Burke 2001: 184), and his insistence that 'we ignore at our peril the variety of images, artists, uses of images and attitudes to images at different periods of history' (and in different places, it should be added) (Burke, 2001: 16), are consonant with discourse analysis I. So too is Ludmilla Jordanova's *The Look of the Past* (2012), which explores a wide range of images and objects and has some very helpful suggestions for further readings on historical contexts. Andersen's (2003) book *Discursive Analytical Strategies* offers a detailed and accessible exegesis of Foucault's own methods, while Phillips and Hardy's (2002) book includes an interesting analysis of a collection of cartoons.

COMPANION WEBSITE

Visit **https://study.sagepub.com/rose4e** for:

- **Links to the best online lectures on Foucault**, which focus on specific aspects of his work. This is useful because he shifted his arguments over the course of his life, some would argue quite radically, in ways this chapter doesn't discuss.
- **Links to a series of podcasts** on the history of museums.
- **An exercise** showing you discourse analysis in action.

9

DISCOURSE ANALYSIS II: INSTITUTIONS AND WAYS OF SEEING

key example: this chapter looks at how museums display images and artefacts, and discusses several studies of the American Museum of Natural History in New York.

It also looks briefly at how some museums and galleries are using social media to picture themselves and their collections.

9.1 Another Introduction to Discourse and Visual Culture

The previous chapter began with a brief introduction to the work of Michel Foucault, and suggested that there are two methodologies that have developed from his work. Although these two are related and overlap – most particularly because both share a concern with power/knowledge as it is articulated through discourse – these two methodologies have tended to produce rather different sorts of research. The first type of discourse analysis, discussed in Chapter 8, works with visual images and written or spoken texts. Although it is certainly concerned with the social positions of difference and authority that are articulated through images and texts as they circulate, it tends to focus on the production and rhetorical organisation of visual and textual materials.

In contrast, the second form of discourse analysis, which this chapter will explore, often works with similar sorts of materials, but is much more concerned with their production by, and their reiteration of, particular institutions and their practices, and their production of particular human subjects.

9.1.1 Discourse analysis II: The institution

The difference between what I am calling 'discourse analysis I' and 'II' can be clarified by looking at how two exponents of these two kinds of discourse analysis use the term 'archive'. In her discussion of the first type of discourse analysis, Tonkiss (1998: 252) describes the material that this sort of analysis works with as an 'archive'.

While Tonkiss herself puts the term in inverted commas, clearly aware that it carries a certain conceptual baggage, she nevertheless uses it to refer to her collection of data, and then moves on to consider what the data shows about certain discursive formations. However, a different kind of discourse analyst, like Alan Sekula (1986, 1989), would spend some time examining the archive itself as an institution, and unpacking the consequences of its particular practices of classification for the meanings of the things placed within it. Referring to archives of photographs in particular, he argues that:

> archives are not neutral; they embody the power inherent in accumulation, collection and hoarding as well as that power inherent in the command of the lexicon and rules of a language ... any photographic archive, no matter how small, appeals indirectly to these institutions for its authority. (1986: 155)

No doubt Tonkiss would agree with this comment. However, Sekula is at pains to explore the effects of 'archivalisation' on texts and images in a way that Tonkiss is not. Sekula and writers like him make that analytical move because they place their understandings of discourses firmly in relation to the account of institutions given by Foucault. Archives are one sort of institution, in the Foucauldian sense, and this second sort of analysis would not treat them as transparent windows onto source materials in the way that Tonkiss seems to. Archives work in quite particular ways that have effects both on what is stored within them, and on those who use them (Frosh, 2003; Rose, 2000; Steedman, 2005), and this is as true of online archives as it is of the sort discussed by Sekula.

As we have seen, several of Foucault's books examine specific institutions and their disciplines: prisons, hospitals, asylums. For writers concerned with visual matters, perhaps the key text is *Discipline and Punish* (Foucault, 1977). Subtitled *The Birth of the Prison*, this is an account of changing penal organisation in post-medieval Europe, in which alterations in the organisation of visuality (and spatiality) are central. The book begins by quoting a contemporary account of a prolonged torture and execution carried out as a public spectacle in 1757. Foucault then quotes from a prison rulebook written 80 years later which is, as he says, a timetable. Foucault's questions are: How (rather than why) did this change in penal style, from spectacular punishment to institutional routine, take place? And with what effects? Through detailed readings of contemporary texts, *Discipline and Punish* traces this shift.

> By the mid-nineteenth century, the punishment–body relation is not the same as it was in the torture during public executions. The body now serves as an instrument or intermediary: if one intervenes upon it to imprison it, or to make it work, it is in order to deprive the individual of a liberty that is regarded both as a right and as a property. The body, according to this penality, is caught up in a system of constraints and privations, obligations and prohibitions. Physical pain, the pain of the body itself, is no longer the constituent element of the penalty. From being

> an art of unbearable sensation punishment has become an econ-
> omy of suspended rights ... As a result of this new restraint, a
> whole army of technicians took over from the executioner, the
> immediate anatomist of pain: warders, doctors, chaplains, psychia-
> trists, psychologists, educationalists ...
>
> (Foucault, 1977: 11)

The prison was born. As well as a new institution and a new understanding of punishment, in *Discipline and Punish* Foucault describes
the emergence of a new set of professions which defined who needed
punishment and who could exercise that punishment, and of a new
subjectivity produced for those so punished – what he called the 'docile
body'. This was the body subjected to these new penal disciplines, the
body that had to conform to its 'constraints and privations, obligations
and prohibitions'.

A key point of Foucault's argument is that in this new regime of
punishment, these docile bodies in a sense disciplined themselves, and
Foucault argues that this was achieved through a certain visuality (for
general discussions of the role of visuality in the work of Foucault, see
Jay [1993] and Rajchman [1988]). Once defined by the new 'expert'
knowledges as in some way deviant, these bodies were placed in an
institution that was 'a machine for altering minds' (Foucault, 1977:
125). Foucault expands this point, and demonstrates the importance of
a visuality to it, by discussing a plan for an institution designed by
Jeremy Bentham in 1791 (1977: 195–228). Bentham called this build-

panopticon ing a **panopticon**, and suggested it could be used as the plan for all sorts
of disciplining institutions – prisons, but also hospitals, workhouses,
schools and madhouses (Figure 9.1). The panopticon was a tall tower,
surrounded by an annular building. The latter consisted of cells, one for
each inmate, with windows so arranged that the occupant was always
visible from the tower. The tower was the location of the supervisor but
because of the arrangement of its windows, blinds, doors and corridors,
the inmates in their cells could never be certain that they were under
observation from the tower at any particular moment. Never certain of
invisibility, each inmate therefore had to behave 'properly' all the time;
thus they disciplined themselves and were produced as docile bodies:
'Hence the major effect of the Panopticon: to induce in the inmate a
state of conscious and permanent visibility that assures the automatic
functioning of power' (Foucault, 1977: 210). This sort of visuality, in
which one subject is seen without ever seeing, and the other sees with-

surveillance out ever being seen, Foucault called **surveillance**, and he argued that,
since it was an efficient means of producing social order, it became

A General Idea of a PENITENTIARY PANOPTICON in an Improved, but as yet (Jan ${23}^d$ 1791), Unfinished State.
See Postscript References to Plan, Elevation, & Section (being Plate referred to as N.° 2).

EXPLANATION.

FIGURE 9.1
Plan for a
panopticon,
first proposed
by Jeremy
Bentham
in 1787
The Bentham
Papers, UCL
Library Services,
Special Collections

a dominant form of visuality throughout modern capitalist societies. Through its operation, says Foucault (1977: 200) (in an echo of Lacan), 'visibility is a trap'.

Foucault suggests that institutions work in two ways: through their apparatus and through their technologies. This is a distinction this chapter will use; however, Foucault was rather inconsistent in his use of these terms, and the distinction made here between them is clearer than that found in his work. An **institutional apparatus** is the forms of power/knowledge that constitute the institutions: for example, architecture, regulations, scientific treatises, philosophical statements, laws, morals and so on, and the discourses articulated through all these (Hall, 1997b: 47). Hence Foucault described Bentham's panopticon as an apparatus: at once an architectural design and a moral and philosophical treatise. The **institutional technologies** (sometimes difficult to differentiate from the apparatus) are the practical techniques used to practise that power/knowledge. Technologies are 'diffuse, rarely formulated in continuous, systematic discourse ... often made up of bits and pieces ... a disparate set of tools and methods' (Foucault, 1977: 26). An example might be the design of the windows and blinds in the panopticon.

institutional apparatus

institutional technologies

9.1.2 The Institution and Photography

It has been argued by some historians of photography that photography must be understood as a technology in this Foucauldian sense. John Tagg, for example, writes:

> Photography as such has no identity. Its status as technology varies with the power relations that invest it. Its nature as a practice depends on the institutions and agents which define it and set it to work ... Its history has no unity. It is a flickering across a field of institutional spaces. It is this field we must study, not photography as such. (1988: 63)

For Tagg, photography is diffuse; it is given coherence only by its use in certain institutional apparatuses. He elaborates this claim by studying photographs as they were used in the nineteenth century by police forces, prisons, orphanages, asylums, local governments' medical officers of health, and newspaper journalists and publicists (Figure 9.2). It is its uses in these institutions that Tagg argues gives photography its status as a unified something rather than a diffuse 'no one thing', and this coherent something is, according to Tagg, the belief that photographs picture the real. (Hence he is very critical of Barthes's (1982) assertion, discussed in Section 6.3.2, that the *punctum* of a photograph is a trace of an uncoded referent.) The apparatus of these various institutions – the police, prisons, orphanages, asylums, local government, the emergent mass media – asserted the truth of their claims to be able to detect, or punish, or cure the criminal, the ill, the orphaned, the mad or the degenerate (in part by relying on the scientific status of the discourses of physiognomy and phrenology, discussed in the previous chapter). Producing a certain regime of truth, these institutions used photography as a crucial technology through which these distinctions were made visible (see also Tagg, 2009).

The related opposite of this, as Sekula (1989) notes, was the detection, celebration and honouring of the moral, the familial and the proper in bourgeois photographic portraiture. Thus the institutional uses of photography make us think photographs are truthful pictures, not photographic techniques themselves. For Tagg, then (and see also Lalvani, 1996; Sekula, 1989), Foucault's emphasis on institutions and power/ knowledge is crucial for understanding the belief that photography pictures the real.

This emphasis on institutional apparatus and technologies gives a different inflection to this second kind of discourse analysis. It shifts attention away from the details of individual images – although both Tagg (1988) and Sekula (1989) describe the general characteristics of particular types of photographs – and towards the processes of their production and use. That is, this type of discourse analysis concentrates most on the sites of *production* and *audiencing*, in their *social modality*. In their discussion of nineteenth century police photography, for example, both Sekula and Tagg pay a good deal of attention to the processes used to classify, file, retrieve and use photographs of those who had been pictured as 'criminal'. They both also argue that photography was only one part of what Sekula (1989: 351) calls 'a bureaucratic-clerical-statistical system of

FIGURE 9.2
'The Bashful
Model':
Photographing
a Prisoner in
Gaol by Sir
Luke Fildes;
published
in The
Graphic in
1873 and
reprinted
in John
Tagg's book
The
Disciplinary
Frame
(2009: xxvii)

"intelligence"', and he suggests that the filing cabinet was actually a more important piece of institutional technology than the camera. They discuss other technologies – such as phrenology and fingerprinting – that were used alongside photography, and they explore other aspects of institutional apparatuses in their studies too. This means that the sources used in their accounts are as eclectic as those of the discourse analysts discussed in Chapter 8. However, certainly in the case of Tagg and Sekula, their work is held together by an insistence on the power relations articulated through these practices and institutions. For both of them, visual images and visualities are articulations of institutional power.

This is one aspect of their work that has been criticised. For although both take care to distinguish their Foucauldian understanding of power from those that see power simply as repressive, nonetheless there is very little sense in either of their work of the possibility of visualities other than those of dominant institutions. Lindsay Smith (1998), for example, takes them to task for not looking at a wide enough range of nineteenth century photographic practices, and in particular for neglecting the kinds of domestic photography practised by a number of women in the mid-nineteenth century (see also Di Bello, 2007). These women photographers can be seen as producing images that do not replicate the surveillant gaze of the police mugshot or the family studio portrait: they thwart that classifying gaze by strategies such as blurred focus, collage and over-exposure. Moreover, like their discourse analyst cousins whose work was discussed in the previous chapter, there is very little reflexivity in this second type of discourse-analytical work. Ironically, considering their critique of truth claims, Tagg and Sekula both make very strong claims themselves about the veracity of their accounts. Tagg (1988: 1–2) in particular is quite scathing about Barthes, implying that Barthes's insistence on the uncoded quality of certain photographs was merely an emotional response to his search for a photograph that would remind him of his mother after she had died. 'I need not point out', says Tagg (1988: 2) 'that the existence of a photograph is no guarantee of a corresponding pre-photographic existent.' Tagg here counterposes the self-evident ('I need not point out …'), which he later expands at great length with the use of much theory, to the emotional need driving Barthes's work. As I read it, Tagg is making an opposition between his masculinised rationality and what he sees as the effeminate emotionality of the grieving Barthes. Hardly a self-reflexive strategy, I think.

9.1.3 Discourse analysis II, the museum and this chapter

As will be clear from discussions in previous chapters, the Foucauldian approach taken towards photographs by Tagg and Sekula is by no means the only way to think about photographs. Chapter 5 described different kinds of content analyses of photographs, and Chapter 6 explored the use of semiology in relation to the photographs found in magazine adverts. So this chapter is not going to look yet again at photos. Instead, it will turn to work that considers two other kinds of institutions that deal with visual objects – the art gallery and the museum – that have also been subject to Foucauldian critique by writers such as Tony Bennett (1995) and Eilean Hooper-Greenhill (1992) (other important discussions include Barker, 1999; Barrett, 2011; Greenberg et al., 1996; Kidd, 2014; Leahy, 2012; Preziosi and Farago, 2004; Sherman and Rogoff, 1994; Starn, 2005; and Vergo, 1989). These accounts explore how visual images and objects are produced in particular ways by institutional apparatuses and technologies (as 'art', for example) and how various embodied subjectivities are also produced, such as the 'curator' and 'the visitor'. Museums and galleries are institutions which, while of course not free from the workings of power, are not as obviously coercive as those examined by Tagg and Sekula. Their disciplines are more subtle, and they thus provide a more fruitful ground for exploring the extent to which this second type of discourse analysis can address questions of conflicting discourses and contested ways of seeing.

The particular case study will be the American Museum of Natural History in New York (hereafter referred to as the AMNH; see Figure 9.3), as seen by Mieke Bal (1996: 13–56), Donna Haraway (1989: 26–58), Timothy Luke (2002), Ann Reynolds (1995), and Michael Rossi (2010). Their accounts will also allow another opportunity to consider the possibility of a reflexive discourse-analytic practice.

Bal's account of the AMNH, however, is not strictly speaking a discourse analysis; she is a semiologist (Chapter 6 discussed some of her work), and she puts semiology to work in the AMNH. This is a useful reminder that there are ways of interpreting museums other than Foucauldian discourse analysis II. Social semiotics has been used to understand museum layout (Stenglin, 2014) and how visitors make sense of museum displays (Heath and von Lehn, 2004), for example; and ethnographic observation and interviews have also been used to interpret visitors' experiences of museums (Handler and Gable, 1997; Macdonald, 2002). In this chapter, though, the status of the art gallery and museum as institution provides a way of examining the methodology of this second kind of discourse analysis. The chapter has six sections:

1. The first is this introduction, which has discussed in more detail what I mean by 'discourse analysis II'.
2. The second discusses what sources are used in 'discourse analysis II'.
3. The third examines the apparatus of the gallery and the museum.
4. The fourth examines the technologies of the gallery and the museum.
5. The fifth explores visitors to galleries and museums.
6. And the final section assesses the strengths and weaknesses of this type of discourse analysis of institutions.

9.2 Finding Your Sources for Discourse Analysis II

The kinds of sources used for this kind of discourse analysis are as diverse as those deployed by the discourse analysis discussed in Chapter 8. A key Foucauldian account of the emergence of the art gallery and the museum as particular kinds of institution is Tony Bennett's *The Birth of the Museum* (1995), and he is typical in his use of a wide range of sources.

He undertakes a careful reading of the many *written texts* that discussed museums and galleries in the second half of the nineteenth century. These were produced by reformers, philanthropists, civil servants and curators who were all arguing, though often in different ways, for the establishment of galleries and museums that were open to the public. Studies of current discussions about museums and their practices could supplement this sort of historical written source with other types of documents available now, such as the annual reports of galleries and museums and their mission statements, as well as their websites, online archives and iPhone apps. *Interviews* with the directors, curators and designers of museums and galleries can also be used in contemporary studies (although Phillips and Hardy [2002: 71] suggest that naturally occurring talk is more valid for discourse analysis than talk produced in the context of a discourse-analytic research project). Both historical and contemporary studies often use photographs or other *visual images* of buildings, rooms and displays too, sometimes simply as illustrations to their written accounts, and both also pay attention to the *architecture* of the institution – its design, decorations, inscriptions, layout and so on. Studies of contemporary museums and galleries also often rely on visits to the institution and *observation* of the way people visit and work in them.

In relation to the studies of the AMNH on which this chapter concentrates, they are all historical accounts of particular halls of that museum, which use written texts such as the autobiographies of curators, the minutes of museum committee meetings, visitor guides, scientific texts and the museum's annual reports; Haraway (1989) supplements this with an account of what the hall she is interested in looks like to the visitor now – or, at least, what it looks like to Haraway now. Several illustrate their arguments using photographs of museum displays and other images. There has been some debate about these sources: Bennett (2004: 114–35) suggests that Haraway should have looked at documents that show the relationship between the AMNH and municipal and state education authorities too, and that this would have made her account of the development of the AMNH more accurate. Bal's (1996) account is a reading of a few halls of the museum based entirely on their layout and the displays on show to the visitor in late 1991. (Her study is also interesting in the way it uses illustrations to make her points, as well as written text.)

focus

Visit a gallery or a museum. Usually when we visit a museum or a gallery, only some of the many objects in the building attract our attention: the paintings, the objects, the items in the shop. This time, spend time looking at other things: the architecture of the building, for example, its floor plan, its warders, the other visitors. Take notes on what you read, see, hear and feel as you walk around, to refer to as you read the rest of this chapter. While many of the accounts of museums discussed here rely on written materials – either archival materials or, for example, museum guides – most also rely on the careful observation of the museum itself.

9.3 The Apparatus of the Gallery and the Museum

As Stephen Bann comments, the history of museums can be interpreted

> *grosso modo* in terms of two conceptually distinct phases. The first, roughly
> speaking up to the end of the eighteenth century, qualifies as a 'prehistory' in the
> sense that the collection and display of objects apears to answer no clear prin-
> ciples of ordering by genre, school, and period. The second, which represents an
> almost irresistible movement towards conformity over the course of the last two
> centuries, is a history in which the museum has developed and perfected its own
> principles of ordering by giving spatial distribution to the concepts of school and
> period, in particular. (Bann, 1998: 231; see also Hooper-Greenhill, 1992)

Bennett's (1995) discussion of museums and galleries focuses on the second of these
phases, and draws much theoretical inspiration from Foucault's *Discipline and
Punish: The Birth of the Prison*. Bennett points out that both prisons and modern
museums were born in broadly the same historical period, and he argues that they
deployed a similar disciplining surveillance. In making this claim, Bennett interprets
his written sources using the kinds of methods discussed in the previous chapter. Thus
he too looks for *key themes*, for *truth claims*, for *complexity* and for *absences* (see
Section 8.4.1). He pays attention to the diversity of ways in which public museums
and galleries were justified by nineteenth century commentators, noting, for example,
that they were defended as an antidote to working-class men's drunkenness, as an
alternative to working-class disaffection and riot, and as a means to civilise manners
and morals. But his overall emphasis is very much on the way this discursive formation produced the museum as a disciplining machine:

> The museum, in providing a new setting for works of culture, also functioned as
> a technological environment which allowed cultural artefacts to be refashioned in
> ways that would facilitate their deployment for new purposes as part of govern-
> mental programmes aimed at reshaping general norms of social behaviour.
> (Bennett, 1995: 6)

His concern, then, is with the power that saturated the museum and gallery, and he
explores that power in terms of those institutions' apparatuses. In particular, he
focuses on particular discourses of culture and science that shaped their design and
practice, and also produced certain subject positions. Hooper-Greenhill (1992: 176),
too, is interested in the way 'new technologies and new subject positions were constituted through the administration of [a museum's] newly acquired material'.

   Bennett argues that there was a specific discourse of 'culture' which saturated the
births of the museum and gallery. Using the sources listed in Section 9.2, he argues
that the power of museums and galleries had the same aim: both use 'culture' as a tool
of social management. He notes that the definition of 'culture' used in the two sorts
of institutions is somewhat different and that it does produce some differences

between them, especially in the sorts of objects they display. In the museum, 'culture' tends to refer to that later nineteenth century understanding of culture as 'a whole way of life', and museums often collect objects that are meant to exemplify the way of life of particular social groups. In the nineteenth century, this often meant that museums collected and displayed the artefacts of colonised peoples, and these peoples were seen as less cultured and more natural than those of the West. (Annie Coombes [1994] discusses nineteenth century displays of African artefacts in European and North American museums in her book *Reinventing Africa*.) Bal's (1996) account of her 1991 visit to the AMNH emphasises its continued articulation of imperialist, white discourse, noting that halls showing the way of life of certain colonised peoples are entered directly after halls displaying stuffed mammals and birds, thus implying that certain groups are closer to nature than others. Galleries, on the other hand, work with an older definition of 'culture' as that which can ennoble the human spirit, and the objects they display are those defined as Art (see Section 9.3.6 for more on this notion of Art). Such objects – usually paintings and sculpture from Western traditions – are then also constituted as 'Art', and as noble and uplifting, by being on display.

Bennett also discusses, more briefly, a specific discourse of science that was part of the museum's apparatus of power. In museums, he notes, objects are always classified according to what are claimed to be 'scientific' or 'objective' principles, whether they be drawn from notions of historical progress, scientific rationality or anthropological analysis. Rossi's (2010) discussion of the creation of a model of a whale by curators at the AMNH in the early twentieth century is relevant here. Rossi (2010) explains how the curators at the AMNH who wanted to build a scientifically accurate model of a sulfur-bottom whale used photographs, notes, measurements and descriptions of an actual dead whale landed in Newfoundland to build their model; when it went on display in 1907, it was hugely impressive in part because these devices were understood to guarantee that the model was a 'true' representation of the real whale (see also Gosden et al., 2007).

Bal (1996) remarks that differentiations made by the complex discourse of culture are expressed in the gallery and museum which flank either side of Central Park in New York. On the one side, the AMNH, on the other, the Metropolitan Museum of Art.

> By this very division of the city map, the universal concept of 'humanity' is filled with specific meaning. The division of 'culture' and 'nature' between the East Side and the West Side of Manhattan relegates the large majority of the world's population to the status of static being, assigning to a small portion only the higher status of art producers in history. Where 'nature', in the [AMNH] dioramas, is a backdrop, transfixed in stasis, 'art', presented in the Met as an ineluctable evolution, is endowed with a story. (Bal, 1996: 15–16)

In his account of the AMNH, Luke (2002) prefers to focus on the parallels between its collecting practices and those of US corporations, suggesting that the museum's 'searches for fossilised bones mimic the quest of large-scale sweeps by American capital through every remote expanse of the world in search of other organic goods from the Paleozoic era, like coal, oil, gas, or pre-Paleozoic inorganic minerals, like gold, silver, copper, bauxite, or iron' (Luke, 2002: 121).

Bennett (1995) is also especially concerned to examine the *social subjectivities* produced through these discursive apparatuses. The strong emphasis he places on how discourse produces social positions, and the consequences for how museums were designed and policed, distinguishes his study from many of those that rely on the type of discourse analysis examined in Chapter 8. He identifies three subject positions produced by the museum and gallery. First, there were the benefactors of these new institutions. Thus he is clear that the emergent 'experts' on museum and gallery policy and patronage were white middle-class men, their social position produced through their claims to 'expertness' as well as through the larger discourses of capitalism, patriarchy and racism. Similarly, Haraway (1989: 54–8), in her discussion of the AMNH as 'institution' in the early twentieth century, carefully explores the intersecting discourses of eugenics, exhibition and conservation that were mobilised to justify the founding of the museum, and also notes that those three discursive themes were all 'prescriptions against decadence, the dread disease of imperialist, capitalist, white culture' (Haraway, 1989: 55). The museum's funders were precisely representatives of 'imperialist, capitalist, white culture', and thus she too is clear on the coincidence between the discourses of the museum and the wider power relations of society. Richard Bolton (1989) offers a more recent example of the effects of exhibition patronage in his discussion of the sponsorship of an exhibition of Richard Avedon photographs at the Institute of Contemporary Art in Boston by a local department store (Figure 9.4).

FIGURE 9.4   A photograph by Roger Farrington from Richard Bolton's essay (1989) on the opening of an exhibition of photographs by Richard Avedon (Bolton, 1989: 275). In using this photo, what might Bolton be suggesting about the relation between the gallery as an institution, the images on display, and the creation of distinct social subjectivities?

Secondly, there were the scientists and curators: the technical experts, if you like, who operationalise those discourses of culture and science in their classifying and displaying practices (Section 9.4.5 will return to these latter practices: Bennett pays them little attention). And thirdly, there are the visitors. The visitor about whom the nineteenth century benefactors of museums and galleries were most concerned was produced as the morally weak, probably drunk, working-class man. The contemplation of art and the appreciation of museums' knowledge was constructed discursively by these patrons as involving particular ways of visiting museums and galleries, and Bennett (1995) argues that these ways involved orderly appreciation rather than unruly entertainment. In ways he less-than-convincingly demonstrates, he argues that both sorts of institution disciplined their visitors into what were seen as civilised ways of behaving. Bennett again pays some attention to the visual and spatial aspects of museums and galleries when making this argument, examining architectural plans and noting the way that surveillance of other visitors was often built into the designs of these institutions; he also reproduces some contemporary photographs of museums and exhibitions taken from positions that he claims again articulate the surveillant quality of these spaces. He thus suggests that museums and galleries worked to regulate social behaviour by producing docile bodies (see also Leahy, 2012). Reynolds (1995) discusses a hall of the AMNH in the 1950s, and notes how it too assumed, addressed and produced a very specific audience, again one in apparent need of education: city dwellers.

Bennett (1995) also makes a distinction between the construction of the gallery visitor and the museum visitor, though. Galleries, he argues, rely on a notion of Art that always remains implicit:

> In art galleries, [Art] theory, understood as a particular set of explanatory and evaluative categories and principles of classification, mediates the relations between the visitor and the art on display in such a way that, for some but not for others, seeing the art exhibited serves as a means of *seeing through* those artefacts to see an invisible order of significance that they have been arranged to represent. (Bennett, 1995: 165)

Following the work of Bourdieu and Darbel (1991), who found that the visitors to art galleries were overwhelmingly bourgeois, he argues that this particular sort of Art theory is understood only by middle-class gallery-goers because only they have been allowed access to the sort of education that considers Art. This is a problematic claim and Bennett himself worries that it is too crude in the class categories it itself uses; nevertheless, Bennett concludes that art galleries remain obscure places to some social groups, and that this is a contradiction at the heart of their institutional apparatus. In contrast, museums often do make their classification systems explicit; Henrietta Lidchi (1997), for example, in her account of an exhibition that opened at the Museum of Mankind in London in 1993, which sought to portray the way of life of the Wahgi people of Papua New Guinea, shows the way the exhibition admitted to its own practices of collection and reconstruction. This admission produced a visitor capable of critique, a possibility Bennett suggests is not available in art galleries. However, the question of how visitors actually do look in museums and galleries is one that neither Reynolds nor Bennett addresses, and this is an absence that occurs in all the studies of the AMNH. Section 9.5 will return to it.

This section's discussion of the discourses that were part of the institutional apparatus of the museum and gallery has been partial. Bennett (1995) ranges more widely in his book; for example, he explores the role of national government in funding public museums and galleries, and notes that this makes the visitors to museums and galleries both citizens instead of, or perhaps as well as, docile bodies, and was therefore a potentially democratising move. Similarly, writers on the AMNH draw on a range of institutions, practices and sites in order to describe the multiplicity of meanings residing in that institution. Haraway (1989), for example, suggests that in order to understand the dioramas in the Akeley African Hall, it is necessary to understand the practices not only of diorama and taxidermy, but also of early twentieth century safaris too, the role played in them by photography, and the wider discourses of nature, culture, patriarchal masculinity, eugenics, conservation and so on that were articulated through them. However, the broad aims of these discussions of the institutional apparatus are, I hope, clear. In their explorations of institutional apparatuses, these discourse analysts of institutional power/knowledge focus both on discourses about museums and galleries but also on how those discourses are materialised. Their concern is always with the intersection of power/knowledge and with the production of differentiated subject positions.

9.4 The Technologies of the Gallery and the Museum

Section 9.1 defined institutional technologies as the practical techniques used to articulate particular forms of power/knowledge: 'the techniques of effecting meanings' (Haraway, 1989: 35). Foucault described them as diffuse and disparate sets of bits and pieces, and this section will enumerate some of these bits and pieces as they work in museums and galleries. The question posed by this second type of discourse analysis is, again, what the effects of certain technologies are in terms of what they produce; and Bann (1998) insists that this question demands carefully detailed and historically sensitive empirical answers. All of the studies of museum and gallery technologies discussed here focus on the public display areas of the institution in question.

9.4.1 Technologies of display

Section 9.3 has already touched on some aspects of how images and objects are displayed in museums and galleries, but at the large scale: how buildings are differentiated into museums or galleries, how whole rooms are labelled, and how this then classifies objects and paintings in particular ways. This section instead will focus on more small-scale techniques of display. These are usually accessed by researchers through visits to museums or galleries, or through historical documentation.

In museums, several technologies of display are available (after Lidchi, 1997: 172):

- display cases, mounted either on walls or on tables;
- open display, with no protective cover;
- reconstructions, which are supposedly life-like scenes. The dioramas discussed by Haraway (1989) and Luke (2002) in the AMNH are a particular sort of reconstruction;
- simulacra: objects made by the museum in order to fill a gap in their collection or to preserve fragile originals;
- immersive displays, which surround the visitor.

Each of these different display techniques may or may not have interactive elements that invite the visitor to do something with the objects on display. And all can have rather different effects. Their precise effects very often depend on their intersection with other technologies, especially written text. For example, Lidchi (1997: 173) suggests that reconstructions in museums usually consist of everyday objects put together with some kind of reference to their everyday use. Reconstructions thus depend on the presence of 'real' artefacts in an 'accurate' combination, and this makes their display seem truthful; although, as Lidchi also points out, this effect also depends on the visitor's prior faith in the accuracy of the anthropological knowledge used to make the display. Glass display cases, on the other hand, produce a truth not in relation to the apparent representational accuracy of what is on display, but in relation to the classification system of the museum. When placed in a case, an object is dislocated from the everyday context that reconstructions attempt to evoke, and is instead placed in the classificatory schema of the museum. Again though, given the truth regime of the museum as an institution, the effect on the visitor is of a truth: an analytic one this time rather than a representational one.

All the discussions of the AMNH pay a good deal of attention to the social meanings produced through the 'truthful' display of exhibits in their cases, and in particular to the dioramas of animals and people that filled many of the museum's rooms (Figure 9.5). These discussions often focus on the effects of the *spatial organisation* of displays: how different objects are placed in relation to one another. Haraway, for example, says that in the dioramas showing stuffed large African mammals against painted backdrops of their natural habitat:

> Most groups are made up of only a few animals, usually a large and vigilant male, a female or two, and one baby … The groups are peaceful, composed, illuminated … Each group forms a community structured by a natural division of function … these habitat groups … tell of communities and families, peacefully and hierarchically ordered. Sexual specialization of function – the organic bodily and social sexual division of labour – is unobtrusively ubiquitous, unquestionable, right. (1989: 30)

FIGURE 9.5
The Akely
African Hall at
the American
Museum of
Natural History,
photographed
in 1962. The
dioramas are
behind glass all
around the room
© American Museum
of Natural History

Thus patriarchy is naturalised, she says. Similarly, Bal (1996: 40–2) looks at a glass display case in the AMNH's Hall of African Peoples, which, according to its caption, contains objects that show the hybridisation of Christianity with indigenous African religions. However, Bal notes that the display is dominated by a large carving in the centre of the case of a Madonna and child: thus 'my overall impression of this exhibit is its emphasis on Christianity' (Bal, 1996: 42).

Reynolds's (1995) discussion of the (Warburg) Hall of Man and Nature in the AMNH, which opened in 1951, is an especially detailed exploration of the way of seeing invited by a particular group of displays. The displays in this hall refuse the apparent reality of the dioramas that Haraway (1989) discusses. Instead, Reynolds shows how they offer a visually and spatially fragmented, and clearly illusionistic, series of views of a landscape that draw the visitor closer in for a detailed look at each of the component parts. The effect, 'through foregrounding the very devices of illusionism', says Reynolds (1995: 99), is to transform 'the visitors' eyes into magnifying glasses, microscopes, or scalpels, which could reveal the invisible workings of a previously familiar but superficially understood natural world'. This is rather different from the awe-inspired gaze that the model of the sulfur-bottom whale was assumed to incite when it was built in 1907, and indeed that model was taken out of display in 1969 and destroyed four years later (Rossi, 2010). The spatial organisation of these displays still produces a reality effect, but it is historically specific; the effects that Haraway (1989) and Bal (1996) describe in the late twentieth century are different again.

In the case of the gallery, consider how the images are *framed* and *hung*. Paintings are now very often hung in a single row around the walls of a room, inviting you to follow them round, looking at each one in turn. That is, they are hung as individual images. This is a twentieth century practice (Celant, 1996; Waterfield, 1991); in the nineteenth century, it was very common instead for the walls of galleries to be packed almost from floor to ceiling with paintings. This change is associated with increasingly detailed modes of classification and changing notions of Art. The discourse of Art as something to be contemplated for universal truths, which Section 9.3 described (see also Section 4.3.6), became widespread in the twentieth century, and it changed hanging practices. If paintings are hung side by side, it is possible to contemplate each of them individually as pieces of Art. This also has an effect on the viewer: to encourage that contemplative way of viewing (Duncan, 1995). The combination of this kind of hanging with the layout of galleries often heightens this effect. As Jean-Francois Lyotard says of the spectator at an exhibition:

> the visitor is an eye. The way he looks, not only at the works exhibited but also at the place where the exhibition takes place, is supposedly governed by the principles of 'legitimate construction' established in the *quattrocento*: the geometry of the domination over perceptual space. (1996: 167)

Thus it could be argued that both the image and the viewer are individualised through this technology of hanging, and that viewers are produced as contemplative eyes and paintings as objects to be contemplated.

Finally, when considering the technologies of display in museums and galleries, you may also need to think about *immersion* and *interaction*. By immersion, I mean the technologies that are used to immerse the gallery or museum visitor in a particular sensory experience. Some artworks invite the viewer to enter a room or a building, and to be surrounded by a combination of lights, colours, sounds and textures. Some museums also do this, using images, smells or sounds as part of efforts to evoke past experiences. Increasingly now, museums are using digital technologies to achieve immersive effects. David Gruber (2014), for example, describes an exhibition of terracotta warriors held at the Hong Kong Museum of History which had an elaborate series of digital displays, including the exhibit's first room, in which visitors were kept for 15 minutes before being allowed to enter the rest of the exhibition; in that 15 minutes, visitors were surrounded by animated images of a warrior and his chariot, birds dancing and a fighting warrior. As Gruber (2014) describes it, this was also an interactive display: as visitors watched the displays and moved around the room, the displays responded. The warriors, for example, waved at visitors or tried to 'shoot' them. Interaction is another mode of museum display, in which visitors are invited to physically engage with museum artefacts. Sometimes this is simply by picking them up. Again, though, digital technologies are changing some of this.

Many museums now have touchscreen displays, or interactive tables, for example, onto which images are projected that change when you touch the table. In 2015 the AMNH was experimenting with a more ambitious project: the creation of a virtual Neanderthal flute that visitors can 'play' when they visit the museum's Hall of Human Origins.

focus

What technologies of display are used in the gallery or museum you visited? Is the list of possibilities provided in this section adequate to their description? Or are there other technologies of display that you want to consider?

9.4.2 Textual and visual technologies of interpretation

These sorts of display effects always work in conjunction with other technologies, especially written and visual ones. There are a number of textual technologies to consider, and they can be interpreted using the tools of the first kind of discourse analysis, described in Chapter 8.

- *labels and captions*. These are a key way in which objects and images are produced in particular ways. For example, in a gallery, a painting will always have a caption with the name of the artist; it will almost always have the date of the painting and its title, and very often the materials it was made with. These apparently innocuous pieces of information nonetheless work to prioritise certain sorts of information about paintings over others. In particular, it makes the artist the most important aspect of the painting, in accordance with the notions of Art and Genius examined in Section 4.3.6, whereas Chapter 2 was at pains to suggest that there are many other aspects of an image that are much more important than who made it. In a museum, labels have similar effects: they make some aspects of the objects on display more important than others. Bal (1991: 32) notes that labels and captions at the AMNH almost always deploy a rhetoric of realism – 'realism, the description of a world so lifelike that omissions are unnoticed, elisions sustained, and repressions invisible' – which makes it difficult for visitors to question the kinds of knowledge they offer.
- *panels*. Both galleries and museums frequently have large display panels of text in their display rooms. These often provide some sort of wider context for the objects or images on display. In the case of the exhibition discussed by Lidchi (1997), the panels were where the exhibition's practices of representation were made explicit. Panels often are more explicitly interpretative than labels and captions.

• *catalogues*. Most larger exhibitions, and many galleries and museums, produce catalogues for sale. These too are part of their technologies of interpretation. Like labels, captions and display panels, though, they convey very particular kinds of knowledge.

focus

Look at the labels and captions in the museum or gallery you are visiting. What might be the effect of taking all the labels and captions away? Take two or three images or objects and invent some new labels for them. What kind of effects are you aiming for in your new text? Bal (1996) also suggests some strategies for undermining the realism of museum labels and captions.

Visual technologies can also shape the effects of a museum or gallery. Museums often use photographs as part of display panels or catalogues to show what the use of an object 'really' was, or to assert the authenticity of an object on display by showing a picture of it, or one like it, in its original context of use. Galleries use photographs in display panels much less often, but their catalogues often have them, again usually as apparently documentary images.

All of these visual and textual technologies can be examined using the method of discourse analysis described in Chapter 8. Read them for their key themes, their claims to truth, their complexities and their silences.

9.4.3 Technologies of layout

Section 9.3 has already touched on aspects of the overall layout of museum and gallery space. Here some of its smaller-scale spatial and visual effects will be explored.

First, there is the layout of an *individual room*. As Kevin Hetherington (1997: 215) says, 'As classifying machines, museums have to deal with heterogeneity through the distribution of effects in space.' Hence the importance of the spatial organisation of displays and buildings, but also of rooms. Haraway's (1989) discussion of the Akely African Hall in the AMNH (Figure 9.5) describes the effect of its spatial organisation by means of an analogy:

The Hall is darkened, lit only from the display cases which line the sides of the spacious room. In the center of the Hall is a group of elephants so lifelike that a moment's fantasy suffices for awakening a premonition of their movement, perhaps an angry charge at one's personal intrusion. The elephants stand like a high altar in the nave of a great cathedral. The impression is strengthened by one's growing consciousness of the dioramas that line both sides of the main Hall and the spacious gallery above. Lit from within, the dioramas contain detailed and lifelike groups of large African mammals – game for the wealthy New York hunters who financed this experience ... each diorama presents itself as a side altar, a stage, an unspoiled garden in nature, a hearth for home and family ... Above all, inviting the visitor to share its revelation, each tells the truth. Each offers a vision. Each is a window into knowledge. (Haraway, 1989: 29)

Here, Haraway considers the relation established between elements in the room, and writes to convey the effect of their combination. She emphasises the coherence of this Hall, both in its spatial organisation and in its effects. Hetherington (1997), on the other hand, reminds us that museum and gallery spaces can also be incoherent. Particular objects can disrupt the symmetry or the clarity of the museum or gallery layout, for example.

One of the most important disciplines of museum and gallery spaces for visitors is the almost universal rule that you cannot touch the exhibits. This is enforced in a number of ways: objects are placed in glass cases; ropes are placed in front of paintings; warders watch visitors. Again, the Foucauldian question must be, what kind of subjectivities does this produce? Obviously, it produces a visitor that looks rather than touches (again).

Rooms can also be *decorated* in particular ways, with particular effects. In galleries of modern art, and also in galleries showing photography as art, the walls are often painted white and any seating is modern and minimal. This practice of display became common after the Second World War, and Duncan (1993) argues that it was encouraged by the insistence of the Museum of Modern Art in New York that that was how its big touring exhibition of post-war abstract expressionist American art should be shown. (Duncan places this exhibition in the context of US attempts to assert its cultural dominance in the Cold War.) The effects of this mode of display are suggested by Brian O'Doherty (1996: 321–2): 'The new god, extensive, homogeneous space, flowed easily into every part of the gallery. All impediments except "art" were removed ... the empty gallery [is] now full of that elastic space we call Mind.' O'Doherty is suggesting that the minimality of the white gallery space again produces the Art-work as something to be contemplated separately from any other distractions; and again, it produces the visitor to such galleries as simply an eye unencumbered by considerations other than looking (see also Grunenberg, 1999).

Then there is the question of how each room in a museum or gallery relates to other rooms. In the case of galleries, for example, paintings are hung in groups in separate rooms according to periods and (often national) schools, and this works to naturalise these periods, schools and nations, and also to produce a narrative of development from medieval painting to the present day (Bal's art production in history; see also Bann, 1998). Charlotte Klonk (2009), meanwhile, offers an account of the interior of modern art galleries from 1800 to 2000. She traces the emergence of what is now taken for granted as the space of the gallery – O'Doherty's 'white cube' (although Klonk is critical of his account; see Klonk, 2009: 218) – to New York's Museum of Modern Art in the 1930s, which was in turn inspired by German design in the 1920s. Klonk (2009: 14) argues that this style produces the art gallery as 'a series of passages from one, subtly lit spacious white room to another', a style that is remarkably similar in galleries in very different places and with very different external architectural forms. Displays of new media art in contemporary art galleries do not challenge this layout, says Klonk, but simply switch off the lights to create a series of black boxes.

focus

By no means all galleries have white walls, and few museums do. In the museum or gallery you visited, what other elements of decoration were important? What about coloured wall coverings, lighting, carpet, screens, other objects? What effects did they produce? If you visited a gallery that had white walls in some of its rooms and not in others, what was the difference between the white and non-white rooms, in terms of their objects on display and the effects created?

9.4.4 Architectural technologies

It is also important to pay attention to the way the *architecture* of museums and galleries articulates various discourses of culture, art and science. For example, there are the imposing *facades* and *entrance halls* of many nineteenth century galleries and museums, which were designed to be as inspiring and uplifting as the understanding of culture and science articulated within. Figure 9.3 shows the exterior of the AMNH, and Haraway considers the effects of its design:

> The facade of the memorial ... is classical, with four Ionic columns 54 feet high topped by statues of the great explorers, Boone, Audubon, Lewis and Clark. The coin-like, bas-relief seals of the United States and of the Liberty Bell are stamped on the front panels. Inscribed across the top are the words TRUTH, KNOWLEDGE, VISION and the dedication to Roosevelt as 'a great leader of the youth of America, in energy and fortitude in the faith of our fathers, in defense of the rights of the people, in the love and conservation of nature and of the best in life and in man'. Youth, paternal solicitude, virile defense of democracy, and intense emotional connection to nature are the unmistakable themes. (1989: 27)

focus

So far, this section has listed a number of technologies that are used in museums and galleries. It has focused on their possible effects in terms of the productivity of their power/knowledge; that is, on how they produce certain knowledges about paintings and objects, and certain subjectivities of visiting and curating.

Does the gallery or museum you have visited use any other technologies to produce particular interpretations of its contents or visitors?

9.4.5 Spaces behind the displays

The rooms in which objects are displayed are of course only some of the spaces through which a museum or gallery's power/knowledge works. There are also the *stores* and the *archives*, the *laboratories* and the *libraries*, and the *offices* and *service areas*. As Hooper-Greenhill (1992: 7) notes, these spaces are not open to the public (although researchers can often gain access) because they are the spaces in which the museums and galleries produce their knowledges. They are the spaces in which the museum professionals such as curators, restorers, designers and managers work – the spaces in which the classification schemes that structure the public display areas are put into practice. Hence:

> a division [is] drawn ... between knowing subjects, between the producers and consumers of knowledge, between expert and layman ... In the public museum, the producing subject 'works' in the hidden spaces of the museum, while the consuming subject 'works' in the public spaces. Relations within the institution are skewed to privilege the hidden, productive 'work' of the museum, the production of knowledge through the compilation of catalogues, inventories and installations. (Hooper-Greenhill, 1992: 190)

Yet very little attention is paid by Foucauldian studies of museums and galleries to these spaces and their particular technologies; indeed Bal (1996: 16) argues that the curators and other museum staff that work in these spaces are 'only a tiny connection in a long chain of subjects' and are therefore not worth studying in any detail. Bann (1998) however demurs, and I too find this rather an odd omission. While writers like Bal (1996) and Hetherington (1997) are happy to explore the discursive contradictions of museums' and galleries' display spaces, they seem uninterested in the possibly more subversive contradictions at work in the behind-the-scenes practices that operationalise those institutions' regimes of truth. If, as Bann (1998: 239) argues, there are 'internal contradictions built into the development of the modern museum', they too require investigation, and might perhaps be best seen in these hidden spaces. Indeed, in a rare exception to this neglect of behind-the-scenes spaces, Sharon Macdonald's (2002) study of the mounting of an exhibition on food at the Science Museum in London demonstrates just this, as she observes a very lively debate among curators about what the exhibit should show, how and why (see also Shaw, 2013).

focus

Few of these accounts of museums and galleries deal in any detail with what are now surely two more key spaces that visitors to these institutions encounter: the *shop* and the *café*. Emilie Cameron (2007) notes that, despite the discursive construction of both art and science as existing in opposition to the world of commerce and consumption, in fact the shops in museums and galleries are a key part of the institution, not least because they are so profitable. Indeed, assessing how much gift shop sales will be generated by a visiting exhibition is an important factor in many galleries' decisions about whether to host an exhibition or not (Cameron, 2007: 556).

What about the shop and café in the museum or gallery you visited: What sorts of discourse are at work here? What sorts of practice? Are they connected to those of the display spaces? If so, how? If not, how not? Could you use the methods used by the discourse analysts in this chapter to examine the productivities of these spaces?

discussion

Foucauldian discussions of the AMNH elaborate how the museum's claims to truth have produced distinct subject positions, which are very clearly differentiated by class, gender and race in particular. The AMNH was not exceptional in this, and during the 1980s museums and galleries themselves began to reflect critically on their practice in similar ways. This led to what Peter Vergo (1989) called the 'new museology'. The new museology was an effort to make museums and galleries both more representative of the diversity of cultures and more open and engaging to their visitors. These efforts have taken many forms, from changes in acquisition and exhibition programming policies, to redesigning displays, to hands-on displays and sensory experiences, and to education and entertainment events; they also include the online archives that many museums and galleries now host. Nowadays, many museums and galleries are also using digital technologies to enhance their visitors' immersion in and interaction with their collections, as Section 9.4.1 noted. Most museums and galleries are using websites and social media to extend their engagement with visitors too. Most have their own website, of course, and many also have sites on other social media: for example, a Facebook page, YouTube channel or Twitter account. So you can follow many museums and galleries on Twitter and like them on Facebook; you can explore their online archives and share what you find. Some encourage you to check in with Foursquare when you visit, and museums' and galleries' online presence is further extended when visitors tag the photos they take there on Instagram, for example. A museum or gallery's online presence thus includes the sites that the institutions host as well as uses of the museum's geolocation and hashtag by visitors. This social media presence may enable more people to engage with – and discuss and even challenge – the museum or gallery's claim to authoritative knowledge.

FIGURE 9.6   The American Museum of Natural History's iPhone app
© American Museum of Natural History

These developments raise some important challenges for the kind of discourse analysis of museums presented here. First, the online activities of museums and galleries may not be best explored using discourse analysis. This is implicit in Jenny Kidd's (2014) discussion of the way that digital technologies are turning the contemporary museum into a 'transmedia text', a notion drawn from the theorisation of 'convergence culture' by Henry Jenkins (2008) and discussed in Section 2.5 of this book. A **transmedia text** extends across multiple media, and implies an active, participatory user who will 'seek out new information and make connections among dispersed media content' (Jenkins, 2008: 3). Kidd's (2014) account of the transmediated museum and its users is based on a study of twenty UK museums. She examines not only how visitors interact with digital technologies located in the museums' buildings, but also a wide range of online encounters with the museums, from the hits and comments on their Facebook pages to uses of their Twitter hashtags. Chapter 5 suggested that the scale of activity on social media encourages a turn to quantitative analytical methods, and this is true in Kidd's case, too. She uses a range of both quantitative and qualitative methods to find out what people say about museums on social media. These methods include discourse analysis but also content analysis of a large number of social media

transmedia text

posts and comments; in addition she uses questionnaire surveys, semi-structured interviews and observations of people interacting with digital displays in museums (Kidd, 2014: 19, 42–3). Following transmediated museums thus seems to require more than the archival work on which much of this chapter's examples of discourse analysis II are based. (Section 9.5 will discuss paying attention to museum and gallery visitors in more detail, and Chapter 10 is also relevant to this topic.)

Secondly, as Gruber (2014) notes, immersive and interactive displays are attempts to induce an embodied, sensory response from museum and gallery-goers. He suggests that discourse analysis may not be the most effective method for exploring those responses either, because they require attentiveness not to discourse but to affect.

9.5 The Visitor

Sections 9.3 and 9.4 have both noted that, according to these Foucauldian accounts of museums and galleries, as well as producing the images and objects in their possession in particular ways, these institutions also produce a certain sort of visitor. Helen Leahy (2012) traces the discursive emergence of the museum and gallery visitor as above all constituted as an 'eye': someone who sees, and, through seeing, understands in specific ways. Museums do this explicitly, precisely offering their objects to their visitors as a kind of educational spectacle. According to Bennett (1995), things are slightly more complicated in the case of galleries, where the knowledge that produces the 'good eye' is kept invisible in order to maintain the gallery as a space where the middle class can distinguish itself from other social groups by displaying apparently innate 'taste'.

There are though more prosaic ways in which visitors to galleries and museums are disciplined. Section 9.4.4 noted some of these in relation to the prohibition on touching objects and images. There are many other *rules* about what visitors can and cannot do in galleries and museums, and these are enforced by warders. Picknicking and playing music, for example, are forbidden: the effect of this prohibition is to reiterate the 'higher', contemplative or pedagogic aims of the institution. Other forms of discipline include the *spatial routing* of visitors. Often galleries and museums invite visitors to follow a particular route, either through the layout of rooms or through the provision of floor plans marked with suggested walks (this is very common for very large galleries which expect visitors with little time: routes are suggested which ensure this sort of visitor will see [what are constructed as] the highlights of the collection). Some galleries also give you a clue as to which paintings are especially deserving of this kind of viewing by providing *seating* in front of them. As Section 9.3 noted, Bal (1996) pays a lot of attention to the effects of this sort of spatial routing of visitors at the AMNH.

Bennett (1995) argues that there are other, less overt forms of disciplining behaviour in museums and galleries, though. From his historical work, he argues that the contemplation of art and the appreciation of museums' knowledge was expected to involve particular ways of visiting these places, and that these ways were policed not only by rules and warders but also by other visitors. That is, he reworks Foucault's discussion of the way surveillance makes the operation of power 'automatic' by suggesting that the regulation of social behaviour in these museums is conducted as much by the visitors' knowledge that they are being watched by other visitors as it is by more obvious forms of discipline.

This emphasis on the productivity of the museum or gallery as institution in relation to its visitors raises a key question though. Just how effective are these disciplining technologies? In her account of modern art galleries, Klonk (2009: 11) is clear that such galleries are intended to produce a certain effect on the viewer: 'They tend to mould experience – the perception, behavior and aesthetic, sometimes even political, judgement of spectators.' Klonk distinguishes her argument from that of Bennett here, suggesting that art galleries were intended to create experiences rather than inculcate values. But she is careful not to claim that such efforts were successful. To make such a claim, she says, 'would be irresponsibly speculative. This kind of causation can never be proven' (Klonk, 2009: 11). Chapter 8 noted that Foucault insisted that wherever there was power, there were counter-struggles, but a common criticism of Foucauldian methods is that they concentrate too much on the disciplining effects of institutions and not enough on the way these disciplines may fail or be disrupted. This is a criticism that can be made of all nearly all the accounts of museums and galleries cited in this chapter. The previous section remarked on their frequent uninterest in exploring the working practices behind-the-scenes in museums and galleries, for example; it seems to be assumed that in those spaces, classifying systems and rhetorics of realism are successfully coherent, even by those writers who question its success in the more public spaces of these institutions. Similarly, few of these studies consider the possibility that visitors may be bringing knowledges and practices to the museum or gallery that are very different from those institutions' knowledges and practices. Bennett is quite clear that this is not an issue his book is concerned to address:

> My concern in this book is largely with museums, fairs and exhibitions as envisaged in the plans and projections of their advocates, designers, directors and managers. The degree to which such plans and projections were successful in organising and framing the experience of the visitor or, to the contrary, the degree to which such planned effects are evaded, side-stepped or simply not noticed raises different questions which, important though they are, I have not addressed here. (1995: 11)

This neglect parallels the critique made by Smith (1998) of the Foucauldian histories of photography offered by Tagg (1988) and Sekula (1986, 1989). There, too, the diversity of engagements with particular fields of power/knowledge is underestimated.

These sorts of questions are not made impossible by this second type of discourse analysis, but they have been pursued only rarely. None of the studies of the AMNH discussed here offer any methodological clues as to how such questions might be answered.

focus

This section has noted the consequence of the emphasis in this second kind of discourse analysis on the institution rather than the visitors. What did your visit to a gallery or museum suggest about the power of the institution over its visitors? Did all the visitors you see behave 'properly'? If not, how not? Were there certain groups allowed to behave differently – children, for example? How were any deviations policed, if at all?

There are a few exceptions to this neglect of visitors as subjects constituted through discourses other than those of the museum or gallery, however. There are a number of case studies that have focused on exhibitions that have been especially controversial (see, for example, Lidchi, 1997). Several exhibitions displaying the artefacts of native peoples, for instance, have been heavily criticised for their continued naturalisation or exoticisation of those peoples, and Elsbeth Court (1999) discusses both this accusation and some artistic and curatorial responses to it in a case study of displays of art by a range of artists from Africa. Much less attention has been paid to less explicit forms of resistance to the museum and gallery's disciplines. An exception is Leahy (2012: 100), who discusses 'numerous examples of recalcitrant bodies that have rebuked the museum's performatives', and does so drawing on historical materials as well as her own observations. Other studies that have paid attention to what visitors to museums and galleries think of what they see have used interviews (Fyfe and Ross, 1996, 2002), ethnographic participant observation (Handler and Gable, 1997), a mix of both, or videoed observation (Heath and van Lehn, 2004), as well as Kidd's (2014) multi-method analysis of what people say about museums online.

These studies invite more general questions about the visitors to museums and galleries. Do they critique the particularity of the sort of knowledge about Art offered by a gallery, for example? If so, how? Through their own experience? Through boredom? Through more formalised kinds of understanding, wondering why almost all the artists produced by galleries as great were men, or white? Do visitors touch objects on display, surreptitiously? Do they find routes around museums they shouldn't, or sneak a sandwich while a warder looks the other way? What are the effects of these possible strategies on the visuality and spatiality of the museum and gallery, and on their paintings and objects? And is the social media activity of museums and galleries allowing visitors to speak back to the institutions effectively? Kidd's (2014) analysis begins with a quotation from Foucault and asserts that examining the workings of power/knowledge are no less important in the transmediated museum. Her analysis reveals that museums are in fact often resistant to the forms of knowledge articulated by visitors on such sites (not least because these sites are usually managed by the museums' marketing departments); nor do online games or apps offer much in the way of agency to their players. However, she suggests that other digitally enabled forms of 'participation', such as user-generated exhibitions or archives, may offer more significant opportunities to create new forms of knowledge that the museum can archive and share. She therefore concludes that the power dynamics enabled by interactive digital media are somewhat more complex than the surveillant discipline discussed by Bennett (1995).

discussion

All the discussion in this chapter has assumed that museums and galleries should be understood as buildings with displays, visitors and workers. However, this is not the only way in which museums and galleries can be understood. In recent decades, several museums and galleries have not only been built as places for the production of certain kinds of subjects and objects, but also as key elements of the regeneration and branding of cities. This means not only that their apparatus and technologies structure ways of seeing within the museum building, but also that images of the building itself become part of quite other visualities.

Perhaps the most famous example of this is the Guggen-

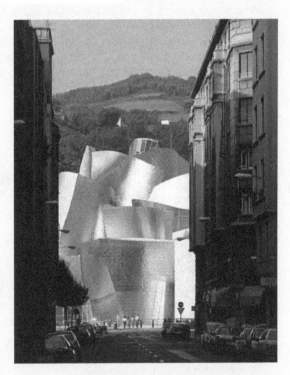

FIGURE 9.7   The Guggenheim Museum in Bilbao

heim Museum in Bilbao, Spain, designed by architect Frank Gehry and opened in 1997 to near-universal acclaim (Figure 9.7). Its spectacular architectural form has become very famous. Anna Maria Guasch and Joseba Zulaika (2005: 8) pose an interesting question when they ask, 'What is really being displayed in Bilbao?' They certainly don't think it's the art inside the building that matters most. Instead, they argue that 'the dominant image is the container, not the content' (Guasch and Zulaika, 2005: 16), and Klonk (2009: 196) also remarks that the radical external appearance of the building is in sharp contrast to its mostly conventional internal design and the modest artwork it houses.

More and more often, spectacular architecture is commissioned as part of urban regeneration projects so that images of that regeneration can be used in city marketing and tourism campaigns. Museums seem a favourite choice, and the Guggenheim Bilbao is just one of many recent examples. The building itself is visually striking, and images of it – in all kinds of media (Figure 9.9) – proliferate. The regional government in Spain paid over $170 million for the Guggenheim Bilbao museum; and in return, images of the building (it is claimed) have attracted nearly two million visitors to what was 'a declining industrial city in northern Spain of which only a very limited number of people outside Spain had previously heard' (Klonk, 2009: 196). The museum as a spectacle was part of a strategy to regenerate Bilbao, and seems to have played a significant role in achieving that goal (Fraser, 2005).

Most of the essays in one of the books exploring the Guggenheim – *Learning from the Bilbao Guggenheim* (Guasch and Zulaika, 2005) – consider the museum in this wider context of the role of museums designed by famous architects in urban regeneration strategies. Only a few pay attention to the way in which such ideas or strategies are materially apparent in this particular museum. Those that

FIGURE 9.8   Some souvenirs of the Guggenheim Museum in Bilbao do, focus on various aspects of its technologies. Andrea Fraser (2005) takes the museum's audio tour and unpacks its implicit discourses; Hans Haacke (2005) explores the sponsorship that funds major Guggenheim exhibitions; and Antoni Muntadas (2005) creates a photo-essay that places images of the Guggenheim next to other images of spectacular architecture, a corporate event, and gift shop items (see Figure 9.8; Chapter 13 discusses photo-essays in more detail).

FIGURE 9.9
One page of *Business as Usual II,* a photo-essay on the Guggenheim Museum in Bilbao, by Antoni Muntadas, 2005
© Antoni Muntadas

9.6 Discourse Analysis II: An Assessment

This second type of discourse analysis follows Foucault in understanding visual images as embedded in the practices of institutions and their exercise of power. It thus pays less attention to visual images and objects themselves than to the institutional apparatus and technologies which surround them and which, according to this approach, produce them as particular kinds of images and objects. This approach is thus centrally concerned with the social production and effects of visual images, and to that extent conforms to one of the criteria set out in Chapter 1 of this book for a critical visual methodology. It offers a methodology that allows detailed consideration of how the effects of dominant power relations work through the details of an institution's practice.

However, this type of discourse analysis pays little attention to the specific ways of seeing invited by an image itself (although it can focus with care on the context of its display). Nor, as Sections 9.4.5 and 9.5 have noted, with its neglect of audiencing and the circulation of images between institutions, does it pay much attention to the way that 'power is exercised from innumerable points, in the interplay of nonegalitarian and mobile relations' (Foucault, 1979: 94). Foucault's own arguments do not rule out these latter topics of research, but they have not so far been developed by these Foucauldian analysts.

Finally, there is the question of reflexivity. The kind of discourse analysis discussed in this chapter does not spend time on reflexive contemplation. This is no doubt for the same reasons as Section 8.5 outlined: many of the assumptions underlying the conventional forms of reflexivity in the social sciences are not tenable within a Foucauldian framework. However, unlike the 'certain modesty in our analytic claims' nonetheless advocated by Tonkiss (1998: 260) in her discussion of the first type of discourse analysis, discussed in Section 8.5, this second type of discourse analysis tends, if anything, to the immodest. The introduction to this chapter noted as an example of this analytical self-confidence the stinging critique of Barthes made by Tagg (1988). But all the writers on museums and galleries cited in this chapter appear equally confident that the claims they make about the effects of these institutions are correct. Haraway's (1989) essay, for example, makes some highly coloured assertions about the effects of the AMNH's Akeley Hall that give me pause. Here's a taster of her style:

> scene after scene draws the visitor into itself through the eyes of the animals in the tableaux. Each diorama has at least one animal that catches the viewer's gaze and holds it in communion. The animal is vigilant ... but ready also to hold forever the gaze of meeting, the moment of truth, the original encounter. The moment seems fragile, the animals about to disappear, the communion about to break; the Hall threatens to dissolve into the chaos of the Age of Man. But it does not. The gaze holds, and the wary animal heals those who will look. (1989: 30)

While Haraway may be attempting, in the Foucauldian manner advocated by Kendall and Wickham (1999: 101–9), to give co-authorship of her encounter with the Akeley Hall to its inanimate objects, she might also be read as offering an account of the effects of the Hall that is somewhat ungrounded in the details of its apparatus or technologies. (This critique has also been made of Luke's [2002] discussion of the AMNH [Rothenberg, 2003].) Moreover, I suspect that this sort of writing makes the AMNH a lot more exciting – and powerful – than it is to the vast majority of its visitors.

This second form of discourse analysis focuses very clearly on the power relations at work in institutions of visual display. However, this focus produces some absences in its methodology, too: an uninterest in images themselves, a lack of concern for conflicts and disruptions within institutional practices, a neglect of the practices of viewing brought by visitors to those institutions, and a lack of any form of reflexivity.

Summary: Discourse Analysis II

- *associated with*:
  Discourse analysis II has most often been used to look at the ways in which various dominant institutions have put images to work.

- *sites and modalities*:
  This type of discourse analysis concentrates most on the sites of production and audiencing, in their social modality.

- *key terms*:
  Key terms include discourse, power/knowledge, surveillance, apparatus and technology.

- *strengths and weaknesses*:
  Discourse analysis II focuses on the articulation of discourses through institutional apparatuses and institutional technologies. It is especially effective at examining the powerful discourses that produce the objects and subject positions associated with various institutions, for example the objects that count as 'art', the art gallery, and subjects such as patrons, curators and visitors. It is much less interested in the site of the image itself, and also in practice seems uninterested in the complexities and contradictions of discourse. Nor is discourse analysis II concerned with reflexive strategies.

Further Reading

There are no methodologically explicit deployments of discourse analysis II that I know of. If the methods of discourse analysis II have to be deduced from the work, try reading some of Foucault himself, especially *Discipline and Punish*, along with Alan Sekula (1986) and John Tagg (1988), and see what you can glean of their process.

 ## COMPANION WEBSITE

Visit **https://study.sagepub.com/rose4e** for:

- **Links to the best online lectures on Foucault**, which focus on specific aspects of his work. This is useful, as he shifted his arguments over the course of his life, some would argue quite radically, in ways this chapter doesn't discuss.
- **Links to a series of podcasts** on the history of museums.
- **An exercise** to help you get to grips with the analytical vocabulary of discourse analysis.

10

TO AUDIENCE STUDIES AND BEYOND

ETHNOGRAPHIES OF AUDIENCES, FANS AND USERS

key example: this chapter looks at studies of how television is watched.

It also explores some of the methodological consequences of the mobility of visual content in convergence culture.

10.1 Audience Studies: An Introduction

The previous six chapters have discussed a range of methods commonly used to interpret visual materials critically. What all these methods have in common, however, as I have discussed them here, is a relative lack of interest in the site of audiencing: that is, in what happens when images are encountered in the social world. That uninterest takes different forms in relation to different methods. Sometimes, it is inherent in the constitution of the method itself. Compositional interpretation, content analysis and cultural analytics, for example, all locate the meaning they recover from visual materials wholly in those materials; these methods simply discount the audience entirely as meaning-makers. Thus, in Catherine Lutz and Jane Collins's (1993) study of the photographs in the magazine *National Geographic*, content analysis was used to explore what the photographs showed, while another method – the group interview – was used to examine how audiences interpreted the photographs. In other methods, or versions of them, the uninterest in audiencing is less understandable, though. Chapter 6 noted Bal and Bryson's (1991) insistence that semiology is centrally about how audiences interpret the meanings of signs. However, it is only necessary to recall Judith Williamson's (1978) argument, that the audiences of adverts are constituted in specific ways by advertising itself, to see that Bal is not necessarily typical in emphasising active meaning-making by images' audiences. (The emergence of social semiotics and multimodal methods was positioned in Chapter 6 as a reaction to precisely this uninterest in audiencing among mainstream semiologists.) Psychoanalytic studies of film, meanwhile, actually pay a lot of attention to the notion of the spectator of a film, as Chapter 7 pointed out. But their initial interest was in how the formal structures of a film create particular spectating positions, as in Laura Mulvey's (1989) claim that everyone is masculinised when they view Hollywood narrative cinema; and although later studies gave more interpretative agency to the audience, no one apparently ever talked to any actual audience of any particular film to discover what positions they were in fact occupying. Discourse analyses of the sorts discussed in Chapters 8 and 9 also tend to be uninterested in the question of audiences, although I can see no reason inherent in discourse analysis that would explain that neglect; audiences too, it might be argued, bring discourses to bear on the visual materials they encounter, and these also could be analysed in order to understand the productive effects of images. But, to date, they mostly haven't been – at least in relation to the sorts of visual materials discussed in those two chapters. Audiencing, then, as something involving specific social actors engaging with visual materials in specific contexts, is neglected in all these approaches to visual materials.

This chapter addresses that omission, and discusses a range of studies and their methods that focus directly on what I have called the site of audiencing. Many academic disciplines have contributed to the study of people watching film and television in particular, and there is now a very rich literature on what is variously called 'effects research', 'audience studies' or 'reception studies' (Nightingale, 2011; Schrøder et al., 2003; Staiger, 2005). This chapter engages only very selectively with this large body of work.

It begins with the approach to the site of audiencing that emerged in the discipline of cultural studies. This body of work traces its lineage to the arguments of Stuart Hall quite specifically, and it is usually referred to as 'audience studies'. This book has already touched upon some of Hall's relevant arguments in Chapter 6. There, Hall's work was used to note how visual signs can affirm the dominant ideological or institutional structure of a society by offering audiences what Hall (1980) called the text's 'preferred meaning'. Audience studies became a core part of cultural studies in the 1980s, and was particularly interested in analysing the audiences of television programmes. 'Audience' in these audience studies meant the audiences for television programmes, who ranged from family viewers to enthusiastic fans. At that point in time, it also inevitably meant the audiences of *broadcast* television: that is, television as part of the mass media. Audience studies use interviews and ethnographies of various kinds in order to assess whether or not TV's mass audiences take up television's preferred meanings – whether viewers affirm the dominant order as it is articulated through an image, or whether they resist it in some way. This approach thus immediately has potential as a critical visual methodology, because it is directly concerned with how visual images can produce and reproduce social power relations. This chapter will also discuss audience studies in relation to the other two criteria established in Chapter 1 for a critical visual methodology: that is, taking images seriously, and reflexivity.

FIGURE 10.1
Watching TV
in the 1970s

However, it is clear that television audiences have changed in various ways since the 1980s, because the nature of television itself has changed. In the early years of that decade, there were far fewer broadcasting and production companies and far fewer channels than there are now; and households owned fewer TV sets. This meant that a great deal of television viewing took place in the living rooms of houses, with the whole family gathered to watch the same programme (at least until the kids went to bed); this in turn meant that when you went to school or to work or to the shops the next day, you could be pretty sure that at least some of the people you met would have watched the same programme the previous day, and you could chat about it with them.

FIGURE 10.2
Watching the
BBC news on
an iPod
© Alamy

Now, of course, there are far more channels to watch, and many households have more than one TV; TV boxes allow you to pause live TV, or to watch programmes when you want to; and digital recorders allow much more flexibility in watching what's been recorded than videos ever did. Television programmes are available to watch in other ways, too (see Figure 10.2): on computers, tablets and smartphones via broadcast companies' websites, or on YouTube, for example, where they might have been uploaded either by those same companies or by what Burgess and Green (2009) call 'users' (see Section 10.2.3 for a discussion of this term). As well as changes in how television is transmitted, TVs themselves are now also used to show many other things apart from TV programmes; connected to other pieces of hardware and/or the Internet, you can play a DVD just like you used to be able to play a video, but you can also display a slideshow of your family snaps from your camera, screen a home video, browse YouTube or play an Xbox game. Television programmes are transmitted not just through TV sets, and TVs are used not just for television programmes. 'Television', therefore, is not what it was. Although it is important not to exaggerate these changes – lots of popular TV programmes continue to gather millions of people in front of their sets at the same time – for many scholars they have prompted a move from thinking about the 'audience' to thinking about 'users'. They also pose a range of methodological challenges to understanding how television is now watched.

FIGURE 10.3
When more and more television is available in more and more places, some production companies go to great lengths to publicise new programmes – or, in this case, the fifth series of *Game of Thrones*, launched at the Tower of London in May 2015.
© Franziska Krug, courtesy of Getty Images

Audience studies often use interviews to explore how audiences interpret what they see on television. Ethnography is also a favoured research approach, and this chapter pays particular attention to ethnographic studies of audiencing. 'Ethnography' involves a range of research methods including participant observation, informal interviewing and careful field notes as ways of exploring everyday settings (Murphy, 2011; see also Gillespie, 1995). This chapter looks both at cultural studies scholars who have used ethnographic approaches to understand audiencing, and also a body of anthropological ethnographic work interested in what people do with images as visual objects (see Rose, 2010). The work of anthropologists like Christopher Pinney (2003), Deborah Poole (1997), and Elizabeth Edwards (2001) explores images as artefacts – objects that are always embedded in specific social practices and are impossible to interpret without understanding that embedding. This work is particularly interested in the circulation of images, and the chapter will examine these ethnographic approaches as candidates for a critical visual methodology of audiencing too.

Of course, ethnography is not the only approach to understanding television. Many television programmes have been interpreted using content analysis, discourse analysis, semiology, or combinations of these. Important work has been undertaken by the Glasgow Media Group, for example, using content analyses of public news broadcasting in the UK to show what values and ideologies are implicit in news programmes (Glasgow Media Group, 1976, 1980; Philo and McLaughlin, 1993). Social semiotics also deals centrally with audiencing. This chapter, though, focuses on interview-based and ethnographic-like studies of television audiencing, and has five sections:

1. The first is this introduction.
2. The second discusses definitions of audiences, as well as fans and users.
3. The third examines the interviews and ethnographies of television audiences, users and fans undertaken by audience studies scholars.
4. The fourth looks at anthropological ethnographies of visual objects.
5. And the final section examines the strengths and weaknesses of ethnographic approaches as a critical visual methodology.

10.2 Audiences, Fans and Users

Like content analysis, the study of audiences emerged as a specific research field in the 1930s, alongside the rapidly expanding mass media. While content analysis looked at the content of media 'messages', other studies were prompted more by both commercial and academic interest in how the audiences for the mass media were reacting to what they heard and saw (McQuail, 1997). In the intervening years, many different theoretical approaches to audiences have developed, with different methodological implications, preferences and traditions, including the use of quantitative as well as qualitative research methods (see for example Brooker and Jermyn, 2003; Livingstone, 2005; Nightingale, 2011; Schrøder et al., 2003; Staiger, 2005). This section contextualises the particular methods that are the focus of this chapter by discussing the development since the 1980s of notions of 'audience', 'fan' and 'user'.

10.2.1 Audiences

Most of the early work on audiences assumed a linear process through which meaning was transmitted, from the producer to the audience (although many researchers also acknowledged that various social factors affected the degree of impact of any particular message on any specific person). Exemplifying this linearity, this body of work described the 'producers' of media as the 'senders', and 'audiences' as the 'receivers'. As Sonia Livingstone (2005) points out, this sort of assumption remains at the heart of much discussion in the contemporary media of its own effects: witness the worries about the effects of violent films or computer games on the young children who watch them. However, in an essay available in mimeograph form in the early 1970s and published in 1980, the Marxist critic Stuart Hall offered what was seen at the time as a radically different approach to understanding how audiences engaged with the mass media. Instead of working with a linear model of meaning transmission, Hall (1980) offered a model in which two distinct processes were going on: encoding and decoding.

encoding   As Section 6.3.4 noted, **encoding** is part of the methodological vocabulary of semiology. A 'code' is a set of conventionalised ways of making meaning that is specific to a particular group of people. The process of encoding, according to Hall (1980), is when a particular code becomes part of the semiotic structure of an image. Chapter 6 mentioned what Hall (1980) called the 'professional code', which patterns how news broadcasts look. The professional code, to remind you, governs things like 'the particular choice of presentational occasions and formats, the selection of personnel, the choice of images, the staging of debates' (Hall, 1980: 136). Hall also argued that the mass media usually encode what he called the 'dominant code', which supports the existing political, economic, social and cultural order. In making this argument, Hall was drawing above all on the work of the Marxist theorist Antonio Gramsci, who, living in Fascist Italy in the 1930s, argued that political, economic, social and cultural order was maintained not only by the coercive power of the state – its police and army – but also by the dominant meanings and values of a society. This sort of power, maintained by culturally constituted norms, was termed **hegemony** by Gramsci. Gramsci also argued that there would be resistance to hegemony, resistance that he called counter-hegemony. Since audience studies was a Marxist-inspired critical project, it was analytically necessary that it should both explore hegemonic values and chart resistance to them.

hegemony

Hall thus used semiological tools to understand how social power relations were encoded into the programmes and publications of the mass media. Crucially for audience studies, however, he also argued in that paper that, as well as the process of encoding, the mass media were also subject to a process of **decoding**. Decoding is the central tenet of audience studies. Hall argued that when people read a newspaper or listened to a radio show or watched a television programme, they actively decoded their texts, voices, images and music. Audiences do not simply passively absorb the messages contained in the media, he insisted; rather, they actively make sense of them. And Hall (1980) argued that they react in three different kinds of way to the messages in, say, a TV news broadcast. Hall described these as different sorts of readings:

decoding

1. *preferred reading*. This is a reading that affirms the hegemonic political, economic, social and cultural order, as was noted in Section 6.4.
2. *oppositional reading*. This is an interpretation of the TV news which understands what the news is saying, but challenges the way it affirms the dominant order of things. It is counter-hegemonic.
3. *negotiated reading*. This kind of reading is a mix of preferred and oppositional reading.

Audiences, then, are constituted in this theory as a discrete site of meaning-making, as they decode the significance of the mass media that they encounter in their everyday lives. And they can do this by bringing their own knowledges and understandings to bear on the products of the media. As Shaun Moores (1993: 16) says, 'While recognising the text's construction of subject positions, [this argument] pointed to readers as the possessors of cultural knowledges and competences that have been acquired in previous social experiences and which are drawn on in the act of interpretation.'

This tripartite model has been subject to various criticisms (Staiger, 2005: 83). Nonetheless, it has been enormously productive as a way of thinking about audiences, not as passive dupes of the media, but as active viewers who, at least in theory, can interpret what they see and hear in their own ways. Subsequent work has gone on to consider the complexities of both encoding and decoding (for one recent study, see Couldry et al., 2010). Another development is work done on fan cultures.

10.2.2 Fans

Many audience studies are particularly interested in fans as a particular sort of audience. According to Jenkins (1988: 88), someone becomes a **fan** 'not by being a regular viewer of a particular program but by translating that viewing into some kind of cultural activity, by sharing feelings and thoughts about the program content with friends, by joining a community of other fans who share common interests'. This book has mentioned the work of Jenkins on fans before, way back in Chapter 2. There I noted how he describes fans as 'active producers and manipulators of meanings ... spectators who transform the experience of watching television into a rich and complex participatory culture' (Jenkins, 1992: 23).

fan

focus

Are you a fan, or do you know a fan, in Jenkins's sense of the word?

If you're not or you don't, try taking an inventory of your belongings that are in some way related to TV programmes. Include the screensavers, jigsaws, clocks, card games, videos, board games, figurines, birthday cards, bookmarked

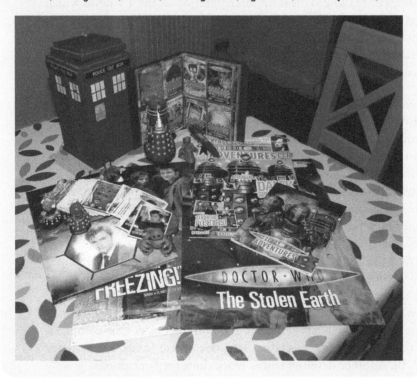

FIGURE 10.4
A collection
of *Dr Who*
stuff, 2010

websites, stationery sets, comics, remote control toys, card collections and albums, DVDs, audio CDs, posters, pens, and magazines – to list items related to the *Dr Who* TV series that my kids have at some point owned. (There was also a birthday cake in the shape of one of the Doctor's arch enemies, I remember, and Figure 10.4 shows their collection in 2010.) How important are the things on your list to you? Which ones – if any – do you think show that you are a fan? What ones don't count? Why?

Jenkins uses the term 'participatory' to emphasise the way fans take elements from their favourite television programmes – a character, let's say – and make something new with it. Perhaps they make a painted or drawn portrait of that character, or edit videos of the programme to make a new story featuring him or her, dress up as a character (Figure 10.5), or put a popular TV character or catchphrase to work in a different context (Figure 10.6). What Jenkins's work implies is that fans are audience members who are paying a particular kind of very careful attention to a TV show, so careful and also so committed that they can design an artwork, or a replica costume, or a Lego animation, based on a detailed understanding of that show. (And of course there is also the possibility of what Jonathan Gray [2003] calls anti-fans, who really dislike the attention given to cult shows or films, designing satires of those shows, and

FIGURE 10.5
Fans of the TV series *Game of Thrones* dressed as their favourite characters at the launch of Series 5.
© News Letter

in the process paying them the same level of attention as fans do.) Along with the work of other cultural studies scholars such as Janice Radway (1984), Ien Ang (1985), and Constance Penley (1991), Jenkins's work has been very influential on audience studies.

FIGURE 10.6
A photograph of British Prime Minister David Cameron has been pasted over the face of a character from the *Game of Thrones* TV series, along with one of the phrases made famous by the show, 'winter is coming', and used at a march to demand action on climate change in London, 2014

discussion

Audience studies have not been immune from the interest in emotion and affect that has gained ground across the social sciences in the past decade or so (see, for example, Gibbs, 2011; Gorton, 2009). However, as Janet Staiger (2005) points out in her review of what she calls 'reception studies', many kinds of studies of audiences have for a long while noticed the importance of emotions to how people engage with the products of the mass media. Feminist discussions of why many women love watching soap operas often focus on the emotions created by the programmes, for example, including the emotions experienced by the cultural studies scholar as she watches the same programmes (Ang, 1985); and feminist accounts of fan activities often emphasise the pleasure that many women gain from reworking a TV serial's characters and plot into even more satisfying versions when they make their fan artwork or literature or video. A classic example is Penley's (1991) essay on the female fans of *Star Trek*, writing and illustrating stories in which the show's two leading male characters fall in love.

Studies of fan culture raise an important methodological point in relation to deciding what it is that an audience study should focus on. For many audience studies, the focus is 'television' in the sense of both the technology *and* its content, which is watched in particular ways. Audience studies of fan culture, instead, concentrate on the *content* of TV and how it is recrafted by fans, very often into a different medium. To simplify, then, the discussion of 'audiences' and 'fans' implies the interpretation of rather different visual materials: audiences watch content delivered via specific communication technologies, while fans are involved in content that crosses different media.

10.2.3 'Users'

There is also a third way of describing 'people who watch television': as 'users'. There are a number of reasons for the emergence of this term, all of which propose that viewing TV is becoming increasingly active. Although viewers have been invited to participate in broadcast TV since its invention, as studio audiences, for example (Holmes, 2008), these invitations are becoming more frequent, particularly as the number of reality TV shows grows and TV viewers are invited to vote either by making a phone call or by pressing a button on their digital set remote control. Another reason for thinking in terms of 'users' is that, as this chapter has already remarked, television is now part of online digital culture, and this enables a range of more active engagements with programmes, from selecting when to watch them and on what device, to 'liking' them or commenting on them on their Facebook page for example. Indeed, as Livingstone (2009: 267) notes, 'People increasingly engage with content more than forms or channels – favourite bands, soap operas or football teams, wherever they are to be found, in whatever medium or platform', such that many people now, like fans, follow content rather than, say, 'television'. This is enabled by the way that media corporations put the visual content of specific TV shows across many media, so you can buy mugs, figurines, posters, board games, chocolate, ringtones, cartoon books, and the duvet and pillowcase set that feature your favourite show or character. All this suggests that the distinctions and alignments between medium, content, producer and consumer are blurred – which is exactly what the notion of convergence culture describes.

The upshot of all this is that many scholars now argue that, while neither the passive or inattentive viewer nor the 'audience' convened by major media events should be forgotten, the term 'user' better captures the many active ways in which people engage with television as both technology and content.

discussion

The use of the term 'user' is not uncontroversial, however. While Livingstone and Das (2013) worry that the term 'user' cannot address collective viewing in the way that 'audience' can, Nick Couldry (2011) is concerned that the emphasis on the creative user can underestimate the power of hegemonic discourses and institutions.

Couldry's point is an important one. Jenkins defined convergence culture like this, remember:

> Convergence does not depend on any specific delivery system. Rather, convergence represents a paradigm shift – a move from medium-specific content towards content that flows across multiple media channels, toward the increased interdependence of communications systems, toward multiple ways of accessing media content, and toward ever more complex relations between top-down corporate media and bottom-up participatory culture. (2008: 254)

The latter comment – about 'ever more complex relations between top-down corporate media and bottom-up participatory culture' – marks an important change in audience studies over the past three decades. Hall was writing in a moment when the possibility of resistant readings seemed theoretically at least reasonably straightforward: surely hegemony would indeed by resisted by audiences' counter-hegemonic readings! Fiske (1994: 192), for example, watched a group of teenagers watch a sitcom and decided that they 'produced a cultural experience within which the show, the behaviour of watching it, and the place where it was watched were all mobilized to produce social identities and social relations that were within their control as opposed to, and in emancipation from, those institutionalized for them in the officially approved family'. While this particular analysis by Fiske may have been correct, Meaghan Morris (1988) had lamented not long before that cultural studies was perhaps too quick to see resistance everywhere. Debates about contemporary media 'users' are thus echoing an ongoing concern in audience studies about the extent to which media meanings are resisted.

Certainly it is important not to assume that 'users' are more creative or more resistant than 'audiences' were. Jenkins (1992: 34) himself emphasised in his earliest work on fans that fans do not necessarily resist hegemonic cultural ideologies, and he has repeated the point in relation to the contemporary 'user' of media (Jenkins, 2014; and see Hay and Couldry, 2011). Moreover, as many cultural critics point out, many of the participatory activities offered by the large corporations who make TV shows are the means by which those corporations carry out at least some of their market research. When you register on your favourite TV show's website and download a cell phone theme, no matter what you think you are doing, even if you are downloading it to spoof it, your details and preferences are recorded and used as data by those corporations to work out what sells best to whom (Napoli, 2010; van Dijck, 2009). To resist the power wielded by contemporary media then is not simply to read their content counter-hegmonically.

The next subsection looks at how interviews and ethnographic methods have been used to explore these various conceptualisations of the site of audiencing.

10.3 Audience Studies Researching Audiences and Fans

Both interviewing and ethnography are very well established in the social sciences, of course, and there are huge literatures discussing them. (Good introductions include Atkinson et al. [2007], Braun and Clarke [2013], Bryman [2012], Gilbert [2008], Hammersley and Atkinson [2007], and O'Reilly [2008].) This section cannot therefore discuss in detail exactly what each method entails, nor examine all its possible implications. Instead, it will focus on the implications of the debates about 'audiences', 'fans' and 'users' for the design of interview-based or ethnography-based studies.

10.3.1 Using interviews to explore decoding

In order to explore the 'cultural knowledges and competences' through which audience members decoded mass media products, many early studies of audiencing turned to interviews with audience members. Interviews are not used in this body of work to discover what people 'actually watch'; other methods are available for that, for example asking people to keep a diary of their viewing (see Couldry et al., 2010). Instead, interviews are used to explore the sense people make of television. One of the most influential of these early studies was written by David Morley (1980) on a popular early evening news programme broadcast by the BBC called *Nationwide*. Morley (1992: 181) advocates the interview method, for example, 'not simply for the access it gives the researcher to the respondents' conscious opinions and statements but also for the access that it gives to the linguistic terms and categories ... through which respondents construct their words and their own understandings of their activities'. It should also be noted, though, that other researchers have used other methods to gain access to audience interpretations. In her study of how viewers of the American soap opera *Dallas* understood the programme, for example, Ang placed a small advertisement in a women's magazine asking people to write to her about why they liked or disliked watching it, saying that she would use their responses in her dissertation. She received 42 replies and used these in her book *Watching Dallas* (Ang, 1985).

Three sorts of interviews are used by researchers interested in how people interpret television programmes. The first sort of interview is the *one-to-one interview*, conducted by the researcher with one interviewee. This is the sort of interview used by Ann Gray (1992) in her study of how women used video cassette recorders (VCRs) in their homes. The second sort of interview is the *group interview*. This has usually involved working with groups that are already constituted. Morley (1980), for example, found his groups by going into classes that were already established at various institutions of higher education, and Buckingham (1987) found his by working with groups of friends established at schools and youth clubs. The third type of interview that has been used is also a kind of group interview: the *family interview*, in which most or all of the members of a family are interviewed together in their home. Clearly these three types do not exhaust the possibilities of interviewing. Group interviews can be carried out with groups brought together especially for the research project, say, though this is often time-consuming to organise and it can be difficult to find an appropriate venue; family members can be interviewed in groups, for example all the adults together and then all the children together; repeat interviews can also be done, perhaps as plotlines in a soap opera develop.

All these sorts of interviews are tape-recorded, transcribed and then analysed. Recording a group interview requires a really high-quality tape recorder, and transcribing group interviews is also notoriously even more difficult and time-consuming than transcribing one-to-one interviews. The analysis of the interviews is also complex and time-consuming. There is no space here to detail the various methods for doing this; they are discussed at length in many textbooks on qualitative methods.

First, more needs to be said about interview methods and especially about the logics underlying the *recruitment* of interviewees. The early work in cultural studies that was concerned with audiences made some assumptions – later to be problematised – about why it was that different audiences decoded television programmes in different ways. The argument was that it was the socio-economic position of the audience member that shaped their reaction to the preferred meaning of a TV show. In his study of how a popular TV news programme was interpreted, Morley (1980) was clear that position did not determine the decoding process, and he stated explicitly that other things might affect it, in particular the audience member's involvement in different cultural frameworks such as a particular youth culture or membership of 'racial minorities' (Morley, 1980: 23). However, Morley did argue that these sorts of social positionings could explain why certain groups reacted in certain ways to the same programme. He recruited his groups accordingly. While he was happy to mix the gendered and racialised composition of his groups, he never mixed the class composition, and thus he found his groups through different higher education institutions with different student bodies. There were groups of mainly white working-class young men found through an apprenticeship course at Birmingham Polytechnic, for example, and groups of mainly white middle-class men found at a bank's training college; he also found mainly black groups through further education classes, and a group of shop stewards through a Trades Union Congress training college. He screened two *Nationwide* programmes for these groups in their established group setting, and then held the group interview. Similarly, in her study of VCR use Ann Gray (1992) assumed that gender was an important analytical category that might well explain video use and therefore chose only to interview women; she did though try also to interview both working-class and middle-class women. Thus theoretical arguments about what structures the diversity of audience reactions are used to inform the choice of interviewees.

Morley (1980: 33) explains his preference for group interviews by suggesting that one-to-one interviews imply that people are 'social atoms', while group interviews allow for the dynamics of social interaction to become evident. It has also been argued that group interviews can replicate, to a degree, everyday talk about TV programmes (Lunt and Livingstone, 2009). Two points could be made here, both drawing on Anne Gray's (1992) work. Gray wanted to explore how women used VCRs as part of their TV viewing, and used one-to-one interviews as her method. Her study is very far from assuming that the women she spoke to are social atoms, though; the whole point of her interviews was to understand the women's VCR use as a consequence of their role in their family. Indeed, it is women's position in their family that might well have been one reason that Gray chose to conduct one-to-one interviews, because there is a difficulty in interviewing family members together that Morley does not mention in his 1980 study, which is the issue of family dynamics. Much feminist research on domestic labour has found that in households where men and women co-habit, men tend to overestimate their contribution to that labour and, moreover, that their version of events often prevails in interviews in which both the man and the woman are present. Gray's own work on VCRs (confirmed by Morley's [1986] own later work on television use in families) suggests that, generally, it is the adult man of the household who controls its use when he is present. This may have been a difficult issue to explore in depth in family interviews – men may have underestimated their control in order not to appear selfish – and thus Gray's choice of one-to-one interviews seems justified as a way of accessing women's views. Indeed, although Morley argues that one of the strengths of group interviews is to make the dynamics of social interaction evident, he does not acknowledge how difficult it can be to make sense of those dynamics. Nor does he mention the potential difficulties an interviewer might have in facilitating an open discussion in a group with complex dynamics; David Buckingham (1991) gives some examples of complicated group interactions in his account of group interviewing children about television. Group interviews are very challenging, both to do and to understand.

Once the interviews have been completed, the interpretation begins. Morley (2006: 75, 77) summarises his approach by commenting, 'You just need to read it again and again … You just have to be prepared to go on doing this kind of work on a project, examining the data for a long time and thinking very hard about it.' Moores (1993: 18) describes the process as finding 'significant clusters' of meaning and then 'charting the lines that join these clusters with the social and discursive positionings of readers'. For Morley (1980: 34), these significant clusters emerged from a close study of the working vocabulary and speech forms of his interviewees. He established from these what he called their 'lexical repertoires', then looked for patterns of argument and evidence, and finally tried to ascertain the ideologies underlying all of these. His conclusion identified two sorts of decodings of the *Nationwide* programmes, which he did relate to two socio-economic groups. The first was a decoding that broadly accepted the preferred meanings of *Nationwide*, and this was produced by the middle-class members of Morley's groups (as well as many of the young apprentices). The second was an oppositional reading, produced by working-class members of his groups but with important differences among them. Thus the shop stewards produced a politically informed 'radical rank-and-file perspective' while the black further education students offered an 'alienated "critique of silence"' (Morley, 1980: 137). Thus Morley could insist that class position alone did not determine the processes of decoding: so too did the cultural constitution of racialised and politicised identities, for example.

In his 1980 study, Morley (1980: 163) admitted that he was unhappy with aspects of his methodology and felt that it needed further development. His later study of *Family Television* (1986) did take his work in new directions. In this work he chose to use family interviews. This was because he was increasingly interested in two issues that his earlier research methodology had made difficult to access. The first of these was the ways in which the actual practices of watching television at home were difficult to access through groups that were not constituted through shared domestic spaces. The second of these was the question of what people chose to watch in the first place. His 1980 study had assumed that all his groups would be familiar with *Nationwide*; but what if the blacks students' 'alienated "critique of silence"' was a consequence of their total uninterest in the programme? Thus in *Family Television*, Morley (1986) interviewed 18 white nuclear families living in south London. All were working class or lower-middle class (as defined by Morley using notions of cultural capital rather than income [Morley, 1986: 52–3]), all had two adults and at least two children less than 18 years old, and all owned at least one television and one video recorder. He used the unstructured interviews (which took place in the family's home and lasted one or two hours each) to explore how the use of television was embedded in the wider family dynamics. How were TVs and videos used? What was watched and with what reaction? How were decisions about what to watch made? Most of his results (again with lots of transcripts reproduced) are recorded family by family, but there is one thematic chapter on television and gendered relations which argues that, in these households, the adult men tend to plan the viewing, control the remote control, watch in silence, watch more TV than anyone else, prefer more factual programmes, work the video, and don't like admitting to talking about TV.

discussion

Versions of the first method used by David Morley (1980) continue – that is, showing mass media images to people in conditions very different from those the images were produced for, and then interviewing them about what they saw. Often described as 'reception research' (Schrøder et al., 2003), it is used both by academic researchers but also by media producers as a way of testing new products on an audience.

Morley's shift to considering the social practices through which watching TV occurs is one that many others interested in audiencing have also advocated. As John Fiske (1994: 198) notes, 'audiencing is a variety of practices, an activity', and exploring that activity is of increasing interest to many researchers. However, many of these other writers have also advocated the use of other methods, in particular ethnography, to access those practices.

10.3.2 Ethnographies observing TV audiences

The trajectory followed by Morley's work in the 1980s was to move from asking audiences to talk about a television programme in an interview situation set up entirely for the purposes of his research project, to asking people to talk about their TV watching in one of the locations where it is usually done: the family home. For Morley, this trajectory followed a logical line of argument concerning how the decoding of television programmes should best be examined. However, if the aim is to explore 'the immediate physical and interpersonal contexts of daily media reception' (Moores, 1993: 7), then it could be argued that any sort of interview format is inappropriate. Instead, the most appropriate methodology would be to go to those contexts and take a close-up view of TV watching as it actually happens. This logic implies a more ethnographic approach to TV watching, which can access the complex detail of decoding as it is in the process of occurring. (Jenkins's [1992, 2006] studies of fans also adopted this immersive ethnographic method.)

Like interviewing, ethnography is a method long established and much discussed in the social sciences, and, again, there are excellent discussions of it elsewhere which I will not repeat here. One of the most fundamental aspects of an ethnography is what ethnographers call 'the field', that is, the location of your ethnographic work. What is the location most relevant to your research topic? Well, very often, given the theoretical importance attached by audience studies to the notion of family viewing and the historical location of most televisions in houses, a frequent answer to that question has been 'the home' (Schrøder et al., 2003: 5).

An ethnographic approach to TV viewing at home would involve the researcher observing an audience in their homes over an extended period of time, and talking with them about their viewing but probably also about many other things too. Not surprisingly perhaps, examples of this sort of ethnography are rare, because it is difficult to get access to people's houses for the length of time that an ethnographic study requires. However, a self-styled 'ethnographic' study by James Lull (1990: 174–85) offers some pointers for other researchers. Lull (1990: 183) defines ethnographic audiencing research as 'an interpretative enterprise whereby the investigator uses observation and in-depth interviewing to grasp the meaning of communication by analysing the perceptions, shared assumptions, and activities of the social actors under scrutiny'. He suggests that there are four things to consider when planning an ethnographic study of audiencing:

- *access to the audience*. Lull (1990: 175) notes that this is very difficult. He suggests going through the committee or board that runs a local institution such as a school or a church. (He notes that this may involve gaining access only to a specific social group.) Explain what you want to do to them (Lull suggests keeping this as vague as possible), ask them to give you access to their membership list, and then contact the names on that list. He suggests that 25 to 30 per cent of families thus contacted will agree to participate in the study.
- *observation techniques*. Lull (1990: 177) advocates the usual ethnographic means of recording what you see and hear: unobtrusive note-taking.
- *data collection*. Lull (1990: 178–80) suggests that spending between three and seven days with a family is enough to give the researcher access to their usual behaviour, and that during this period there are different stages of data collection. The first one or two days he suggests spending in collecting the more obvious kinds of data: what the house looks like, family history, biographical sketches. The next couple of days should focus on recording the dynamics of the family, especially by participating in its important routines. The final stage is to interview each family member separately.
- *analysing data*. As Lull (1990: 180) comments, ethnographic work generates lots of data. He rather briefly recommends interpreting it by organising it into internally coherent topics that can be used to illustrate conceptual points. Judith Okely (1994), in her discussion of interpreting ethnographic data, is more detailed about the challenges of dealing with observational notes and interview material.

Lull (1990) puts these precepts to work in large-scale studies the aim of which is the objective study of family viewing habits. According to him, 'The observer must create and sustain rapport with family members while maintaining the disinterested eye and ear of the objective observer-reporter' (Lull, 1990: 179).

In order to observe television watching as it occurs naturally, Lull recommends that the researcher does not reveal at any stage in the fieldwork process that their real object of interest is TV viewing. This raises an issue concerning the ethics of research. As Chapter 14 discusses at greater length, ethical research assumes as its starting point that research participants are fully informed about the aims and purpose of any research project, and explicitly consent to participate in it; there have to be very strong reasons indeed not to tell your participants what you are doing with them. In his advocacy of deceiving research subjects in the name of objective research, Lull shows little concern for the power relations between the researcher and researched. Thus there is no reflexive consideration of how those relations might affect his research findings either.

Another example of ethnographic research of an audience in its home – and one that Lull (1990: 16–17) dismisses for being too personal – is Valerie Walkerdine's (1990) account of watching a family watch a video of *Rocky II*. Walkerdine is certainly very personal in this essay, but she is so in order to explore just those issues that Lull's methodological orientation evades: her own complicity in the power dynamics between an academic researcher and, in this case, a working-class man who cheers as he watches the boxer Rocky smash his opponent into pulp. Walkerdine watched him do this when she was in the family living room, ethnographically observing their activities, and she describes her own revulsion at this scene and also her revulsion at the man's pleasure in it. Later though, she describes how she watched the video herself in the privacy of her office and found herself breaking down in tears as she watched the same scene in another way; this time as a woman herself from a working-class background absolutely at one with Rocky's brutal determination to succeed, to get out, to fight his way free. What her own changed audiencing suggests to Walkerdine is her own complicity with the ways in which the academy so often denigrates working-class understandings. In that living room, she says, she was acting as a feminist academic horrified at male violence, and in that position she could not see any other way; in particular, the class dynamics of the situation were invisible to her.

Lull (1990) and Walkerdine (1990) offer two, very different, ways of researching audiencing in homes (and, in Walkerdine's case, reflecting on the academic as an audiencer too). A third model for ethnographic audience studies is offered by Gillespie's (1995) account of television and video use by Asian young people in Southall, London. She chose to undertake her research in the area of London in which she had already been working for some time as a teacher. In fact, she lived there for two years, which poses another question in relation to Lull's (1990) work: is studying a family for at most a week enough to explore adequately the everyday 'microprocesses' of audience activity? However, Gillespie did not use that family home as the main site of her ethnography. Instead, she used a range of places where young people gathered together – morning registration and classes at school, 'cruising' around Southall at weekends, weddings – as well as a number of families' homes. In all these locations, she listened to how what had been watched on television and video got talked about. The emphasis in her study is thus very much on talk about television. In brief, Gillespie (1995) argues that watching and, crucially, talking about TV programmes is a vitally important way in which social identities are made. In particular, the challenge for the young people with which she worked is to become competently 'cosmopolitan' as a means of articulating their diasporic and hybrid cultural identity. For Gillespie, not only does 'the learning and testing of these competences [shape] talk among peers and in families about news on TV' (Gillespie, 1995: 21), but also '"TV talk" – the embedding of TV experiences in conversational forms and flows – becomes a feasible object of study only when fully ethnographic methods are used' (1995: 23). Given this argument about the importance of talk about TV programmes, it was logical for Gillespie to choose the locations of such talk as her field; and these included family homes but also a range of other places.

discussion

One rich strand of ethnographic audience studies focuses on how racialised, ethnic, national and minority identities are articulated through particular practices of watching – and sometimes making – television. One classic study is the work of the anthropologist Eric Michaels (1995), who in the 1980s examined how Aboriginal Australians started to make their own kind of television. Another example discussed by Dhaenens (2012) is the editing of a German soap opera by gay fans to give it a more explicit queer storyline; the edited version is shared on YouTube. There is also an extensive body of work looking at how migrants create complex cultural identities by viewing the television broadcast in other countries via satellite dishes and websites (for a review, see Madianou, 2011).

One implication of this work is worth making explicit here: that what I have been calling the 'site of audiencing' is more than just a metaphor for a specific set of social and cultural processes. The 'site' of audiencing is also always literally a site – a physical location where people actually look at visual things. This book has remarked on this in passing before now, but ethnographies of audiencing make it explicit. Television was once viewed almost entirely in homes, and so ethnographies were done in homes. But television is also talked about in all sorts of other places, so some ethnographers go to those places too in order to listen to how the meanings of TV programmes were discussed, negotiated and defined. And of course the same logic applies to sites of production: they too are physical locations, and significant studies have been made of the production of several television drama serials (Tulloch, 2000). Indeed, the notion that there are two different but equally theoretically significant sites of meaning-making – the site of audiencing and the site of production – is implicit in Hall's foundational model of the two parallel processes of encoding and decoding (Tulloch, 2000: 6).

focus

The same television programme (if it is indeed the same) can be watched in very different ways depending on where you are. The social conventions of viewing are different in homes, in bars and in airport departure lounges, for example.

See if you can watch the same programme – or something very similar – in two quite different circumstances. Watch a big sporting event with a group of friends at home and another in a sports bar; watch a 24-hour news channel on your own in an airport

FIGURE 10.7   Watching television coverage of the Wimbledon tennis tournament, at Wimbledon on a large screen

departure lounge and at home. Are you watching the programmes differently in different places and with different people? How are the people around you watching it? Are there similarities, and is that to do with the programme itself or the social conventions of watching TV?

10.4 Ethnographies of Visual Objects

One way of thinking about the recent changes in television viewing is to consider how the sites of audiencing have diversified as modes of delivery and contexts of watching have multiplied. What, and where, television 'is' is no longer as straightforward as it once was. This leads to a body of work that pays close attention to how people encounter particular kinds of visual images in specific social situations and locations: a body of work developed by a group of anthropologists interested in things like photographs and art objects (anthropologists have paid less attention to the mass media, it must be said; Askew and Wilk [2002] and Ginsburg et al. [2002] are exceptions).

Now, as I have suggested, audience studies are concerned with social identity and its relation to the meaning of images. They explore how that identity affects the decoding of that meaning, and how the process of decoding is itself part of making identity. Their emphasis is on the process of interpretation undertaken by audiences on images. The anthropologists I want to discuss are certainly concerned with these questions, too. But what interests them most is what is *done* with things like TV shows, and what effects result from that doing (which may or may not include the interpretative creation 'meaning'). To

visual objects do that, these anthropologists pay attention to what they call **visual objects**: material objects that can be seen, watched, touched, carried and decorated. Alfred Gell (1998: 6) writes about art objects, for example, arguing that they are 'intended to change the world rather than encode symbolic propositions about it', and that he is therefore more interested in 'the practical mediatory role of art objects in the social process, rather than with the interpretation of objects "as if" they were texts'. This aligns such work with the theoretical interest in the materiality of the visual that was described in Chapter 1, and it is a useful approach for considering television under conditions of convergence culture, I think, because it can pay close attention both to the diversity of visual objects that such convergence creates, and to what people do with such objects in a variety of locations. This section examines it in a little detail.

discussion

Along with those found on televisions and smartphones, family photos are probably one of the most common kinds of visual images found in everyday spaces (Figure 10.8). While there are many accounts of family snaps that use compositional interpretation to evoke their affective qualities, and discourse analyses that examine the very particular ways in which familiality is represented in this sort of image, there are now a number of studies that approach family photos as particular kinds of object with which specific things are done, with particular social effects. In my own work, for example, I argue that family snaps, in the ways that they are made, stored, displayed and circulated, are objects that are fundamental to the performance of domestic spaces, kinship networks and mothering (Rose, 2003, 2004, 2005, 2010). Others have discussed the importance of the display of family snaps to social status (Chalfen, 1987) and of their exchange to friendship networks among mothers (Lustig, 2004).

FIGURE 10.8
Family snaps
displayed on a
mantelpiece

10.4.1 Techno-anthropology

This chapter has already noted that television programmes can be seen in many different places, on different kinds of screens: small screens, like mobile phones, and big screens, as when local authorities erect large screens in public places to show TV coverage of major sporting events like the Olympics. Not only this, but televisions can also work with other technologies like DVD players, satellites, game consoles and video cameras. All this suggests that 'television' might best be approached as 'not so much a visual medium, more a visual object' (Morley, 2006: 275). Indeed, Morley (2006) coins the term 'techno-anthropology' to describe the ethnographic study of communication technologies as objects.

For Morley, 'techno-anthropology' means the anthropology of technology. The term refers to visual communication technologies in particular, and it also refers to a particular kind of anthropology inspired by Arjun Appadurai's (1986) book on *The Social Life of Things*. In that book, 'things' means any kind of material object, and it is this notion of a thing that underlies Morley's emphasis on visual *objects*. This is not a conceptualisation of an object as something inert and lifeless, though. Instead, in Appadurai's account, objects are absolutely integral to human life: to identity, and to social, economic and political relations and institutions. We humans surround ourselves with objects; we are who we are, and we do what we do, only in co-operation with a multitude of objects. For Appadurai, the relation between things and social identities and relations is so close that he talks about the 'intercalibration of the biographies of persons and things' (Appadurai, 1986: 2). The vital visual objects that Morley's techno-anthropology examines are the communication technologies that display images (Figures 10.1, 10.2, 10.7 and 10.8).

This emphasis on the social life of visual objects has two significant features (Dudley, 2010; Edwards, 2001; Gell, 1998; Myers, 2001; Pinney, 2003; Poole, 1997).

First, and perhaps most importantly, it pays careful attention to exactly what sort of thing a particular visual object is. And in giving this attention to the *materiality* of a visual object, techno-anthropological approaches are immediately attentive to both the image and the technology that is displaying it. For example, it matters a great deal to techno-anthropology whether a television news programme is watched on a huge screen in a busy train station, or on a TV in a living room during a family meal, or on a smartphone during a daily commute. The different materialisations of an image matter because techno-anthropology insists that the material qualities of an image intervene in the world, particularly the world of people. The argument here is a *performative* one. 'Images are not representations in the sense of a screen onto which meaning is projected,' notes Pinney (2004: 8); they are instead 'compressed performances'. That is, the significance of an object does not pre-exist its social life. Any object is always actualised in a specific moment of use, which produces both the object and the sort of person looking at it.

Appadurai (1986), for example, is interested in how practices of economic exchange bestow certain values on commodities; no thing is a commodity before it is put into specific economic circuits. His more general claim that it is what is done with things that produces their significance was extended to visual images in Thomas's influential book *Entangled Objects* (1991), where Thomas argued that it is what is done with an image, rather than its inherent meaning, that gives it significance. Thomas (1991: 4) remarked there that 'objects are not what they were made to be but what they have become'. An image may have a range of material qualities – the term "affordance" is often used to refer to these – but it is only when someone uses the image in some way that any of those qualities become activated, as it were, and significant. It may have a range of potential meanings, but they are latent until mobilised in a specific context. And while any person is a rich and complex subject, they are momentarily shaped by the visual object as they look at it. This suggests that the significance of objects is not entirely determined by the meanings people place on them. In his account of the relations between indigenous art and colonial culture in Australia and New Zealand, for example, Thomas (1999) explores the way certain artworks have intervened in the cultural identities of, and relations between, white settlers and indigenous peoples; 'I have presumed that art is effective in defining those relations and meanings, and may radically redefine them', he notes in his introduction (Thomas, 1999: 18). More generally, he argues that the agency of objects means that this co-constitution of people and objects is not always a predictable process. 'Objects and contexts not only define each other,' he writes, 'but may change and disrupt each other' (Thomas, 1999: 18). And Thomas (1991) strongly advocates the empirical investigation of specific encounters between objects and people in order to delineate properly the effects of those unpredictable encounters. This point deserves emphasis because it is an important difference between this approach and that of the audience-studies ethnographers discussed in the previous section, who very much tend to give agency to the viewers of television. The notion that the materiality of the television might also intervene in viewers' identities is not often considered in that work. (It does resonate, however, with the debate in visual culture studies, mentioned in Section 1.4.2, about whether, and how, images exceed the cultural.)

FIGURE 10.9   To emphasise his argument that photographs are visual objects deeply embedded in social practices, Pinney (1997: 173) chooses to reproduce this photograph of Sitabai holding a photograph of his son rather than show only the visual content of the photograph
Courtesy of University of Chicago Press

Secondly, visual objects are understood as *mobile*. Many visual objects travel, of course, and if conventional TV sets are not particularly easy to move around with, TV programmes, smartphones and tablets certainly are; and both audience-studies scholars and anthropologists are agreed that a visual object's value or significance often changes as it makes those various moves through time and across space. This is because, as Appadurai (1986) makes clear, although in theory any meaning could be given to any object, in practice the play of meanings is constrained by the cultural context in which an image is placed, and these are (radically or partially) different in different places and periods (see for example Danny Miller's [2011] discussion of the use of Facebook in Trinidad, and Helen Grace's [2014] on migrant workers sharing cameraphone photos in Hong Kong). The importance of that context lies both in its shaping of an object's value and in what is done with a visual object. This claim allows Thomas (1991) to emphasise the **recontextualisation** of objects. In its social life and travels, an object **recontextualisation** passes through different cultural contexts which may modify or even transform what it means: 'What we are confronted with is never more or less than a succession of uses and recontextualisations' (Thomas, 1991: 29); and Myers (2001: 54) suggests that recontextualisation has become a 'reigning concept' for this anthropological approach to visual objects. What Thomas (1991: 28) called the 'mutability of things in recontextualisation' is the theme of much anthropological work on visual objects.

The ethnographic methods adopted by these anthropologists means that the context for viewing a visual object is taken to be the particular social practices in which a particular kind of viewing takes place. There are cultural differences here – Lakshmi Srinivas (2002) discusses the shouting and singing that accompanies films in cinemas in India, for example – but there are also differences depending on exactly where an image is viewed and what the appropriate viewing practices are in that location – the same film may be watched very differently in domestic settings. As this chapter has already suggested, the same visual content can be viewed very differently depending on where it is seen, and techno-anthropology is sensitive to these differences.

On the face of it, focussing on 'recontextualisation' is a very useful approach to TV audiencing in convergence culture, where TV programmes can be watched in many kinds of ways, via all sorts of devices, and in all sorts of places; it pays direct attention to the site of an image's circulation. So what would be involved in doing a techno-ethnography of TV audiencing?

10.4.2 A brief guide to doing a techno-ethnography

There are four elements to this sort of ethnography.

First, consider *the materiality of the visual object*. The assertion that material objects have their own particular physical properties is one place to start an anthropological study of visual objects. One way to elaborate on these material properties would be to use compositional interpretation; that is, to take a visual object and subject it to a detailed description using the sort of vocabulary examined in Chapter 4. Edwards (2002) suggests that there are three aspects to their materiality:

- *visual form*, or content. This refers to what the image shows. A television screen may show just a TV show, or it may have some sort of menu displayed too; a YouTube page may be screening a TV show fullscreen or the show may be surrounded by all the elements of the standard YouTube page, including adverts and comments.
- *material form*, or the physical qualities of the visual object itself. In the case of television, we can think about the qualities of the screen: its size, its definition, its colour range.
- *presentational form*, or the particular way in which an image is presented to the person looking at it. Is the television that's screening the show large or small? Flat screen or analogue? Or is it being watched on a touchscreen phone or a laptop? How does that affect how it is seen and what effects that seeing has?

Secondly, examine *what is done with a visual object in a particular location*. Since the visual object and viewer are co-constituted, it is very important to pay attention to those material qualities that the viewers emphasise or enact when they do things with the object, since the materiality of an image in context is in part about how its 'objectness' is constructed by those people doing things with it. So observe what is actually done with a specific visual object. What affordances are mobilised? In the case of a TV programme on a television in the kitchen of a house, is it watched intently, or glanced at occasionally? Is it on all the time, or only when the dishes are being done? It can also be important to consider how an individual object is placed in relation to other objects. Is a TV in pride of place in a living room, or tucked away in a corner? Is it surrounded by DVD players, MP3 players, CDs and an Xbox, by ornaments and knick-knacks, or by a pair of huge speakers? Ondina Leal (1990) discusses televisions in working-class Brazilian homes, which are placed in front rooms so that they can be seen from the street; they are symbols of the owners' status. But they are also surrounded by sacred family possessions, notes Leal (1990: 21), including in one case family photographs, a religious picture, a fake gold vase, plastic flowers and a broken radio. Who dusts these precious objects? Who decides on such elaborate arrangements? Why? With what effects?

focus

One way of accessing the audiencing of television programmes watched on the Internet is to focus on websites that allow viewers to post comments about programmes on the site, and then analyse those comments. Susan Antebi (2009) did just this, examining reactions to the Peruvian chat show *Laura en America*, hosted by Laura Bozzo.

But are the comments on webcast TV programmes an adequate substitute for the full act of audiencing which, as all the ethnographers discussed in this chapter agree, is an embodied and social experience? Can you rely on interpreting just the comments, without knowing the circumstances in which they were posted?

Thirdly, consider *the mobility of the visual object: where it travels* and how it changes as it does so. This anthropological approach to images suggests that tracking objects as they move is necessary in order to understand their significance. Appadurai was explicit on this point:

We have to follow the things themselves, for their meanings are inscribed in their forms, their uses, their trajectories. It is only through the analysis of these trajectories that we can interpret the human transactions and calculations that enliven things. Thus, even though from a *theoretical* point of view human actors encode things with significance, from a *methodological* point of view it is the things-in-motion that illuminate their human and social context. (Appadurai, 1986: 5)

In the context of convergence culture, this is a useful contribution: follow some television as it travels, and locate the audiences it gathers in its different sites, and compare the sites the better to understand the specificity of each one.

These sites may be very diverse, and Livingstone (2009: 268) notes that some may be even more difficult to access than people's living rooms: people watching TV on their computers in their bedrooms, or on their iPhones on the bus, are harder to observe, not least because they may be doing other, private things at the same time: instant messaging, or texting.

discussion

Ethnography as a method can be used to study sites other than that of audiencing, including the television studios where TV programmes are made (see Tulloch, 2000). There are also ethnographies of sites where other kinds of visual objects are created: James Ash (2015) bases his account of the effects of computer games on their players on a careful ethnography of how they are made and tested; and with Monica Degen and Clare Melhuish, I have recently been exploring the making of digital visualisations of new urban development projects by, in part, watching visualisers at work (Degen et al., 2015; Rose et al., 2014). Indeed, it might be argued that with the dispersal of sites of audiencing into anywhere where someone has a smartphone, ethnographies of production have the practical advantage of suggesting a clear and limited number of sites at which ethnographic work can be carried out.

Ethnography can also be used to approach other kinds of visual materials. One of the most important sociological studies of art objects, in fact, is a sort of ethnography (though rather light touch) of how art objects are both produced and then circulate. This is the book *Art Worlds* by Howard Becker, first published in 1982. The 'art world' is the network of large numbers of people cooperating, often routinely, to produce and consume what we know as art, or, in Becker's (1982: x) words, 'the network of people whose cooperative activity, organized via their joint knowledge of conventional means of doing things, produces the kind of art works that the art world is noted for' (and see Rothenberg, 2014). That 'network of people' includes the people making art works, but also the agents, gallery owners, curators, critics, commissioners and collectors whose various activities produce, distribute, publicise, display, sell and comment on art works.

Sarah Thornton (2008) takes a slightly different approach to Becker in her entertaining study of *Seven Days in the Art World*. Like Becker, she is interested in how some objects are produced as art by a range of social actors and organisations, but her book is organised with a chapter on what happens in one day at seven specific locations, including an artist's studio, an art magazine's editorial office, the meeting of a major art prize jury, a major international art fair, and a university's fine art programme seminar. Thornton's work thus suggests (more explicitly than Becker) that multi-sited ethnographies can be used to explore how art objects – but not only art objects – circulate between different locations, as discussed in Section 10.4.1.

The work of both Becker (1982) and Thornton (2008) raises a question about how the sites of the 'production' of images should be defined. The site of production might be understood simply as the location of the creation of a visual object: an artist's studio or a digital visualiser's office. Or it might be understood, as in Becker and Thornton's work, as distributed among a number of sites where different social actors and organisations operate to recontextualise an object as an artwork.

Becker (1982) makes another interesting methodological point. He says that his focus on the social organisation of the art world means that he is not interested in thinking about the images that artists create in aesthetic terms. Indeed, he says explicitly that aesthetic judgements are produced by the collective social activity he is interested in studying, especially by critics and curators of various kinds. Thus while he is very interested in the material objects that members of the art world use to do their various kinds of work (and is thus often cited approvingly by those concerned to assert the importance of that materiality), unlike the anthropologists cited in the previous section he is not arguing that the objects that become defined as art in art worlds have any agency themselves.

Finally, interpret *the effect of the visual object by putting it all together*. Examining the effects of these materialities, practices and mobilities is complex. At the level of discourse, ethnographic fieldnotes or interview materials can be interpreted using discourse analysis I, gradually finding recurring practices, effects and taken-for-granted assumptions that produce both a certain kind of television and a certain kind of user. Anna McCarthy's (2001) study of televisions in public spaces is exemplary at putting together the mobile visual content of these TVs with the materiality both of the TV sets and their specific locations; however, the one thing she does not do in her study is to talk to any kind of audience about the various televisions she discusses. Lisa Taylor's (2008) study of the relation between gardeners and garden media, on the other hand, is an account of how gardening television programmes and gardening journalism are received by gardeners in a town in the north of England. Her focus on both TV and gardening magazines could be seen as acknowledging an aspect of convergence culture, since some TV programmes have their own magazines, and the same gardening celebrities appear across different media. Her study, which is 'ethnographic in intention' (Taylor, 2008: 9), pays a lot of attention to how the meanings taken from this range of gardening media affect how her research participants garden (concluding that they are not impressed, generally, and very little of the media's recommendations about 'good' gardening appears to impact on any actual gardening); but she does not pay detailed attention to exactly how these various media are encountered. Pulling the materiality of the TV programme, its mobilities and its effects together is not easy, then.

discussion

Taylor's (2008) account of gardening media raises an interesting question about what to track when following mobile images. In the case of a TV programme, it is perhaps quite easy to identify when that programme, as a specific block of visual content, is mobile between different devices at different times in different places with different viewers. But if we take the argument about convergence culture seriously, just as a museum is no longer the building and its collections (recall the discussion of the transmediated museum in Section 9.4.5), the TV programme is no longer just the TV programme: it is also its social media presence, its spin-off magazine, and its branded live gardening shows. But how to track who follows the programme on Facebook or Twitter? Does the spin-off magazine count as part of the programme? What about its celebrity presenters, who may appear in all sorts of other media, about gardening but also about other things?

10.4.3 A final comment, on users and non-media-centric media studies

Techno-anthropology is one productive direction in which to explore the consequences of convergence culture, particularly as it focuses so clearly on that culture's modality of circulation.

However, some media studies scholars are taking the logic of convergence culture in a slightly different direction, towards what has been

non-media-centric media studies

dubbed **non-media-centric media studies**. Media studies – like audience studies – has tended to organise itself through studies of particular media: film studies, new media studies, game studies, TV studies. Indeed, techno-anthropology's focus on the various materialisations of specific visual content might be said to be organised in the same way, as it studies how a visual object like a photograph or a TV programme travels. However, if the distinctions between different media are breaking down as content converges across them, then that form of organising our understanding of media audiencing may be out of date. The idea of a non-media-centric media studies – and indeed a non-media-centric audience studies – is to examine audiencing not in relation to just one medium, like TV, but in terms of the full range of what people do with all sorts of media and its content. As Shaun Moores (2012) points out, many kinds of media are central to many, many kinds of ordinary, different everyday routines: listening to the news while driving to work, sitting down with your kids to watch their favourite after-school broadcast TV show, catching up on your favourite Internet-streamed show as a way to wind down on a Friday evening, checking Instagram while you take a coffee break; and many young people now do these things simultaneously, checking Twitter while watching a TV programme on catch-up, for example; multiple media content are accessed, more or less simultaneously, on various devices, often while on the move. Couldry (2011: 220) describes this situation as a 'media manifold'. This complexity also means that it is no longer clear just what constitutes a 'media', nor what happens when it is watched – hence the emergence of non-media-centric media studies.

Both Moores (2012) and Couldry (2011) suggest that non-media-centric media studies involves a three-fold methodology: exploring 'the rhythms, density, and patterning of what people do to access or use media' (Couldry, 2011: 223); examining what visual content is accessed and how it is watched; and how that accessing and watching are related to broader social processes and practices. Couldry (2011) for one argues that this is the most important task for understanding media audiences now: gaining a better understanding of the diversity of audiencing. And although neither Moores nor Couldry elaborate much more on what might be appropriate methods to achieve this, it seems that ethnography – of some kind – would remain a good choice.

10.5 Ethnographic Studies of Audiencing: An Assessment

The work cited here explores an issue mentioned frequently in the preceding chapters of this book but not so far addressed directly – audiencing – and offers a number of theoretical and methodological resources for understanding its dynamics. Its first contribution to a critical visual methodology is obviously to make audiences – or users – central to the effects of images. In doing so, audience studies have made the whole notion of audiencing rather more complex than this book has so far acknowledged. What is an audience? What different kinds of audience are there? What are they watching and how? And where are they? These questions have been raised consistently by audience studies scholars as they have studied audiences, fans and users over the past three decades or so. And they have offered specific answers to these questions and others.

This chapter has only addressed some of the work on audiences carried out in the discipline of cultural studies, along with that of some anthropological fellow-travellers. But it is clear from this discussion that audience studies can fulfil the three requirements for a critical visual methodology. It takes images seriously; while audience studies sometimes pays less attention to the preferred meaning of television images in order to pay more attention to the audiences' meanings, the anthropologists discussed here take the visuality and materiality of visual objects very seriously indeed; and all of these scholars are centrally concerned with the power relations in which visual objects and their viewer are embedded, and which are performed as audiencing is done.

For some of these scholars – though not for all – reflexivity is core to their work. Many ethnographers from very different disciplinary backgrounds would argue that reflexivity is central to their method, and Patrick Murphy (2011) forcefully concurs. Unlike Lull (1990), both Walkerdine (1990) and Gillespie (1995) advocate full disclosure and the careful, not to say painful, exploration of the researcher's position in relation to those she is researching. That position is understood in the same way as the social position or identity of the audience: in terms of class, gender, race and so on. Walkerdine (1990) and Gillespie (1995) use their reflexive self-descriptions in rather different ways, however. Gillespie (1995) reflects carefully on her position as a white researcher of Irish descent in relation to her research subjects. While not perhaps as powerful or revelatory as Walkerdine's essay, Gillespie's discussion nevertheless does a solid job of allowing the reader to evaluate the reliability of her account. Gillespie's methodological explicitness affirms both the validity of her interpretation and the ethical nature of her project. Walkerdine's essay, instead, seems to me to be conveying a critical theoretical insight into the complex and sometimes ambiguous work of critical interpretation. Reflexivity, then, is not a necessary component of audience studies (it was not part of Hall's [1980] early account of encoding); and when it is used, it is used to various ends.

There are, however, various questions to be asked of the approaches to audiencing explored in this chapter. One of these, directed at the earlier audience studies specifically, concerns the way in which the site of audiencing is approached almost exclusively in its social modality. Both Mark Jancovich (1992) and Virginia Nightingale (1996) remark that as a consequence of the attention it pays to audiencing, this body of work neglects the image itself and its production. That is, 'the textual processes through which television establishes social, cultural and political agendas' are ignored (Jancovich, 1992: 136). As an example of this, Gillespie's (1995) introduction to her ethnography takes 13 pages to get back to television after its opening mention, discussing in the meanwhile questions of identity, race, hybridity, cosmopolitanism, fieldwork, diaspora, the subaltern and youth culture. While her more detailed discussions do pay attention to specific scenes in TV programmes, her overall approach is very much to subordinate the semiotic detail of the programme to the sociological situation of its audiences. Indeed, the emphasis on the social modality of TV watching is so strong in work of this kind that Moores (1993: 54) wonders whether studies that aim to embed TV watching firmly in the dynamics of classed, racialised and gendered social relations end up being more about those relations than about television. Jancovich (1992: 136) pursues this worry when he says that it is not clear in Morley's (1986) study of family television precisely how those dynamics of family interaction affect the decoding of TV programmes. Clearly they do affect crucial aspects of television use, such as who decides to watch what and when; but their effect on who interprets what and how is much less clear. The same issue may appear as non-media-centric media studies develop more fully.

The theoretical assumptions of audience studies done as a part of cultural studies also have some questionable implications. Ang (1989) argues that much of the early work on audiencing assumed the authoritative researcher who knew more, or better, about TV programmes than the people they were interviewing. Moores (1993: 65) responds that some of her critique is misplaced, since authors like Morley (1980) explicitly invited their readers to make their own sense of their interview material by including large amounts of interview transcripts in their accounts. In this way, Morley is somewhat more modest in his interpretative claims than Ang allows, since his readers can reach their own conclusions (though still on the basis of the materials provided by Morley). However, on one point Ang's (1989) critique does seem fair. She says that the assumption that there is a preferred meaning contained in a visual image implies that only the researcher can access it, and that it can act as a kind of baseline from which other audience interpretations can be assessed. Morley (1980: 22) actually deploys a number of ideas from mainstream semiology to describe the preferred meanings of the TV programme *Nationwide*, or, as he puts it, 'to establish provisional readings of their main communicative and ideological structures'. But as Moores (1993: 28) asks of these 'communicative and ideological structures': 'Can we be sure we didn't put it there ourselves while we were looking?' Thus the notion of a preferred meaning is vulnerable to the same kind of questioning as all non-reflexive semiological claims to access the hidden meanings in images (see Section 6.5). (And recall that similar questions were posed in relation to content analysis and its claim to access the real meanings of images in Chapter 5.)

Other concerns about the role of the researcher in audience studies relates more to the methods used. In relation to interviewing, the issue is the impact of the researcher on their research subjects during the interview. As Buckingham (1991: 229) notes, all talk is done in a specific context, and this context affects what sort of talk is done. This is true of all social interactions, as those discourse analysts discussed in Chapter 7 here insist. However, Buckingham (1991) suggests that those researching audiencing should pay a little more attention to the effects of the interview context on what is said in the interview. I have already suggested that Gray (1992) might have considered this issue when making her decision to interview women VCR users on a one-to-one basis rather than in family groups. Obviously one-to-one interviews have their own specificities (which Gray [1992: 34] does explore), but it is rare to find any consideration of the way the researcher might have affected group or family interviews. The example Buckingham (1991: 229–32) uses is from his own work with school-age children. He notes that he interviewed these children at school and was introduced to them by their teacher, so that the children in those groups most likely associated him with teachers. In the group interviews, the children were very critical of TV advertising, and also discussed the racism and sexism of some kids' cartoon series; but the question Buckingham asks is, were these children employing an 'interpretative repertoire' that they thought was appropriate to the situation (see Section 7.3.1), a situation in which an adult was listening to them, and when they know many adults, especially teachers, disapprove of television? Buckingham (1991) is not suggesting that the children were not saying what they thought, still less that they were lying; he is simply considering what effect the interview situation itself might have had on the material he gathered there. Concerns about the impact of the researcher on the material gathered are obviously relevant to ethnographic work as well. Hanging around in a living room, a school or indeed anywhere where you suspect something like television perhaps is being watched may, in some circumstances, affect what the people you are observing do; and talking to them about what they are doing will perform a particular kind of social interaction as much as allow you a window into their audiencing (Schrøder et al., 2003: 16).

Ethnography as a method is bedevilled by its own challenges. One is the time required to do an ethnography adequately. Clearly, given enough time and resources, researchers can embed themselves in many sites of audiencing in all their modalities in great detail, examining their co-constitution and the working of recontextualisation across them. But researchers with less time and resources will not have the luxury of extended, close-up ethnographic observation, and they will therefore have to make choices about what aspect of the social life of their chosen images they wish to concentrate on. Time and resource constraints place limits on many studies, and I imagine that such constraints affect many researchers. And since the quality of the findings of the anthropological approach do depend on detailed and extensive empirical evidence, such constraints may affect this method more perhaps than others this book has discussed (see Murphy [2011] for further discussion about the quality of some media ethnography).

Many of these issues, however, are endemic to any kind of social research: the role of the researcher and the definition of the field are questions any research project has to address. In that light, it is possible to conclude that this body of work on audiencing strongly emphasises the importance of the social modality of the sites of images' circulation and audiencing, but can also pay attention to its technological modality. In terms of a critical visual methodology, some of this work can pay too little attention to the power of images themselves, and, although it can be strongly and productively reflexive, it is not necessarily so.

Summary: Audience Studies

- *associated with*:
  The sort of audience studies discussed here have been used most often in relation to the audiences of television programmes; the anthropologists discussed have examined a wider range of visual objects.

- *sites and modalities*:
  Audience studies focus most strongly on the site of audiencing in its social modality; anthropologists emphasise the site's technological modality, as well as the circulation of images.

methods that use the ways in which the web itself organises its data, to examine that data (Rogers [2014] gives a useful overview of a wider range of digital research). Digital methods thus examine 'natively digital objects' (2013: 1): things that are only found on the web, including 'specific digital media' (Rogers' examples in his introduction [2013: 15] are a blog post and a Wikipedia edit). And digital methods analyse those 'objects' using techniques that are only used on web data: searching for hyperlinks, tags, user locations, hits, datestamps and likes, for example. He suggests that using digital methods on digital objects not only allows us better to understand how the web is organised; he argues that such methods can also help us to answer questions about social life now. For example, Lisa Nakamura (2014) studied the extensive spread of a type of online image created at the behest of 'scambaiters'. Scambaiters are self-styled Internet vigilantes who pose as potential victims to online scammers in order to waste their time and resources by demanding that they create bizarrely posed photographs. The photos almost always show African (apparent) scammers, even though most online scammers are not African. Nakamura (2014: 261) suggests that 'an analysis of the origins and meanings of overtly racialized and sexist viral images such as these can tell us much about how racial and ethnic difference are enacted on the internet through visual means', and she uses Google Images search to locate such images and then to explore their circulation and audiencing. In this way, digital methods 'build upon existing, dominant [digital] devices themselves, and with them perform a cultural and societal diagnostics' (Rogers, 2013: 1–3).

There certainly seems to be a case to be made that understanding the pervasive presence of digital images in everyday life requires new methods. For most people in the Global North – and a good many in the Global South too – digital technologies are ubiquitous. They saturate everyday life, whether we are aware of them or not. Think of all the things that are done with a smartphone: calls (including calls made over 3G and 4G networks and VoIP services like Skype and Facetime) and messages are made and sent (emails and texts [SMS] as well as other messaging services like iMessage, WhatsApp and Snapchat); streets are navigated (using online maps like Google Maps); music is listened to (either downloaded or streamed) and photographs are taken and shared (on platforms like Instagram and Snapchat); tweets are tweeted; games are played; not to mention the apps that tell you the weather forecast, track how far you walk each day, let you book a taxi, record your weight, and check your bank account balance. Many of these apps and services invite you to respond to them: to like an Instagram photo or a YouTube video, to favourite a tweet, or to make a location found on Google Maps your home. And then there's your desktop, laptop or tablet, which does some of the same as your phone and more: emailing for work and leisure; googling for information; shopping; reading newspapers, magazines and ebooks; playing more games, listening to more music, watching films and TV programmes … as well as using word processing packages and other software for work and study. A great many of these apps and software packages involve images. From the app icons on your phone screen, to video calls, to attaching a photo to a message or a tweet, to using your cameraphone to share images on Instagram, to the banners on websites – quite apart from all the video and photography sites like Vimeo, YouTube, Flickr, Pinterest etc. – there are images everywhere. And increasingly, as well as the screens of your computer and your phone, there are larger screens in more-or-less public spaces like shopping malls and piazzas, showing news programmes, advertising and, sometimes, artworks (Berry et al., 2013; Casetti, 2013; McQuire et al., 2009; McQuire, 2010; Verhoeff, 2012). This is the 'media manifold' described by Nick Couldry (2011: 220), as Section 10.4.3 noted, and, to quote the title of danah boyd's (2014) recent study of how teenagers in the US use social media, 'it's complicated'.

The vast numbers of images on various online platforms is often used as evidence of the saturation of everyday life with images. In November 2014, for example, 100 hours of video were uploaded to YouTube every minute and 60 million photographs were uploaded to Instagram every day, figures which were dwarfed by the 350 million images uploaded onto Facebook and the 400 million photos sent to Snapchat. And while many of these images are made and shared quickly and casually, many of the digital images that we see have gone through elaborate revision using image-editing software like Photoshop. Chapter 5 discussed the usefulness of content analysis and cultural analytics in this context. Given such vast numbers of images, quantitative methods continue to offer valuable insights. 'We need to understand cultural, creative, and knowledge-systems across whole populations', insists John Hartley (2012: 54); 'at the very least that we need to focus on probabilities in large-scale systems (e.g. "what can I find on YouTube?") rather than on essences found in single texts (e.g. the signed work of art in a museum)' (2012: 57).

For many scholars, though, the ubiquity of digital technologies – including 'ubiquitous photography' (Hand, 2012) – is about more than just the amount of digital stuff that is now being created. It is also about how the production, circulation and audiencing of digital materials (digital images, say) affect social and cultural life. Many argue that the technologies that enable all those YouTube videos and Snapchat photos are part of the emergence of new forms of social and cultural practice. Chapter 1 touched on one aspect of this argument in its discussion of the claim that a particular 'digital vision' is emerging that is visible in very many kinds of professionally produced digital imagery (Elsaesser, 2013). A more general argument has been articulated by Evelyn Ruppert, John Law and Mike Savage (2013). Drawing on the work of Bruno Latour (2007), they see 'digital devices as increasingly the very stuff of social life in many locations … reworking, mediating, mobilizing, materializing and intensifying social and other relations' (Ruppert et al., 2013: 24). This is very similar to the anthropological work discussed in Section 10.4.1, although it owes more to Latour's somewhat stronger emphasis on the agency of objects: certain affordances shape what can be done with the technology.

Exploring just how digital 'devices' may rework social and other relations entails a number of methodological decisions, of course. For many scholars, it is important to focus on everyday interactions with technologies, and explore how people are using technologies to do what they want to do. Section 10.4.3 suggested that ethnographic approaches to this task could be effective. A somewhat different approach is taken by Jill Walker Rettberg (2014) in her book on *Seeing Ourselves Through Technology*. Hers is a more discursive account, mixing discussions of specific apps and platforms from media reports and academic discussions with her own experiences. Digital methods are not the only way of studying digital images, then; as ever, the appropriate method depends on your research question.

However, other scholars have argued that, if digital technologies and social and cultural identities and relations are co-produced, it is necessary to look not only at what people do with technologies, but also at what the technologies themselves are doing. They are interested in how platforms for image sharing, for example, or social media platforms, have their own forms of internal organisation (Halavais, 2013; Ruppert et al., 2013). Hartley (2012), among many other new media scholars, emphasises how platforms like Facebook and Google depend on internal algorithms to sift their data, and that this structures what their users see in quite particular ways: for example, Google Maps prioritises in its search results those locations that have received most 'likes' (Graham et al., 2013), and it may therefore be shaping who goes where. Hartley (2012) argues that this means we need to understand online platforms and databases as more than the sum of their individual parts; we also need to understand them as systems that organise themselves – through their software – in quite particular ways.

This is the understanding that drives Rogers' (2013) definition of digital methods. To summarise: if, as it is claimed, digital devices are making us through new ways of organising all sorts of data about us, including images, we need to use those same devices and their methods to work out the effects of that organisation on social and cultural life.

Rogers makes a clear distinction between digital methods and other kinds of methods that use digital technologies. On his definition, methods that examine objects that are not natively digital are not digital methods, even if those objects have been scanned and uploaded to the web. So, for example, an analysis of eighteenth-century portrait paintings may have relied on looking at portraits in the online archives of many art galleries. While their online availability has changed the research because it has made many more portraits available for study, their interpretation cannot be a digital method because the portraits were not created digitally. Nor, on Rogers' definition, do digitised versions of pre-digital methods count as properly digital methods. Thus, according to Rogers (2013: 15), the cultural analytics discussed in Chapter 5 is not a digital method. Partly this is because it does not always study digitally created objects. Cultural analytics has been deployed on digitised versions of films, Impressionist paintings, manga comics and magazine covers, for example, none of which were created digitally. And even when it does analyse digitally created objects – it has also been used on Instagram photos of cities and selfies – cultural analytics does not use Instagram's distinctively digital objects for organising its photographs. It does not, for example, use tags

tags (very short textual descriptions of an image), likes or follows to understand how Instagram's photographs are organised: it only analyses their visual content. Indeed, this was a criticism of cultural analytics made in Chapter 5. Cultural analytics treats digital photographs as isolated objects, and analyses them by identifying patterns in very large numbers of them; it does not examine the ways in which Instagram's software structures their distribution. Thus even when it analyses digitally created images, cultural analytics is not a digital method on Rogers' definition.

'Digital methods' must therefore be deployed on those digital images that are fully embedded in online image-sharing (and social media) platforms and apps. Given that they pay particular attention to the ways that those platforms and apps organise the millions of photos that they host in order to present a specific selection on any one phone or PC screen, it also becomes apparent that digital methods focus particularly on the sites of the *circulation* and the *audiencing* of images. They look at online data – that is, data (like images) that has been uploaded to the web and is available for study there (Section 11.4 will mention the issues of privacy that this raises) – and they explore how that data is organised by the conventions and techniques of its platform using those same techniques.

discussion

image recognition software

There are also a large number of **image recognition software** programmes that can explore the *content* of digital images. They can search large collections of digital images and generate textual descriptions of those images; and researchers are also working on programmes that will be able to undertake searches for images based on the images' visual content rather than on the tags that have been attached to them (*New York Times*, 2014). Such software is commercial and currently very expensive, so will not be discussed further in this book.

This chapter will discuss digital methods in relation to an analysis of YouTube by Jean Burgess and Joshua Green (2009) and a discussion of Instagram by Tim Highfield and Tama Leaver (2014; see also Weller et al., 2013). Both of these studies look at digitally produced images – photographs and videos – and explore how the digital objects of their respective platforms (for example, Instagram's tags and YouTube's 'like/dislike' buttons) affect how the images on that platform become visible.

This definition of digital methods creates something of a paradox for this chapter, however, because digital methods for analysing visual images are currently still emergent. Burgess and Green's (2009) methods are not fully digital, and Highfield and Leaver (2014) are reporting on the early stages of their Instagram analysis. What this means is that this chapter cannot point to a selection of off-the-shelf software tools for analysing digital visual materials using digital methods as defined by Rogers. Currently, to use a digital method for analysing images, you need to know how to write software, or to work with someone who does. So this chapter does not contain a discussion of how to do a specific digital method for analysing digital images. Nonetheless, in a book like this it seems important to address the methodological issues that these methods raise, for three reasons. First, there are various projects afoot working to invent and share digital methods for working with images, and their results will surely be available in the lifetime of this book. Secondly, some readers may well be able to code, or know someone who can, and may want some methodological guidance on how to proceed. And thirdly, digital methods raise some interesting questions about visuality and digitality which are not simply technical and are therefore of interest to anyone concerned with how to study contemporary visual culture.

So, despite not discussing a specific digital method, this chapter discusses digital methods more generally in five sections:

1. The first is this introduction.
2. The second examines some of the issues surrounding how to access digital images.
3. The third examines some of the questions that digital methods examining digital images might usefully ask.
4. The fourth explores some of the ethical issues involved in using digital methods.
5. And the fifth assesses the usefulness of digital methods for analysing images, using the criteria established in Chapter 1.

11.2 How to Access Digital Objects for Digital Methods

The first step in deploying a digital method to interpret online images is to figure out what images you are interested in and why. Your research question should 'perform a cultural and societal diagnostics' (Rogers, 2013: 1–3), remember. And the images must be both digitally produced and digitally organised.

One important means by which digital objects are organised is by their **metadata**. Metadata is data that adds information to other data. To take   metadata
the example of an image file: if you take a digital photograph with a camera, that photo's metadata may include the camera's make and model,

whether a flash was used or not, when it was taken, and its location. (It is the date and time in this metadata that enables photo management software like Picasa and iPhoto to sort your photos in date order.) If you then tweet that photograph when you have turned on the 'Add a location to my Tweets' option in your Twitter account settings, the image file will be stripped of its original metadata by Twitter, but among the tweet's 32 pieces of metadata will be its location. Thus an image's metadata can be created by the device that created the image, and it can also be created by subsequent things that are done to that image – by Twitter's software, in the previous example, but also for example by you when, after you've tweeted it, you add a tag to that photo in the application you use to organise your digital photo collection on your desktop computer. The data carried by digital images, then, vary as a photograph (that is, an image file plus its metadata) circulates through different media. (Rogers' [2013] discussion of digital methods describes a much wider range of digital objects, but at the moment it seems that image files' metadata is the focus for most efforts to develop digital methods that can analyse images.) The first step in figuring out what digital objects you want to base your analysis on, then, is to understand what digital information is attached to the specific images you are interested in.

The next step is to decide which of those combinations of images and metadata are relevant to answering your research question. In their study of YouTube, Burgess and Green (2009: 7) describe their interest in understanding how YouTube, as a platform, functions as 'a mediated cultural system'. How is YouTube structured by its particular interface? What are its dominant patterns of use? What sorts of visual and other practices are becoming the norm on such sites? What is their 'shared and particular common culture' (Burgess and Green, 2009: 39)? In line with Rogers' argument, they assume that to answer those questions, they needed to use YouTube's distinctively digital objects. These were not simply the videos on YouTube, but the videos that YouTube itself had calculated were its 'most viewed', 'most favourited', 'most responded' and 'most discussed' over a particular period in 2007, and tagged as such. That is, they chose videos with certain kinds of metadata (the 'most viewed' tag) to study.

Once you've identified both the images and their relevant metadata, you then need to extract them from their online source, and turn them into your own dataset. This can be done manually, with a large enough team (Burgess and Green [2009] imply that this is how they downloaded the 4,320 YouTube videos that form the basis of their YouTube study). Or it can be done by using or designing a software programme **scrape** that can extract – or **scrape** – specified data from a platform automatically.

The digital method described by Highfield and Leaver (2014) for exploring Instagram functions like this. It involved writing code that hooks into Instagram's API, or application programming interface. The code in effect poses questions to Instagram's API, querying Instagram's digital objects. Highfield and Leaver (2014: n.p.), like Burgess and Green (2009), focus on the tags attached to images, in their case the photographs on Instagram, and report that 'the information about the tagged images returned through the Instagram API allows us to examine patterns of use around publishing activity (time of day, day of the week), types of content (image or video), and locations specified around these particular terms.' Highfield and Leaver's (2014) work builds on similarities between Instagram's digital objects and Twitter's. For a number of reasons, doing large-scale, quantitative analyses of tweets is relatively straightforward, and Highfield and Leaver suggest that using what has been learnt about tweets is a good starting point for analysing Instagram photographs, particularly given the similarities between the use of the tag in Instagram to label photos, and the use of the hashtag in Twitter to signify a particular issue. However, what they cannot currently do is analyse Instagram's visual content directly: their analysis is restricted to Instagram's images' metadata.

discussion

The queries that can be directed at online images include:

- queries that will retrieve images of specific form or shape or colour;
- queries that will retrieve images that have been tagged in similar ways by their users;
- queries that will retrieve images if their surrounding text is similar.

focus

A project which does not use digital methods because it does not analyse born-digital images, but which nonetheless gives a good idea of the process of digital methods, is *The Real Face of White Australia*. This project has extracted photographs from a part of the digitised National Archives of Australia. In the early twentieth century, the Australian government was asserting that Australia was white, which, quite apart from the treatment meted out to Aboriginal Australians, meant that thousands of Chinese, Japanese, Indian, Afghan, Syrian and Malay immigrants and their families were surveilled and policed in various ways; this often included having their photographs taken and being held in police or immigration records (remember the discussion of photography

the real face of white australia
home • about

FIGURE 11.1 Screenshot from *The Real Face of White Australia*. http://invisible australians.org/faces

in Chapter 9). These photos are the ones scholars Kate Bagnall and Tim Sherratt have scraped from the National Archives of Australia (NAA) and placed onto *The Real Face of White Australia* website, where you can click on the photograph to see the original record, 'revealing', as the website says, 'the real face of White Australia'. Here is a shortened version of Tim describing how he scraped the images:

> It didn't take long to find a python script that used the OpenCV library to detect faces in photographs. I tried the script on a few of the NAA documents and was impressed ... So then the excitement kicked in. I modified the script so that instead of just finding the coordinates of faces it would enlarge the selected area by 50px on each side and then crop the image. This did a great job of extracting the portraits ...

> Once the script was working I had to assemble the documents. I already had a basic harvester that would retrieve both the file metadata and digitised images for any series in the NAA database. Acting on Kate's advice, I pointed it at [the relevant section of the archive] and downloaded 12,502 page images. All I then had to do was loop the facial detection script over the images. Simple! ... after running for several hours, my faithful old laptop finally worked its way through all the documents. The result was a directory full of 11,170 cropped images. There were still quite a lot of false positives and so I simply worked my way through the files, manually deleting the errors. I ended up with 7,247 photos of people ... Then it was just a matter of building a web app to display the portraits ... It's important to

11.5 Digital Methods: An Assessment

This section cannot be a proper assessment of digital methods for analysing the online organisation of digital images, because few such methods currently exist for researchers to use. Nonetheless, even at this stage of their development, some aspects of the usefulness or otherwise of digital methods for a critical visual methodology are clear.

To begin with, it is evident that digital methods focus on the sites of the image itself, its circulation and its audiencing, and they do so by focussing on their technological modality in particular. Digital methods thus sit very comfortably with those accounts of the impact of digital technologies on social and cultural life which suggest that the machines – to use Rettberg's (2014) phrasing – are active agents in this life; that is, with approaches to visual culture that emphasise the importance of the material agency of digital hardware and software. Coming from a Latourian position, for example, Ruppert et al. (2013) explicitly endorse what they describe as Rogers' (2013) ontological claim about the organisation of social life by distinctively digital processes. In an odd way, then, digital methods do satisfy the first criteria for such a methodology that this book has so far used, which is that, to be critical, a visual methodology must pay close attention to the image. Digital methods do not do this by paying close attention to visual content of images in the same way as the other methods discussed in this book do, though. In fact, they pay attention to the visual content in very particular and rather limited ways, as we have seen both in this chapter and in Section 5.3 on cultural analytics, because software can only detect certain elements of the data contained in, or associated with, image files. Nonetheless, digital methods are based entirely on that data, and in this sense can be said to be very attentive to the image itself.

If Ruppert et al. (2013) are also to be believed, digital methods may be able to say important things about new, monadic forms of social difference that are emerging as digital technologies of many kinds intervene in many aspects of everyday life. As for reflexivity: digital methods simply do not discuss reflexivity, in the sense it was discussed in Chapter 2. There is no discussion of how the researcher's social position might affect a digital methods analysis. Indeed, Rogers' (2013) recommendation, noted in Section 11.3.2, that researchers should use a 'clean' version of Google as a research tool, is precisely about removing any impact you may have on its results. Paradoxically, though, this suggests that digital methods may be open to a certain kind of reflexivity. After all, the data trail left behind by everyone who uses Google is what constitutes (part of) the 'post-demographic' or 'monadic' sociality that online activity co-produces between technologies and people, and that includes researchers. Digital methods may therefore enable reflexivity about how the research results generated by digital methods are situated by the particular online profile of a researcher.

Digital methods certainly have potential as a critical visual methodology, then. However, there are also various issues that need some thought in relation to digital methods. One is the instability of web data and objects: a platform may disappear (as Myspace did), or an API be discontinued (Rogers, 2015).

Another is its particular definition of what counts as a digitally produced image. Rogers (2013) does not spend a lot of time elaborating on this. It is though rather less straightforward than he seems to assume. Take the example of the high-quality digital visualisations that are found on the hoardings around building sites, showing what the building will look like when it is finished (Figure 11.3). They weren't very common even five years ago, but they're now to be found on the billboards of even quite small building projects. Their production is certainly digital from its inception (Rose et al., 2014; Degen et al., 2015). These images are derived from the 3D computer model that is the architect's design for the building: sometimes the design software creates images as it designs the building, and sometimes the computer model is imported into visualisation software. Either way, software is used to create that intensely detailed and immersive imagery which Chapter 1 suggested was perhaps becoming typical of a contemporary 'digital vision'. These images are therefore digital at their site of production, for sure, and arguably at the site of the image itself too.

FIGURE 11.3
A digital visualisation on a billboard in Cambridge, UK

However, visualisers often try quite hard to make their visualisations look like photographs. Many visualisations contain bits of photographs cut and pasted into them, in fact, particularly photos of people, trees and other particularly complex objects. And many architectural photographs now are mimicking the intensity of the digital visualisations, with a preference for dusk or night scenes that allow lots of glowing light and dazzling effects, not least by using post-production software like Photoshop. The result is that it's often not possible now to differentiate between a photo and a visualisation of a new building. In terms of the image itself and its compositional qualities, then, this sort of visualisation remediates (analogue) photography in a number of significant ways. So can it be said to be a purely digital object? This returns us to some of the debates rehearsed in Chapter 1. For materialists focused on the ontology of objects, the answer would be yes, because the production of these images relies entirely on digital technologies. Indeed, Rogers (2013: 25) cites both McLuhan and Hayles as he develops an ontological claim for the distinctiveness of digital methods, although he argues not that such methods are materially distinctive (as do McLuhan, Hayles and other materialists discussed in Chapters 1 and 2) but that they are structured by distinctive software processes. For those more interested in the discursive framing of images, though – discourse analysts, for example – the answer might be more equivocal. If such visualisations are often described as 'photographs' when they are reproduced in newspapers – and they often are – and if the billboards on which they appear carry warnings reminding their viewers that a 'Computer Generated Image is indicative only' – which seems to imply that they might be taken as images of real scenes – are their digital qualities irrelevant so that they should be understood as photographs after all?

It also remains to be seen just how digital methods will be able to deal with the 'expressive content' of images. While image software is becoming increasingly adept at recognising what photographs show and even generating captions for photos automatically, as Section 5.4 noted, the mood or feel of an image is something else. But it is as important for digital images as for any other. Many digital images are created with the immersive, intense aesthetic of a contemporary 'digital vision', and that is crucial to images intended to sell urban redevelopment projects to would-be buyers, for example. But elsewhere, quite other expressive content is valued. A great deal of web content adopts what Nick Douglas (2014) calls the 'internet ugly aesthetic' in which 'it's meant to look like shit'. Whether polished and atmospheric or sloppy and amateurish, digital methods do not (yet?) provide a means for examining the compositional modality of the image itself.

Finally, many scholars remain sceptical that digital methods can address questions of cultural meaning. The same doubt appeared in Chapter 5's discussion of content analysis and cultural analytics; for many researchers, especially those schooled in the cultural turn, these automated and/or large-scale methods simply cannot focus on what matters in contemporary visual culture: people doing all sorts of complex, thoughtful, creative, 'idiotic' (Goriunova, 2013) things with all sorts of anticipated and unanticipated effects.

Summary: Digital Methods

- *associated with*:
  The analysis of digitally produced objects, using digitally distinctive forms of organising data.

- *sites and modalities*:
  Digital methods are most concerned with the sites of the image itself – its circulation and audiencing, in their technological modality

- *key terms*:
  Key terms include metadata, tag, folksonomy, image searches and scrape

- *strengths and weaknesses*:
  Digital methods that can analyse online images are not currently fully developed. Potentially, though, they will be able to analyse patterns in the content and distribution of online images, particularly in what they suggest about forms of social and cultural activity.

 COMPANION WEBSITE

Visit **https://study.sagepub.com/rose4e** for:

- **A link to the Digital Methods Initiative at the University of Amsterdam**, led by Richard Rodgers, the author of the key text discussed in this chapter. On their website, you'll find lots of tutorials on, and discussion about, how to do digital methods.

12

MAKING IMAGES AS RESEARCH DATA

PHOTO-DOCUMENTATION AND PHOTO-ELICITATION

key examples: the examples discussed in this chapter all use photographs, as part of either photo-documentation or photo-elicitation methods, in order to explore urban environments.

The chapter also looks more briefly at a range of other visual materials created as research data in the course of research projects.

12.1 Making Images as Research Data: An Introduction

This chapter looks at a range of methods attracting more and more attention in social sciences such as sociology, health studies, anthropology, education and human geography. These methods are distinct from all the other approaches to visual materials discussed in this book so far, because they do not work with *found* images that already exist distinct from a research project like Hollywood films, YouTube videos or family snaps. Instead, they work with images that are *made* as part of a research project. Such images can be made by the researcher, or they can be made by the people they are researching; and they can take many forms, including film, video, photographs, maps, diagrams, paintings, models, drawings, memory books, diaries and collages. Importantly, these are not visual objects that simply illustrate some aspect of the research project, what Marcus Banks (2001: 144) calls a 'largely redundant visual representation of something already described in the text'. Instead, in these methods, the images are used actively in the research process, as one type of data amongst others generated usually by interviews or ethnographic fieldwork. They are what is often called 'visual research methods'.

The two methods this chapter will explore are photo-documentation and photo-elicitation. As their names suggest, each uses photographs as its key visual element.

In photo-documentation, a researcher takes a carefully planned series of photographs to document and analyse a particular visual phenomenon. Photo-elicitation asks research participants to take photographs which are then discussed in an interview with the researcher; the data generated in this case consists of both the photographs and the interview. However, the chapter will also mention work that uses other visual media and briefly explore the specific contributions that those other media can make.

Many of the methods discussed so far in this book flow directly from a clear theoretical position. Semiology, psychoanalysis, discourse analysis I and II, and audience studies in particular are clearly predicated on specific theoretical frameworks that understand the visual in particular ways. This is somewhat less true of the anthropological approach discussed in Chapter 10, whose theoretical bases are materiality, performativity and mobility rather than visuality. But neither compositional interpretation nor content analysis are based on any particular theoretical position, no matter how broad, and this is also true of the three methods discussed in this chapter. They do not emerge from specific theoretical contexts, and so they can be used to answer a very wide range of research questions. In particular, such visual methods can and often are put to use to answer a research question that has nothing to do with visuality or the visible.

However, for its key examples this chapter chooses to concentrate on a number of studies that use photo-elicitation and photo-documentation as ways of understanding social relations and identities in contemporary urban spaces. Clearly, towns and cities are hugely complex, and visual methods can be deployed to access only certain aspects of them (Dicks et al., 2006; Emmison and Smith, 2000). Nonetheless, images such as photographs are seen as especially valuable in urban research because they can convey something of the feel of urban places, space and landscapes, specifically of course those qualities that are in some way visible: they can suggest the layout, colour, texture, form, volume, size and pattern of the built environment, for example, and can picture people too. Photographs can thus capture something of the sensory richness and human inhabitation of urban environments (though not all, of course: they cannot convey sound and can only suggest touch). The chapter thus looks at a body of work that uses visual methods to explore specific aspects of what is visible in urban environments.

It is also argued by many researchers that urban environments are experienced very differently by different people. Not all spaces are equally safe to everyone; not everyone has the power or resources to use towns and cities as they want; processes of deprivation, marginalisation and privilege profoundly affect how urban spaces are used and seen by different social groups. And many visual methods – photo-elicitation in particular, as we will see – are deployed with the aim of generating evidence about the ways in which social positions and relations are both produced by, and produce, distinct urban experiences. In that sense, all these methods are part of a critical social science aiming to explore and account for social difference and hierarchy. And, having said that they do not share a common theoretical source, it is nonetheless interesting that they have become much more popular over the past ten years at the same time as academic interest in the everyday uses of urban spaces (Highmore,

2002; Jacobsen, 2009) and in the sensory experiencing of urban spaces (Degen, 2008; Mizen and Wolkowitz, 2012; Pink, 2015) has grown.

This book has already explored photography as a specific medium in several places. Chapter 5 briefly discussed its complicity with colonialism; Chapter 6 rehearsed the debate about whether the photograph contained an indexical trace of the real or not; Chapter 9 described John Tagg's (1988: 63) Foucauldian account of photography as 'a flickering across a field of institutional spaces'; and the arguments in Section 10.4 imply that photographs can also be understood as performative visual objects whose affordances are activated, as it were, only by specific social practices. So how are photographs understood to be contributing to the efficacy of photo-elicitation and photo-documentation?

Surprisingly, the debates among theoreticians of photography are rarely cited in the social science literature discussing the use of photography as a research tool (Rose, 2014). Many researchers simply use photographs as records of what was really there when the shutter snapped. One of the first to argue for the use of photographs alongside interviews – John Collier – claimed that 'photographs are precise records of material reality' (Collier, 1967: 5) and that their value lay in the way this precision provided data for analysis. John Grady (2004: 20) agrees: 'Pictures are valuable because they encode an enormous amount of information in a single representation.' Photos are valuable too for the way they convey 'real, flesh and blood life', according to Howard Becker (2002: 11), making their audiences 'bear witness' to that life (Holliday, 2004: 61; see also Mizen and Wolkowitz, 2012). Others, however, argue that it is less the visual content of a photograph that matters and more how it is made and interpreted in the context of a specific research project. Now, even Collier's early argument for photo-elicitation claimed that it is only through interviewing that the information carried by a photo can be accessed by the researcher (Collier, 1967: 49). But more recent arguments suggest a more radical contextualisation of the knowledge that a photograph carries. The editors of one collection of essays on using visual methods for social research, Caroline Knowles and Paul Sweetman (2004a), for example, claim that they are uninterested in theorising exactly what photography in general is or does. Instead, they suggest that the photographs used by social science researchers are simply means to certain ends. They emphasise 'the analytical and conceptual possibilities of visual methods' in terms of 'what it is that visual methods are able to achieve' (Knowles and Sweetman, 2004a: 6), rather than in terms of what photographs inherently are. Given such debates over the significance of the site of the image and the site of its audiencing, it is not surprising that there remains no clearly established methodological framework to discuss the uses of photography in social science research (Becker, 2004; Rose, 2014; but see Pauwels [2010] and Wagner [2007] for attempts).

Such differences make the question of whether these methods constitute a critical visual research methodology rather hard to answer. Clearly, the criterion that images must be considered carefully, and as having their own agency, seems to be met by both those who see photographs as evidence of the real, as well as by those who argue that the interpretation of photos is always context-specific. In both cases, the role of the photograph itself is clearly present, either as self-evident evidence, or as evidence whose significance is established through the research process. The second criterion – that the research considers the social conditions and effects of visual objects – needs approaching rather differently when considering these methods, however. None of the studies I will discuss in this chapter uses photographs to examine the social effects of imagery (though such a use of photo-elicitation and photo-documentation could be imagined). And though some do explore the social effects of particular visualities, as I have already noted, the methods discussed in this chapter are not always directed at examining the social effects of visual materials in the same way as many of the other methods in this book are. Nonetheless, the question of the social effects of the visual remains relevant to these methods: not so much in relation to what their images do in the wider social world, but in relation to the social relations embedded in the research process itself. That is, the social effects of images with which these methods are most concerned centre on the relations between the researcher, those people they are researching, and the photos. And this means that the question of research ethics is much more overt in these methods than in others. Research ethics is precisely about ensuring that the social relations of a research project are ethical. A consequence of this concern with research ethics is that the third criterion for a critical visual methodology – reflexivity – is also usually quite central to research projects using photographs. Just how reflexivity has been argued to be part of ethical research practices using photographs will be examined in relation to each of the methods discussed in this chapter. Research ethics more broadly will be discussed in the penultimate chapter of this book.

In order, then, to assess the usefulness of these methods in relation to this slightly modified understanding of a critical visual methodology, this chapter has four sections:

1. The first is this introduction.
2. The second examines photo-documentation as a research method.
3. The third examines photo-elicitation as a research method.
4. And the final section assesses the strengths and weaknesses of these approaches.

12.2 Photo-documentation

Photo-documentation is a method that assumes photographs are accurate records of what was in front of the camera when its shutter snapped – 'a precise record of material reality' – and takes photographs in a systematic way in order to provide data which the researcher then analyses. A good example of this approach being put to work on urban environments is Charles Suchar's work on gentrification in the neighbourhoods of Lincoln Park in Chicago and Jordaan in Amsterdam (1997, 2004; see also Suchar, 2006). Gentrification is a process of change in long-established, rather run-down, but quite central urban neighbourhoods; new people, attracted by relatively low house prices and the centrality of the location, start to move in, with subsequent changes to a range of the neighbourhood's features. Suchar's earlier work was interested in the detailed physical, social and cultural changes that gentrification brought to the urban environment, both externally, to the streets and gardens, and to the internal decoration of homes. It focused on the individuals who moved into the areas recently as well as on long-term residents, using photographs of shops, roads, buildings and homes, and portraits of individuals.

discussion

One visual research method that this chapter does not discuss is **video-documentation**: the video-recording of naturally occurring social situations. Section 6.4 noted that this was a method often used by social semiologists, and referenced detailed discussions by Hubert Knoblauch (2009; Knoblauch and Tuma, 2011) and Christian Heath, Jon Hindmarsh and Paul Luff (Heath et al., 2009; Hindmarsh et al., 2010), which this chapter will not summarise. Other uses of video to create research data include asking research participants to carry video cameras as they do something, for example cameras mounted on the handlebars of bikes as part of research on cycling mobilities (Myrvang, 2008). Indeed, wearable technologies in general are beginning to make their debut as social science research tools (see for example Paterson and Glass, 2015).

It should be noted here that, while video has a long history of being treated as a descriptive tool that documents social activities, several scholars take a different approach to it and argue that it is a particularly effective tool for capturing the affective and non-representational aspects of social life. Charlotte Bates (2014) has recently edited an interesting collection of essays making this case, as does the ongoing work of Sarah Pink (2013, 2015; Pink et al., 2015).

video-documen-tation

Key to the successful use of photo-documentation, as Jon Rieger (1996) makes clear, is the careful conceptualisation of the link between the research topic – in Suchar's case, those changes associated with gentrification – and the photographs being taken. Suchar (1997) achieves this by using what he calls a **shooting script**. Shooting scripts depend on the initial research question being addressed. They are lists of sub-questions, if you like, generated by that overall question, and they guide a first go at taking photographs relevant to the research question. Suchar (1997: 34) uses scripts so that the 'information within [a photo] can be argued as putative facts that are answers to particular questions'. For example, one of the things that changes when an urban area is undergoing gentrification are the shops. They often go more upmarket, or more trendy. So the list of questions Suchar (1997: 37) set himself in relation to the aspect of gentrification was:

shooting script

- What variety of shops are found in the different areas of the neighbourhood?
- What do they sell, or what services do they provide?
- Who are the customers? Are they locals or do they come from outside the neighbourhood?
- Who works in, owns or manages these shops?

While Suchar does not discount taking photos in a more intuitive kind of way, a shooting script of this sort guides what photographs he takes and, most importantly, why: Suchar rightly insists that to serve as evidence for social science research, the photos must be clearly connected to a research question, and in his work this is achieved by the shooting script.

Such an initial shooting script guides the first stage of taking photographs. The photographs thus made, however, do not speak for themselves. To further develop their links to the research question, Suchar (1997) adds field notes to each photo he takes. This includes factual information (date, time, location for example), but also a paragraph or two of commentary on how each photo relates to the shooting script questions. Suchar also attaches labels to each photo, which he describes as a kind of coding (Suchar, 1997: 38).

The second stage of the process then begins. Attaching codes to his photos allows Suchar to begin to compare photographs. He could compare the same sort of stores, and compare different kinds of stores; he evaluated their storefronts, advertising and clientele. And from this process of comparison, facilitated by the first stage of coding, further codes begin to emerge. These codes might contribute to answering the research question; but they might themselves require further exploration. Suchar (1997: 39) also says that the photos themselves might throw up interesting issues that the questions of the initial shooting script didn't address. So a third stage of this process is to develop a second shooting script, to develop and refine the insights generated by the first.

Suchar (1997) develops his method by comparing it to a grounded theory approach to social science research (on grounded theory, see Strauss and Corbin, 2008). Grounded theory builds iteratively from detailed field evidence, and this is exactly Suchar's approach to using photographs as evidence; he says that he finds 'that reference to very detailed visual documents, and the information they contain, allows for a closer link between the abstractive process of conceptualizing and experientially derived observations' (Suchar, 1997: 52). And although the photographs show him patterns that would not otherwise be evident, their significance depends on Suchar's systematic coding of what they show. They are used as descriptive devices, the meaning of which must be established by the researcher. For example, although his photos of gentrifiers' houses allowed him to establish the importance of a certain style of their housing which he called 'urban romantic', the significance of that style in terms of its relation to social change is established by the interpretative work he does with the photos (and with photo-elicitation interviews with residents [Suchar, 1997]). The status of the photographs is clear in many of Suchar's (1997, 2004) published accounts of his work, where his photos are presented as illustrations of typical changes in these two urban neighbourhoods. They have captions explaining what they show, but those captions usually downplay any peculiarity in favour of presenting each photo as a typical example of the wider changes with which he is concerned. In his published work therefore, his photos serve to confirm and validate his analysis of gentrification.

FIGURE 12.1 From Suchar's study of gentrification in Chicago. The original caption reads '900 W. block of Concord Place. A typical collection of older cottages and new construction/housing units that have replaced torn-down structures. Spring 2001' (Suchar, 2004: 158)
Courtesy of Routledge

Photo-documentation can also be used to track changes in the urban environment over time. Change in urban environments can be tracked by repeated photographing – or **rephotography** – of the same place over days, months or years (Rieger, 2011). **Time-lapse photography** – where a series of photos are taken from the same place at regular, frequent intervals, and then spliced together – can track much faster changes in the urban environment, for example how crowds come and go over the course of a day. Paul Simpson (2012) used this method to track how a crowd gathered and then dispersed around a street performer over a period of around 45 minutes. He used a camera on a tripod and took a photo every 15–20 seconds; he also made notes about the event, especially what the performer was saying. He analysed the resulting 151

rephotography

time-lapse photography

photos by creating a time-lapse video of the photographs and then, playing it at different speeds, identified the rhythms of the crowd's movement as the performer intervened in the usual flow of pedestrians.

Photo-documentation as described here is not a widely used method in the social sciences (though, as Mizen and Wolkowitz [2012] point out in their introduction to a special issue of *Sociological Research Online* on visual research methods, many social scientists take photographs in a much less considered way as a means of 'realistically' documenting social life). However, it can be a rigorous and careful way of documenting visual appearances and relating them to social processes, which, with a reflexive discussion of the coding process, can certainly work as a critical visual methodology. Without that discussion though (as in Suchar's 2006 essay), it risks creating photographs that appear to be simply illustrative.

focus

You know that a local town always has a lantern parade down its high street three weeks before Christmas each year, to coincide with the Christmas lights being switched on. You are also interested in notions of 'community', a key term in the social sciences from their foundation in the late nineteenth century to today. Develop a shooting script that would begin to answer the question: does that parade generate a sense of community among its participants?

Things you need to consider include what theorisation of community you will be working with, what the visible effects of such a parade are, and how they might relate to that theorisation. You also need to think about what information and evidence you need about the parade and how you will get it: will you need to do interviews, for example, or participate in the local workshop events where the lanterns get made?

Finally, how does Suchar's iterative approach to photo-documentation work when you are interested in a one-off event?

12.3 Photo-elicitation

Photo-elicitation is, as Douglas Harper notes, 'based on the simple idea of inserting a photograph into a research interview' (Harper, 2002: 13). While the photo inserted into a research interview can be one taken by the researcher, or indeed an image found elsewhere, most photo-elicitation studies ask research participants to take some photos – and it is their photos that are then discussed in the photo-elicitation interview. It is a widely used method across a range of social science disciplines.

discussion

There is sometimes some confusion in the literature on visual methods between
photo-elicitation and **photovoice**, so it is useful to clarify the differences between
these two methods. Photovoice is a method developed in particular by Carolyn
Wang and Mary Anne Burris (Baker and Wang, 2006; Wang, 1999; Wang and Burris,
1997; see also de Lange et al., 2007), and comes in part from a specific tradition
of action research with disadvantaged and marginalised social groups inspired by
the Brazilian activist Paulo Freire. The point of action research is not just to study
something, but to engage research participants and researchers in a process of
social learning, analysis and empowerment, in the hope of eventually changing the
social situation itself. Visual images can be a powerful tool in this process (Carlson
et al., 2006), and a key difference between photovoice and photo-elicitation is that
the former is a process of ongoing and cumulative work with a group of people that
takes place over a long period of time. Photo-elicitation, in contrast, usually involves
just one or two interviews between the researcher and the research participant.
Photo-elicitation takes place over a period of a few weeks rather than the months
and years of an ongoing and long-term photovoice community empowerment project. And while photo-elicitation also speaks about empowering research participants,
this usually refers to the relation between the researcher and the researched, not
the relation between participants and the wider society.

photovoice

Photo-elicitation as a method is argued by its users to have four key
strengths. First, it is claimed that, since photographs carry a great deal
of information, they are 'an opportunity to gain not just more but different insights into social phenomena, which research methods relying
on oral, aural or written data cannot provide' (Bolton et al., 2001: 503;
Mannay, 2016). So it is argued that while ordinary interview talk can
explore many issues, discussing a photograph or a drawing with an
interviewee can prompt talk about different things, things that researchers hadn't thought about and places that researchers can't go (what
Louisa Allen [2012] calls 'unknown unknowns'). One project exploring
the importance of consumption to young people's identity in the UK, for
example, found that it was only when the young people were talking
about the photographs they had been asked to take that they directly
raised issues of race, ethnicity and religion (Croghan et al., 2008).

Secondly, it is argued that these sorts of interviews can prompt different
kinds of talk from other interview methods. In particular, it is often
suggested that photo-elicitation encourages talk that is more emotional,
more affective, more 'ineffable' (Bagnoli, 2009: 548). Namiko Kunimoto
(2004), for example, was researching the experience of Japanese-Canadians

interned during and after World War II. Although not initially designed as a photo-elicitation study, her essay demonstrates especially clearly how photos can evoke quite different kinds of memories in her interviews. She recounts that at the beginning of an interview, things would feel rather restrained and formal – until she asked to see any photographs from the internment camps that her interviewee had. Once the photos were retrieved, she found the whole interview changing, becoming much more intense and emotional as the photos stirred deep and often painful memories. Other researchers emphasise the ability of photo-elicitation methods to evoke the affective materiality of social life (Hunt, 2014; Pink, 2013; Pink et al., 2015). Thus for many researchers, photo-elicitation interviews evoke different kinds of knowledge from their participants than just talking would do (Darbyshire et al., 2005), and this richness of interview material is often emphasised by advocates of these sorts of visual methods.

Thirdly, many researchers also argue that elicitation interviews with participant-generated visual materials are particularly helpful in exploring everyday, taken-for-granted things in their research participants' lives. Asking them to take photographs of that life, and then to talk about the photos, allows the participants to reflect on their everyday activities in a way that is not usually done; it gives them a distance from what they are usually immersed in and allows them to articulate thoughts and feelings that usually remain implicit (Blinn and Harrist, 1991; Holliday, 2004; Latham, 2003; Liebenberg, 2009; Mannay 2010).

Fourthly, elicitation interviews with participant-generated images are also often argued to empower research participants. Getting research participants to say why they took a photo and what it means gives them a clear and central role in the research process, and also positions them as the 'expert' in the interview with the photographs as they explain the images to the researcher. Given the centrality of the research participant's expertise, several researchers also claim that photo-elicitation demands collaboration between the researcher and the research participants in ways that other methods do not (Allen, 2012; Liebenberg, 2009; Mannay, 2010; Rasmussen and Smidt, 2003; White et al., 2010). These claims have become considerably more nuanced in recent years, however, as researchers have used visual methods in a wider variety of settings and begun to reflect in more detail on the complex dynamics between researchers, research participants and the broader contexts in which research is undertaken (see Allen, 2012; Joanou, 2009; Lomax, 2012; Packard, 2008).

discussion

participatory

Many visual research methods are used in research projects that also describe themselves as **participatory**. Participatory research methods are those that attempt to hand over to research participants the creative and interpretative work involved in conducting research; they are often members of a community group or organisation. (Photovoice can therefore be described as a participatory method.) There is a very rich literature discussing the complexities of such participation, to which justice cannot be done here. However, both Claudia Mitchell in her book *Doing Visual Research* (2011) and Dawn Mannay (2016) in her *Visual, Narrative and Creative Research Methods* focus directly on participatory visual research methods, and there is also the very useful *Handbook of Participatory Video* (Milne et al., 2012; see also de Lange et al., 2007).

These four key strengths of photo-elicitation are in fact argued to be strengths of elicitation methods using any sort of visual materials. Advocates of photo-elicitation also add two further factors to the specific strengths of photo-elicitation. First, they emphasise the detailed information that photographs are understood to record, as noted in Section 12.1. Secondly, they report that asking people to take photographs is a good way to enrol participants into a research project because taking photographs is perceived as easy and fun, and participants get something from their involvement: the photos (Darbyshire et al., 2005; Wright et al., 2010). Indeed, taking photographs does seem easier for most people than, for example, asking them to draw, map, paint or work as a graphic novelist. Researchers using the latter methods all note that potential participants often need a lot of reassurance that any kind of drawing, no matter how unskilled, is perfectly acceptable and useful (Bagnoli, 2009; Crilly et al., 2006; Galman, 2009); indeed, participants in photo-elicitation projects may also need reassuring that they do not have to take photos that (they think) the researcher will find 'interesting' (Frith and Harcourt, 2007).

It is now possible to see more clearly why photo-elicitation is proving a popular method among researchers interested in the experiencing of urban environments, and particularly in how towns and cities are experienced by less powerful groups in society, for example the homeless (Hodgetts et al., 2007b; Johnsen et al., 2008; Klitzing, 2004) and children (Barker and Smith, 2012; Clark, 2010; Clark and Moss, 2001; Clark-Ibanez, 2007; Croghan et al., 2008; Darbyshire et al., 2005; Dennis et al., 2009; Dodman, 2003; Fleer and Ridgway, 2014; Jorgenson and Sullivan, 2009; Lomax, 2012; Mannay, 2010; Mitchell et al., 2007; Rasmussen, 2004; Rasmussen and Smidt, 2003; Thomson, 2008; White et al., 2010; Young and Barrett, 2001). Children's experiences of urban environments in the global North are often highly constrained by adults, and the past 20 years has seen a body of work emerge that listens to children's own views about the implications of their often-disempowered social position. Such work has quite often used photo-elicitation as a way of hearing children's views about the urban places they inhabit. This choice of method has been made not, as Philip Darbyshire and his colleagues (2005) make clear, because children are seen as inarticulate verbally, but for all the reasons listed above: the method is effective at recruiting children and young people and at recording the details of the places children use; it empowers children by allowing them to picture what they want to show and by making adults listen to their explanations and interpretations of their world; and the interview talk becomes rich and multi-layered when photographs are being discussed. The rest of this section draws on this body of work with children in cities in order to explore photo-elicitation as a method in more detail.

The first thing that looking at the use of photo-elicitation for researching children's experiences of urban spaces shows is that there are many permutations of the method. However, once the initial research question has been formulated and the research participants recruited – and it is important to note here that getting access to, and consent to work with, children often requires following extensive ethical protocols (Matthews et al., 1998) – there are six stages to a photo-elicitation project. Marylis Guillemin and Sarah Drew (2010) also offer a good discussion of the process.

discussion

Photo-elicitation is the most popular form of visual method currently in use across the social sciences. However, many researchers are experimenting with other kinds of participant-generated visual material, and argue that these other kinds of material can be especially effective at producing particular kinds of evidence.

Asking participants to draw diagrams, for example, is good for getting an overview of an issue because it encourages more abstract kinds of thinking and talk (Crilly et al., 2006). Maps of different kinds can explore relationships between different things (Clark, 2011; Jung, 2014); relational maps, for example, in which the research participant is given a pen and paper, asked to put themselves in the centre of the page, and then to add important people and places to the map – putting the most important closest to them and the least important furthest away – are a useful method for exploring relationships between people (Bagnoli, 2009). Getting participants to draw timelines can focus on significant events in their biographies (Sheridan et al., 2011), and asking them to make collages (Mannay, 2010), self-portraits (or 'visual autobiographies' [Esin and Squire, 2013]), or drawings can help in discussions of identity (Bagnoli, 2009; Garner, 2008; Kearney and Hyle, 2004; Theron et al., 2011).

Giving participants a camera and asking them to film a journey or a place is a way to explore both the corporeal and sensory engagement with environments (Bates, 2014; Pink, 2013; Pink et al., 2015), and to explore aspects of mobility (Murray, 2009). Participants' video-diaries have been used to explore questions of identity and visual appearance (Holliday, 2004). Asking participants to make a collage from all sorts of visual materials can give interesting insights into their visual culture, as they mix their own photos and drawings with those culled from the Internet and print media (Mannay, 2010; O'Connor, 2007). And memory books (Thomson and Holland, 2005), graphic novels (Galman, 2009), and 'diary-photographs' (Latham, 2003), which ask participants to write and create and/or collect images, have also all been advocated as ways of exploring social identity.

Many of the researchers using these methods openly admit that they are some-what experimental; but each also explains very carefully why the particular method they decided to use was appropriate for generating evidence to answer their research question. So you too should feel free to experiment – just make sure that when you write up your research, you are very clear about what you hoped your particular experiment would achieve and why.

12.3.1 Photo-elicitation: planning the practicalities

It is important before you start your photo-elicitation project that you give some thought to its practicalities. For a start, you need to think about how many partici-pants you need. In the studies of children's experiences of urban places cited above, the number of children involved ranged from 6 to 88, and the number of photographs from 57 to nearly 1000. So photo-elicitation projects can be quite small and focus in-depth on a limited number of participants, or be quite large. Deciding on the size of yours depends on a number of factors, not least how much time you have for the project; and this relates to another point: photo-elicitation projects are more time-consuming than research projects based on one-off interviews. You need to find your participants, meet them, wait for them to take their photographs, get the photos printed, arrange another interview, do that interview, chase up those participants who have not returned their camera, transcribe the interviews, and then analyse both pho-tographs and transcripts.

Then there is the camera to sort out. It appears to be common practice to give a camera to project participants, who take the photos for the project on that camera. These cameras are usually single-use, disposable cameras. The reason for this seems to be that they are simple to use, take decent pictures, and are cheap, so if they get lost or damaged it is not a big problem. This is particularly a consideration when working with younger children. However, Quaylan Allen (2012) says that for his research participants – middle-class Black men in high school – disposable cameras were not felt to be 'cool' enough to be seen using, so he bought cheap digital cameras to recruit students to his project. Whether disposable or digital, you need to buy the cameras, and think about how you are going to get them back from the participants and print the photographs fairly quickly so that you can then interview them about the photos while the process of taking them is still fresh in their minds. You might also want to consider the advantages and disadvantages of asking participants to use their own cameraphones.

You need to consider too where you are going to undertake the two interviews needed in a photo-elicitation project: an initial briefing interview and then the longer photo-elicitation interview proper. In many cases, interviewing in the participant's home would seem the obvious choice, but many projects that work with children access the children through their school. In the latter case, you need to be flexible enough to respond to the school's timetable requirements.

Finally, you need to prepare some documentation. One vital piece of paperwork is a consent form. The ethics of working with images is something Chapter 14 will discuss in more detail. For now, it is important to note that you should ask your participants to sign a form that says they are aware of what the project is about and they agree to participate, and if you want to reproduce the photographs they have taken, you should take care to ascertain that they also agree to that (and can change their minds later). Working with children produces some particularly complex questions about who can and should consent to research being done with them; researchers agree that as well as the child's consent, the consent of their parents or carers is also vital to obtain. Another piece of paperwork is an information sheet for your research participants, which may or may not be part of your consent form. Marisol Clark-Ibanez (2007) reproduces an information sheet she prepared for the children she worked with in South Central Los Angeles, briefly explaining what she wanted the children to do, how she was going to collect the cameras, and how to contact her with any questions.

12.3.2 Photo-elicitation: the initial briefing

All photo-elicitation projects start off with an initial interview with the research participants. The aim of this interview is for the researcher and the person they are interviewing to meet and establish some initial trust, for the researcher to explain the overall aims of the research project and what is expected from the participant, and for the participant to agree to sign the consent form you have already prepared.

This initial briefing interview will also obviously involve explaining what you want the participant to do with the camera. You might need to show your participant how the camera works. You also need to tell them what kind of photographs you are hoping for. Most photo-elicitation projects give their participants a fairly broad remit in terms of what they should photograph: a typical day (Hodgetts et al., 2007b), things or places that are most important to them (Clark-Ibanez, 2007; Dennis et al., 2009; Liebenberg, 2009), their world inside and outside their home (Mannay, 2010). Some projects set more focused tasks though: a project on the relation between young people's identity and consumption asked participants to photograph their favourite consumer goods (Croghan et al., 2008), and a project on how children perceived their journey to school asked them (rather leadingly) to take photographs of whatever they thought was dangerous (Mitchell et al., 2007). Disposable cameras place an upper limit of 39 on the number of photographs taken; if you decide to use a digital camera you may want to choose a maximum number of snaps. And don't forget to give your participants the information sheet to remind them what you are expecting and when and how to return the camera to you.

focus

Given that many children now, certainly in the global North, own either a camera-phone or a digital camera or both, and that they take a lot of pictures with them, what sorts of research questions could be answered by gaining permission to interview them about the photographs they choose to take outside the context of a research project?

In some projects it might also be useful to gather some preliminary data from the participant that is relevant to the project, or even to have a longer interview.

12.3.3 Photo-elicitation: printing the photos

The photographs are usually turned into prints, so that they can all be seen together by both the researcher and the research participant in the photo-elicitation interview. Once they are developed, some researchers suggest returning them to their makers without looking at them, before the photo-elicitation interview is held. There are two reasons for this. One is that the person who took the photographs may not, on reflection, want to show the researcher all the photos they took: some may be embarrassing, or show illicit activities, for example. Returning the photos to their creator before the interview gives them an opportunity to remove any they do not wish to discuss (Clark-Ibanez, 2007: 176; Croghan et al., 2008). The second, quite different, reason for returning the photos to the participant before the photo-elicitation interview is that it allows the participant to write a caption for each photograph, and in so doing the participant begins to reflect on the process of taking photographs in a way that then enriches the subsequent interview (Blinn and Harrist, 1991).

Whether the photos have gone back to the participant or not, it is a good idea to number each one so that you can refer to specific photographs in the interview (Clark-Ibanez, 2007).

12.3.4 Photo-elicitation: the photo-elicitation interview

The researcher then conducts another interview (or interviews) with their interviewees, discussing the photos with them in detail. All researchers using this method agree that this stage is vital in clarifying what photos taken by interviewees mean to them; by themselves the photos are meaningless. Some choose to show the photographs to the participant one by one, asking for comments on each; some spread all the photographs out together and the interview starts from there; some do both. The prompt questions are quite broad – often simply 'What does this show?' or 'Why did you take this one?' – and the interviewer then pursues and develops whatever topics emerge. It is also useful to allow the participant to reflect on the taking of the photographs as a process, rather than focus only on the photographs' content. As Darrin Hodgetts and his collaborators explain in relation to their photo-elicitation work with homeless men and women in London:

> In its most straightforward form, a participant might photograph an object such as a can of cider and then move, in discussion with the researcher, beyond this depiction to talk about drinking schools and other social formations often inherent to cultures of homelessness. It is common for photo-production participants to offer stories that take off from photographs, moving well beyond the depiction, and raising issues about the history of depicted events, relationships and places. (2007b: 266)

This is exactly why photo-elicitation (Hodgetts et al. prefer the term 'photo-production') is argued to be so productive: even the most banal of photographs – a can of cider! – can prompt participants to give eloquent and insightful accounts of their lives.

Doing photo-elicitation work with children – even children as young as three years old (Clark, 2010; Clark and Moss, 2001) – similarly produces very rich accounts of their worlds. Clark-Ibáñez (2007: 181) reports dreading an interview with one girl who had taken 38 pictures of her new kitten, her *gatito*, and nothing else (see Figure 11.2). But in

FIGURE 12.2
Janice's *gatito*, reproduced from the photo-elicitation study of inner-city children by Marisol Clark-Ibáñez (2007: 186)
© Clark-Ibáñez

talking about the kitten, the girl also talked about the pets she had had in Mexico, before her family's move to Los Angeles, which then prompted more talk about her immigrant journey. Darbyshire et al. (2005: 424) note that pets appeared very frequently in the photographs and maps made by children in their study, too. This was a large study of children's physical activity as it related to their health, and in particular to obesity, in Australia. Pets were hardly ever mentioned in interviews with children about their sports and play, but it was clear from the photos and maps that playing with pets was an important part of children's physical activities. Both these examples suggest how photo-elicitation interviews can produce very informative accounts by participants of their lives.

They also suggest that in talking about how urban spaces were experienced – in these cases through interactions with pets – these children were also presenting particular versions of their own identity to the researchers. This point has been discussed at length by Hodgetts et al. (2007b) and Croghan et al. (2008), and relates to how the photographs are understood in these photo-elicitation interviews. Clearly, photographs are used as evidence of material reality by all researchers to some extent: they record what was there when the shutter snapped. All researchers, in their assumption that the meaning of what is pictured in a photo can only be understood by talking with the person who took the photograph, also assume that the photograph is a representation of something. A can of cider can represent drinking schools, a cat a journey from Mexico to the USA. The image has a meaning: it represents something else, and the interview explores those representations. In these assumptions it is possible to see the two understandings of what a photograph is that this book has already touched on: the photograph as a trace of the real, and the photograph as a culturally encoded image. However, Hodgetts et al. (2007b) and Croghan et al. (2008) both argue that the photographs of photo-elicitation should also be seen in a third way, similar to the previous chapter's discussions of photographs: as visual objects put to work to perform social identities and relations. Indeed, Hodgetts et al. suggest that the photograph has no inherent meaning, even to its maker, because its significance depends entirely on the context in which it is being viewed:

> Photographs are things that people work with, use to explain and to show. Photographs provide a vehicle for invoking and considering situations, events and issues. The meaning of a photograph is thus more fluid and variable in response to the changing circumstances of the photographer, the viewers, and what is being done in the interaction between them. (Hodgetts et al., 2007b: 266–7; see also Barker and Smith, 2012)

That is, photo-elicitation interviews are sites in which the interviewees (and interviewers) perform their social identity by, in part, making and talking about the photographs they have taken. This leads Croghan et al. (2008: 347) to describe such interviews as 'forms of self-accounting', in which identity work is done that focuses particularly on the special features of the photographs. They note that 'the photo-elicited interviews in our study were often used to clarify and repair any problems in the presentations of self in the photographs, and of the consequences of that presentation in a broader social context' (Croghan et al., 2008: 351). A project working with schoolchildren in Ireland comments on how photographs discussed in the classroom had clearly been taken as ways of presenting particular versions of the children to their peers as well as to the researchers (White et al., 2010); and these accounts of the importance of the interview context also recall David Buckingham's (1991) discussion of the dynamics of group interviews with schoolchildren in their schools, discussed at the end of Chapter 10 (see also Buckingham, 2009). At the very least, this suggests the need for some reflection on the relationship being established between the researcher and the researched in the context of the photo-elicitation interview, and some consideration given as to how that is shaping the discussion of the photographs.

Some researchers also comment on the usefulness of asking interviewees about what photos they wanted to take as part of the photo-elicitation project, but could not (Allen, 2011; Allen, 2012; Guell and Ogilvie, 2015; Hodgetts et al., 2007b). The reasons given for not taking photographs vary wildly, but all can be insightful. Sometimes it matters to know that something isn't pictured because the camera broke down, or couldn't zoom, or, in the case of Cornelia Guell and David Ogilvie's (2015) study of commuters, because something that usually appeared in an interviewee's daily commute happened not to appear on the days they were carrying the camera. Participants' discussion of what would have been in a photo that was not made for practical reasons can be as rich as their discussions of photographs they were able to take. Sometimes, though, the reasons for not photographing something are more complex. For example, Hodgetts et al. (2007b) point to the way in which photographs themselves are also part of the 'self-accounting' just discussed. Participants' desire to picture themselves in particular ways to the researcher, or to the outside world, might lead them to deliberately choose to avoid photographs of less socially acceptable – or even illegal – activities, or to avoid repeating what they see as media stereotyping (see also Holgate et al., 2012). Discussing what photographs were not taken as part of the photo-elicitation project is thus an important part of the second interview.

Finally, some more practical points about the photo-elicitation interview. Ideally these interviews should be recorded. As the interviewer, always remember to say the number of the photo you are discussing out loud so you can cross-refer between the interview transcript and the photographs later. However, researchers working with children often point out that obtaining a decent audio recording in a noisy classroom is often impossible, so you may need good note-taking skills if you are discussing photos in that situation.

12.3.5 Photo-elicitation: analysing the interview and photographs

Once the photo-elicitation interview has been transcribed (if it was recorded), the transcript and the photographs are interpreted using conventional social science techniques.

There are a number of options here. If you are faced with a large number of photographs, you should consider doing some kind of content analysis to begin to get a sense of what they show. Several of the studies of children's photographs already cited use some kind of frequency count of the content of the photographs. Clark-Ibanez (2007: 178), for example, recommends categorising photographs either as inventories (or events that are part of institutional paths, such as photos of schools), or as 'intimate dimensions of the social' (such as photos of family), though I find these categories rather hard to distinguish between. Croghan et al. (2008) use a different approach and categorise their photos more simply into those that show commodities, people (subdivided into photos of friends and photos of family), and significant places. (In the process they discovered that, despite having asked their participants to photograph consumer goods that mattered to them, only 17.9 per cent of photos showed such goods, while no less than 71.8 per cent showed people instead – a good example of photo-elicitation allowing participants to shape the research project to their own ends.) Kim Rasmussen and Soren Smidt (2003) also divide photos into simple categories, in their large-scale study of Swedish children's understandings of their neighbourhood: places to be used by children in neighbourhoods (such as playgrounds), means of transportation, nature spots or nature objects, public buildings, private buildings and places, special persons with a connection to neighbourhood, and animals.

These frequency counts can occur alongside more qualitative analysis. Such analysis usually seems to involve some kind of coding process quite close to the discourse analysis I outlined in Chapter 8 of this book, although detailed discussions of this coding process in the literature are rare. Most researchers seem to treat the photographs and interview transcripts as one body of data, and devise a coding system that includes both of them, although some researchers work with their participants to develop the codes (see, for example, Dodman, 2003). An exception, however, is Patrice Keats's (2009) account of the analysis of textual and visual materials that formed part of the same research project. She suggests first taking a careful overview of all the data you have collected; then analysing the textual data and the visual data separately; and then exploring the relationship between the written and visual texts. This seems a useful approach with photo-elicitation, because it allows the specific roles of the photographs and the talk, and the relation between them, to be considered more directly.

Codes should reflect the status of the photographs in the interview: as inventories of material reality, as representations of social identity, and as objects whose meaning is negotiated in the context of the photo-elicitation interview. Codes need to acknowledge the complexities of the photographs as well as the talk. For example, it is important to recognise that, as well as what they show, some photographs are intended to signal what is no longer in a place. Rasmussen (2004), for example, discusses one photograph taken by a boy of the site where he and his friend had a play town out of mud and sticks, until it was washed away by the rain; Rasmussen (2004: 157) says, 'I have to admit that as an adult coming from outside this community, I cannot see what Anders "sees"', but does not explain how a picture that refers to something no longer visible was coded.

Finally, when analysing photo-elicitation photographs it is also necessary to explore whether the form the photographs take is influenced by other kinds of visual practice. For example, the relation between the photographs taken as part of a photo-elicitation project and the research participants' experience of family photography should be considered; Frith and Harcourt (2007) report that some of their participants' photo-elicitation activity was turned into a kind of family photography, shaping what was pictured and how. In relation to research with children and young people, the influence of mass media images of young people has been noted by several researchers (Croghan et al., 2008; Mannay, 2010; Woodward, 2008). Young people seem to want to picture themselves in the way that the media picture them, creating 'a particular view of teen-age identity as a fun time in which friendships are paramount' (Croghan et al., 2008: 349). In contrast, other groups may wish to picture themselves very differently from their representation in the mass media. Hodgetts et al. (2007b) argue that homeless adults deliberately emphasise the ordinary and the mundane aspects of their lives in their photo-elicitation work, to counteract the exaggeration of the extreme aspects of their lives in the media.

Clearly, interpreting the data generated by photo-elicitation interviews is complex. In particular, the relationship between the talk and the photograph needs careful consideration.

12.3.6 Photo-elicitation: presenting the results

Chapter 13 discusses the use of images in the presentation of research findings in some detail. However, writing up a photo-elicitation project entails some final methodological decisions which are worth mentioning here, particularly in relation to how the research participant photographs will be used.

It is fair to say that most photo-elicitation studies do not reproduce very many of the photographs taken by their participants, and indeed many studies do not reproduce any at all. An exception is Clark-Ibanez (2007), who includes 26 of her participants' photos (from a total of 959). Her choice of photos – which she does not discuss – seems often to emphasise the positive and engaging aspects of her young participants' lives; and, with her written text, the assertive presence of these photographs conveys a strong sense of the social agency of the children with whom she worked. Another strategy for reproducing participants' photographs is adopted by Rasmussen (2004), whose essay includes just a few photographs, chosen as good examples of the various analytical points being made about children's places in urban environments. These two strategies might be described as evocative and exemplary respectively: one uses photographs to evoke the social world of their participants, and the other uses photographs to exemplify how the photographs contribute to analytical understanding.

What of those who choose not to reproduce any of the photographs they worked with? This is not a decision that any of the studies cited in this chapter explains. I assume there may be several reasons. Perhaps the anonymity of the participants has been guaranteed; perhaps the participants refused permission for the photos to be reproduced; perhaps the argument that the value of the photographs in generating rich and complex talk means the results tend to pay more attention to the talk; perhaps the argument that the photographs create meaning in specific contexts of display and talk mean that reproducing them in a different context – that is, in the pages of an academic journal – would change their meaning and thus render them tangential to the paper's arguments. Whatever the reason – and there may be others I am unaware of – it is clear that as much thought needs to go into the decision about why, whether and how to reproduce photo-elicitation photographs as needs to go into any other aspect of this method.

12.3.7 Photo-elicitation: a critical visual methodology?

Photo-elicitation has a large number of enthusiastic advocates across a wide range of social science disciplines. It seems clear that it is a productive method, but also a complex one, in which the conceptualisation of the status of the photograph – as inventory, as evocation and as performance – has significant implications for all aspects of the method. For both these reasons, photo-elicitation practitioners tend to be highly reflexive in their use of the method, making clear their own role in the photo-elicitation work and carefully exploring the impact of the various 'contexts, genres and sites of elicitation' (Croghan et al., 2008: 346) in which they work. This attentiveness to the role of the image, to the research process, and to the researcher's role in the method certainly suggest that photo-elicitation can be a valuable critical visual methodology.

12.4 Making Photographs as Research Data: An Assessment

This chapter has discussed two methods that depend on making photographs as part of the research process, rather than using found images as the focus of research. It has identified the characteristics of photos that these researchers put to work, and looked at how those characteristics are related to the researcher's arguments and knowledge claims.

Advocates of both photo-documentation and photo-elicitation make photographs and then use them as data, subjecting them to specific forms of analysis: what they show can be interpreted via forms of content analysis, or by different kinds of qualitative coding, and interpretation usually takes place in the context of other research data that has been gathered by the researcher, very often interviews.

A challenge faced by both methods is the relation of the photograph to the social phenomenon being investigated by the researcher. The value of visual research methods is usually claimed to be revelatory: that is, images can show things that other forms of analysis cannot. However, photographs can only show 'embodied and material manifestations' of social phenomena (Allen, 2011: 488; see also Barker and Smith, 2012). Not everything that is of interest to a social scientist is necessarily visible in a photo, and projects using photographs as part of visual research methods therefore have to think quite carefully about the relation between the visible and the social. As Rieger (2011: 144–5) notes, 'The strength of the relationship between visual and social change ... varies: some visual changes seem to have little social significance, and there are social changes that may not have very obvious or prominent visual manifestations.' Another significant issue that may require careful thought is the relation between the photographs and the other data gathered as part of the research project, including the interviews with the photos. While photo-documentation and photo-elicitation methods rely on the unique abilities of visual materials to convey information or affect in ways that words find hard or impossible, both also rely on some kind of spoken or written work to make the effects of those visual materials evident, and many photo-elicitation methods also depend on other forms of data. However, data gathered by these various means can confirm, complement, elaborate or contradict each other, and the researcher must evaluate their different claims (O'Connell, 2013). Moreover, the relation between images and what is said about them in interviews perhaps requires more careful thought than it is often given, because such interview talk explicates images in complex ways (for discussion see Esin and Squire, 2013; Hodgetts et al., 2007b; Jenkings et al., 2008).

One further challenge that all visual research methods face is the question of research ethics (Allen, 2012). Research projects using visual research methods are subject to the same research ethics requirements as all social science research, but the visual research methods are often perceived to face particular ethical challenges, especially around the anonymity of research participants. This is discussed at some length in Chapter 14.

The final question to pose to these methods is whether photo-documentation and photo-elicitation are valuable as critical visual methodologies. Certainly many studies using these methods pay careful attention to the agency of the image and what exactly it can show and do in the specific research situation. Many of these studies are also methodologically explicit, explaining carefully what they chose to do and why, so there is an element of reflexivity too in very many of them. And finally, many use these visual methods to explore marginalised or disempowered people and places: children, the homeless. It seems, then, that these research methods have ample potential to work as critical visual methodologies.

Summary: Making Images as Research Data

- *associated with*:
  These methods usually use either photographs taken by the researcher, or images – which might be photos but could also be drawings or maps, for example – made by the research participants.

- *sites and modalities*:
  These methods can pay careful attention to the sites of production and the image, and to the site of audiencing in the form of the research participants. Interest in how the images may circulate beyond the research process is generally confined to a concern with the ethics of showing images.

- *key terms*:
  Documentation, elicitation, participation time-lapse photography, video-documentation.

- *strengths and weaknesses*:
  Images can show things and prompt talk that other interview types may not, and can therefore be used as evidence to develop and support, or to supplement, other forms of research data.

Further Reading

There are three collections of essays that contain a wide range of useful examples of visual research methods being put to work: one is a book edited by Caroline Knowles and Paul Sweetman (2004b), one a special issue of the online journal *FQS: Forum Qualitative Social Research* edited by Susan Ball and Chris Gilligan (2010), and the third is a special issue of *Sociological Research Online* edited by Philip Mizen and Carol Wolkowitz (2012).

COMPANION WEBSITE

Visit **https://study.sagepub.com/rose4e** for:

- **Resources relating to visual research methods**, and specific methods including photo-documentation, photo-elicitation, participatory mapping, participatory video-making, photovoice and digital storytelling.
- **Links to a number of projects that have used these various methods**, so that you can see them in action in more detail, which is invaluable if you are thinking of using some kind of visual research method yourself.

13

USING IMAGES TO DISSEMINATE RESEARCH FINDINGS: CIRCULATION AND AUDIENCING

key examples: the types of image discussed in this chapter as means of disseminating the results of research projects include data visualisations, photo-essays, films, interactive documentaries and exhibitions.

13.1 Using Images to Disseminate Research: An Introduction

This chapter looks at ways to use images to share the results of your research with different kinds of audiences. Showing research results in visual form is not new, of course. Geographers have drawn maps and anthropologists have made films since their founding as academic disciplines, and the graphs, diagrams and charts of quantitative social science also have a long history. In recent years, though, interest in disseminating research results by using visual images has been growing among social researchers across a much wider range of disciplines, and the kind of visual material that might be used to convey research results has also expanded. There are five main reasons for these changes.

The first reason is one that has appeared repeatedly throughout this book: for many researchers, images carry different kinds of information from the written word. The hoary cliché that 'a picture is worth a thousand words' is often used in support of this claim. More rigorously, researchers like Sarah Pink (2013, 2015) argue that still and moving images are particularly good at conveying aspects of the social world that may elude written description: colour, movement, arrangement, gesture, texture, sound. The discussion of photo-elicitation as a visual research method in Section 12.2 noted that this is the reason it is chosen by many researchers: they think that the images themselves are often more evocative of the sensory, as well as richer in information, than interview talk or written text can be, and that research participants' talk about images can be particularly revealing about the affective aspects of their experiences. These claims parallel a wider theoretical turn in the social sciences towards the concepts of affect, embodiment, the sensory and the emotional, as discussed in Chapter 1. All this suggests not only that images are useful in evoking affect, but also that affect is a particularly important thing to try to convey as part of research findings. And if it is indeed the case that an image and only an image can convey an important aspect of the topic under investigation, then it seems logical that images should also be used when the research findings are being presented. Which, as this chapter will explore, is one reason why many researchers are now choosing to create their own visual materials as a means of accurately conveying their research findings.

A second reason for social scientists turning to data visualisation is the recent interest in what is often called 'big data'. As Chapters 1, 5 and 11 have all discussed, the availability of very large datasets is encouraging something of a resurgence in quantitative and computational methods in the social sciences (although, as Chapter 11 pointed out, the technical difficulties in accessing the large numbers of images circulated on social media has meant that the full implications of that particular kind of big data have not really impacted on visual research methods as yet). Analyses of big datasets are often presented visually.

The third reason that many researchers are turning to visual materials to present their research findings is a claim that research conveyed in the form of images can reach more audiences, and different kinds of audiences, than the usual academic research output of a paper in a scholarly journal or a chapter in a book (Puwar and Sharma, 2012). Sometimes this is advocated on the grounds that visual images communicate their messages very powerfully, either because they can carry lots of information, or because images can be more affectively powerful than academic writing. Susan Thieme (2012: np) claims both about making a film, suggesting that 'representing research in moving pictures and sound can be far more evocative, immediate and detailed than in a written text'. Images may also communicate the results of research more directly because the format in which they are presented is more familiar to more people than academic work. If an argument is expressed not in the often-arcane vocabulary of the social sciences, but instead as a film or a cartoon (Bartlett, 2013), it may be much more accessible to non-academic audiences.

This relates to the fourth reason often given for showing research results visually, which is that most of us live in a very visual world. If more and more communication is happening through visual media, the argument goes, then academic research also needs to start communicating visually. Jessica Jacobs (2013: 714) opens her discussion of the use of film by geographers by making just this point: 'the Internet and digitisation are disrupting the hegemony of the printed word', she says, because platforms and apps include so many images, and she concludes from this that geographers (and other social researchers) should not only get better at interpreting films (and other visual materials), but also get better at making them in order to communicate their research more appropriately in the current moment (see also Hunt, 2014; Newbury, 2011).

The fifth reason that visual materials might be used to share the results of a research project is specific to participatory research projects. Participatory research projects – using methods like photovoice, or image-elicitation methods, both discussed in Chapter 12 – are concerned to empower the people who participate in those projects, and one way to achieve this is to make public the images that they have created to express their views. This could take the form of a film screening or an exhibition. Or it could take the form of a more focused presentation: a slideshow presented to a specific group of policymakers, for example.

Mentioning participatory research projects, and the importance they place on showing the results of their work to various audiences, raises an important point about the relation between this chapter and Chapter 12. Chapter 12 explored creation of visual materials as research data, particularly as part of photo-documentation and photo-elicitation methods. This chapter focuses on using visual materials to disseminate research results. Putting these two discussions into separate chapters might imply that there is a clear distinction between images studied as research data, including images created as data is analysed, and images created to disseminate the findings of a research project. This is not always the case, however. Sometimes the images that are treated as data, or as a way of analysing that data, are also used when the research findings are turned into some kind of output, academic or otherwise. This is particularly the case for participatory research because the whole point of participatory visual research projects is to facilitate research participants to create images that will be disseminated once the project has ended. It is also true, for example, of the graphs and bar charts reproduced as Figures 5.2 and 5.3, which were generated in order to analyse the data generated by the first stages of a content analysis, and then reappear in the book that summarised the insights of that research project. Hence, as Darren Newbury (2011) points out, the same image can serve as data, be merely illustrative of a written argument, or express part of the findings of a project. For many research projects, then, the distinction between images-as-data, images-as-analysis and images-as-dissemination is not clear.

discussion

arts-based research

The distinction between images-as-data and images-as-dissemination is also blurred in **arts-based research**. Arts-based research is 'an effort to utilize the forms of thinking and forms of representation that the arts provide as a means through which the world can be better understood' (Barone and Eisner, 2012: xi). It is a wide field, sometimes encompassing versions of some of the methods referred to in this book: photo-elicitation and collage, for example (Butler-Kisber, 2010; Leavy, 2009). Arts-based research also includes more specialised forms of arts practice though, such as sculpture, theatre, installation art and painting (all discussed in Knowles and Cole, 2008). It can be participatory, with the research process facilitated by an artist, or it can be conducted by the artist/researcher alone. The end product is usually 'something that is close to a work of art' (Barone and Eisner, 2012: 1) and is therefore created as something to put on display or to perform: it is created for audiences of some kind. (It is therefore also sometimes claimed that arts-based research can reach wider audiences than more conventional kinds of research [Boydell et al., 2012].) Arts-based research is thus not a report of findings derived by other means – it is not a dissemination technique.

Since arts-based research creates insights specifically through the creative possibilities enabled by the medium of a specific art form, its projects depend on arts techniques rather than social science research methods. So this book does not discuss arts-based research specifically. For readers interested in the field, Tom Barone and Elliot Eisner (2012) give a very good introduction and overview.

However, in some cases, and more and more often, researchers do decide to make images specifically in order to disseminate their research findings to various audiences. This chapter focuses on some of the ways to do that, and on some of the issues it raises. The chapter uses the four sites that have organised the book's discussion of visual methodologies, because the sites of the production of images, the image itself, the circulation of images, and their audiencing are as relevant to understanding academic uses of images as they are to any other kind. The chapter's examples are of different kinds of images, produced and circulated in different ways, and with different (anticipated) relationships to their audiences.

This chapter has six sections:

1. The first is this introduction.
2. The second looks at data visualisation.
3. The third looks at photo-essays.
4. The fourth looks at making films.
5. The fifth section examines multimedia websites.
6. And the final section explores the strengths and weaknesses of using images to disseminate research findings.

13.2 Data Visualisation

Data visualisation means representing data in a visual format in order to discover its patterns (Manovich, 2011); sometimes the term **infographic**   infographic is used to refer to the same thing. Visualising data, especially quantitative data, is a common practice in the social sciences. Chapter 5 on content analysis and cultural analytics showed examples of how quantitative visual methods might generate visualisations of data. Data visualisations are also increasingly popular in other fields: both *The Guardian* and the *New York Times* newspapers design striking data visualisations as part of their online news analysis. Many of these online infographics are animated and many are interactive: that is, the viewer can alter the data they show by clicking on a menu option or hovering over different parts of the screen. Many online datasets are now also accompanied by visualisation tools to help users make sense of the data they contain. This section briefly reviews some debates about data visualisation, and some of the issues at stake in using data visualisations as part of social science research.

13.2.1 Visualisation and the spectacularisation of research findings

John Grady's (2011) discussion of visualisation in social analysis suggests that visualising data is a craft, and an essential one for social researchers, because it allows them to draw on what he calls 'the cognitive competency of the eye' (Grady, 2011: 495).

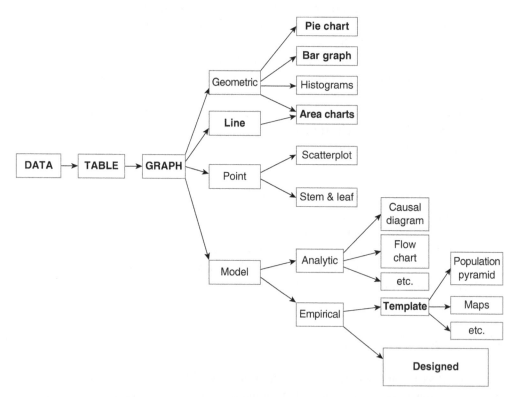

FIGURE 13.1   A typology of non-animated visual displays of information (Grady, 2011: 496)

He suggests that turning quantitative data into pictures allows the researcher to see patterns and thus to make discoveries about that data that would otherwise remain obscure. He is thus advocating visualising data as a means of analysing it more effectively. Grady (2011) focuses on quantitative data (survey data in particular), and he discusses the various kinds of graphs and charts that can be made using Microsoft's Excel spreadsheet. As he points out, to create a bar chart that is both useful and understandable is a skill that cannot entirely be delegated to the software, so he pays some attention to questions of layout and readability. However, he is mostly concerned with how different ways of displaying different data can yield analytical insight. His charts and graphs are therefore all pretty basic. It could be said that his interest in what might be called the aesthetics of data visualisation is subordinate to the usefulness of the analytical insights the visuals can generate (which is not to say that his visuals do not have an aesthetic).

This is somewhat different from the recent popular interest in data visualisation, especially among journalists. There, the claim is both that 'information is beautiful' (McCandless, 2012) and that beauty can be a tool for improving the understanding and analysis of information. The emphasis is thus on 'the explanatory power of beauty' (McCosker and Wilken, 2014: 155). Some academics are also utilising that power to create gorgeous data visualisations, many of which are based on different kinds of mapping. Figure 13.2 is an example of a different kind of aesthetic: brutal (the central data visualisation looks like a bleeding bullet hole), to show data about some of those who died in the First World War.

FIGURE 13.2   This interactive data visualisation uses data from the Commonwealth War Graves Commission to show the numbers of men and women from Commonwealth countries who died fighting in the First World War; http://codehesive.com/commonwealthww1/ data based on Commonwealth War Graves Commission Records; design by James Offer

discussion

If you are interested in learning the basics of designing data visualisations, the classic texts are by Edward Tufte, especially his *Envisioning Information* (1991) and *The Visual Display of Quantitative Information* (2001).

Grady (2011) rightly emphasises that the beautiful visualisations produced by professional designers for newspapers require excellent skills in both design and in using graphics software, as well as a good understanding of the data to be visualised. While a social science researcher will understand the data, they are very unlikely to have the design or technical skills necessary to produce those sorts of complex visualisation. Grady (2011) thus raises an important issue that will recur throughout this chapter – whether social science researchers have the skills necessary to create effective kinds of visualisation. With the exception of anthropologists who learn how to make ethnographic films, neither filmmaking nor photography – let alone graphic design – are part of the training of social science researchers (although some geographers might learn about mapmaking). This is the reason for Grady's (2011) decision to focus on a well-known and widely available spreadsheet package for his discussion of using visualisations to analyse data. He is suggesting, in effect, that social researchers should stick to what we know best, which is the careful analysis of data, and that we should more-or-less rely on software to make the visual presentation of that analysis clear and legible. Other social science researchers discussed in this chapter, facing a similar skills gap, make a different decision, and choose to collaborate with professionals who have those skills.

discussion

The basic process of data visualisation is a translation from data to visual format. Generally,

> we map the properties of our data that we are most interested in onto a topology and geometry. Other less important properties of the objects are represented through different visual dimensions – tones, shading patterns, colours or transparency of the graphical elements. (Manovich, 2011: 39)

However, Lev Manovich (2011) argues that his own data visualisations – produced as part of the cultural analytics method discussed in Chapter 5 – are rather different from this. Rather than translating just some specific properties of a larger dataset into visual form, cultural analytic visualisations (and some other data visualisation formats like tag clouds) are 'direct visualisations' (Manovich, 2011: 47). They do not 'reduce' data before visualising it, as happens when the specific properties of a dataset to be visualised are selected, or the data summarised and then visualised; instead, cultural analytics creates new representations built directly from all the existing data.

Views about the data visualisations that can be generated to show research findings are diverse. In their discussion of data visualisations of big data, Anthony McCosker and Rowan Wilken (2014) suggest that the insight to be derived from this sort of often-spectacular image is not in fact the clarity of analytical patterns as suggested by Grady (2011), but rather the evocation of intensity and flow that corresponds most closely to the specifically Deleuzian notion of 'the diagram'. Deleuze's discussions of 'the diagram' do not take the diagram to be an explanatory tool but rather a form of indicating non-representational fields of affective intensity and flow.

Johanna Drucker (2011), however, is rather suspicious of that affective intensity. In a polemical essay, she argues that many data visualisations are so focussed on their spectacular effects that they do not pay enough attention to the data itself. She suggests that data visualisations tend to focus too closely on doing things with the data without paying enough attention to who generated that data and why, how reliable it is, what categories it assumes, and so on. Data visualisations – especially the visually seductive ones – thus tend to gloss over the crucial fact that data is not equivalent to the real world, she claims: 'Rendering *observation* (the act of creating a statistical, empirical, or subjective account or image) as if it were *the same as the phenomena observed* collapses the critical distance between the phenomenal world and its interpretation' (2011: n.p.). For Drucker, data visualisations therefore need to get much better at foregrounding questions of interpretation in the audience's mind, and Figure 13.3 reproduces two images from a project aiming to do just that in relation to what can be found on Wikipedia. Drucker herself suggests some ways in which the kinds of graphics that Grady (2011) discusses might be rendered more obviously interpretative:

> the most striking feature distinguishing humanistic, interpretative, and constructivist graphical expressions from realist statistical graphics is that the curves, bars, columns, percentage values would not always be represented as discrete bounded entities, but as conditional expressions of interpretative parameters – a kind of visual fuzzy logic or graphical complexity. Thus their edges might be permeable, lines dotted and broken, dots and points vary in size and scale or degree of ambiguity of placement, and so on. These graphical strategies express interpreted knowledge, situated and partial, rather than complete. (Drucker, 2011: n.p.)

While Grady (2011) does discuss the production of the data he uses at some length in his text, Drucker (2011) is advocating embedding indications of the situatedness and partiality of the data into its graphical representation. These debates have implications for the design of data visualisations.

FIGURE 13.3A
A map showing the location of the geotags attached to Wikipedia articles written in English

FIGURE 13.3B
A map showing the location of the geotags attached to Wikipedia articles written in Egyptian Arabic

FIGURE 13.3   One form of the partiality of data is the language that information is written in, which shapes who can create information, what can be said, and who can interpret what is said. Here, two maps show which places in the world are described in Wikipedia in two different languages. It is clear that many more places are described in English (for a fuller discussion, see Graham et al., 2014)

13.2.2 Designing a data visualisation

Section 13.2.1 suggested that visualising data is by no means straightforward – even if there are an increasing number of software tools that allow you to do so in an increasing variety of formats. There are therefore a number of issues to consider when visualising data (see also Figure 13.4):

- What are the key research findings you want your visualisation to display?
- How will your visualisation embed specific knowledge claims? For example, do you want it to be a 'direct' or a 'reduced' visualisation, to use Manovich's (2011) terms? Do you want it to refer to the partiality or situatedness of its data? If so, how will you do that?
- Who is the intended audience for your visualisation? Will that audience have certain skills in understanding particular kinds of visualisation? Will the site of the visualisation's display make a difference to what it should be?

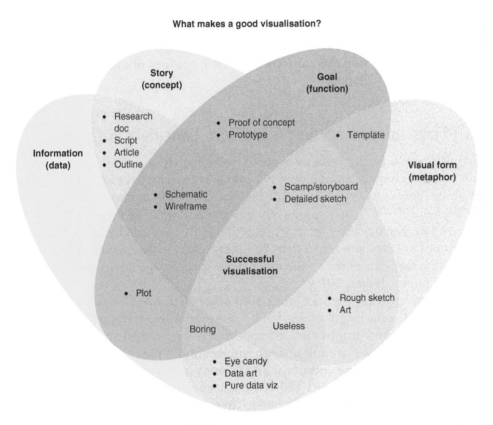

FIGURE 13.4 The important things to consider when visualising data, according to David McCandless (2015)

- Only now should you start to think about the visual format that might best show your findings. Is a bar chart, a diagram, or map the most appropriate format? Still or animated? Do you want to convey diagrammatic intensity or representational clarity? Interactive or not? Tufte (1991, 2001) has lots of food for thought here.
- Design your visualisation.

13.3 Photo-essays

A photo-essay is a combination of writing with photographs. The writing can range from extended captions to book-length studies, and the photographs must be at least as important as the text to the photo-essay's impact (Newbury, 2011). W.J.T. Mitchell (1994: 290) says that the photo-essay is 'a truly composite form' because of this equality between text and image. Being able to take (and edit) really good photographs – like designing good data visualisations – is not a skill that social researchers necessarily have, and some photo-essays are therefore collaborations between a photographer and a researcher. However, digital cameras do now enable most people to take at least decent photographs; and on that basis, making a photo-essay is probably one of the least difficult ways of showing the findings of a research project visually. This section therefore spends a bit more time discussing this method than the others in this chapter.

13.3.1 Photo-essays: some preliminary considerations

So why might you consider creating a photo-essay as part of your research project? Well, photo-essays rely on the ability of photographs to carry large amounts of information about 'how culture and social life looks … that's difficult to represent in text alone' (Wagner, 2007: 47); they can display 'the taken-for-granted moments that communicated ethnographic meaning' (Harper, 2006: 158). They also build on the ability of photographs to carry more than that. Photo-essays are also argued to be powerful devices because they can evoke a wide range of sensory and affective responses in the viewer of the photos (Hunt, 2014).

One of the foremost exponents of the photo-essay method is Douglas Harper, and he has reflected at some length on his book *Changing Works* (Harper, 2001), which uses both his own photographs and archival images. He is insistent on the ways in which both sets of images are full of both information – they show specific places and people – but also representations, always making particular arguments. And following Harper, Marcus Banks (2008: 47) argues that one of the things that photo-essays can do is present an argument. They can offer an analysis of a particular social situation, as Muntadas (2005) did in his photo-essay on the Guggenheim

Bilbao, part of which was reproduced in Figure 9.9. Indeed, Carol Marley's experience in starting to take photographs as part of a research project about immigration is that you have to have an argument – or at least a conceptual framework – to enable you to work out what you want to photograph (Gilligan and Marley, 2010).

The other thing that Banks (2008) suggests a photo-essay can do is to offer a sense of the subjective experiencing of a social situation. What does it feel like to be there? While most photo-essays contain elements of both of these, perhaps a first step in considering how to put a photo-essay together is to decide whether you want it to analyse something, or to evoke something. Do you want to create an argument or a feeling for your audience, or both? And of course, answering this depends on the larger theoretical context in which your project is grounded.

An example of a city being photographed as both an 'inventory' and as 'a way into the macrosocial process through which the global world is organized' is Hong Kong, in a book by Harper and sociologist Caroline Knowles (Knowles and Harper, 2009). However, I think it is fair to say that photographs have mostly been used to evoke the sensory experience and feel of urban environments, or what Alan Latham (2003) calls their 'texture'. Geographers and others have long been interested in the elusive qualities that define senses of place, and some are now using photography to convey the feel of particular places. Tim Edensor's (2005) book about industrial ruins is exemplary here (see also Liggett, 2007). Edensor uses photographs throughout his book to evoke excessive qualities of ruins. In fact, he uses photographs in two ways. First, he records ruins themselves, before they are demolished or renovated or disintegrate entirely, noting that photos 'can reveal the stages and temporalities of decay' (Edensor, 2005: 16). Secondly, he suggests that photographs convey some of the experiential qualities peculiar to ruins:

> Photographs are never merely visual but in fact conjure up synaesthetic and kinaesthetic effects, for the visual provokes other sensory responses. The textures and tactilities, smells, atmospheres and sounds of ruined spaces, together with the signs and objects they accommodate, can be empathetically conjured up by visual material. (Edensor, 2005: 16)

Occasionally, the ruins' decay seems to have infected the form of Edensor's photos. They too sometimes lose definition and meaning, and it is impossible to make out what they are 'of' (Figure 13.5 reproduces one of these). Edensor also induces the feel and texture and strange obscurity of ruins by inserting the photos uncaptioned into his text. There they work as a kind of visual supplement to his arguments, hanging unreferenced, perhaps 'utilised as an alternative source of information independent from the text' (Edensor, 2005: 16), and in any case always suggesting that there is more to ruins than Edensor's textual interpretation can convey.

A photo-essay can have two effects, then: the analytical and the evocative. To achieve either, or both, it is crucial to consider the relation between the photographs and the text. As I have already noted, in a photo-essay the photographs are as important as the text in conveying the meaning of the photo-essay. But as W.J.T. Mitchell (1994: 281–322) makes clear, the relation between text and photographs can take different forms, and it is that form that requires careful consideration.

The text and the photographs may, for example, be doing the same thing: making the same argument, evoking the same feeling. Often this is achieved either by captioning the photographs fully or referring to them directly in the text. Certainly in analytical photo-essays I think this explicit cross-referencing is vital. Hence Helen Liggett (2007: 22–3) takes care in her photo-essay on urban space to explain just what she intends the reader to see in the photos. However, Howard Becker (2002) has discussed an example of a photo-essay in which the photographs work to support the arguments of the text without any explicit cross-referencing between them – a book written by John Berger and heavy with photographs by Jean Mohr, called *A Seventh Man* (Berger and Mohr, 1975), about the experiences of men migrating from poorer to more affluent parts of Europe. The photos are never referred to directly by the text, and their minimal captions are listed at the end of the book rather than next to the relevant photo. Nonetheless, the photos ask the reader to work to make sense of them; they are not all easy to respond to; there is a depth to the engagement they invite that again suggests a seriousness of purpose to Mohr's work. Becker (2002) thus calls Mohr's photographs 'specified generalizations'. They add something to Berger's generalisations about migration and its effects: they specify them. They show what they really are, what they look like, what they do – they make them believable. And Becker argues it is the peculiar ability of photos to do this, to show 'flesh and blood' as if for real:

> What can you do with pictures that you couldn't do just as well with words (or numbers)? The answer is that I can lead you to believe that the abstract tale I've told you has a real, flesh and blood life, and therefore is to be believed in a way that is hard to do when all you have is the argument and some scraps and can only wonder if there really is anyone like that out there. (Becker, 2002: 11)

Becker is arguing that the effect of Mohr's photos is, in the end, to affirm the veracity of Berger's text. The photos do not simply illustrate the researcher's arguments; they work more actively to convince us that those arguments are correct. The visual qualities of the photographs are being used to make the reader believe what the text of the book is telling us.

Another strategy for photo-essays, though, is for the photographs and text to work against each other in some way. Perhaps the photographs suggest that there is more to a situation than the text is offering; perhaps the text points to wider social relations that the photographs cannot show.

So, in thinking about a photo-essay, you need to consider whether it will tend towards the analytical or the evocative or both; and what the relation between the photographs and the text will be.

discussion

In their project *Small is Beautiful?*, geographers Caitlin DeSilvey and James Ryan travelled with photographer Steven Bond around the south-west of England looking for 'broken things and the people who mend them'. Their interpretation of the relations between the craftspeople they met, the things they mended, and the tools they used have appeared in a number of different forms: as a blog and a website (*Celebration of Repair*, 2015), as exhibitions, as a book (Bond et al., 2013), and as a paper in the journal *Cultural Geographies* (DeSilvey et al., 2014).

They describe the relation between Steven's photographs and the text written by Caitlin and James like this:

> As we sorted, the images fell into relation with each other in resonant triptychs, and we let them. For each photo we made a small text box and we filled until it was full, the words settling in place like handfuls of screws or buttons in a square tin ... The words try to inhabit (and illuminate) the peculiar space created by each photograph, a space which is, as Walter Benjamin intuited,

immense and unexpected. Whole worlds are contained in a fleck of paint, a twist of loose thread. We find ourselves wandering through landscapes where odd textures and atmospheres remind us of something or some place we can't quite name – the smell of a grandfather's workshop, perhaps, or a tactile childhood memory of the greasy resilience of smooth leather, the shock of cold steel. (DeSilvey et al., 2014: 657)

This method of working with the photographs depends on the argument that photographs evoke the affective. One part of one of their triptychs of photographs is reproduced as Figure 13.6. Compare it to Figure 9.9, which is an extract from another photo-essay and which seems to me to be an attempt at an analysis in visual form.

And on the tailor's table, two pairs of steel shears lie side by side, both close to a foot long, and weighing over a pound each. One pair, which has a worn leather sheath around the loop of one handle, was manufactured in Sheffield; the other came from Newark, New Jersey. How does the tailor decide which of the two to use when faced with a piece of fabric that needs cutting? What fine distinctions of edge and angle does he set against considerations of weave and weight? The equivalence of the shears is illusory; each pair has specific capacities and proficiencies, learned (and shaped) by the tailor over the 72 years since he was trained as a young boy in Birmingham in what he calls 'the art of cutting'.

R. Pavely, Fortuneswell, Dorset

FIGURE 13.6   A photograph and its text from DeSilvey, Ryan and Bond's essay '21 Stories' (2014: 670–1)
© Steven Bond

13.3.2 Photo-essays: putting one together

All this suggests that the sorts of question you need to consider when making a photo-essay might include the following:

- What's the conceptual framework you've been working with, and what is it you want the photographs to do in relation to that framework?
- Related to this, do you want to tend towards making an argument or evoking a feeling, or both? Why?
- Will the photographs speak for themselves, or do you want to tie them tightly into the text? So do you need a draft of that text already? Or will you start writing after you've taken some photos?
- What will the relationship between the photographs and the text be? What layout do you want? How large should photographs be? Where will they be placed on each page and in relation to each other? What sort of text, if any, should accompany each? Do you need – or are you being asked to work with – some kind of designer

to make these decisions? Newbury (2011: 655–62) has an interesting discussion about these sorts of choices.

- Who are you assuming will be looking at and reading your photo-essay? Who is its audience? This question is only rarely addressed in the discussions of photo-essays mentioned in this section; Section 13.6 will return to this point.
- What format are you going to use to create the photo-essay? Will it be a paper, a dissertation, a book? A printed pamphlet? A download-able pdf? An exhibition?
- Given all that, what photographs do you want to use? Becker (2002) points out that in *A Seventh Man*, there are enough of Mohr's photos, from different places and showing different things, to give an impression of properly comprehensive coverage (see also Wagner, 2007: 47–8). What photographs do you need to similarly convince your reader that your photographs are credible? Why do you want to photograph specific things? What kinds of content, framing, focus, colour, perspective and so on might help you achieve the effects you want? (It might be useful to go back here to Chapter 4 on compositional analysis to get some ideas.) Would some comparisons be effective (Harper, 2003: 259)? Between what and why?
- Do you want to include photographs that you haven't taken? If you do, will you need to get copyright clearance? (Chapter 14 discusses copyright in a little more detail.)
- Are there any ethical considerations relating to any of the photographs you are considering using?
- Finally, following Newbury (2011: 662), take a look at some photo-essays that you like and see what you can learn from them.

In short, creating a social science photo-essay is not the same as being a documentary photographer, as Wagner (2007) discusses at some length, and you need to be clear about what you are doing and why: how does your photo-essay articulate the social science argument you are making for the wider audience you are imagining?

13.4 Films and Videos

Another possibility for making a visual account of a research project is to make a film.

13.4.1 Ethnographic film as a context

Anthropology as an academic discipline has a long tradition of high-quality, 50- or 90-minute **ethnographic films**, and excellent accounts of

ethnographic films

ethnographic filmmaking are available (see for example Banks, 2001; Banks and Ruby, 2011; Barbash and Taylor, 1997; Pink, 2013; and on filmmaking more generally see Thurlow and Thurlow, 2013). Making this sort of film is a specialised and technically demanding process which requires a lot of expensive equipment as well as a production team (getting good-quality sound recording is a different task from directing the filming, for example, and a film editor will have an entirely different skillset again). All this is unlikely to be accessible to most readers of this book and indeed to most researchers in the social sciences.

There have however been some collaborations between researchers and film-makers to make such extended films. Susan Thieme (2012) discusses her experience of such a collaboration in relation to a film called *The Other Silk Road*, about migrant workers within and from Kyrgyzstan in Central Asia. The 28-minute film (with some other accompanying visual material) took 15 months to make. She describes the collaboration in terms of a series of 'interfaces' with her research participants, with the various members of the filmmaking crew, and with the film's sponsor, a media-focussed NGO. These began in the pre-production phase, when her research project got underway, continued through the film's production phase, when the film was being planned and filmed, and through its post-production phase, when the film was edited by the film crew's editor and then re-edited after discussions with her research project's sponsor (see Franzen [2013: 421] for another discussion of collaborative re-editing). The film was then released for distribution. Thieme's (2012) detailed account of this process gives a very useful insight into its complexity and demands.

Thieme's (2012) discussion focuses mostly on the sites of the production of her film and its imagery. She says less about its distribution and audiences (though notes that her decision to make a shorter film was driven by her desire to screen it to busy policy-makers). Ethnographic filmmaking has its own circuits of distribution – festivals and repositories from which films can be borrowed for teaching or other kinds of screening – which suggest diverse kinds of audiences, from the interested general public to anthropology students. However, as Sarah Franzen (2013) discusses, it can be very useful to have a more specific idea of who the audience for your film is, how you are going to reach them, and what kind of audiencing you want to encourage. She notes that ethnographic filmmakers tend not to be very concerned about how their films are interpreted by their audiences; but some of the little research that has been done suggests that, far from increasing understanding of the people in the film, some audiences of ethnographic films watch them in ways that affirm various kinds of cultural stereotypes (Franzen, 2013: 417). To counter this, Franzen suggests a more collaborative approach not only to the production but also to the audiencing of ethnographic films. In her own practice, for example, she attends screenings of her films and hosts question-and-answer sessions after they've been shown, so that she can engage with audiences and encourage interpretations of the films that match what she and her collaborators were hoping to achieve.

13.4.2 Making and showing a short digital film

With the advent of relatively cheap digital video cameras and digital film-editing software, though, making a high-quality, extended film with filmmaking professionals is not the only option for researchers interested in film as a medium for disseminating their research results. It is possible to make a short film now just using your smartphone, some apps and a bit of extra hardware; and online platforms like YouTube and Vimeo provide easy and free ways to share the film.

If you are thinking of making a short film, you can find useful advice on making simple films in many guides to home movie-making (see, for example, Cope, 2007a, 2007b), as well as the guides to ethnographic and other filmmaking mentioned in Section 13.4.2. Even though you can use just your phone to make and edit a film, other equipment might also be desirable: a tripod almost certainly, perhaps a separate audio-recorder and microphone, and perhaps some more sophisticated editing software. The subsequent steps are not that dissimilar to making a photo-essay:

- First of all think carefully about what you want your film to show. Yolanda Hernandez-Albujar (2007) discusses a short film that she made called *Voices*, which was made to evoke the feelings of Latin American migrants in Italian cities. She emphasises the importance of thinking carefully about what you want to film and why, given your research questions and emergent findings.
- Think too about who you want to show it to and how you want them to react. How might that affect what you film?
- Start a storyboard: put the outlines of key scenes onto separate index cards or PowerPoint slides, and move them around until you have them in the most effective order to create the effect you are seeking. Add other scenes that seem necessary.
- Take any ethical considerations into account.
- Script a voice-over commentary if needed.
- Then go shoot the film. Remember to pay as much attention to the quality of the sound as to the quality of the image.
- Edit the film to match the storyboard shape and add the voice-over.
- Put your film into circulation. This might mean uploading it to Vimeo, inserting it into a website or a blog accompanied by some text that encourages your audience to approach it in a particular way, or it might mean organising live screenings.

13.5 Multimedia Websites

Another form of disseminating research results more widely than the conventional academic paper or book is to design a multimedia website. A website could of course be a way in which a photo-essay or a film could find its audiences. You could upload your film to Vimeo and also make it the centrepiece of a website, for example, and many blogs are designed show off photographs. However, websites can carry all sorts of media, including any kind of still image, written text, animations and sound, as well as film, and websites have other possibilities. The arrangement of the website's pages can put different things into various relationships; a search box can make a complex website easily navigable; a website can be updated regularly; and it can be integrated with social networks like Twitter.

13.5.1 Multimedia websites: an overview

Many of these possibilities are now being explored by researchers interested in using visual means to convey their research, and a number of different ways of doing this seem to be emerging. There are some fairly simple websites that work just as hosts of things like photo-essays or films. Having said 'fairly simple', of course this still means that a lot of thought has gone into how the site is structured and how it can be searched.

Some websites have been designed as repositories for the visual and other materials made or collected as part of a research project. In terms of how these materials are organised and searchable, these websites tend to be more complex than the previous kind. One example is the *Invincible Cities* website, which contains essays, maps and photographs (see Figure 13.7). The photographs have been taken by Camilo José Vergara over a number of years in Harlem in New York, Richmond in California, and Camden in New Jersey. The website's home page invites the visitor to choose one of those locations, and the next page offers the introduction to the site by Vergara and an essay about urban change in that place either by Vergara or by sociologist Howard Gillette. Vergara's aim is to document the evolution of the urban ghetto over time, and the site hosts hundreds of photographs taken by him in the three cities. Many of these are repeat photographs of the same place (see Section 12.2). They can be searched by date, by location via the maps on each city page, and by photo type, for example 'panorama' or 'interior'.

There are also websites that have a more explicitly interactive design, which not only organises an extensive collection of material but also aims to 'transform how users engage with materials' (Coover, 2011: 617; see also Favero, 2013; Nash et al., 2014). Roderick Coover (2011) calls these 'interactive media representations', and the term **interactive documentary** – or i-docs – is also used to refer to similar things. Coover argues that digital technologies, particularly software, not only draw on older forms of communication like writing and photography, but also offer new ways of communicating, particularly

interactive documentary

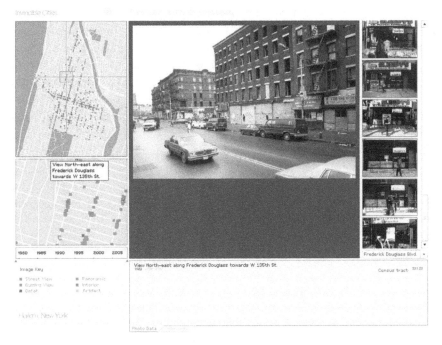

FIGURE 13.7
Screenshot
from the
Invincible Cities
website, http://
invinciblecities.
camden.rutgers.
edu/intro.html
© Camilo José
Vergara

'layered tropes, juxtaposed paths, modally varied arguments, and active choice-making' (Coover, 2011: 618). He thus proposes that these new forms allow for a new way of disseminating the results of research. It means dissemination can be 'multimodal': it can include written text but also audio recordings and video. It can also include more material: all the audio recordings of entire interviews (not just a selection of transcribed quotations), and all the video that was made as part of a project (not just the bits that might make it into a 50-minute film). Paths and links between materials can be created that can show how particular interpretations might be made. Most importantly, though, this new way of dissemination can create opportunities for those interacting with such an interactive media site to take their own routes through the material. Coover (2011), then, is advocating inter-active media representations because they can host most, if not all, of the different kinds of research data generated during a research pro-ject; they can host most if not all of that data; they can show something of how the researcher came to their conclusions; and they can allow the visitor to engage with the evidence so they can make their own interpretations. In this way, 'i-docs generate new, creative, non-linear forms of engagement and interaction between viewers, authors and the material itself' (Favero, 2013: 260).

There are many possible ways to achieve this interactivity. Coover's own technique for allowing the users of his sites to create their own pathways through them is to create panoramas, which are images annotated with various kinds of text. These panoramas also contain linked and layered materials that connect to the panoramic image 'whether directly or by juxtaposition … offer[ing] points of disruption, encounter, and difference by creating paths into the image' (Coover, 2011: 629): these are accessed by clicking on the panorama. Coover suggests that this method allows for a coherent argument to be made, through the panorama, but also allows visitors to question that coherence by exploring other kinds of data. As he says, 'these environments promote re-interpretation, contextualized by agency, exploration, path-making, and choice-making' (Coover, 2011: 636).

discussion

Exhibitions share with multimedia web projects the ability to show a wide range of different kinds of material. An exhibition can show framed photographs with minimal captions, or it can be an immersive experience using film, sound projection, music and even performance. An exhibition is not an unusual way of sharing research results with a wider audience. You need to identify a venue, decide which images to display and how (taking any ethical or copyright issues into account), build the display, and publicise the exhibition to the appropriate audiences.

A multimedia exhibition can be an ambitious undertaking. Sociologists Nirmal Puwar and Sanjay Sharma (2012) discuss their collaboration with filmmaker Kuldip Powar, poet Sawarn Singh, musician Nitin Sawhney, and composer Francis Silkstone to make *Noises of the Past*, a mix of music, poetry and film launched in Coventry Cathedral in 2011. The installation explored the experiences of Indian men who fought in the British army during the Second World War. Puwar and Sharma (2012) note that sociologists have done a lot of work on 'the vexed issue of postcoloniality, memory and belonging in relation to national(ist) commemoration ceremonies and proliferating "global wars"' (Puwar and Sharma, 2012: 52). This work has often been critical of the ways that soldiers' experiences have been assimilated into a celebratory account of the British Empire. They wanted to make these sociological analyses more public, but not in a way that was didactic, accusatory or exclusionary. Drawing on sociology's history of using inventive and creative methods to share sociological insight with non-academic audiences, they decided that a creative installation would be a good way:

> to productively intervene in public debates concerned with reimagining a British nation able to come to terms with its colonial past, in the present (contested) multicultural moment. In this respect, the project aimed to engage with existing currents of nationalist sentiment and remembrance, and *reroute* these towards more immersive, open-ended ways of belonging to a multicultural nation. (Puwar and Sharma, 2012: 53)

They describe the complex process of creating *Noises of the Past* at some length; it is clear that such a large-scale public intervention involves a huge amount of work, and a willingness to engage actively with the creative insights and processes of non-academics too.

As well as reaching new audiences, scholars who have been involved in mounting exhibitions point to two other ways in which an exhibition can be a productive way to share research insights. The first is how the exhibition design process can enhance research findings. Felix Driver (2013) reflects on this in his discussion of an exhibition based on his research called *The Hidden Histories of Exploration*. The second is evident in Katherine Johnson's (2011) account of a much less elaborate exhibition she helped to run as part of a participatory research project on LGBT mental health; she suggests that an exhibition can also be particularly valuable to the research participants who made the images that appeared in the exhibition, in this case 'showcasing the the experiences of lesbian, gay, bisexual and transgendered people living with and managing mental health issues' (Johnson, 2011: 176).

13.5.2 Building a multimedia website

Designing a simple website to host research outputs is not hard; there are several softwares or platforms that offer more or less flexible templates into which your own digital files can be inserted. As with filmmaking, there are plenty of 'how to design a website' books that will be very useful for designing a simple website as part of a research project. An excellent discussion of integrating a research project with a website is that offered by Stephen Papson, Robert Goldman and Noah Kersey (2007).

Elaborate multimedia projects are more challenging to implement, however. They require considerable skills in both design and programming (and Banks [2008: 107–11] works through some of the complications in both structuring a site and making it searchable). As with making complex data visualisations, extended films, or a complex installation, working with other creative professionals may be necessary.

Some basic pointers to designing a site using these sorts of packages:

- Decide where the site will be hosted and, if necessary, purchase a domain name.
- As with all the uses of visual images discussed in this section, think about what you want them to achieve for the audience you have in mind (and what any other media can best achieve [Dicks et al., 2006]).
- Consider any ethical or copyright issues as you decide what you want the site to carry (Chapter 14 says a bit more about this).
- The basic unit of website design is the page, so think about what each page should do, one page at a time.
- Think about what else you want on the site: a search facility for example, or a news feed.
- Think about how the pages should link together in a robust and clear way.

13.6 Using Images to Disseminate Research: An Assessment

This chapter has discussed a range of different kinds of image that can be used to disseminate the results of your research. Interest in such forms of dissemination is growing for a range of different reasons, as Section 13.1 discussed. Perhaps the most consistent reason given by advocates of these various means of visual dissemination is that well-designed images – whether bar charts, data visualisations, photo-essays, films, interactive websites or an exhibition – can all reach audiences that conventional academic outputs do not, and can reach them in ways that have real impact. In order to reach those audiences in such a powerful kind of way, all these techniques require the researcher to ask similar questions: What research findings do I want to convey? Who do I want to convey them to? And what visual design or format is therefore the best to use?

Given their claims to reach those audiences that other forms of academic output cannot, these various dissemination techniques should also be subjected to interrogation in the context of this book's concern with critical visual methodologies. Section 1.3 outlined four criteria for such a critical visual methodology: a critical approach to visual culture is one that takes images seriously, thinks about the social conditions and effects of visual objects, and is reflexive. All the techniques discussed in this chapter take images seriously, clearly. Thinking about how the images that disseminate research findings are produced and about their effects has also been central to the chapter's discussion of each technique. Questions about audience – about where to display these images – have also been raised consistently. And it is certainly possible to think about ways in which reflexivity can be built into these uses of images. Section 13.2.1 discussed Drucker's (2011) concern that some data visualisations do not reflect enough on the data that they use, and her essay suggests some ways in which such visualisations might suggest the situatedness of that data; likewise Jacobs (2013) argues that reflexivity must be part of critical filmmaking, and shows how she achieves this in her own filmmaking practice. It certainly seems, then, that disseminating the results of research using visual materials can be part of a critical visual methodology.

Exciting as all of this potentially is, though, there are a number of issues that need careful consideration before deciding to invest a lot of time and energy in creating a visual summary of a research project.

Several of these considerations are practical. Although many of the technologies necessary to create the kinds of visual materials discussed in this chapter are rapidly becoming more accessible both in terms of price and skill, producing good-quality visual outputs still takes considerable investment. You may need to learn – and practise – a whole new skillset, and have to buy – and practise using – at least some decent kit, whether for producing images or editing them. Even with digital cameras that correct for your wobbling grip, and editing software that can sharpen images that are out of focus, using photographic or moving images in the way discussed in this chapter still requires good-quality images. Although 'good' is a rather hard quality to define, it does seem to me that these approaches to dissemination require a fairly high level of visual skill to really be effective. While this is a skill that can be developed and improved (Grady, 2004), there is no doubt that some researchers are just better at, for example, taking the sort of photos that work to convey lots of information or to convey a mood or an affect, than others. If in your heart of hearts you know you are not one of them, then you would need to think seriously about undertaking a project that relied on you making photographs, for example.

Or – you could choose to work with someone who has the skills you lack. Several of the projects mentioned in this chapter were achieved as collaborations between researcher(s) and one or more creative professionals. Susan Thieme (2012) discusses the benefits and the challenges of this, as does Ruth Bartlett (2013) in her account of working with a professional cartoonist to create five cartoons to summarise the results of her research into dementia activism. Working with a photographer, filmmaker or cartoonist can give you access to their technical skills, but it also requires a good deal of careful discussion about your research so that the professional understands what you are trying to achieve and also any ethical considerations you may have about the kinds of images they may create. Conversely, researchers also need to appreciate that creative professionals will have specific expectations and assumptions about producing something they are happy with visually. And of course many visual professionals will rightly expect payment for their input, which you will need to source.

If there are issues to consider in relation to the production of images to disseminate your research, there are also practical issues related to its distribution. Disseminating the results of research in visual form to other academics remains somewhat fraught. Including a photo-essay instead of a chapter in a research dissertation is fairly straightforward, if your supervisor is supportive. But when it comes to publishing research with images, the situation remains a little trickier. While all social science journals are now online, and online can carry, in principle, many high-quality colour images, in practice the guidance on submitting images still often seems to be dictated by the requirements of the printed versions of journals. Indeed, even achieving good quality reproduction of a single image can be difficult in some journals, let alone a photo-essay.

And most social science journals continue not to carry photo-essays, for example, because they are not seen as legitimate research outputs (Newbury, 2011). While much of this may be a short-sighted reaction against innovation (Newbury, 2011), there are also issues about the rigour and reliability of visual outputs that are genuinely challenging, I think. Many academics would not be clear how to judge the quality of, say, a series of collages as part of a journal's peer review process. In their discussion of arts-based research, Barone and Eisner (2012: 148–54) suggest six criteria for judging such research:

- incisiveness
- concision
- coherence
- generativity
- social significance
- evocation and illumination.

As Barone and Eisner (2012) themselves say, though, this list is just a starting point for wider discussion among visual researchers; it is not a usable checklist that journal reviewers can easily use.

The question of how visual research outputs are received brings this discussion to the site of the audiencing of images. Academics are one audience for such outputs, when and if they appear in journals or in books. But one of the major claims for disseminating research findings visually, remember, was that this was a way in which those findings would reach many more people, and also non-academic kinds of people, than the standard academic outputs of a paper or book. Again, there are a number of questions to think about here.

Many visual dissemination projects rely on reaching 'the general public', either by using the web or by mounting an exhibition. It is clear that some well-resourced and high-quality visual projects clearly do reach out to new audiences and have considerable impact on how they think about the research topic. *Noises of the Past* seems to have been one of these. However, the impact of even the most brilliant installation or exhibition is limited to the number of people who walk through the door, and that may not, in the end, be very many. It may also be a particular group of people, those that tend to go to exhibitions in art galleries and museums (particularly if you are using the gallery or museum space on your university campus; this may be free to use but limit your audience in quite specific ways). Putting work online may appear to be a solution to this problem, but it also has drawbacks. There is an awful lot of stuff online, and people need to be able to find yours easily; multimedia projects hosted on their own unique websites are very difficult to find unless you know what you are looking for, and they can also disappear if their funding is not secure.

Another issue that the dissemination of research using visual materials needs to pay more attention to, I think, is just what audiences make of a research project's visual output. Some of the research projects mentioned in this chapter note that their exhibition or installation had a 'visitors' book', which invited visitors to comment on what they had seen; and Franzen (2013) describes the question-and-answer sessions she ran with her film screenings. But most of the examples of visual research outputs in this chapter do not seem particularly interested in considering their audiences' reactions to their work (Boydell et al. [2012] note a similar absence in arts-based research in health studies). This is somewhat perplexing. I at least remain convinced that interpreting images is not an easy task. Images without any text are very hard to make head or tail of (and Banks [2001: 139–51] confirms this; see also Gilligan and Marley, 2010).

Without wanting to undermine the valid point that images can do work that written text cannot, nor disallow (even if that were possible) the kinds of interaction with evidence and interpretation that interactive documentaries invite, audiences for such visual projects still need some guidance on how to treat the images that they are being offered. If they are not, one risk is that the viewers of the work will simply be baffled, rather than convinced by them or sensorily stimulated by them or whatever. Or they could come to conclusions that are counter-productive to the research's findings. Drucker's (2011) worries, that all too often data visualisations are seen as straightforward abstractions from reality, are also relevant here. If visualisations of quantitative data risk being taken too readily as descriptive and truthful, qualitative visualisations risk being too obscure to communicate the findings of a research project effectively. Johnson's (2011: 185) account of the exhibition organised as part of a participatory photography offers a further salutory warning: one comment in the visitors' book was highly abusive about the experiences shown in the exhibition. To be effective as means of conveying research findings, then, and particularly as a *critical* visual research method, visual outputs need accompanying text that explains their aims effectively; obviously this won't entirely control an audience's reactions to the work, but it may provide a framework for interpretation. So visual projects should consider how that guidance is best provided, I think.

discussion

Darren Newbury glosses one use of photographs in his book on photography during the apartheid era in South Africa like this:

> At the end of one chapter, a magazine page spread showing a photograph of a funeral that followed the Sharpeville Massacre is juxtaposed with a musician seated at a piano. The visual echo of the row of coffins in the piano keyboard was intended to summarize one of the themes of the chapter, which counter-posed the oppression of the apartheid state with culture as a form of resistance and escape. (Newbury, 2011: 657)

Without such help, there is a much higher risk than usual that the images will be ignored or else read in ways entirely different from those intended by the researcher.

Finally, disseminating the results of research projects using visual materials – particularly if the point of making those materials is to share them with a wide and general audience – raises the question of research ethics. The next chapter discusses this much more fully.

Summary: Using Images to Disseminate Research

- *associated with*:
  Many kinds of images can be used to disseminate the results of research.

- *sites and modalities*:
  Making such images requires consideration of the images' production, content, circulation and audiencing.

- *key terms*:
  There are no key terms.

- *strengths and weaknesses*:
  It is claimed that images can convey the results of research more directly and more affectively to non-academic audiences. This claim is tempered by concerns about the effective distribution and actual audiencing of the visual outputs of research projects.

Further Reading

Marcus Banks (2008: 92–112) offers a useful discussion of presenting visual research.

 COMPANION WEBSITE

Visit **https://study.sagepub.com/rose4e** for:

- **Links to resources** on engaging non-academic audiences with the process and outcomes of academic research, as well as resources on how to create your own images from (or as) your research results, using free data visualisation software and online platforms.
- **Examples of research projects** that have used various visual means to disseminate their findings. Looking at how other researchers have done this is a useful way to reflect on exactly what you want to achieve if you are thinking of doing something similar.
- **An exercise** asking you to make quite a different kind of visual object as a way of communicating your research results.

14

RESEARCH ETHICS AND VISUAL MATERIALS

key examples: the chapter pays special attention to the ethical issues raised when photographs are created as part of a research project.

14.1 Research Ethics and Visual Materials: An Introduction

Chapter 12 discussed a range of different methods that involved either researchers or research participants making visual images as part of a research project, and Chapter 13 explored a number of ways in which such images could be made public. Over the past couple of decades, it has become more and more necessary for such activities to consider the ethics of their practice. This is so for a number of reasons, not least the fact that for some time now (in the UK, the USA and elsewhere), conducting social science research – particularly funded research, or research for university degrees – has had to gain formal approval from university ethics review boards. These boards are constituted differently in different universities but they all review the ethics of proposed research projects and come to a judgement about their adequacy. If judged inadequate, the project should either never happen, or be altered in some way so that it is deemed to be ethical.

So what is ethical research? All discussions of research ethics agree that there are very few absolutely hard and fast rules about what constitutes ethical research in all situations; every research project must consider the particular circumstances it will encounter and create, and then decide what is ethical in those circumstances (Clark, 2012). Absolute rules of ethical conduct are hard to find, then; instead, many social science research organisations offer principles or guidelines for ethical research. The Economic and Social Research Council (ESRC), for example, which is a major funder of social science research in the UK, says that ethical research is based on six key principles (Economic and Social Research Council, 2015: 4):

- Research participants should take part voluntarily, free from any coercion or undue influence, and their rights, dignity and (when possible) autonomy should be respected and appropriately protected.
- Research should be worthwhile and provide value that outweighs any risk or harm. Researchers should aim to maximise the benefit of the research and minimise potential risk of harm to participants and researchers. All potential risk and harm should be mitigated by robust precautions.
- Research staff and participants should be given appropriate information about the purpose, methods and intended uses of the research, what their participation in the research entails, and what risks and benefits, if any, are involved.
- Individual research participant and group preferences regarding anonymity should be respected, and participant requirements concerning the confidential nature of information and personal data should also be respected.
- Research should be designed, reviewed and undertaken to ensure that recognised standards of integrity are met, and quality and transparency are assured.
- The independence of research should be clear, and any conflicts of interest or partiality should be explicit.

These principles should inform every stage of the research process, from its design, to the selection of both participants and materials, to the collection and analysis of data, to the dissemination of the project's results, to the archiving of its data.

While most of the principles of ethical social science research are exactly the same whether you are dealing with interview transcripts, ethnographic observation notes, or participant-generated collages, working with some kinds of visual material can pose specific ethical dilemmas that general discussions of social science research ethics tend to overlook. The ESRC's *Framework for Research Ethics* has a list of research that would normally require a full ethics review because there is a 'more than minimal risk' that ethics guidelines may be breached (ESRC, 2015: 9), and included in this list is research using 'visual/vocal methods' (ESRC, 2015: 10). Why are visual methods mentioned here? The list clarifies its concern when it notes that it is concerned about methods 'where participants or other individuals may be identifiable in the material (e.g. images, sound recordings) used or generated' (ESRC, 2015: 10). Not all visual methods create or work with images of identifiable individuals, of course, but photographs, films, drawings and videos are particularly likely to create data where individuals are identifiable, and this recognisability may be in conflict with the fourth principle of ethical research, which states that 'preferences regarding anonymity should be respected' (ESRC, 2015: 4). This is why visual research methods can be seen to involve 'more than minimal risk' of breaching ethical principles.

While there are a number of very helpful guides to the ethics of social science research using written or spoken texts (see, for example, Denzin and Giardina, 2007;

Iphofen, 2009; Mertens and Ginsberg, 2009), until quite recently there were far fewer dealing with the ethics of visual research. With the growing popularity of visual research methods, this has changed, and there are now several important statements and discussions. Almost all pay most attention to research projects generating new visual materials, whether by researchers or by research participants. However, I would suggest that many of the principles developed for research with such photographs should also apply to found photographs. All research should be ethical, whether you are working with visual materials generated in the course of your research project, or working with visual materials that you have found ready-made; research should be ethical if the people who made those visual materials, or who are pictured in them, are alive, or if they are long dead. Photographs, film and video images can pose ethical difficulties whether generated a day ago, a decade ago, or a century ago. All research using visual materials, then, should consider its ethical implications.

This chapter's discussion of the ethics of visual research methods is based on the overview provided by Rose Wiles et al. (2011). They suggest that there are now four factors that shape the making of ethical decisions when using visual research methods (see Figure 14.1): the critical issues of anonymity, guidelines and consent; frameworks and ethics review boards; laws, including copyright law; and the researcher's own personal moral framework. This chapter has a section on each of these five factors that impact on making ethical decisions when

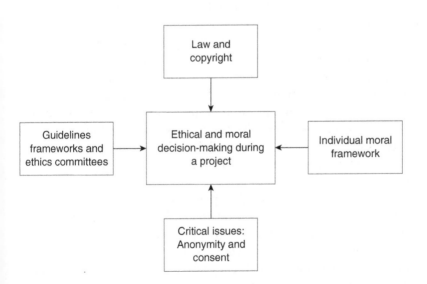

FIGURE 14.1
Current forces shaping ethical decision-making on a research project (adapted from Wiles et al., 2011: 687)

conducting visual research, and each one discusses an example of a researcher exploring the factor in detail:

1. The first of the chapter's sections is this introduction to research ethics in general.
2. The second explores the dilemma that anonymity imposes on visual research with video and photographs.
3. The third discusses the issue of research participant consent.
4. The fourth discusses some of the formal regulations and committees with which ethical research must engage.
5. The fifth examines the implications of law and copyright for the use of visual materials in research.
6. The sixth reflects on the research's own moral framework.
7. Finally, the seventh section concludes by reflecting on these ethical debates in the light of some of the changes in contemporary visual culture broached in the first chapter of this book.

14.2 Anonymity and Confidentiality

As a focus group of researchers using visual methods convened by Wiles and her team (2012) confirms, it is in relation to concerns about the anonymity of research participants that visual research methods often face their most severe challenges (and see Banks, 2001: 128–35; Pink, 2013; Warren, 2002; Wiles et al., 2011). Videos, films and photographs usually create images that identify individuals; they also create images that identify specific places. If an ethics review board insists that a project must fully anonymise both its participants and the places in which the research took place, is it even worth considering using visual methods?

Well, yes. It might be possible to make or use photographs as part of a photo-elicitation project, providing participants are shown only those photographs that they themselves made, and that the photos are not shown to anyone else at any stage of the research (Section 13.6 noted that this could be another reason why so few published photo-elicitation studies contain photographs taken by research participants). And it might be possible to anonymise the images made or found. Eyes or other identifying features could be blocked out, and digital photographs that picture people could be anonymised using software that turns them into cartoon-like images, or drawings (Wiles et al., 2012).

However, visual methods researchers have also questioned the assumption that all images that identify individuals are in some way unethical. They suggest, for example, that the wealth of information that a photograph of a person or a film of a place can convey can be so important to retain that it overrides the right to anonymity of the people and places pictured (Wiles et al., 2011). They also suggest that obscuring faces or landmarks can be dehumanising and thus disrespectful to those pictured (Jordan,

2014; Nutbrown, 2011; Wiles et al., 2012). Indeed, some research projects are designed precisely in order to allow their participants to articulate some aspect of their identity; it might then be very important to the participants themselves that they are clearly identified with the images made with or by them.

discussion

Ruth Holliday (2004), for one, has insisted that using identifiable images of research participants can enhance their power in the research process (see also Sweetman, 2009). For Holliday, this is part of reflexivity about the role of the researcher in relation to the researched. She shares the scepticism of various post-structuralist schools of thought about forms of reflexivity that involve the researcher reflecting on his or her position and identifying its effects, a reflexivity that assumes a stable identity that can be reflected upon (Holliday, 2004: 56; Rose, 1997). Instead, she argues that both researcher and researched are positioned by discourses external to themselves, as well as in relation to each other. While this is a differentiated relationship, she argues that writing up research from it that includes images of the participants renders that relationship visible to a more sustained kind of scrutiny than texts authored by the researcher alone, because, according to Holliday, the voices and the images of the research participants are there to 'talk back', as it were, from their photos. Holliday (2004: 60) says of her participants that 'their reflections seem to be much more present within the authorial text I have constructed through video than if I were simply reciting their accounts in my own words'. It is as if the veracity of the visual demands that due attention be paid to the research participants. So for Holliday, identifiable images have more ethical potential than anonymised images.

Some researchers therefore make the case that it is more ethical to use visual methods that identify specific individuals and places, than it is to anonymise them. Indeed, the Code of Research Ethics developed by the International Visual Sociology Association states quite clearly that 'various research methods do not require anonymity. Among these are: community/participatory research, and individual case studies involving individuals who consent to using identifying information (e.g. own names and visual representations)' (Papademas and IVSA, 2009: 254). And there is some evidence that in the UK at least, many ethics committees, particularly in universities, are happy to be persuaded of this, provided the case is a robust one, carefully made (Wiles et al., 2010). Anonymity, then, is not necessarily obligatory when using visual research methods; but its absence requires careful consideration. Wiles and her team (2012: 48) suggest that there are three key criteria to consider: research participants' status and 'vulnerability'; the nature of the research; and the ways that the visual data will be used and presented.

There is one situation, however, in which research participants should not remain anonymous, regardless of their own wishes, according to the principles of ethical research: when the researcher uncovers evidence of illegal activity. The guidelines produced by the British Sociological Association's Visual Sociology Study Group are particularly clear on this point:

> Images depicting illegal activities, including criminal damage, sexual violence and hate crime do not have the privilege of confidentiality. The BSA-Visual Sociology Group believe that members have a responsibility and duty to give images depicting serious crime (including sexual violence, terrorism or child abuse) to the relevant authorities. Furthermore, the members have a professional responsibility to assist the police in matters of criminal activity. This is as much to protect the researcher, as it is to protect vulnerable individuals in society. (British Sociological Association, VSSG, 2006: 3)

The same statement also reminds researchers that:

> Research data given in confidence do not enjoy legal privilege; that is they may be liable to subpoena by a court and research participants should be informed of this. Retaining images of serious crime (including child abuse, sexual violence and hate crime) is deemed criminal under British law and researchers should therefore contact the relevant authority and hand over any materials to the relevant authorities in such cases. (British Sociological Association, VSSG, 2006: 3)

Anonymity, then, is something to be considered carefully in research using visual methods.

14.3 Consent

The principle of informed consent is one of the most important in all kinds of research. That is, the people you are researching should be aware of what the research is about, what you are hoping they will do if they agree to participate, and what you intend to do with the research results; they should then explicitly agree to participate. (Hence the problem with the ethnographies of television viewing by James Lull [1990] discussed in Section 10.3.2; Lull did not inform his participants about what he was really interested in researching when he negotiated access to their homes. Hence too the worries about using data scraped from social media platforms discussed in Chapter 11.) In the context of visual research methods, the 'people you are researching' can include both individuals you are recruiting for an organised photo-elicitation project, say, as well as those people who end up being pictured in the images that your research finds or generates.

Sometimes verbal consent might be sufficient, but ethical review boards usually expect researchers to create written consent forms for all research participants to sign at the beginning of the research project. A typical consent form would include a summary of the research project, and various boxes for participants to tick, agreeing to a range of different activities and to a range of things that you may want to do with the data they help you to generate. In terms of visual research methods, consent forms would be expected to include a short description of what you hope the participants will do (for example, 'make a collage', 'keep a photo-diary') and a range of options about what you plan to do with the images (for example, 'use for analysis only', 'reproduce only in my dissertation', 'reproduce in academic publications', 'use in a public exhibition'). Consent forms also often explicitly offer anonymity to research participants, which the next sub-section will address. In thinking about consent, then, you should think about the whole research project, not just the data collection stage, and gain consent for all the uses of the images that the whole project will entail.

An ethical issue particularly relevant to methods asking participants to consent to generate their own images is the age of the participant. Visual research methods are often used with children, as Chapter 12 discussed. However, children under the age of 16, or sometimes 18, are assumed not to be capable of making informed judgements about their participation in research projects (hence they are very often described, somewhat controversially, as 'vulnerable' research participants). To prevent any possible risk to them, research with children usually requires the consent of both the child (often verbally, especially with younger children) and their parent or legal guardian. In the UK, researchers working with children also have to undergo vetting by the Criminal Records Bureau to ensure they have no record of child abuse (for discussions of this in the UK context, see Farrell, 2005; Matthews et al., 1998).

There are a number of issues in relation to gaining informed consent to visual research methods (Wiles et al., 2011). One I have already mentioned: is informed consent from everyone pictured in an image generated as part of a research project necessary? Although the legal situation is not crystal clear, in the UK and the USA, anyone is allowed to take photographs in public places, even if the photo shows a private place. Legally, then, consent from people pictured in public places is not required. Hence the IVSA Code of Ethics states that 'visual researchers may conduct research in public places or use publicly-available information about individuals (e.g. naturalistic observations in public places, analysis of public records, or archival research) without obtaining consent' (Papademas and IVSA, 2009: 255). However, if clearly identifiable individuals are pictured, in some circumstances you may feel it is appropriate (and indeed simply polite) to ask them if it is OK if they appear in your photograph or film.

Another issue relating to consent is the use of images on social media sites. Images visible to researchers on social media platforms like Facebook, Instagram, Twitter and Pinterest, for example, are visible because the people who uploaded them agreed to make them 'public' when they did so. However, they did not explicitly agree to allow their images to be used as part of a researcher's dataset. So is using their images for research purposes appropriate?

focus

Take a look at Figure 14.2, which was taken by photographer Martha Cooper as part of a research project directed by university professor David Halle and reproduced in his book *Inside Culture* (Halle, 1993). How many people in this picture might have to give informed consent, in order to reproduce it in a book like this?

FIGURE 14.2   One of Martha Cooper's photographs in *Inside Culture: Art and Class in the American Home* (Halle, 1993: 95). Its original caption was 'The "den" of a Manhattan house'
© University of Chicago Press

focus

Look at some of the debates generated in many different countries about Google's effort to photograph streets for Google Maps Street View. For some, Google is within its rights, since it is filming from a public place – the street – and it blurs any faces or car licence plates that appear in its photos. For others, its camera's gaze into front gardens and living rooms is intrusive.

Would you use Google's Street View photos as part of a research project that wanted to explore contemporary patterns in the design of house fronts? (You might have difficulty doing this in Germany, where nearly 250,000 people asked Google to blur the fronts of their homes in Street View.) Think about your answer specifically in terms of the IVSA and BSA-VSSG statements.

Another issue about informed consent concerns the fact that many research projects start out planning to do one thing, only to end up doing another. For example, organising a community mapping workshop with a group of young people might seem like a great research method to explore their sense of local belonging; the young people might agree to it in principle and sign the consent forms, but when you get them together around a table with blank sheets of paper and lots of marker pens, it just doesn't work: they're not interested, it's boring, they don't see their neighbourhood like a map ... but what they do want to do is create a collage about their neighbourhood using photos they take with their cameraphones. Great, you think (while also pondering the practicalities and the ethics of downloading cameraphone images) – but they haven't formally consented to making a collage: they consented to making a map. These sorts of situations are not that rare in relation to visual methods, because the methods are sometimes very different from participants' everyday experiences. Participants might agree in principle to something unusual, but when it comes to actually doing it, they might not be so keen; or it might be seen to require specific skills that research participants do not feel they have (this is a challenge often faced by researchers who want to use drawing as a visual research method, as Chapter 12 noted). In this situation, you will have to change what you were planning to do and will thus have to gain the participants' consent once more, this time for the new activity.

Another circumstance in which consent might need renegotiating is in relation to the audiencing of images. Research participants should be asked to consent to specific uses of the images that are part of the research project they are involved in. Here, it is important to consider carefully what audience each image will have and what that audience might do with it. Is it better that some images are only viewed by the researcher and the research participant who made them? Making such decisions can be done in principle at an early stage of the research, but may need to be revisited once the actual images are made or found – if participants make particularly intimate or private photos of their children, for example. And what about the various audiences that might see images once the research is being presented to those not involved in its production? Asking for consent to use images in public places – whether your undergraduate dissertation, a published, peer-reviewed paper, an exhibition or a website – is crucial. But *informed* consent to the consequences of displaying an image is difficult to achieve. Consent might be gained for specific sorts of dissemination, and might assume an informed and sympathetic audience. But once an image has gone public – and online, in particular – it is very hard to ensure that it will only be seen by particular audiences, or in the context in which you have carefully placed it (any caption might well disappear if an image is cut and pasted elsewhere or, for example, reblogged on Tumblr). Section 13.6 discussed this in its assessment of disseminating the results of research using images. Given these complexities, it might be better to negotiate consent to displaying images when it is clearer which images you and your participants want to show, where and why, and who the likely audiences might be (Jordan, 2014). In fact, many visual researchers suggest thinking about consent as a rolling process, rather than a once-and-for-all event that happens at the beginning of data collection.

discussion

Laura Lewis (2004) offers a salutary tale in her discussion of the photographs taken by Maya Goded of the inhabitants of a village in Guerrero, Mexico. Goded stayed in the village in the early 1990s and took many intimate portrait photographs, with the permission of the villagers. When the photos appeared in a book and exhibition some time later, Lewis took a copy of the book to the village. She found that the villagers barely recognised themselves in the photos. They had been pictured in ways that they found degrading and inappropriate, while Goded's career as an up-and-coming documentary photographer advanced. Lewis (2004: 491) describes Goded's photography as an unethical 'optical violence' inflicted upon the villagers. Clearly, in an ethical research project, the process of consent has to extend beyond the site and moment of *producing* an image, to the sites of its *content* and *audiencing* as well.

Lewis's (2004) essay also asks another ethical question of visual research. What do you do when you are researching found images – like those taken by Maya Goded – that you consider to be unethical in some way? Specifically, do you reproduce them in your own work so that your readers can see what it is you are criticising, or do you refuse to circulate them yet more widely? Lewis (2004) does not reproduce any of Goded's photographs (though she does note that they can easily be found on the Internet). She describes them instead; yet even that gave her pause for thought. She notes that she hesitated about writing her paper, concerned about 'the sensitive nature of some of the photographs' (2004: 494). In the end though, she went ahead because, in her words, 'the issues I hope to have laid out fairly here are, I believe, important ones to bring to light' (2004: 494).

Consent, then, is a requirement of ethical research. However, it is better thought of as a process than a one-off event.

14.4 The Formal Framework: Regulations and Committees

All of the professional bodies for social science researchers, as well as some funders like the ESRC, have developed statements about the principles or guidelines – or sometimes regulations – for conducting ethical research. Some of these are quite general, such as the ESRC's *Framework for Research Ethics* (2015), or the American Sociological Association's *Code of Ethics* (n.d.), and this chapter has already mentioned two clear statements of ethical principles and guidelines for visual researchers, one drawn up in 2006 by the Visual Sociology Study Group of the British Sociological Association (British Sociological Association, VSSG, 2006), and the second by the International Visual Sociology Association in 2009 (Papademas and International

Visual Sociology Association, 2009). These guidelines are not exactly the same; for example, the BSA-VSSG guidelines are rather more prescriptive than the IVSA's.

Any research project planning to collect or create visual materials is now required to gain formal ethics approval from the researcher's institution; and if you are a freelance researcher, you should comply with the relevant professional body's ethical research guidelines. If you are a researcher based in a university – whether as an undergraduate or a professor – your research proposal will need to go through a formal process of review by your university's ethics committee or institutional review board before you can proceed. Ethics committees now usually have clear processes and procedures, but, again, these are not the same everywhere, or for every sort of research project. Research with people deemed to be 'vulnerable' – for example, children, or people with dementia – will be subject to a greater degree of scrutiny.

It is important to proactively think through the position of your research proposal in relation to both the principles of ethical research and the process of gaining consent. To repeat Andrew Clark's (2012) argument, each research project is dealing with a unique situation and must be thought through in the round and on its merits. On the one hand, following principles and processes to the letter may not necessarily guarantee an ethical project (what if, for example, your ethics committee insists on anonymising data but your research participants insist they want an exhibition of their self-portraits at the end of your work together?). On the other hand, ethics principles and processes are not just another administrative burden placed on the poor researcher: they are there to prevent the abuse of the researcher's power.

discussion

Liz Tilley and Kate Woodthorpe (2011) discuss another, more or less formal 'framework', but one that applies to a lot of funded research: the expectation that the researcher will disseminate the results of their research as widely as possible. Certainly research projects funded by the ESRC in the UK are expected to have 'impact' on non-academic users, and as Tilley and Woodthorpe (2011) discuss, this can have implications for maintaining the anonymity of research participants. Although neither of them used visual research methods, their discussion of why they decided to make the sites of their research public is very useful in highlighting the way in which the funders of research may have expectations – or even formal conditions – about how research results will be publicised and acted on that make maintaining the anonymity of research participants difficult.

14.5 Copyright

Copyright is a legal term that refers to the ownership of a specific visual image (see Lowe, 2011; Prosser et al., 2008: 6–9). Generally, the person who made the image is the person who owns it (sometimes, though, their employer owns the copyright). Copyright may also be transferred to the maker's family, their employer, their estate, or an authorised representative. If the photos in the photo-essay of your research project were taken by the people you were researching, for example, they are the copyright owners and you will need to seek their consent to reproduce the photos in any presentations or publications (Barker and Smith, 2012). Similarly, if you are studying webpage banner advertisements or documentary films or whatever, you will need to locate the copyright owner of specific images and request their permission before reproducing any of their work in published work of your own. However, you are the copyright owner of photographs you take yourself (although you may still want to gain consent from anyone pictured in your photographs for their public use).

Most discussions of copyright in relation to visual research ethics stop here. However, as Marita Sturken and Lisa Cartwright (2009: 204–20) and Jeremy Lowe (2011) make clear, copyright and associated laws about the right of publicity, trademark practice, and (in the USA) the Fair Use doctrine are legally very complex. They have been challenged by a number of artists concerned to problematise notions of authenticity, originality and authorship; and, as they say, 'the digital image raises questions of reproduction and copyright to new levels of intensity' (Sturken and Cartwright, 2009: 212), because images can so easily be copied.

discussion

Copyright is a restrictive condition attached to the use of images, which makes their sharing and re-use difficult. In response to this, the Creative Commons organisation has established a licensing system which supplements that of copyright. Under the Creative Commons system, the copyright of an image still resides with its owner. However, the copyright holder can choose to add Creative Commons licences to their work too, which allow it to be shared in different ways. A Creative Commons licence always contains an attribution licence, but can also include a number of other options relating to the sharing, modification and commercial exploitation of your work. If you have created visual images as part of your research project, you may wish to share them under a Creative Commons licence. You can find out more about Creative Commons licences at their website, creativecommons.org.

Permissions might also be needed to undertake various other aspects of visual research. For example, while you are legally entitled to take photographs in public places, many places are not clearly either 'public' or 'private' and you will most likely need to get permission to take photographs there. Examples include shopping malls and museums.

14.6 The Researcher's Own Moral Framework

Research ethics is clearly a complex area. Beyond copyright laws there are no hard and fast rules, and each research project will have its own specificities. When reaching ethical decisions, a researcher might also, in the end, rely on their own convictions and commitments as to the proper course of action.

For example, as Chapter 12 pointed out, visual research methods are very often used as part of participatory research projects. Researchers who advocate participatory research methods usually do so because they want to try to empower the people who take part in their projects. Often working with marginalised or oppressed groups and communities, they see participatory research as a means of giving their research participants skills and confidence, perhaps enabling them to present their views in public, and perhaps to those with more power and the ability to influence. This is one way in which the researcher's own moral framework may shape their research activity. In this example, it may be that the researcher's personal commitment to their research participants may encourage them to challenge their ethics review board guidelines in relation to anonymity, for example. Conversely – as in the case of Laura Lewis's (2004) research discussed above – a researcher's convictions may compel them to refuse to reproduce images that they consider demeaning to their research participants.

14.7 Conclusions: Ethics, Visual Research and Contemporary Visual Culture

Designing, undertaking and disseminating research that uses visual materials in ethical ways is clearly not straightforward. The issues raised by consent and anonymity are complex; laws, guidelines, frameworks and ethics review boards are not straightforward; and researchers have their own convictions too. There are ethical guidelines available, more now than there used to be; but they do not, and cannot, offer cast-iron rules that guarantee ethical research. Each research project must devise its own ethical practices, based on the specifics of its situation. Hence, all the guidelines cited by this chapter – by the ESRC, the IVSA and the BSA-VSSG – start by emphasising the need for social science researchers to uphold the highest professional standards. For many researchers using visual methods, this means that reflexivity is a prerequisite for ethical research. By this they simply mean a constant, careful and consistent awareness of what the researcher is doing, why, and with what possible consequences in terms of the power relations between researcher and researched, both during and after the research process (Mannay 2016). Many researchers also find that discussing particularly recalcitrant ethical dilemmas (appropriately) with colleagues can be very helpful.

It might also be important to place your ethical concerns in the wider context of contemporary visual cultures. Sarah Pink (2013: 49–52) makes the point that different people, places and cultures have different notions of ethical practice (as does the

BSA-VSSG statement). As Pink says (2013: 50), 'this problematizes the idea that there is one set of rules that defines *the* ethical way to undertake ethnographic research.' Indeed, it may well be the case that you encounter quite different uses of images in your own everyday life. As I have been writing this chapter, reflecting on my own research practices in the light of its discussions, I have also participated in a number of photographic practices that bear little relation to the ethical principles discussed here. I live in a town in the UK that is full of tourists all year round, and I am sure that I must have been photographed by one or two of them – without my consent! – as I was walking to the library to look for books for this chapter. I also live in a country with the highest number of closed-circuit television cameras per head of population in the world, so it is most likely I was also videoed in the last few days when I was in town. My kids have been doing homework most days and, like millions of others, are experts at searching with Google Images and downloading what they find to illustrate their school projects, regardless of copyright laws. And a few days ago, I got an email from a friend with a link to a photosharing website where she has uploaded some photos she took of my daughter and hers going trick-or-treating this Halloween. None of this activity has involved anyone asking the consent of anyone else to take or share these various images. Indeed, Gunther Kress (2010) has argued that contemporary visual culture now is composed of image-making, circulating, sharing and mashing so profligate that, in many situations, to talk of consent, privacy, copyright and anonymity is simply irrelevant to many people (see also Flores and James, 2013).

Or is it? While it is certainly the case that what the IVSA or the BSA-VSSG would see as unethical practices exist in contemporary visual culture, it is also the case that specific dilemmas in how to deal ethically with images are often hotly debated there. Think of the public controversies over Facebook's privacy rules, or whether news photographs have been faked; think of the care taken to educate young people about how to present themselves online, or what to do about cyberbullying. As Clark (2012) points out, there are many conventions in contemporary visual culture about how to deal appropriately with various kinds of images, including, for example, family snaps. Researchers in a project looking at family resemblances, for instance, asked several of their interviewees if they could take copies of some of the family snaps that had been discussed as part of their interviews (Wiles et al., 2011). What they got as answers revealed a nuanced set of sensibilities about who could give permission to copy which family photographs: the owner of the photo in question, who had just been interviewed; or the people who were pictured; or the parents of the people in the picture if those people were not adult; or the nearest surviving relative of the person pictured. Thus even an apparently banal practice like family photographs is highly regulated by accepted ways of making, sharing and displaying family snaps (Rose, 2010). Caroline Scarles (2013) draws a similar conclusion about holiday snaps from her study of UK tourists taking photographs of local people in Peru. Similarly elaborate ethical conventions may be emerging in digital media like cameraphone videomessaging, Facebook pages and friending (Livingstone, 2008), and video games (Bainbridge, 2010; Flores and James, 2013; Sicart, 2009). Ethical discourse is alive and well in many locations of contemporary visual culture, and to ignore it as a researcher may be to enact a kind of 'paternalism' that negates research participants' agency (Wiles et al., 2012: 48).

Of course, it may not look much like the sort of ethical discourse that this chapter has explored; and this does suggest that the concepts used by social science researchers to talk about the ethics of visual research methods are rather restricted. Social science researchers tend to discuss ethical issues implicitly in terms of rights (Gross et al., 2003; Mitchell, 2007). Copyright protects the rights of the owner of a photograph; the right to anonymity protects the research participant; the right to consent (and to withdraw consent) likewise. This language of 'rights' is central to modernist ethics, and various assumptions inhere in it, primary among them 'confidence in a determinable calculus of harms and benefits [and] fixed principles of right and wrong action' (Shildrick, 2005: 3). While many situations do demand such calculations, principles and judgement, this chapter has already suggested that many scholars working with visual methods argue strongly that there is a need to develop other kinds of ethics, in which the aim is to explore continually the dynamic and relational grounds upon which relations between researcher and researched are played out. Ethical relations between them then become a more open-ended, ongoing process of reflection and provisional assessment, which is perhaps better described as an ethics of care, or dignity (Langmann and Pick, 2014) than an ethics of rights. And what about ethics based on other kinds of principles? Of recognition, for example, or intervention (Rose, 2010)? As visual research methods continue to gain ground, these questions will no doubt become more pressing.

Summary: Research Ethics and Visual Materials

- *associated with*:
  All research with visual materials should consider its ethics.

- *sites*:
  The ethics of working with visual materials play out at all four sites: the site of the image's production, its circulation, its audiencing and the image itself.

- *key terms*:
  Key issues include the confidentiality, anonymity and consent of research participants, and any copyright issues relating to the images.

- *strengths and weaknesses*:
  Current discussions of research ethics are very often phrased in terms of rights, and driven by the institutional imperatives of ethics review boards. This may encourage researchers to neglect other possible forms of ethical research practice.

Further Reading

The chapter written by Rose Wiles, Andrew Clark and Jon Prosser is a very good overview of many of the issues this chapter has touched on, with some helpful case study discussions (Wiles et al., 2011). There are also a number of books exploring the ethics of various visual media: film (Downing and Saxton, 2010), video games (Sicart, 2009), the Web (Gross et al., 2003), the mass media (Mitchell, 2007; Silverstone, 2007), and museums (Marstine, 2011), for example.

 COMPANION WEBSITE

Visit **https://study.sagepub.com/rose4e** for:

- **Links to online resources** that discuss research ethics in general, as well as some that focus on research ethics in relation to visual research methods in particular.
- **An exercise** which takes you through the complications of creating and displaying potentially controversial photos, as a way of thinking through the ethics of visual research.

15

VISUAL METHODOLOGIES: A REVIEW

15.1 Introduction

This chapter ends the book by rehearsing its central themes. Almost all the chapters have explored a particular method for working with just one or two kinds of visual imagery, and the first section of this chapter will compare the methods a little more systematically than previous chapters have done. For each of these methods has its strengths and weaknesses not only in relation to the criteria for a critical visual methodology laid out in Chapter 1, but also in terms of what it is most effective in exploring empirically. These empirical foci do not concern the kinds of visual image on which each method can be deployed; although most chapters have concentrated on only one sort of visual image, every method discussed here can be applied to images other than the sort discussed in that method's chapter, and the first section of each chapter gave examples of this. Rather, the specificity of the empirical orientations of these methods concerns the sites and modalities of visual meaning-making, and this specificity leads to the other topic of this chapter: the possibility of mixing methods – in order to broaden the empirical scope of a study.

Thus this chapter has just three sections:

1. this introduction;
2. a brief reiteration of the arguments of Chapter 2 about the sites and modalities of the meanings of visual images, and how the methods the chapters have discussed relate to them;
3. and the final section, which discusses the merits of mixing methods.

15.2 Sites, Modalities and Methods

Chapter 2 commented that the large body of work exploring the meanings of found visual images suggests that there are four sites at which their meanings are made: the site of *production*, the site of the *image or object itself*, the site of its *circulation*, and the site of its *audiencing*. That is, how an image is made, what it looks like, where and how it travels, and how it is seen are the four crucial ways in which a visual image becomes culturally meaningful. (I use the term 'image' in this discussion, but that should also imply the notion of a visual 'object', as discussed in Chapter 10.) Chapter 2 also suggested that each of those four sites could be understood in terms of three modalities, which it termed the *technological*, the *compositional* and the *social*. The technological concerns the tools and equipment used to make, structure and display an image; the compositional concerns the visual construction, qualities and reception of an image; and the social concerns the social, economic, political and institutional practices and relations that produce, saturate and interpret an image.

Clearly, these sites and modalities are in practice often difficult to distinguish neatly from each another. Because of that, Figure 2.1 in Chapter 2, which pictured sites and modalities in a circular grid, is an image that draws boundaries between things that are rarely so neatly divided one from another. Its lines are misleadingly solid; and, if you've been reading steadily through this book, by this point you may feel that a list of questions like the one that follows is a more appropriate way of approaching the complexity and richness of meaning in a visual image than the demarcated sectors offered in Figure 2.1.

Some questions about the production of an image

- When, where and why was it made?
- Who made it?
- Was it made for someone else?
- What technologies does its production depend on?
- What technologies does its transmission depend on?
- What were the social identities of the maker, the owner and the subject of the image?
- What were the relations between the maker, the owner and the subject?
- Does the genre of the image address these identities and relations of its production?
- Does the form of the image reconstitute those identities and relations?

Some questions about the image

- What is being shown? What are the components of the image? How are they arranged?
- What is its material form?
- Is it one of a series?
- Where is the viewer's eye drawn to in the image, and why?
- What is the vantage point of the image?
- What relationships are established between the components of the image visually?
- What use is made of colour?
- How has its technology affected the text?

- What is, or are, the genre(s) of the image? Is it documentary, soap opera, or melo-drama, for example?
- To what extent does this image draw on the characteristics of its genre?
- Does this image comment critically on the characteristics of its genre?
- What do the different components of the image signify?
- What knowledges are being deployed?
- Whose knowledges are excluded from this representation?
- Does this image's particular look at its subject disempower its subject?
- Are the relations between the components of this image unstable?
- Is this a contradictory image?

Some questions about the circulation of an image

- What transports this image?
- In what form(s) does this image circulate?
- Must it change form in order to circulate?
- In what forms is it materialised in different places?
- Is its circulation organised in any way, and if so, how?
- How is its circulation organised and controlled?
- Who controls its circulation?

Some questions about audiencing

- Who were the original audience(s) for this image?
- Where and how would the image have been displayed originally?
- How is it stored?
- How is it re-displayed?
- Who are the more recent audiences for this text?
- Where is the spectator positioned in relation to the components of the image?
- What relation does this produce between the image and its viewers?
- Is the image one of a series, and how do the preceding and subsequent images affect its meanings?
- Would the image have had a written text to guide its interpretation in its initial moment of display, for example a caption or a catalogue entry?
- Is the image represented elsewhere in a way that invites a particular relation to it, in publicity materials for example, or in reviews?
- Have the technologies used to display it affected the audiences' interpretations of this image?
- What are the conventions for viewing this technology?
- Is more than one interpretation of the image possible?
- How actively does a particular audience engage with the image?

- Is there any evidence that a particular audience produced a meaning for an image that differed from the meanings made at the site of its production or by the image itself?
- How do different audiences interpret this image?
- How are these audiences different from each other, in terms of class, gender, 'race', sexuality and so on?
- How do these axes of social identity structure different interpretations?

Such a long list of questions addressed to a particular visual image may be a useful starting point for your study. It may prompt new ideas because the questions ask about something you have not thought about before; or your image may suggest other questions to you that become more interesting by their absence from this list.

However, this list of questions is very eclectic. It does not suggest that any one series of questions is any more important than any other. And the usefulness of Table 3.1 is precisely to suggest that the theoretical debates in which many of the methods discussed in this book are embedded are important because they do claim that certain sites or certain modalities are more fundamental for understanding the meaning of an image than others. Thus, Table 3.1 locates the methods this book discusses in relation to Figure 2.1's grid, emphasising to which sites and modalities various methods are most attentive. In so doing, Table 3.1 suggests that, for each method, some questions in that list are more important than others. So, as Chapter 2 also insisted, you need to engage with these more theoretical debates about how images mean, or how they do things, before deploying any of the methods discussed in this book.

Since many of the methods discussed here are related to specific arguments about how images become significant, it is not surprising that many of them produce quite specific empirical foci when they are used, as well as implying their own conceptual understanding of imagery. Table 3.1 suggests what these empirical foci are – although, as has been noted at various moments in this book, in some cases these foci are more a matter of what has been done so far by those researchers interested in visual matters than what the method itself might allow. This is the case, for example, in relation to the neglect of audiencing by the second type of discourse analysis discussed in Chapter 9; there does not seem to be anything in the founding arguments of discourse analysis II that precludes exploring the site of audiencing, but very few of its proponents have carried out that kind of research. Instead, the practitioners of discourse analysis II have focused on the institutional sites of image production, use and display, and on particular genres of images. On the other hand, mainstream semiology and much psychoanalysis also neglect to explore the processes of audiencing, but this is because both claim that it is the image itself that produces its audiences' positions. Since both these theories conceptualise the image as productive of spectatorship, both have developed complex and elaborate ways of interpreting what their proponents argue are the effects of those images by looking only at the images in question. The notion that different audiences might react differently to the same image is rarely emphasised conceptually by either mainstream semiology or psychoanalysis, and the methodologies that flow from that conceptualisation therefore also neglect the processes of audiencing. Hence it would be difficult, using those methods as they are usually deployed, to explore how actual audiences make sense of images.

These sorts of considerations might suggest that mixing one method with another is a useful strategy for widening the empirical focus of a research project, because what one method neglects can be given attention by another. Whether this is in fact the case is considered in the next section.

15.3 Mixing Methods

Most of the methods discussed in this book, then, have been applied, either necessarily or contingently, on only one of the sites at which the meanings of images are made. This raises the question of mixing different methods to explore more fully the range of meanings invested in an image at its different sites.

This book has already mentioned some studies that choose to use more than one method in order precisely to explore the diverse meanings that particular images carry at their various sites of production, circulation, image and reception. Catherine Lutz and Jane Collins (1993), for example, used a different method to access each of these three sites in their study of the photographs of the *National Geographic* magazine. At the site of the photographs' *production*, they studied the archives of the magazine and interviewed editors, journalists and photographers. At the site of the *photographs* themselves, they used content analysis, as Chapter 5 examined. And at the *audiencing* site, they used group interviews, showing different groups the same few key photographs and examining their reactions. Similarly, in her study of an exhibition in a museum, Henrietta Lidchi (1997) suggests using discourse analysis II to interpret the institutional processes that *produced* the exhibition's effects, and semiology for interpreting the effects of the technologies of *display* themselves. Section 12.3 also noted that some advocates of photo-elicitation studies use content analysis to interpret their informants' photographs and then use qualitative methods on the transcripts of their interviews. All these strategies then link together the various data that has been gathered in some way (Mason, 2006).

Using more than one method in this manner clearly has some benefits. It allows a richly detailed picture of images' significance to be developed, and in particular it can shed interesting light on the contradictory meanings an image may articulate. The visualities articulated by producers, images and audiences may not coincide, and this may in itself be an important issue to address. Making images (as well as studying them) as part of research into the workings of visual culture could be a very productive research strategy. Using more than one method could also be appropriate for certain examples of the recontextualisation of visual content in convergence culture (Schrøder et al., 2003).

There are, however, a couple of warning notes that should be sounded too. First, if you decide to use more than one method, take care that the theoretical assumptions implicit in both are compatible. Putting together a Hansen-esque affective account of a digital art exhibition with, say, a Foucauldian account of the art gallery system could risk incoherence at the theoretical level, for example in terms of how bodies are conceptualised; and combining large-scale quantitative analysis with in-depth, small-scale qualitative work also has its difficulties (Hall, 2013; Lewis et al., 2013). Secondly, simply discovering that different sites produce different meanings may be a rather obvious finding. And this kind of argument can easily shift into a claim that 'everyone sees things in their own way', a claim that obscures the very real power relations in which visual images – and all social life – participate. As Ang (1989: 107) argues in the context of audience studies, the critical task is to assess what the significance of diverse audience interpretations might be, not simply to mark their existence. Here, the emphasis on circulation in the anthropological approach to interpreting visual materials discussed in Chapter 10 is obviously useful. Instead of just pointing to the existence of three different sites, that approach focuses precisely on the movements of specific visual objects between different locations, which could include the sites of production and audiencing, and it examines the consequences of their effects as they travel. It is perhaps therefore better equipped to respond to Ang's (1989) concern than some more eclectic methodological strategies.

My assessments of methods in this book have depended on an argument about the power relations articulated through visual images. Hence the critique of compositional interpretation, mentioned in Section 4.3.6, which, in its turn to universalised notions of Art and Genius, ignores the social modality of art entirely. Hence, too, the criticism of audience studies, mentioned in Section 10.4.2, that audience participation may not be the same thing as audience empowerment. And then there are the problems with Lutz and Collins's (1993) use of content analysis (discussed in Section 5.3), where their advocacy of that method as the most 'objective' means of avoiding the unconscious interpretation of images implies that researchers are more analytically powerful than other sorts of audiences. These criticisms all depend for their force on an abiding concern for the power relations that saturate all ways of seeing: producers', images', and audiences', including researchers like us. This is important to bear in mind when mixing methods, then. Be methodologically eclectic or, even better, methodologically innovative; but do so bearing in mind the power relations that structure the connections between the different sites and modalities you want to bring together.

Finally then, I would like to reiterate the implications of the critical visual methodology outlined in Chapter 1. Precisely because images matter, because they are powerful and seductive, it is necessary to consider them critically. Whatever method you choose to use, make sure that your account acknowledges the differentiated effects of both an image's way of seeing and your own.

USEFUL READING ON VARIOUS VISUAL MATERIALS

This is a very partial list of just a few of the huge number of books that address specific visual media and genres, to be used only as a starting point.

Fine Art

Carr, D.W. and Leonard, M. (1992) *Looking at Paintings: A Guide to Technical Terms*. London: J. Paul Getty Museum in association with the British Museum Press.

Harris, J. (2006) *Art History: The Key Concepts*. London: Routledge.

Hope, C. and Ryan, J.C. (2014) *Digital Arts: An Introduction to New Media*. London: Bloomsbury Academic.

Kromm, J. and Bakewell, S.B. (eds) (2010) *A History of Visual Culture: Western Civilisation from the 18th to the 21st Century*. Oxford: Berg.

Roberts, H.E. (ed.) (1998) *Encyclopedia of Comparative Iconography: Themes Depicted in Works of Art*, 2 vols. London: Fitzroy Dearborn.

Turner, J. (ed.) (1996) *The Dictionary of Art*, 34 vols. London: Macmillan.

van Straten, R. (1994) *An Introduction to Iconography*, translated by P. de Man. Yverdon. Switzerland: Gordon and Breach.

Photography

Barthes, R. (1982) *Camera Lucida: Reflections on Photography*, translated by R. Howard. London: Jonathan Cape.

Bate, D. (2009) *Photography: The Key Concepts*. Oxford: Berg.

Bolton, R. (ed.) (1989) *The Contest of Meaning: Critical Histories of Photography*. London: MIT Press.

Bull, S. (2012) *Companion to Photography*. Oxford: Wiley-Blackwell.

Edwards, S. (2006) *Photography: A Very Short Introduction*. Oxford: Oxford University Press.

Hand, M. (2012) *Ubiquitous Photography*. Cambridge: Polity Press.

Pinney, C. and Peterson, N. (eds) (2003) *Photography's Other Histories*. Durham, NC: Duke University Press.

Sontag, S. (1979) *On Photography*. Harmondsworth: Penguin.

Wells, L. (ed.) (2015) *Photography: A Critical Introduction*, 5th edition. London: Routledge.

Film

Bordwell, D. and Thompson, K. (2010) *Film Art: An Introduction*, 9th edition. London: McGraw–Hill.

Bordwell, D., Staiger, J. and Thompson, K. (1988) *The Classical Hollywood Cinema: Film Style and Mode of Production to 1960*. London: Routledge.

Ellis, J. (1992) *Visible Fictions: Cinema, Television, Video*, revised edition. London: Routledge.

Monaco, J. (2009) *How to Read a Film: Movies, Media, Multimedia*, 30th anniversary edition. Oxford: Oxford University Press.

The British Film Institute publishes a series of books on individual films, called 'Classics'. Films discussed include *Pulp Fiction, Star Wars, Jaws, The Godfather, Vertigo, The Matrix* and many more.

The film journal *Screen* celebrated its 50th anniversary in 2009 with a special issue of short essays reviewing different aspects of film theory and criticism, and it gives an interesting overview of the state of the field.

Advertising

Arvidsson, A. (2006) *Brands: Meaning and Value in Media Culture*. London: Routledge.

Dyer, G. (1982) *Advertising as Communication*. London: Methuen.

Leiss, W., Kline, S., Jhally, S. and Botterill, J. (2005) *Social Communication in Advertising: Consumption in the Mediated Marketplace*, 3rd edition. London: Routledge.

Television

Bignell, J. (2008) *An Introduction to Television Studies*, 2nd edition. London: Routledge.

Ellis, J. (1992) *Visible Fictions: Cinema, Television, Video*, revised edition. London: Routledge.

Silverstone, R. (1994) *Television and Everyday Life*. London: Routledge.

Williams, R. (1989) *Raymond Williams on Television: Selected Writings*, edited by A. O'Connor. London: Routledge.

Mass Media

Allan, S. (2010) *News Culture*, 3rd edition. Maidenhead: Open University Press.

Curran, J. (2010) *Media and Society*, 5th edition. London: Bloomsbury Academic Press.

Lacey, N. (2009) *Image and Representation: Key Concepts in Media Studies*, 2nd edition. Basingstoke: Palgrave Macmillan.

Thornham, S., Bassett, C. and Marris, P. (eds) (2009) *Media Studies: A Reader*, 3rd edition. Edinburgh: Edinburgh University Press.

Digital Media

Ash, J. (2015) *The Interface Envelope: Gaming, Technology, Power*. London: Bloomsbury.

Buckingham, D. and Willett, R. (2009) *Video Cultures: Media Technology and Everyday Creativity*. Basingstoke: Palgrave Macmillan.

Dovey, J. and Kennedy, H.W. (2006) *Game Cultures: Computer Games as New Media*. Maidenhead: Open University Press.

Egenfeldt-Nielsen, S., Smith, J.H. and Tosca, S.P. (2008) *Understanding Video Games: The Essential Introduction*. London: Routledge.

Gane, N. and Beer, D. (2008) *New Media: Key Concepts*. Oxford: Berg.

Grace, H. (2014) *Culture, Aesthetics and Affect in Ubiquitous Media: The Prosaic Image*. London: Routledge.

Hjorth, L. (2011) *Games and Gaming: An Introduction to New Media*. Oxford: Berg.

Juul, J. (2010) *A Casual Revolution: Reinventing Video Games and Their Players*. Cambridge, MA: MIT Press.

Mäyrä, F. (2008) *Introduction to Game Studies: Games and Culture*. London: Sage.

Rettberg, J.W. (2014) *Seeing Ourselves Through Technology: How We Use Selfies, Blogs and Wearable Devices to See and Shape Ourselves*. Basingstoke: Palgrave Macmillan.

Vernallis, C. (2013) *Unruly Media: YouTube, Music Video, and the New Digital Cinema*. New York: Oxford University Press.

REFERENCES

Acton, M. (2008) *Learning to Look at Paintings*, 2nd edition. London: Routledge.

Adler, J. (1989) 'Origins of sightseeing', *Annals of Tourism Research* 16: 7–29.

Allen, L. (2011) '"Picture this": Using photo-methods in research on sexualities and schooling', *Qualitative Research* 11: 487–504.

Allen, Q. (2012) 'Photographs and stories: Ethics, benefits and dilemmas of using participant photography with Black middle-class male youth', *Qualitative Research* 12: 443–58.

Alpers, S. (1983) *The Art of Describing: Dutch Art in the Seventeenth Century*. London: John Murray.

Ambrose, D. (2007) 'Gilles Deleuze (1925–1995)', in D. Costello and J. Vickery (eds), *Art: Key Contemporary Thinkers*. Oxford: Berg. pp. 117–20.

American Sociological Association (n.d.) *Code of Ethics*, www.asanet.org/about/ethics.cfm (accessed August 26, 2015).

Anden-Papadopoulos, K. (2009) 'Body horror on the internet: US soldiers recording the war in Iraq and Afghanistan', *Media, Culture and Society* 31: 921–38.

Andersen, N.A. (2003) *Discursive Analytical Strategies: Understanding Foucault, Koselleck, Laclau, Luhmann*. Bristol: Policy Press.

Andrews, S. (1995) *Story and Space in Renaissance Art*. Cambridge: Cambridge University Press.

Ang, I. (1985) *Watching Dallas*. London: Methuen.

Ang, I. (1989) 'Wanted: Audiences. On the politics of empirical audience studies', in E. Seiter, H. Borchers, G. Kreutzner and E.-M. Warth (eds), *Remote Control: Television, Audiences, and Cultural Power*. London: Routledge. pp. 96–105.

Antebi, S. (2009) 'The talk show uploaded: YouTube and the technicity of the body', *Social Identities* 15: 297–311.

Appadurai, A. (1986) 'Introduction: Commodities and the politics of value', in A. Appadurai, (ed.), *The Social Life of Things: Commodities in Cultural Perspective*. Cambridge: Cambridge University Press. pp. 3–63.

Armstrong, C. (1996) 'Visual culture questionnaire', *October* 77: 26–8.

Armstrong, C. (1998) *Scenes in a Library: Reading the Photograph in the Book*. London: MIT Press.

Arroyo, J. (2000) 'Mission: Sublime', in J. Arroyo (ed.), *Action/Spectacle Cinema: A Sight and Sound Reader*. London: British Film Institute. pp. 21–5.

Arscott, C. (2007) 'William Powell Frith's *The Railway Station*: Classification and the crowd', in M. Bills and V. Knight (eds), *William Powell Frith: Painting the Victorian Age*. London: Yale University Press. pp. 79–94.

Arvidsson, A. (2005) 'Brands: A critical perspective', *Journal of Consumer Culture* 5: 235–58.

Arvidsson, A. (2006) *Brands: Meaning And Value in Media Culture*. London: Routledge.

Ash, J. (2015) *The Interface Envelope: Gaming, Technology, Power*. London: Bloomsbury.

Askew, K. and Wilk, R.R. (eds) (2002) *The Anthropology of Media: A Reader*. Oxford: Blackwell.

Atkinson, P., Coffey, A. and Delamont, S. (eds) (2007) *Handbook of Ethnography*. London: Sage.

Bagnoli, A. (2009) 'Beyond the standard interview: The use of graphic elicitation and arts-based methods', *Qualitative Research* 9: 547–70.

Bainbridge, W.S. (2010) *The Warcraft Civilization: Social Science in a Virtual World*. London: MIT Press.

Baker, T. and Wang, C. (2006) 'Photovoice: Use of a participatory action research method to explore the chronic pain experience in older adults', *Qualitative Health Research* 16: 1405–13.

Bal, M. (1991) *Reading Rembrandt: Beyond the Word-Image Opposition*. Cambridge: Cambridge University Press.

Bal, M. (1996) *Double Exposures: The Subject of Cultural Analysis*. London: Routledge.

Bal, M. (2003) 'Visual essentialism and the object of visual culture', *Journal of Visual Culture* 2: 5–32.

Bal, M. and Bryson, N. (1991) 'Semiotics and art history', *Art Bulletin* 73: 174–208.

Bal, M. and Bryson, N. (eds) (2001) *Looking In: The Art of Viewing*. London: Routledge.

Ball, M.S. and Smith, G.W.H. (1992) *Analyzing Visual Data*. London: Sage.

Ball, S. and Gilligan, C. (2010) 'Visualising migration and social division: Insights from social sciences and the visual arts', *FQS: Forum Qualitative Social Research* 11. http://www.qualitative-research.net/index.php/fqs/article/view/1486 (accessed August 27, 2015).

Banks, M. (2001) *Visual Methods in Social Research*. London: Sage.

Banks, M. (2008) *Using Visual Data in Qualitative Research*. London: Sage.

Banks, M. and Ruby, J. (eds) (2011) *Made to Be Seen: Perspectives on the History of Visual Anthropology*. Chicago: University of Chicago Press.

Bann, S. (1998) 'Art history and museums', in M.A. Cheetham, M.A. Holly and K. Moxey (eds), *The Subjects of Art History: Historical Objects in Contemporary Perspective*. Cambridge: Cambridge University Press. pp. 230–49.

Barbash, I. and Taylor, L. (1997) *Cross-Cultural Filmmaking: A Handbook for Making Documentary and Ethnographic Films and Video*. Berkeley, CA: California University Press.

Barker, E. (ed.) (1999) *Contemporary Cultures of Display*. London: Yale University Press in association with the Open University.

Barker, J. and Smith, F. (2012) 'What's in focus? A critical discussion of photography, children and young people', *International Journal of Social Research Methodology* 15: 91–103.

Barker, M. (2009) 'Fantasy audiences versus fantasy audiences', in W. Buckland (ed.), *Film Theory and Contemporary Hollywood Movies*. London: Routledge. pp. 286–309.

Barnard, M. (2001) *Approaches to Understanding Visual Culture*. Houndmills: Palgrave Macmillan.

Barnet, B.A. (2009) 'Idiomedia: The rise of personalized, aggregated content', *Continuum: Journal of Media & Cultural Studies* 23: 93.

Barone, T. and Eisner, E.W. (2012) *Arts Based Research*. Thousand Oaks, CA: Sage.

Barrett, J. (2011) *Museums and the Public Sphere*. Oxford: Wiley Blackwell.

Barrett, M. (1991) *The Politics of Truth: From Marx to Foucault*. Cambridge: Polity Press.

Barthes, R. (1973) *Mythologies,* translated by A. Lavers. London: Paladin.

Barthes, R. (1977) *Image–Music–Text*, edited and translated by S. Heath. London: Fontana.

Barthes, R. (1982) *Camera Lucida: Reflections on Photography,* translated by R. Howard. London: Jonathan Cape.

Bartlett, R. (2013) 'Playing with meaning: Using cartoons to disseminate research findings', *Qualitative Research* 13: 214–27.

Bates, C. (ed.) (2014) *Video Methods: Social Science Research in Motion*. London: Routledge.

Battersby, C. (1994) *Gender and Genius: Towards a Feminist Aesthetics*. London: Women's Press.

Baudrillard, J. (1988) *Selected Writings*, edited by M. Poster. Cambridge: Polity Press.

Becker, H. (1982) *Art Worlds*. Berkeley, CA: University of California Press.

Becker, H. (2002) 'Visual evidence: A Seventh Man, the specified generalization, and the work of the reader', *Visual Studies* 17: 3–11.

Becker, H. (2004) 'Afterword: Photography as evidence, photographs as exposition', in C. Knowles and J. Sweetman (eds), *Picturing the Social Landscape: Visual Methods and the Sociological Imagination*. London: Routledge pp. 193–7.

Bedaux, J.B. (1986) 'The reality of symbols', *Semiolus* 16: 5–28.

Beer, D. (2013) *Popular Culture and New Media: The Politics of Circulation*. Basingstoke: Palgrave Macmillan.

Bell, E., Warren, S. and Schroeder, J. (eds) (2014) *The Routledge Companion to Visual Organisation*. London: Routledge.

Bell, P. (2001) 'Content analysis of visual images', in T. van Leeuwen and C. Jewitt (eds), *Handbook of Visual Analysis*. London: Sage. pp. 10–34.

Benjamin, W. (1973) 'The work of art in the age of mechanical reproduction', in H. Zohn (trans.) *Illuminations*. London: Fontana. pp. 219–53.

Bennett, T. (1995) *The Birth of the Museum: History, Theory, Politics*. London: Routledge.

Bennett, T. (2004) *Pasts Beyond Memory: Evolution, Museums, Colonialism*. London: Routledge.

Bennett, T. (2009) *Culture, Class, Distinction*. London: Routledge.

Berger, J. (1972) *Ways of Seeing*. London: British Broadcasting Corporation, and Harmondsworth: Penguin.

Berger, J. and Mohr, J. (1975) *A Seventh Man*. Harmondsworth: Penguin.

Bermejo, F. (2009) 'Audience manufacture in historical perspective: From broadcasting to Google', *New Media and Society* 11: 133–54.

Berry, C., Harbord, J. and Moore, R. (eds) (2013) *Public Space, Media Space*. Basingstoke: Palgrave Macmillan.

Beugnet, M. and Ezra, E. (2009) 'A portrait of the twenty-first century', *Screen* 50: 77–85.

Bignell, J. (2002) *Media Semiotics: An Introduction*, 2nd edition. Manchester: Manchester University Press.

Bird, J., Curtis, B. and Mash, M. (eds) (1996) *The BLOCK Reader in Visual Culture*. London: Routledge.

Blinn, L. and Harrist, A.W. (1991) 'Combining native instant photography and photo-elicitation', *Visual Anthropology* 4: 175–92.

Böck, M. and Norbert, P. (eds) (2013) *Multimodality and Social Semiosis: Communication, Meaning-Making and Learning in the Work of Gunther Kress*. London: Routledge.

Bogue, R. (2003) *Deleuze on Cinema*. London: Routledge.

Bolter, J.D. and R.A. Grusin (1999) *Remediation: Understanding New Media*. Cambridge, MA: MIT Press.

Bolton, A., Pole, C. and Mizen, P. (2001) 'Picture this: researching child workers', *Sociology* 35: 501–18.

Bolton, R. (1989) 'In the American West: Richard Avedon Incorporated', in R. Bolton (ed.), *The Contest of Meaning: Critical Histories of Photography*. London: MIT Press. pp. 261–82.

Bond S., DeSilvey C. and Ryan, J.R. (2013) *Visible Mending: Everyday Repairs in the South West*. Axminster: Uniform Books.

Boothroyd, D. (2009) 'Touch, time and technics: Levinas and the ethics of haptic communications', *Theory, Culture and Society* 26: 330–45.

Bordo, S. (1993) *Unbearable Weight: Feminism, Western Culture, and the Body*. Berkeley, CA: California University Press.

Bourdieu, P. (1984) *Distinction: A Social Critique of the Judgement of Taste*, translated by R. Nice. London: Routledge and Kegan Paul.

Bourdieu, P. and Darbel, A. with Schnapper, D. (1991) *The Love of Art: European Art Museums and Their Public*. Cambridge: Polity Press.

Bowie, M. (1991) *Lacan*. London: Fontana.

boyd, d. (2014) *It's Complicated: The Social Lives of Networked Teens*. London: Yale University Press.

Boydell, K.M., Gladstone, B.M., Volpe, T., Allemang, B. and Stasiulis, E. (2012) 'The production and dissemination of knowledge: A scoping review of arts-based health research', *Forum Qualitative Sozialforschung / Forum: Qualitative Social Research* 13. http://www.qualitative-research.net/index.php/fqs/article/view/1711 (accessed August 25, 2015).

Braun, V. and Clarke, V. (2013) *Successful Qualitative Research: A Practical Guide for Beginners*. London: Sage.

British Sociological Association, VSSG (2006) 'Statement of ethical practices for the British Sociological Association', www.visualsociology.org.uk/BSA_VS_ethical_statement.pdf (accessed August 25, 2015).

Brooker, W. and Jermyn, D. (2003) *The Audience Studies Reader*. London: Routledge.

Brooksby, A. (2008) 'Exploring the representation of health in videogames: A content analysis', *Cyberpsychology and Behavior* 11: 771–3.

Bruno, G. (1993) *Streetwalking on a Ruined Map: Cultural Theory and the City Films of Elvira Notari*. Princeton, NJ: Princeton University Press.

Bruno, G. (2002) *Atlas of Emotion: Journeys in Art, Architecture and Film*. London: Verso.

Bryman, A. (2012) *Social Research Methods*, 4th edition. Oxford: Oxford University Press.

Bryson, N. (1988) 'The gaze in the expanded field', in H. Foster (ed.), *Vision and Visuality*. Seattle, WA: Bay Press. pp. 87–108.

Bryson, N. (1991) 'Semiology and visual interpretation', in N. Bryson, M.A. Holly and K. Moxey (eds), *Visual Theory: Painting and Interpretation*. Cambridge: Polity Press. pp. 61–73.

Bryson, N., Holly, M.A. and Moxey, K. (1994) 'Introduction', in N. Bryson, M.A. Holly and K. Moxey (eds), *Visual Culture: Images and Intepretations*. London: Wesleyan University Press of New England. pp. xv–xxix.

Buchanan, I. and P. MacCormack (2008) *Deleuze and the Schizoanalysis of Cinema*. London: Continuum.

Buckingham, D. (1987) *Public Secrets: EastEnders and Its Audience*. London: British Film Institute.

Buckingham, D. (1991) 'What are words worth? Interpreting children's talk about television', *Cultural Studies* 5: 228–45.

Buckingham, D. (2009) 'Creative visual methods in media research: Possibilities, problems and proposals', *Media, Culture and Society* 31: 559–77.

Burgess, J. and Green, J. (2009) *YouTube: Online Video and Participatory Culture*. Cambridge: Polity Press.

Burgess, M., Stermer, S. and Burgess, S. (2007) 'Sex, lies, and video games: The portrayal of male and female characters on video game covers', *Sex Roles* 57: 419–33.

Burgin, V. (1986) *The End of Art Theory: Criticism and Postmodernity*. Basingstoke: Macmillan.

Burgin, V. (1992) 'Fantasy', in E. Wright (ed.), *Feminism and Psychoanalysis: A Critical Dictionary*. Oxford: Blackwell. pp. 84–8.

Burke, P. (2001) *Eyewitnessing: The Uses of Images as Historical Evidence*. London: Reaktion.

Butler, J. (1990) *Gender Trouble: Feminism and the Subversion of Identity*. London: Routledge.

Butler-Kisber, L. (2010) *Qualitative Inquiry: Thematic, Narrative and Arts-Informed Perspectives*. Thousand Oaks, CA: Sage.

Cameron, E. (2007) 'Exhibit and point of sale: Negotiating commerce and culture at the Vancouver Art Gallery', *Social and Cultural Geography* 8: 551–73.

Caple, H. (2013) *Photojournalism: A Social Semiotic Approach*. Basingstoke: Palgrave Macmillan.

Carlson, E., Engebretson, J. and Chamberlain, R. (2006) 'Photovoice as a social process of critical consciousness', *Qualitative Health Research* 16: 836–52.

Carpentier, N. (2009) 'Participation is not enough: The conditions of possibility of mediated participatory practices', *European Journal of Communication* 24: 407–20.

CarsUK (2010) 'Alfa Romeo Giulietta; Uma Thurman; William Shakespeare. Mix & Serve', http://www.carsuk.net/alfa-romeo-giulietta-uma-thurman-william-shakespeare-mix-serve/ (accessed August 16, 2015).

Casetti, F. (2013) 'What is a screen nowadays?', in, C. Berry, J. Harbord, and R. Moore (eds), *Public Space, Media Space*. Basingstoke: Palgrave Macmillan. pp. 16–40.

Casid, J.H. and D'Souza, A. (eds) (2014) *Art History in the Wake of the Global Turn*. Williamstown, MA: Sterling and Francine Clarke Art Institute.

Celant, G. (1996) 'A visual machine: Art installation and its modern archetypes', in R. Greenberg, B.W. Ferguson and S. Nairne (eds), *Thinking About Exhibitions*. London: Routledge. pp. 371–86.

Celebration of Repair (2015) http://projects.exeter.ac.uk/celebrationofrepair/homepage/ (accessed June 17, 2015).

Chalfen, R. (1987) *Snapshot Versions of Life*. Bowling Green, OH: Bowling Green State University Popular Press.

Chandler, D. (2007) *Semiotics: The Basics*. Abingdon: Routledge.

Cheetham, M.A., Holly, M.A. and Moxey, K. (2005) 'Visual studies, historiography and aesthetics', *Journal of Visual Culture* 4: 75–90.

Clark, A. (2010) *Transforming Children's Spaces: Children's and Adults' Participation in Designing Learning Environments*. London: Routledge.

Clark, A. (2011) 'Multimodal map making with young children: Exploring ethnographic and participatory methods', *Qualitative Research* 11: 311–30.

Clark, A. (2012) 'Visual ethics in a contemporary landscape', in S. Pink (ed.), *Advances in Visual Methodology*. London: Sage. pp. 17–35.

Clark, A. and Moss, P. (2001) *Listening to Young Children: The Mosaic Approach*. London: National Children's Bureau.

Clark-Ibanez, M. (2007) 'Inner-city children in sharper focus: Sociology of childhood and photo elicitation interviews', in G.C. Stanczak (ed.), *Visual Research Methods: Image, Society, and Representation*. London: Sage. pp. 167–96.

Clough, P.T. (2008) 'The affective turn: Political economy, biomedia and bodies', *Theory, Culture and Society* 25: 1–22.

Clough, P.T. and Halley, J.O. (eds) (2007) *The Affective Turn: Theorizing the Social*. Durham, NC: Duke University Press.

Cohan, S. and Hark, I.R. (eds) (1993) *Screening the Male: Exploring Masculinities in Hollywood Cinema*. London: Routledge.

Coleman, R. and Ringrose, J. (2013) *Deleuze and Research Methodologies*. Edinburgh: Edinburgh University Press.

Collier, J. (1967) *Visual Anthropology: Photography as a Research Method*. New York: Holt, Rinehart and Winston.

Colman, F. (2011) *Deleuze and Cinema: The Film Concepts*. Oxford: Berg.

Coombes, A. (1994) *Reinventing Africa: Museums, Material Culture and Popular Imagination in Late Victorian and Edwardian England*. London: Yale University Press.

Coover, R. (2011) 'The digital panorama and cinemascapes', in T. Bartscherer and R. Coover (eds), *Switching Codes: Thinking Through Digital Technology in the Humanities and the Arts*. Chicago: University of Chicago Press. pp. 199–217.

Cope, P. (2007a) *Teach Yourself Digital Home Movie Making*. London: Hodder Education.

Cope, P. (2007b) *Get the Most from Your Digital Home Movie Making*. Newton Abbot: David and Charles.

Copjec, J. (1989) 'The orthopsychic subject: Film theory and the reception of Lacan', *October* 49: 53–72.

Costello, D. and Vickery, J. (eds) (2007) *Art: Key Contemporary Thinkers*. Oxford: Berg.

Couldry, N. (2009) 'Does "the media" have a future?', *European Journal of Communication* 24: 437–49.

Couldry, N. (2011) 'The necessary future of the audience ... and how to research it', in V. Nightingale (ed.), *The Handbook of Media Audiences*. Chichester: Wiley Blackwell. pp. 213–29.

Couldry, N., Livingstone, S.M. and Markham, T. (2010) *Media Consumption and Public Engagement: Beyond the Presumption of Attention*, revised edition. Basingstoke: Palgrave Macmillan.

Court, E. (1999) 'Africa on display: Exhibiting art by Africans', in E. Barker (ed.), *Contemporary Cultures of Display*. London: Yale University Press in association with the Open University. pp. 147–73.

Cowie, E. (1990) 'Fantasia', in P. Adams and E. Cowie (eds), *The Woman in Question: m/f*. London: Verso. pp. 149–96.

Cowling, M. (1989) *The Artist as Anthropologist: The Representation of Type and Character in Victorian Art*. Cambridge: Cambridge University Press.

Crary, J. (1992) *Techniques of the Observer: Vision and Modernity in the Nineteenth Century*. London: MIT Press.

Crilly, N., Blackwell, A.F. and Clarkson, P.J. (2006) 'Graphic elicitation: Using research diagrams as interview stimuli', *Qualitative Research* 6: 341–66.

Croghan, R., Griffin, C., Hunter, J. and Phoenix, A. (2008) 'Young people's constructions of self: Notes on the use and analysis of the photo-elicitation methods', *International Journal of Social Research Methodology* 11: 345–56.

Cubitt, S. (2006) 'Analogue and digital', *Theory, Culture and Society* 23: 250–1.

Cubitt, S. (2014) *The Practice of Light: A Genealogy of Visual Technologies*. London: MIT Press.

Curtis, L.P. (2001) *Jack the Ripper and the London Press*. London: Yale University Press.

D'Alleva, A. (2010) *How to Write Art History*, second edition. London: Laurence King.

Darbyshire, P., MacDougall, C. and Schiller, W. (2005) 'Multiple methods in qualitative research with children: More insight or just more?', *Qualitative Research* 5: 417–36.

Davis, W. (2011) *A General Theory of Visual Culture*. Princeton, NJ: Princeton University Press.

de Lange, N., Mitchell, C. and Stuart, J. (2007) *Putting People in the Picture: Visual Methodologies for Social Change*. Rotterdam: Sense.

de Lauretis, T. (1994) *The Practice of Love: Lesbian Sexuality and Perverse Desire*. Bloomington, IN: Indiana University Press.

de Lauretis, T. (1995) 'On the subject of fantasy', in L. Pietropaulo and A. Testaferri (eds), *Feminisms in the Cinema*. Bloomington, IN: Indiana University Press. pp. 63–5.

deAgonia, M. (2015) 'Apple "springs forward" with more than just the Watch', Computerworld. http://www.computerworld.com/article/2895055/apple-springs-forward-with-more-than-just-the-watch.html (accessed August 16, 2015).

Debord, G. (1983) *Society of the Spectacle*. Detroit, MI: Black and Red.

Degen, M.M. (2008) *Sensing Cities: Regenerating Public Life in Barcelona and Manchester*. London: Routledge.

Degen, M., Melhuish, C. and Rose, G. (2015) 'Producing place atmospheres digitally: Architecture, digital visualisation practices and the experience economy', *Journal of Consumer Culture*. doi: 10.1177/1469540515572238

Deleuze, G. (2005) *Cinema*. 2 vols. Continuum Impacts. London: Continuum.

Dennis, S., Jr, Gaulocher, S., Carpiano, R. and Brown, D. (2009) 'Participatory photo mapping (PPM): Exploring an integrated method for health and place research with young people', *Health and Place* 15: 466–73.

Denzin, N.K. and Giardina, M.D. (eds) (2007) *Ethical Futures in Qualitative Research: Decolonizing the Politics of Knowledge*. Walnut Creek, CA: Left Coast Press.

DeSilvey, C., Ryan, J.R. and Bond, P. (2014) '21 stories,' *Cultural Geographies* 21: 657–72.

Deutsche, R. (1991) 'Boys town', *Environment and Planning D: Society and Space* 9: 5–30.

Dhaenens, F. (2012) 'Queer cuttings on YouTube: Re-editing soap operas as a form of fan-produced queer resistance', *European Journal of Cultural Studies* 15: 442–56.

Di Bello, P. (2007) *Women's Albums and Photography in Victorian England: Ladies, Mothers and Flirts*. Aldershot: Ashgate.

Dicks, B., Soyinka, B. and Coffey, A. (2006) 'Multimodal ethnography', *Qualitative Research* 6: 77–96.

Doane, M.A. (1982) 'Film and the masquerade: Theorising the female spectator', *Screen* 3: 74–87.

Doane, M.A. (1987) *The Desire to Desire: The Woman's Film of the 1940s*. Bloomington, IN: Indiana University Press.

Doane, M.A. (1991) *Femmes Fatales: Feminism, Film Theory, Psychoanalysis*. London: Routledge.

Dodman, D.R. (2003) 'Shooting in the city: An autophotographic exploration of the urban environment in Kingston, Jamaica', *Area* 35: 293–304.

Doisneau, R. (1990) *Renault: In the Thirties*, edited by M. Koetzle. London: Dirk Nishen.

Doisneau, R. (1991) *Robert Doisneau: Interview with Robert Doisneau by Sylvain Roumette*. London: Thames and Hudson.

Douglas, N. (2014) 'It's supposed to look like shit: The internet ugly aesthetic', *Journal of Visual Culture* 13: 314–39.

Dowler, L. (2002) 'Women on the frontlines: Rethinking war narratives post-9/11', *Geojournal* 58: 59–65.

Downing, L. and Saxton, L. (2010) *Film and Ethics: Foreclosed Encounters*. London: Routledge.

Driver, F. (2013) 'Hidden histories made visible? Reflections on a geographical exhibition', *Transactions of the Institute of British Geographers* 38: 420–35.

Drucker, J. (2011) 'Humanities approaches to graphical display', *Digital Humanities* 5. http://www.digitalhumanities.org/dhq/vol/5/1/000091/000091.html (accessed August 27, 2015).

Dudley, S.H. (ed.) (2010) *Museum Materialities: Objects, Engagements, Interpretations*. London: Routledge.

Duncan, C. (1993) *The Aesthetics of Power: Essays in Critical Art History*. Cambridge: Cambridge University Press.

Duncan, C. (1995) *Civilising Rituals: Inside Public Art Museums*. London: Routledge.

Dyer, G. (1982) *Advertising as Communication*. London: Methuen.

Dyer, R. (1982) 'Don't look now: The male pin-up', *Screen* 23: 61–73.

Dyer, R. (1990) *Now You See It: Historical Studies on Lesbian and Gay Film*. London: Routledge.

Dyer, R. (1997) *White*. London: Routledge.

Economic and Social Research Council (2015) *ESRC Framework for Research Ethics*. Swindon: Economic and Social Research Council. http://www.esrc.ac.uk/_images/framework-for-research-ethics_tcm8-33470.pdf (accessed August 26, 2015).

Edensor, T. (2005) *Industrial Ruins: Space, Aesthetics and Modernity*. Oxford: Berg.

Edgerton, S.Y. (1975) *The Renaissance Rediscovery of Perspective*. New York: Harper and Row.

Edwards, E. (2001) *Raw Histories: Photographs, Anthropology and Museums*. Oxford: Berg.

Edwards, E. (2002) 'Material beings: Objecthood and ethnographic photographs', *Visual Studies* 17: 67–75.

Edwards, E. (ed.) (1992) *Anthropology and Photography, 1860–1920*. London: Yale University Press and the Royal Anthropological Institute.

Elkins, J. (1991) 'On the *Arnolfini Portrait* and the *Lucca Madonna*: Did Jan van Eyck have a perspective system?', *Art Bulletin* LXXIII: 53–62.

Elkins, J. (1994) *The Poetics of Perspective*. Ithaca, NY: Cornell University Press.

Elkins, J. (1998) *On Pictures and the Words That Fail Them*. Cambridge: Cambridge University Press.

Elkins, J., Valiavicharska, Z. and Kim, A. (eds) (2010) *Art and Globalization*. Pennsylvania University Park: Pennsylvania State University Press.

Elsaesser, T. (2013) 'The "return" of 3-D: On some of the logics and genealogies of the image in the twenty-first century', *Critical Inquiry* 39: 217–46.

Emmison, M. and Smith, P. (2000) *Researching the Visual: Images, Objects, Contexts and Interactions in Social and Cultural Inquiry*. London: Sage.

Emmison, M., Smith, P. and Mayall, M. (2012) *Researching the Visual*, 2nd edition. London: Sage.

Esin, C. and Squire, C. (2013) 'Visual autobiographies in east London: Narratives of still images, interpersonal exchanges, and intrapersonal dialogues', *Forum Qualitative Sozialforschung / Forum: Qualitative Social Research* 14. http://www.qualitative-research.net/index.php/fqs/article/view/1971 (accessed August 27, 2015).

Evans, H. and Evans, M. (2006) *Picture Researcher's Handbook: An International Guide To Picture Sources And How To Use Them*, 8th edition. Leatherhead: Pira International.

Evans, J. and Hall, S. (1999) *Visual Culture: The Reader*, 2nd edition. London: Sage, in association with the Open University.

Fairclough, N. (2010) *Critical Discourse Analysis: The Critical Study of Language*, 2nd edition. Harlow: Longman.

Fanon, F. (1986) *Black Skin, White Masks*. New York: Grove Press.

Farrell, A. (2005) *Ethical Research with Children*. London: Open University Press.

Favero, P. (2013) 'Getting our hands dirty (again): Interactive documentaries and the meaning of images in the digital age', *Journal of Material Culture* 18: 259–77.

Fernie, E. (1995) *Art History and Its Methods: A Critical Anthology*. London: Phaidon.

Fishman, W.J. (1988) *East End 1888*. London: Duckworth.

Fiske, J. (1994) 'Audiencing', in N.K. Denzin and Y.S. Lincoln (eds), *Handbook of Qualitative Methods*. London: Sage.

Fleer, M. and Ridgway, A. (eds) (2014) *Visual Methodologies and Digital Tools for Researching with Young Children: Transforming Visuality*. London: Springer.

Flores, A. and James, C. (2013) 'Morality and ethics behind the screen: Young people's perspectives on digital life', *New Media & Society* 15: 834–52.

Foster, H. (1988) 'Preface', in H. Foster (ed.), *Vision and Visuality*. Seattle, WA: Bay Press. pp. ix–xiv.

Foster, H. (1996) 'The archive without museums', *October* 77: 97–119.

Foucault, M. (1972) *The Archeology of Knowledge*, translated by A.M. Sheridan Smith. London: Tavistock Publications.

Foucault, M. (1977) *Discipline and Punish: The Birth of the Prison*, translated by A. Sheridan. London: Allen Lane.

Foucault, M. (1979) *The History of Sexuality, Volume I: An Introduction*, translated by R. Hurley. London: Allen Lane.

Franzen, S. (2013) 'Engaging a specific, not general, public: The use of ethnographic film in public scholarship', *Qualitative Research* 13: 414–27.

Fraser, A. (2005) 'Isn't this a wonderful place?' (A tour of the Guggenheim Bilbao)', in A.M. Guasch and J. Zulaika (eds), *Learning from the Bilbao Guggenheim*, Reno, NV: Center for Basque Studies, University of Nevada. pp. 37–58.

Frith, H. and Harcourt, D. (2007) 'Using photographs to capture women's experiences of chemotherapy: Reflecting on the method', *Qualitative Health Research* 17: 1340–50.

Frosh, P. (2003) *The Image Factory: Consumer Culture, Photography and the Visual Content Industry*. London: Berg.

Fyfe, G. and Law, J. (1988) 'Introduction: On the invisibility of the visible', in G. Fyfe and J. Law (eds), *Picturing Power: Visual Depiction and Social Relations*. London: Routledge. pp. 1–14.

Fyfe, G. and Ross, M. (1996) 'Decoding the visitor's gaze: Rethinking museum visiting', in S. MacDonald and G. Fyfe (eds), *Theorizing Museums*. Blackwell: Oxford. pp. 127–50.

Gage, J. (1993) *Colour and Culture: Practice and Meaning from Antiquity to Abstraction*. London: Thames and Hudson.

Gaimster, J. (2011) *Visual Research Methods in Fashion*. Oxford: Berg.

Gaines, J. (1988) 'White privilege and looking relations: Race and gender in feminist film theory', *Screen* 29: 12–27.

Galman, S.A. (2009) 'The truthful messenger: Visual methods and representation in qualitative research in education', *Qualitative Research* 9: 197–217.

Gane, N. and Beer, D. (2008) *New Media: Key Concepts*. Oxford: Berg.

Garner, S. (ed) (2008) *Writing on Drawing: Essays on Drawing Practice and Research*. Bristol: Intellect.

Gee, J.P. (2013) 'Proactive design theories of sign use: Reflections on Gunther Kress', in M. Böck and N. Pachler (eds), *Multimodality and Social Semiosis: Communication, Meaning-Making and Learning in the World of Gunther Kress*. London: Routledge. pp. 43–53.

Gell, A. (1998) *Art and Agency: An Anthropological Theory*. Oxford: Clarendon Press.

Geuens, J.-P. (2013) 'Angels of light', in C. Vernallis, A. Herzog and J. Richardson (eds), *The Oxford Handbook of Sound and Image in Digital Media*. Oxford: Oxford University Press. pp. 45–60.

Gibbs, A. (2011) 'Affect theory and its audience', in V. Nightingale (ed.), *The Handbook of Media Audiences*. Chichester: Wiley Blackwell. pp. 251–66.

Gilbert, N. (2008) *Researching Social Life*, 3rd edition. London: Sage.

Gilbert, R. (1995) *Living with Art*, 4th edition. London: McGraw–Hill.

Gill, R. (1996) 'Discourse analysis: Practical implementation', in J.T.E. Richardson (ed.), *Handbook of Qualitative Methods for Psychology and the Social Sciences*. Leicester: British Psychological Society. pp. 141–56.

Gillespie, M. (1995) *Television, Ethnicity and Cultural Change*. London: Routledge.

Gillespie, M. (2005) 'Television drama and audience ethnography', in M. Gillespie (ed.), *Media Audiences*. Maidenhead: Open University Press. pp. 137–82.

Gillespie, T. (2014) 'The relevance of algorithms', in *Media Technologies: Essays on Communication, Materiality, and Society*, edited by T. Gillespie, P.J. Boczkowski and K.A. Foot. London: MIT Press. pp. 167–93.

Gilligan, C. and Marley, C. (2010) 'Migration and divisions: Thoughts on (anti-) narrativity in visual representations of mobile people', *FQS: Forum Qualitative Social Research* 11. http://www.qualitative-research.net/index.php/fqs/article/view/1476.

Gilman, S. (1985) *Difference and Pathology: Stereotypes of Sexuality, Race and Madness*. Ithaca, NY: Cornell University Press.

Gilman, S. (1990) '"I'm down on whores": Race and gender in Victorian London', in D. Goldberg (ed.), *The Anatomy of Racism*. Minneapolis, MN: Minnesota University Press. pp. 146–70.

Ginsburg, F.D., Abu-Lughod, L. and Larkin, B. (eds) (2002) *Media Worlds: Anthropology on New Terrain*. Berkeley, CA: University of California Press.

Glasgow Media Group (1976) *Bad News*. London: Routledge and Kegan Paul.

Glasgow Media Group (1980) *More Bad News*. London: Routledge and Kegan Paul.

Goldman, R. (1992) *Reading Ads Socially*. London: Routledge.

Goldman, R. and Papson, S. (2011) *Landscapes of Capital*. Cambridge: Polity Press.

Good, J. (2015) *Photography and September 11th: Spectacle, Memory, Trauma*. London: Bloomsbury Academic.

Goodwin, C. (2001) 'Practices of seeing: Visual analysis: An ethnomethodological approach', in T. van Leeuwen and C. Jewitt (eds), *Handbook of Visual Analysis*. London: Sage. pp. 157–82.

Goriunova, O. (2013) 'New media idiocy', *Convergence: The International Journal of Research into New Media Technologies* 19: 223–35.

Gorton, K. (2009) *Media Audiences: Television, Meaning and Emotion*. Edinburgh: Edinburgh University Press.

Gosden, C., Larson, F. and Petch, A. (2007) *Knowing Things: Exploring the Collections at the Pitt Rivers Museum 1884–1945*. Oxford: Oxford University Press.

Grace, H. (2014) *Culture, Aesthetics and Affect in Ubiquitous Media: The Prosaic Image*. London: Routledge.

Grady, J. (2004) 'Working with visible evidence: An invitation and some practical advice', in C. Knowles and J. Sweetman (eds), *Picturing the Social Landscape: Visual Methods and the Sociological Imagination*. London: Routledge. pp.18–32.

Grady, J. (2011) 'Numbers into pictures: Visualization in social analysis', in E. Margolis and L. Pauwels (eds), *The Sage Handbook of Visual Research Methods*, London: Sage. pp. 494–529.

Graham, M., Hogan, B., Straumann, R.K. and Medhat, A. (2014) 'Uneven geographies of user-generated information: Patterns of increasing informational poverty', *Annals of the Association of American Geographers* 104: 746–64.

Graham, M., Zook, M. and Boulton, A. (2013) 'Augmented reality in urban places: Contested content and the duplicity of code', *Transactions of the Institute of British Geographers* 38: 464–79.

Graham-Brown, S. (1988) *Images of Women: The Portrayal of Women in Photography of the Middle East, 1860–1950*. London: Quartet.

Gray, A. (1992) *Video Playtime: The Gendering of a Leisure Technology*. London: Routledge.

Gray, J. (2003) 'New audiences, new textualities: Fans and anti-fans', *International Journal of Cultural Studies* 6: 64–81.

Green, N. (1990) *The Spectacle of Nature: Landscape and Bourgeois Nature in Nineteenth-Century France*. Manchester: Manchester University Press.

Greenberg, R., Ferguson, B.W. and Nairne, S. (eds) (1996) *Thinking About Exhibitions*. London: Routledge.

Gross, L., Katz, J.S. and Ruby, J. (2003) *Image Ethics in the Digital Age*. Minneapolis, MN: University of Minnesota Press.

Gruber, D.R. (2014) 'The (digital) majesty of all under heaven: Affective constitutive rhetoric at the Hong Kong Museum of History's multi-media exhibition of terracotta warriors', *Rhetoric Society Quarterly* 44: 148–67.

Grunenberg, C. (1999) 'The modern art museum', in E. Barker (ed.), *Contemporary Cultures of Display*. London: Yale University Press in association with the Open University. pp. 26–49.

Guasch, A.M. and Zulaika, J. (2005) 'Introduction', in A.M. Guasch and J. Zulaika (eds), *Learning from the Bilbao Guggenheim*. Reno, NV: Center for Basque Studies, University of Nevada. pp. 1–28.

Guell, C. and Ogilvie, D. (2015) 'Picturing commuting: Photovoice and seeking well-being in everyday travel', *Qualitative Research* 15: 201–18.

Guillemin, M. (2004) 'Understanding illness: Using drawings as a research method', *Qualitative Health Research* 14: 272–89.

Guillemin, M. and Drew, S. (2010) 'Questions of process in participant-generated visual methodologies', *Visual Studies* 25: 175–88.

Haacke, H. (2005) 'The Guggenheim Museum: A business plan', in A.M. Guasch and J. Zulaika (eds), *Learning from the Bilbao Guggenheim*, Reno, NV: Center for Basque Studies, University of Nevada. pp. 113–24.

Hagelin, S. (2008) 'Bleeding bodies and post-Cold War politics: *Saving Private Ryan* and the gender of vulnerability', in K. Randell and S. Redmond (eds), *The War Body on Screen*. London: Continuum. pp. 102–19.

Halavais, A. (2013) 'Search and networked attention', in J. Hartley, J. Burgess and A. Bruns (eds), *A Companion To New Media Dynamics*. Chichester: Wiley-Blackwell. pp. 249–60.

Hall, E. (1994) *The Arnolfini Betrothal*. Berkeley, CA: California University Press.

Hall, G. (2013) 'Towards a postdigital humanities: Cultural analytics and the computational turn to data-driven scholarship', *American Literature* 85: 781–809.

Hall, S. (1980) 'Encoding/decoding', in Centre for Contemporary Cultural Studies Culture (ed.), *Media, Language: Working Papers in Cultural Studies*. London: Hutchinson. pp. 128–38.

Hall, S. (1996) 'Introduction: Who needs identity?', in S. Hall and P. du Gay (eds), *Questions of Cultural Identity*. London: Sage. pp. 1–17.

Hall, S. (1997a) 'Introduction', in S. Hall (ed.), *Representation: Cultural Representations and Signifying Practices*. London: Sage. pp. 1–12.

Hall, S. (1997b) 'The work of representation', in S. Hall (ed.), *Representation: Cultural Representations and Signifying Practices*. London: Sage. pp. 13–74.

Hall, S. (1999) 'Introduction: Looking and subjectivity', in J. Evans and S. Hall (eds), *Visual Culture: The Reader*. London: Sage. pp. 309–14.

Halle, D. (1993) *Inside Culture: Art and Class in the American Home*. Chicago: University of Chicago Press.

Hamburger, J.F. (1997) *Nuns as Artists: The Visual Culture of a Medieval Convent*. Berkeley, CA: California University Press.

Hamilton, P. (1997) 'Representing the social: France and Frenchness in post-war humanist photography', in S. Hall (ed.), *Representation: Cultural Representations and Signifying Practices*. London: Sage. pp. 75–150.

Hamilton, P. (2006) *Visual Research Methods*. London: Sage.

Hammersley, M. and Atkinson, P. (2007) *Ethnography: Principles in Practice*, 3rd edition. London: Routledge.

Hand, M. (2012) *Ubiquitous Photography*. Cambridge: Polity Press.

Handler, R. and Gable, E. (1997) *The New History in an Old Museum: Creating the Past at Colonial Williamsburg*. Durham, NC: Duke University Press.

Hansen, M.B. (2004) *New Philosophy For a New Media*. Cambridge, MA: MIT Press.

Hansen, M.B. (2008) 'Benjamin's aura', *Critical Inquiry* 34 (2): 336–75.

Haraway, D. (1989) *Primate Visions: Gender, Race, and Nature in the World of Modern Science*. London: Routledge.

Haraway, D. (1991) *Simians, Cyborgs, and Women: The Reinvention of Nature*. London: Free Association Books.

Harper, D. (2001) *Changing Works: Visions of a Lost Agriculture*. Chicago: University of Chicago Press.

Harper, D. (2002) 'Talking about pictures: A case for photo-elicitation', *Visual Studies* 17: 13–26.

Harper, D. (2003) 'Framing photographic ethnography: A case study', *Ethnography* 4: 241.

Harper, D.A. (2006) *Good Company: A Tramp Life*, updated and expanded edition. Boulder, CO: Paradigm.

Hartley, J. (2012) *Digital Futures for Cultural and Media Studies*. Chichester: John Wiley.

Harvey, D. (1989) *The Condition of Postmodernity*. Oxford: Blackwell.

Hay, J. and Couldry, N. (eds) (2011) 'Rethinking convergence culture', *Cultural Studies* special issue 25 (4–5).

Hayles, K. (1999) *How We Became Posthuman: Virtual Bodies in Cybernetics, Literature, and Informatics*. Chicago: University of Chicago Press.

Hayles, K. (2004) 'Print is flat, code is deep: The importance of media-specific analysis', *Poetics Today* 25: 67–90.

Hayles, K. (2006) 'Unfinished work: From cyborg to cognisphere', *Theory, Culture and Society* 23: 159–66.

Hayles, K. (2012) *How We Think: Digital Media and Contemporary Technogenesis*. Chicago: University of Chicago Press.

Heath, C. and von Lehn, D. (2004) 'Configuring reception: Looking at exhibits in museums and galleries', *Theory, Culture and Society* 21: 43–65.

Heath, C., Luff, P. and Hindmarsh, J. (2009) *Audio Visual Methods in Social Research*. London: Sage.

Hernandez-Albujar, Y. (2007) 'The symbolism of video: Exploring migrant mothers' experiences', in G.C. Stanczak (ed.), *Visual Research Methods: Image, Society, and Representation*. London: Sage. pp. 281–306.

Hetherington, K. (1997) 'Museum topology and the will to connect', *Journal of Material Culture* 2: 199–218.

Heywood, I. and Sandywell, B. (eds) (2012) *Handbook of Visual Culture*. Oxford: Berg.

Higgin, T. (2009) 'Blackless fantasy: The disappearance of race in massively multiplayer online role-playing games', *Games and Culture* 4: 3–26.

Highfield, T. and Leaver, T. (2014) 'A methodology for mapping Instagram hashtags', *First Monday* 20. doi: http://dx.doi.org/10.5210/fm.v20i1.5563

Highmore, B. (2002) *Everyday Life and Cultural Theory: An Introduction*. London: Routledge.

Hill, A. (2009) *Re-imagining the War on Terror: Seeing, Waiting, Travelling*. Basingstoke: Palgrave Macmillan.

Hindmarsh, J., Luff, P. and Heath, C. (2010) *Video in Qualitative Research*. London: Sage.

Hitchcock, T. (2008) 'Digital searching and the re-formulation of research knowledge', in M. Greengrass and L. Hughes (eds), *The Virtual Representation of the Past*. Farnham: Ashgate. pp. 81–90.

Hodge, R. and Kress, G. (1988) *Social Semiotics*. Cambridge: Polity Press.

Hodgetts, D., Chamberlain, K. and Radley, A. (2007a) 'Considering photographs never taken during photo-production projects', *Qualitative Research in Psychology* 4: 263–80.

Hodgetts, D., Radley, A., Chamberlain, K. and Hodgetts, A. (2007b) 'Health inequalities and homelessness: Considering material, spatial and relational dimensions', *Journal of Health Psychology* 12: 709–25.

Holgate, J., Keles, J. and Kumarappan, L. (2012) 'Visualizing "community": An experiment in participatory photography among Kurdish diasporic workers in London', *The Sociological Review* 60: 312–32.

Holliday, R. (2004) 'Reflecting the self', in C. Knowles and J. Sweetman (eds), *Picturing the Social Landscape: Visual Methods and the Sociological Imagination*. London: Routledge. pp. 49–64.

Holly, M.A. (1996) *Past Looking: Historical Imagination and the Rhetoric of the Image*. Ithaca, NY: Cornell University Press.

Holmes, S. (2008) '"The viewers have ... taken over the airwaves?"': Participation, reality TV and approaching the audience-in-the-text', *Screen* 49: 13–31.

Hooper-Greenhill, E. (1992) *Museums and the Shaping of Knowledge*. London: Routledge.

Hooper-Greenhill, E. (1994) *Museums and Their Visitors*. London: Routledge.

Howells, R. (2003) *Visual Culture*. Cambridge: Polity Press.

Howells, R. and Negreiros, J. (2012) *Visual Culture*, 2nd edition. Cambridge: Polity Press.

Hughes, J. (ed.) (2012) *SAGE Visual Methods*. London: Sage.

Hunt, M.A. (2014) 'Urban photography/cultural geography: Spaces, objects, events', *Geography Compass* 8: 151–68.

Hyndman, J. (2003) Beyond either/or: A feminist analysis of September 11th. *ACME: An International E-Journal for Critical Geographies* 2: 1–13.

Iginla, B. (1992) 'Black feminist critique of psychoanalysis', in E. Wright (ed.), *Feminism and Psychoanalysis: A Critical Dictionary*. Oxford: Blackwell. pp. 31–3.

Iphofen, R. (2009) *Ethical Decision-Making in Social Research: A Practical Guide*. Basingstoke: Palgrave Macmillan.

Irigaray, L. (1985) *This Sex Which Is Not One*, translated by C. Porter. Ithaca, NY: Cornell University Press.

Iversen, M. (1986) 'Saussure v. Pierce: Models for a semiotics of visual art', in A.L. Rees and F. Borzello (eds), *The New Art History*. London: Camden Press. pp. 82–94.

Jacobs, J. (2013) 'Listen with your eyes: Towards a filmic geography', *Geography Compass* 7: 714–28.

Jacobsen, M.H. (ed.) (2009) *Encountering the Everyday: An Introduction to Sociologies of the Unnoticed*. Basingstoke: Palgrave Macmillan.

Jameson, F. (1984) 'Postmodernism, or the cultural logic of late capitalism', *New Left Review* 146: 53–92.

Jancovich, M. (1992) 'David Morley, The *Nationwide* studies', in M. Barker and A. Beezer (eds), *Reading into Cultural Studies*. London: Routledge. pp. 134–47.

Jay, M. (1993) *Downcast Eyes: The Denigration of Vision in Twentieth-Century French Thought*. Berkeley, CA: California University Press.

Jenkings, K.N., Woodward, R. and Winter, T. (2008) 'The emergent production of analysis in photo elicitation: Pictures of military identity', *Forum: Qualitative Social Research* 9. http://www.qualitative-research.net/index.php/fqs/article/viewArticle/1169/2582 (accessed August 25, 2015).

Jenkins, H. (1988) 'Star Trek rerun, reread, rewritten: Fan writing as textual poaching', *Critical Studies in Media Communication* 5: 85–107.

Jenkins, H. (1992) *Textual Poachers: Television Fans and Participatory Culture*. New York: Routledge.

Jenkins, H. (2006) *Fans, Bloggers, and Gamers: Exploring Participatory Culture*. New York: New York University Press.

Jenkins, H. (2008) *Convergence Culture: Where Old and New Media Collide*, updated edition. New York: New York University Press.

Jenkins, H. (2014) 'Rethinking "Rethinking Convergence/Culture"', *Cultural Studies* 28 (2): 267–97.

Jenkins, H., Ford, S. and Green, J. (2013) *Spreadable Media*. New York: New York University Press.

Jenks, C. (1995) 'The centrality of the eye in Western culture', in C. Jenks (ed.), *Visual Culture*. London: Routledge. pp. 1–12.

Jewitt, C. (2005) 'Multimodality, "Reading", and "Writing" for the 21st Century', *Discourse: Studies in the Cultural Politics of Education* 26: 315–31.

Jewitt, C. (2009) *The Routledge Handbook of Multimodal Analysis*. London: Routledge.

Jewitt, C. (2014a) 'An introduction to multimodality', in C. Jewitt (ed.), *The Routledge Handbook of Multimodal Analysis*, 2nd edition. London: Routledge. pp. 14–25.

Jewitt, C. (ed.) (2014b) *The Routledge Handbook of Multimodal Analysis*, 2nd edition. London: Routledge.

Jewitt, C. and Oyama, R. (2001) 'Visual meaning: A semiotic approach', in T. van Leeuwen and C. Jewitt (eds), *Handbook of Visual Analysis*. London: Sage, pp. 134–56.

Joanou, J. (2009) 'The bad and the ugly: Ethical concerns in participatory photographic methods with children living and working on the streets of Lima, Peru', *Visual Studies* 24: 214–23.

Johnsen, S., May, J. and Cloke, P. (2008) 'Imag(in)ing "homeless places": Using auto-photography to (re)examine the geographies of homelessness', *Area* 40: 194–207.

Johnson, F.L. (2008) *Imaging in Advertising: Verbal and Visual Codes of Commerce*. London: Routledge.

Johnson, K. (2011) 'Visualising mental health with an LGBT community group: Method, process, theory', in P. Reavey (ed.), *Visual Methods in Psychology: Using and Interpreting Images in Qualitative Research*. London: Routledge. pp. 173–89.

Jones, G.S. (1976) *Outcast London: A Study in the Relationship between Classes in Victorian Society*. London: Peregrine Books.

Jones, G.S. (1989) 'The "cockney" and the nation, 1780–1988', in D. Feldman and G.S. Jones (eds), *Metropolis London: Histories and Representations since 1800*. London: Routledge. pp. 272–324.

Jordan, S.R. (2014) 'Research integrity, image manipulation, and anonymizing photographs in visual social science research', *International Journal of Social Research Methodology* 17: 441–54.

Jordanova, L. (2012) *The Look of the Past: Visual and Material Evidence in Historical Practice*. Cambridge: Cambridge University Press.

Jorgenson, J. and T. Sullivan (2009) 'Accessing children's perspectives through participatory photo interviews', *Forum Qualitative Sozialforschung* 11. www.qualitative-research.net/index.php/fqs/issue/view/447 (accessed August 25, 2015).

Joselit, D. (2012) *After Art*. Princeton, NJ: Princeton University Press.

Jung, H. (2014) 'Let their voices be seen: Exploring mental mapping as a feminist visual methodology for the study of migrant women', *International Journal of Urban and Regional Research* 38: 985–1002.

Juul, J. (2010) *A Casual Revolution: Reinventing Video Games and Their Players*. Cambridge, MA: MIT Press.

Kearney, K.S. and Hyle, A.E. (2004) 'Drawing out emotions: The use of participant-produced drawings in qualitative inquiry', *Qualitative Research* 4: 361–82.

Keating, P. (1976) 'Introduction', in P. Keating (ed.), *Into Unknown England 1866–1913: Selections from the Social Explorers*. London: Fontana. pp. 11–32.

Keats, P.A. (2009) 'Multiple text analysis in narrative research: Visual, written, and spoken stories of experience', *Qualitative Research* 9: 181–95.

Kendall, G. and Wickham, G. (1999) *Using Foucault's Methods*. London: Sage.

Kidd, J. (2014) *Museums in the New Mediascape: Transmedia, Participation, Ethics*. Farnham: Ashgate.

Kittler, F.A. (1999) *Gramophone, Film, Typewriter*. Stanford, CA: Stanford University Press.

Klitzing, S. (2004) 'Women living in a homeless shelter: Stress, coping and leisure', *Journal of Leisure Research* 36: 483–512.

Klonk, C. (2009) *Spaces of Experience: Art Gallery Interiors from 1800 to 2000*. London: Yale University Press.

Knoblauch, H. (2009) *Video Analysis Methodology and Methods: Qualitative Audiovisual Data Analysis in Sociology*, 2nd edition. Frankfurt am Main: Peter Lang.

Knoblauch, H. and Tuma, R. (2011) 'Videography: An interpretative approach to video-recorded micro-social interaction', in E. Margolis and L. Pauwels (eds), *The Sage Handbook of Visual Research Methods*. London: Sage. pp. 414–29.

Knowles, C. and Harper, D.A. (2009) *Hong Kong Migrant Lives, Landscapes, and Journeys*. Chicago: University of Chicago Press.

Knowles, C. and Sweetman, P. (2004a) 'Introduction', in C. Knowles and P. Sweetman (eds), *Picturing the Social Landscape: Visual Methods and the Sociological Imagination*. London: Routledge. pp 1–17.

Knowles, C. and Sweetman, P. (eds) (2004b) *Picturing the Social Landscape: Visual Methods and the Sociological Imagination*. London: Routledge.

Knowles, G. and Cole, A. (2008) *Handbook of the Arts in Qualitative Research: Perspectives, Methodologies, Examples and Issues*. London: Sage.

Kress, G. (2010) *Multimodality: A Social Semiotic Approach to Contemporary Communication*. London: Routledge.

Kress, G. and van Leeuwen, T. (2006) *Reading Images: The Grammar of Visual Design*, 2nd edition. London: Routledge.

Krippendorff, K.H. (2013) *Content Analysis: An Introduction to Its Methodology*, 3rd edition. London: Sage.

Kunimoto, N. (2004) 'Intimate archives: Japanese-Canadian family photography, 1939–49', *Art History* 27: 129–55.

Lacan, J. (1977) *The Four Fundamental Concepts of Psychoanalysis*, translated by A. Sheridan. London: Hogarth Press.

Lalvani, S. (1996) *Photography, Vision and the Production of Modern Bodies*. Albany, NY: SUNY Press.

Langmann, S. and Pick, D. (2014) 'Dignity and ethics in research photography', *International Journal of Social Research Methodology* 17: 709–21.

Latham, A. (2003) 'Research, performance, and doing human geography: Some reflections on the diary-photograph, diary-interview method', *Environment and Planning A* 35: 1993–2017.

Latour, B. (2007) *Reassembling the Social: An Introduction to Actor-Network-Theory*, new edition. Oxford: Oxford University Press.

Leahy, H.R. (2012) *Museum Bodies: The Politics and Practices of Visiting and Viewing*. Farnham: Ashgate.

Leal, O. (1990) 'Popular taste and erudite repertoire: The place and space of television in Brazil', *Cultural Studies* 4. doi:10.1080/09502389000490021

Leavy, P. (ed) (2009) *Method Meets Art: Arts-Based Research Practice*. New York: Guilford Press.

Leiss, W., Kline, S., Jhally, S. and Botterill, J. (2005) *Social Communication in Advertising: Consumption in the Mediated Marketplace*, 3rd edition. London: Routledge.

Leszczynski, A. (2015) 'Spatial media/tion', *Progress in Human Geography,* December (10). doi: 10.1177/0309132514558443

Lewis, L.A. (2004) 'Modesty and modernity: Photography, race and representation on Mexico's Costa Chica (Guerrero)', *Identities: Global Studies in Culture and Power* 11: 471–99.

Lewis, S.C., Zamith, R. and Hermida, A. (2013) 'Content analysis in an era of big data: A hybrid approach to computational and manual methods', *Journal of Broadcasting & Electronic Media* 57: 34–52.

Lidchi, H. (1997) 'The poetics and politics of exhibiting other cultures', in S. Hall (ed.), *Representation: Cultural Representations and Signifying Practices*. London: Sage. pp. 151–222.

Liebenberg, L. (2009) 'The visual image as discussion point: Increasing validity in boundary-crossing research', *Qualitative Research* 9: 441–67.

Liggett, H. (2007) 'Urban aesthetics and the excess of fact', in L. Frers and L. Meier (eds), *Encountering Urban Places: Visual and Material Performances in the City*. Aldershot: Ashgate. pp. 9–23.

Lister, M. and Wells, L. (2001) 'Seeing beyond belief: Cultural studies as an approach to studying the visual', in T. van Leeuwen and C. Jewitt (eds), *Handbook of Visual Analysis*. London: Sage: pp. 61–91.

Livesy, R. (2004) 'Reading for character: Women social reformers and narratives of the urban poor in late Victorian and Edwardian London', *Journal of Victorian Culture* 9: 43–67.

Livingstone, S. (2005) 'Media audiences, interpreters and users', in M. Gillespie (ed.), *Media Audiences*. Maidenhead: Open University Press. pp. 9–50.

Livingstone, S. (2008) 'Taking risky opportunities in youthful content creation: Teenagers' use of social networking sites for intimacy, privacy and self-expression', *New Media and Society* 10: 393–411.

Livingstone, S. (2009) 'The challenge of changing audiences: What is the audience researcher to do in the age of the internet?', in B. Gunter and D. Machin (eds), *Media Audiences Volume 1: History of Audience Study*. London: Sage: pp. 263–71.

Livingstone, S. and R. Das (2013) 'The end of audiences?', in J. Hartley, J. Burgess and A. Bruns (eds), *A Companion To New Media Dynamics*. Chichester: Wiley-Blackwell. pp. 104–21.

Lomax, H. (2012) 'Contested voices? Methodological tensions in creative visual research with children', *International Journal of Social Research Methodology* 15: 105–17.

Lombard, M. (2013) 'Using auto-photography to understand place: Reflections from research in urban informal settlements in Mexico', *Area* 45: 23–32.

Lowe, J. (2011) 'Legal issues of using images in research', in E. Margolis and L. Pauwels (eds), *The Sage Handbook of Visual Research Methods*. London: Sage. pp. 707–22.

Luckurst, R. (2003) 'Traumaculture', *New Formations* 50: 28–47.

Luke, T.W. (2002) *Museum Politics: Power Plays at the Exhibition*. Minneapolis, MN: Minnesota University Press.

Lull, J. (1990) *Inside Family Viewing: Ethnographic Research on Television's Audiences*. London: Routledge.

Lunt, P. and Livingstone, S. (2009) 'Rethinking the focus group in media and communication research', in B. Gunter and D. Machin (eds), *Media Audiences Volume 2: Measurement of Audiences*. London: Sage. pp. 157–74.

Lurie, S. (2006) 'Falling persons and national embodiment: The reconstruction of safe spectatorship in the photographic record of 9/11', in T. Nardin and D.H. Sherman (eds), *Terror, Culture, Politics: Rethinking 9/11*. Bloomington, IN: Indiana University Press. pp. 44–68.

Lury, C. (2004) *Brands: The Logos of the Global Economy*. London: Routledge.

Lustig, S.F. (2004) 'Baby pictures: Family, consumerism and exchange among teen mothers in the USA', *Childhood* 11: 175–93.

Lutz, C.A. and Collins, J.L. (1993) *Reading National Geographic*. Chicago: University of Chicago Press.

Lyman, C.M. (1982) *The Vanishing Race and Other Illusions: Photographs of Indians by Edward S. Curtis*. Washington, DC: Smithsonian Institution.

Lyotard, J.-F. (1996) 'Les immaterieux', in R. Greenberg, B.W. Ferguson and S. Nairne (eds), *Thinking About Exhibitions*. London: Routledge. pp. 113–31.

Macdonald, S. (2002) *Behind the Scenes at the Science Museum*. Oxford: Berg.

Madianou, M. (2011) 'Beyond the presumption of identity? Ethnicities, cultures, and transnational audiences', in V. Nightingale (ed.), *The Handbook of Media Audiences*. Chichester: Wiley Blackwell. pp. 444–58.

Malefyt, T.D. (2010) 'From rational calculation to sensual experience: The marketing of emotions in advertising', in B. Moeran (ed.), *Advertising: Critical Readings, Volume 3: Communication*. Oxford, Berg. pp. 209–25.

Manghani, S. (2013) *Image Studies: Theory and Practice*. Abingdon: Routledge.

Manghani, S., Piper, A. and Simons, J. (2006) *Images: A Reader*. London: Sage.

Mannay, D. (2010) 'Making the familiar strange: Can visual research methods render the familiar setting more perceptible?', *Qualitative Research* 10: 91–111.

Mannay, D. (2016) *Visual, Narrative and Creative Research Methods: Application, Reflection and Ethics*. London: Routledge.

Manovich, L. (2001) *The Language of New Media*. Cambridge, MA: MIT Press.

Manovich, L. (2011) 'What is visualisation?', *Visual Studies* 26: 36–49.

Manovich, L. (2013) *Software Takes Command*. London: Bloomsbury.

Manovich, L. and Douglass, J. (2011) 'Visualizing change: Computer graphics as a research method', in O. Grau and T. Veigl (eds), *Imagery in the 21st Century*. London: MIT Press. pp. 315–38.

Margolis, E. and Pauwels, L. (eds) (2011) *The Sage Handbook of Visual Research Methods*. London: Sage.

Marks, L.U. (2000) *The Skin of the Film: Intercultural Cinema, Embodiment, and the Senses*. Durham, NC: Duke University Press.

Marks, L.U. (2002) *Touch: Sensuous Theory and Multisensory Media*. Minneapolis, MN: University of Minnesota Press.

Marrati, P. (2008) *Gilles Deleuze: Cinema and Philosophy*. Baltimore, MD: Johns Hopkins University Press.

Marres, N. (2012) 'The redistribution of methods: On intervention in digital social research, broadly conceived', *The Sociological Review* 60 (issue supplement S1, Live Methods): 139–65.

Marstine, J. (ed) (2011) *The Routledge Companion to Museum Ethics: Redefining Ethics for the Twenty-First Century Museum*. London: Routledge.

Martins, N., Williams, D., Harrison, K. and Ratan, R. (2009) 'A content analysis of female body imagery in video games', *Sex Roles* 61: 824–36.

Mason, J. (2006) 'Mixing methods in a qualitatively driven way', *Qualitative Research* 6: 9–25.

Matthews, H., Limb, M. and Taylor, M. (1998) 'The geography of children: Some ethical and methodological considerations for project and dissertation work', *Journal of Geography in Higher Education* 22: 311–24.

McCandless, D. (2012) *Information is Beautiful*, 2nd edition. London: Collins.

McCandless, D. (2015) http://www.informationisbeautiful.net/visualizations/what-makes-a-good-data-visualization/ (accessed May 15, 2015).

McCarthy, A. (2001) *Ambient Television: Visual Culture and Public Space*. Durham, NC: Duke University Press.

McCosker, A. and Wilken, R. (2014) 'Rethinking "big data" as visual knowledge: The sublime and the diagrammatic in data visualisation', *Visual Studies* 29: 155–64.

McLuhan, M. (1964) *Understanding Media: The Extensions of Man*. London: Routledge and Kegan Paul.

McQuail, D. (1997) *Audience Analysis*. London: Sage.

McQuire, S. (2010) 'Rethinking media events: Large screens, public space broadcasting and beyond', *New Media & Society* 12: 567–82.

McQuire, S., M. Martin, and S. Neiderer (eds) (2009) *The Urban Screens Reader*. Amsterdam: Institute of Network Cultures.

Mertens, D.M. and Ginsberg, P.E. (2009) *The Handbook of Social Research Ethics*. Thousand Oaks, CA: Sage.

Metz, C. (1975) 'The imaginary signifier', *Screen* 16, 14–75.

Michaels, E. (1995) 'The Aboriginal invention of television in Central Australia, 1982–1986', in P. D'Agostino and D. Tafler (eds), *Transmission: Toward a Post-Television Culture*. London: Sage.

Miller, D. (2011) *Tales from Facebook*. Oxford: Berg.

Millington, B. (2009) 'Wii has never been modern: "Active" video games and the "conduct of conduct"', *New Media and Society* 11: 621–40.

Milne, E.-J., Mitchell, C. and De Lange, N. (2012) *Handbook of Participatory Video*. Lanham, MD: AltaMira Press.

Mirzoeff, N. (1998) 'What is visual culture?', in N. Mirzoeff (ed.), *The Visual Culture Reader*. London: Routledge. pp. 3–13.

Mirzoeff, N. (1999) *An Introduction to Visual Culture*. London: Routledge.

Mirzoeff, N. (2005) *Watching Babylon: The War in Iraq and Global Visual Culture*. London: Routledge.

Mirzoeff, N. (2009) *An Introduction to Visual Culture*, 2nd edition. London: Routledge.

Mirzoeff, N. (2011) *The Right to Look: A Counterhistory of Visuality*. Durham, NC: Duke University Press.

Mitchell, C. (2011) *Doing Visual Research*. London: Sage.

Mitchell, H., Kearns, R. and Collins, D. (2007) 'Nuances of neighbourhood: Children's perceptions of the space between home and school in Auckland, New Zealand', *Geoforum* 38: 614–27.

Mitchell, J. (1974) *Psychoanalysis and Feminism*. London: Allen Lane.

Mitchell, J.P. (2007) *Media Violence and Christian Ethics*. Cambridge: Cambridge University Press.

Mitchell, T. (1988) *Colonising Egypt*. Cambridge: Cambridge University Press.

Mitchell, W.J.T. (1986) *Iconology: Image, Text, Ideology*. Chicago: University of Chicago Press.

Mitchell, W.J.T. (1994) *Picture Theory: Essays on Verbal and Visual Representation*. Chicago: University of Chicago Press.

Mitchell, W.J.T. (1996) 'What do pictures *really* want?', *October* 77: 71–82.

Mitchell, W.J.T. (2005a) *What Do Pictures Want? The Lives and Loves of Images*. Chicago: University of Chicago Press.

Mitchell, W.J.T. (2005b) 'There are no visual media', *Journal of Visual Culture* 4: 257–66.

Mizen, P. and Wolkowitz, C. (2012) 'Visualising changing landscapes of work and labour', *Sociological Research Online* 17: 25.

Modleski, T. (1986) 'Feminism and the power of interpretation', in T. de Lauretis (ed.), *Feminist Studies/Critical Studies*. Basingstoke: Macmillan.

Modleski, T. (1988) *The Women Who Knew Too Much: Hitchcock and Feminist Theory*. London: Methuen.

Monaco, J. (2009) *How to Read a Film: Movies, Media, Multimedia*, 30th anniversary edition. London: Oxford University Press.

Moores, S. (1993) *Interpreting Audiences: The Ethnography of Media Consumption*. London: Sage.

Moores, S. (2012) *Media, Place and Mobility*. Basingstoke: Palgrave Macmillan.

Morley, D. (1980) *The Nationwide Audience: Structure and Decoding*. London: British Film Institute.

Morley, D. (1986) *Family Television*. London: Routledge.

Morley, D. (1992) *Television, Audiences and Cultural Studies*. London: Routledge.

Morley, D. (2006) *Media, Modernity and Technology: The Geography of the New*. London: Routledge.

Morley, D. and Robins, K. (1995) *Spaces of Identity: Global Media, Electronic Landscapes and Cultural Boundaries*. London: Routledge.

Morris, M. (1988) 'Banality in cultural studies', *Discourse* 10: 3–29.

Mulvey, L. (1989) *Visual and Other Pleasures*. London: Macmillan.

Muntadas, A. (2005) 'Business as usual II ... a series of notes', in A.M. Guasch and J. Zulaika (eds), *Learning from the Bilbao Guggenheim*. Reno, NV: Center for Basque Studies, University of Nevada. pp. 125–32.

Murphy, P. D. (2011) 'Locating media ethnography', in V. Nightingale (ed.), *The Handbook of Media Audiences*. Chichester: Wiley Blackwell. pp. 380–401

Murray, L. (2009) 'Looking at and looking back: Visualization in mobile research', *Qualitative Research* 9: 469–88.

Myers, F.R. (2001) 'Introduction: The empire of things', in F.R. Myers (ed.), *The Empire of Things: Regimes of Value and Material Culture*. Oxford: James Currey. pp. 3–61.

Myers, K. (1983) 'Understanding advertisers', in H. Davis and P. Walton (eds), *Language, Image, Media*. Oxford: Blackwell. pp. 205–23.

Myrvang, B.K., Dilley, R. and Marshall, K. (2008) 'Using a head-mounted video camera to understand social worlds and experiences', *Sociological Research Online* 13. http://www.socresonline.org.uk/13/6/1.html (accessed August 27, 2015).

Nakamura, L. (2002) *Cybertypes: Race, Ethnicity, and Identity on the Internet*. London: Routledge.

Nakamura, L. (2008) *Digitizing Race: Visual Cultures of the Internet*. Minneapolis, MN: University of Minnesota Press.

Nakamura, L. (2009) 'Don't hate the player, hate the game: The racialization of labor in World of Warcraft', *Critical Studies in Media Communication* 26: 128–44.

Nakamura, L. (2014) '"I WILL DO EVERYthing that am asked": Scambaiting, digital show-space, and the racial violence of social media', *Journal of Visual Culture* 13: 257–74.

Napoli, P. (2010) 'Revisiting "mass communication" and the "work" of the audience in the new media environment', *Media, Culture and Society* 32: 505–16.

Nash, K., Hight, C. and Summerhayes, C. (eds) (2014) *New Documentary Ecologies: Emerging Platforms, Practices and Discourses*. Basingstoke: Palgrave Macmillan.

Nead, L. (1988) *Myths of Sexuality: Representations of Women in Victorian Britain*. Oxford: Blackwell.

Nead, L. (2000) *Victorian Babylon: People, Streets and Images in Nineteenth-Century London*. London: Yale University Press.

Neale, S. (1983) 'Masculinity as spectacle', *Screen* 24 (60): 2–17.

Neuendorf, K.A. (2002) *The Content Analysis Guidebook*. London: Sage.

New York Times (2014) http://www.nytimes.com/2014/11/18/science/researchers-announce-breakthrough-in-content-recognition-software.html?partner=rss&emc=rss&_r=1 (accessed September 24, 2015).

Newbury, D. (2009) *Defiant Images: Photography and Apartheid South Africa*. Pretoria: University of South Africa (UNISA) Press.

Newbury, D. (2011) 'Making arguments with images: Visual scholarship and academic publishing', in E. Margolis and L. Pauwels (eds), *The Sage Handbook of Visual Research Methods*. London: Sage. pp. 651–64.

Nightingale, V. (1996) *Studying Audiences: The Shock of the Real*. London: Routledge.

Nightingale, V. (ed) (2011) *The Handbook of Media Audiences*. Oxford: Wiley-Blackwell.

Nitsche, M. (2008) *Video Game Spaces: Image, Play, and Structure in 3D Game Worlds*. Cambridge, MA: MIT Press.

Nochlin, L. (1989) *Women, Art and Power and Other Essays*. London: Thames and Hudson.

Nutbrown, C. (2011) 'Naked by the pool? Blurring the image? Ethical issues in the portrayal of young children in arts-based educational research', *Qualitative Inquiry* 17: 3–14.

O'Connell, R. (2013) 'The use of visual methods with children in a mixed methods study of family food practices', *International Journal of Social Research Methodology* 16: 31–46.

O'Connor, P. (2007) '"Doing boy/girl" and global/local elements in 10–12 year olds' drawings and written texts', *Qualitative Research* 7: 229–47.

O'Doherty, B. (1996) 'The gallery as gesture', in R. Greenberg, B.W. Ferguson and S. Nairne (eds), *Thinking About Exhibitions*. London: Routledge. pp. 321–40.

O'Reilly, K. (2008) *Key Concepts in Ethnography*. London: Sage.

O'Toole, M. (1994) *The Language of Displayed Art*. Leicester: Leicester University Press.

Okely, J. (1994) 'Thinking through fieldwork', in A. Bryman and A. Burgess (eds), *Analyzing Qualitative Data*. London: Routledge. pp. 18–34.

Oldridge, D. (2007) 'Casting the spell of terror: The press and the early Whitechapel murders', in A. Warwick and M. Willis (eds), *Jack the Ripper: Media, Culture, History*. Manchester: Manchester University Press. pp. 46–55.

Packard, J. (2008) '"I'm gonna show you what it's really like out here": The power and limitation of participatory visual methods', *Visual Studies* 23: 63–77.

Packer, J. and Crofts Wiley, S.B. (2012) 'Introduction: The materiality of communication', in J. Packer and S. B. Crofts Wiley (eds), *Communication Matters: Materialist Approaches to Media, Mobility and Networks*. London: Routledge. pp. 3–16.

Panofsky, E. (1953) *Early Netherlandish Painting: Its Origin and Character, Volume I*. Cambridge, MA: Harvard University Press.

Panofsky, E. (1957) *Meaning in the Visual Arts*. New York: Doubleday Anchor.

Papademas, D. and International Visual Sociology Association (IVSA) (2009) 'IVSA – Code of Research Ethics and Guidelines', *Visual Studies* 24: 250–7.

Papson, S., Goldman, R. and Kersey, N. (2007) 'Website design: The precarious blend of narrative, aesthetics and social theory', in G.C. Stanczak (ed.), *Visual Research Methods: Image, Society, and Representation*. London: Sage. pp. 307–44.

Paterson, M. and Glass, M.R. (2015) 'The world through Glass: Developing novel methods with wearable computing for urban videographic research', *Journal of Geography in Higher Education* 39: 275–87.

Pauwels, L. (2010) 'Visual sociology reframed: An analytical synthesis and discussion of visual methods in social and cultural research', *Sociological Methods and Research* 38: 545–81.

Penley, C. (1991) 'Brownian motion: Women, tactics, and technology', in C. Penley and A. Ross (eds), *Technoculture*. Minneapolis, MN: University of Minnesota Press. pp. 135–62.

Phillips, N. and Hardy, C. (2002) *Discourse Analysis: Investigating Processes of Social Construction*. London: Sage.

Philo, G. and McLaughlin G. (1993) *The British Media and the Gulf War*. Glasgow: Glasgow University Media Group.

Pine, B.J. and Gilmore, J.H. (1999) *The Experience Economy: Work is Theatre and Every Business a Stage*. Boston, MA: Harvard Business School.

Pink, S. (2013) *Doing Visual Ethnography: Images, Media, and Representation in Research*, 3rd edition. London: Sage.

Pink, S. (2015) *Doing Sensory Ethnography*, 2nd edition. London: Sage.

Pink, S. (ed.) (2012) *Advances in Visual Methodology*. London: Sage.

Pink, S., Mackley, K.L. and Moroşanu, R. (2015) 'Researching in atmospheres: Video and the "feel" of the mundane', *Visual Communication* 14: 351–69.

Pinney, C. (1997) *Camera Indica: The Social Life of Indian Photographs*. London: Reaktion Books.

Pinney, C. (2003) 'Introduction: How the other half ... photography's other histories', in C. Pinney and N. Peterson (eds), *Photography's Other Histories*. Durham, NC: Duke University Press. pp. 1–14.

Pinney, C. (2004) *'Photos of the Gods': The Printed Image and Political Struggle in India*. London: Reaktion Books.

Pisters, P. (2003) *The Matrix of Visual Culture: Working with Deleuze in Film Theory*. Stanford, CA: Stanford University Press.

Pole, C.J. (2004) *Seeing Is Believing? Approaches to Visual Research*. Amsterdam: Elsevier.

Pollock, G. (1988) *Vision and Difference: Femininity, Feminism and the Histories of Art*. London: Routledge.

Pollock, G. (1992) 'Art', in E. Wright (ed.), *Feminism and Psychoanalysis: A Critical Dictionary*. Oxford: Blackwell. pp. 9–16.

Pollock, G. (1994) '"With my own eyes'": Fetishism, the labouring body and the colour of its sex', *Art History* 17: 342–82.

Pooke, G. and Newall, D. (2007) *Art History: The Basics*. London: Routledge.

Poole, D. (1997) *Vision, Race and Modernity: A Visual Economy of the Andean Image World*. Princeton, NJ: Princeton University Press.

Poole, D. (2005) '"An excess of description": Ethnography, race and visual technologies', *Annual Review of Anthropology* 34: 159–230.

Potter, J. (1996) 'Discourse analysis and constructionist approaches: Theoretical background', in J.T.E. Richardson (ed.), *Handbook of Qualitative Methods for Psychology and the Social Sciences*. Leicester: British Psychological Society. pp. 125–40.

Potter, J. and Wetherell, M. (1987) *Discourse and Social Psychology*. London: Sage.

Potter, J. and Wetherell, M. (1994) 'Analyzing discourse', in A. Bryman and R.G. Burgess (eds), *Analyzing Qualitative Data*. London: Routledge. pp. 47–66.

Pratt, M.L. (1992) *Imperial Eyes: Travel Writing and Transculturation*. London: Routledge.

Preziosi, D. and Farago, C.J. (eds) (2004) *Grasping the World: The Idea of the Museum*. Aldershot: Ashgate Press.

Prosser, J. (1998) *Image-based Research: A Sourcebook for Qualitative Researchers*. London: Falmer.

Prosser, J., Clark, A. and Wiles, R. (2008) 'Visual Research Ethics at the Crossroads', National Centre for Research Methods/Realities Working Paper. Available from http://eprints.ncrm.ac.uk/535/ (accessed August 27, 2015).

Pryce, D. (1997) 'Surveyors and surveyed: Photography out and about', in L. Wells (ed.), *Photography: A Critical Introduction*. London: Routledge. pp. 55–102.

Puwar, N. and Sharma, S. (2012) 'Curating sociology', *The Sociological Review* 60: 40–63.

Radway, J.A. (1984) *Reading the Romance: Women, Patriarchy, and Popular Literature*. Chapel Hill, NC: University of North Carolina Press.

Rajchman, J. (1988) 'Foucault's art of seeing', *October* 44: 89–117.

Ramamurthy, A. (2009) 'Spectacles and illusions: Photography and commodity culture', in L. Wells (ed.), *Photography: A Critical Introduction*. London: Routledge. pp. 231–88.

Rampley, M. (2005) *Exploring Visual Culture: Definitions, Concepts, Contexts*. Edinburgh: Edinburgh University Press.

Rasmussen, K. (2004) 'Places for children – children's places', *Childhood* 11: 155–73.

Rasmussen, K. and Smidt, S. (2003) 'Children in the neighbourhood: The neighbourhood in the children', in P. Christensen and M. O'Brien (eds), *Children in the City: Home, Neighbourhood and Community*. London: Routledge. pp. 82–100.

Reavey, P. (ed.) (2011) *Visual Methods in Psychology: Using and Interpreting Images in Qualitative Research*. London: Routledge.

Rettberg, J.W. (2014) *Seeing Ourselves Through Technology: How We Use Selfies, Blogs and Wearable Devices to See and Shape Ourselves*. Basingstoke: Palgrave Macmillan.

Reynolds, A. (1995) 'Visual stories', in L. Cooke and P. Wollen (eds), *Visual Display: Culture Beyond Appearances*. Seattle, WA: Bay Press. pp. 82–108.

Rieger, J.H. (1996) 'Photographing social change', *Visual Sociology* 11: 5–49.

Rieger, J.H. (2011) 'Rephotography for documenting social change', in E. Margolis and L. Pauwels (eds), *The Sage Handbook of Visual Research Methods*. London: Sage. pp. 132–49.

Riviere, J. (1986) 'Womanliness as masquerade', in V. Burgin, J. Donald and C. Kaplan (eds), *Formations of Fantasy*. London: Methuen. pp. 35–44.

Rizzo, T. (2012) *Deleuze and Film: A Feminist Introduction*. London: Bloomsbury.

Roberts, H.E. (ed.) (1998) *Encyclopedia of Comparative Iconography: Themes Depicted in Works of Art*, 2 vols. London: Fitzroy Dearborn.

Rodowick, D.N. (1997) *Gilles Deleuze's Time Machine*. Durham, NC: Duke University Press.

Rodowick, D.N. (2001) *Reading the Figural, or, Philosophy After the New Media*. Durham, NC: Duke University Press.

Rodowick, D.N. (2007) *The Virtual Life of Film*. Cambridge, MA: Harvard University Press.

Rodowick, D.N. (2010) *Afterimages of Gilles Deleuze's Film Philosophy*. Minneapolis, MN: University of Minnesota Press.

Rogers, R. (2013) *Digital Methods*. London: MIT Press.

Rogers, R. (2014) 'Political research in the digital age', *International Public Policy Review* 8: 73–87.

Rogers, R. (2015) 'Digital methods for web research', in R. Scott and S. Kosslyn (eds), *Emerging Trends in the Social and Behavioural Sciences*. Hoboken, NJ: John Wiley.

Rogoff, I. (1998) 'Studying visual culture', in N. Mirzoeff (ed.), *The Visual Culture Reader*. London: Routledge. pp. 14–26.

Rorty, R. (1980) *Philosophy and the Mirror of Nature*. Oxford: Blackwell.

Rose, G. (1997) 'Situating knowledges: Positionality, reflexivities and other tactics', *Progress in Human Geography* 21: 305–20.

Rose, G. (2000) 'Practising photography: An archive, a study, some photographs and a researcher', *Journal of Historical Geography* 25: 555–71.

Rose, G. (2003) 'Domestic spacings and family photography: A case study', *Transactions of the Institute of British Geographers* 28: 5–18.

Rose, G. (2004) '"Everyone's cuddled up and it just looks really nice": The emotional geography of some mums and their family photos', *Social and Cultural Geography* 5: 549–64.

Rose, G. (2005) '"You just have to make a conscious effort to keep snapping away, I think": A case study of family photos, mothering and familial space', in S. Hardy and C. Wiedmer (eds), *Motherhood and Space: Configurations of the Maternal Through Politics, Home, and the Body*. Basingstoke: Palgrave Macmillan. pp. 221–40.

Rose, G. (2009) 'Who cares for which dead and how? British newspaper reporting of the bombings in London, July 2005', *Geoforum* 40: 46–54.

Rose, G. (2010) *Doing Family Photography: The Domestic, the Public and the Politics of Sentiment*. Farnham: Ashgate.

Rose, G. (2012) 'The question of method: Practice, reflexivity and critique in visual culture studies', in I. Heywood and B. Sandywell (eds), *The Handbook of Visual Culture*. Oxford: Berg. pp. 542–58.

Rose, G. (2014) 'On the relation between "visual research methods" and contemporary visual culture', *The Sociological Review* 62: 24–46.

Rose, G., Degen, M. and Melhuish, C. (2014) 'Networks, interfaces, and computer-generated images: Learning from digital visualisations of urban redevelopment projects', *Environment and Planning D: Society and Space* 32: 386–403.

Rose, J. (1986) *Sexuality in the Field of Vision*. London: Verso.

Rose, N. (1998) *Inventing Our Selves: Psychology, Power, and Personhood*. Cambridge: Cambridge University Press.

Rose, N. (2007) *The Politics of Life Itself: Biomedicine, Power, and Subjectivity in the Twenty-First Century*. Princeton, NJ: Princeton University Press.

Rossi, M. (2010) 'Fabricating authenticity: Modeling a whale at the American Museum of Natural History, 1906–1974', *Isis* 101: 338–61.

Rothenberg, J. (2014) *Sociology Looks at the Arts*. London: Routledge.

Rothenberg, M. (2003) 'Museum politics: Power plays at the exhibition', *ISIS: Journal of the History of Science in Society* 94: 504–5.

Rowe, J. (2011) 'Legal issues of using images in research', in E. Margolis and L. Pauwels (eds), *The Sage Handbook of Visual Research Methods*. London: Sage. pp. 707–22.

Rubio, F.D. (2012) 'The material production of the spiral jetty: A study of culture in the making', *Cultural Sociology* 6: 143–61.

Rubio, F.D. and E.B. Silva (2013) 'Materials in the field: Object-trajectories and object-positions in the field of contemporary art', *Cultural Sociology* 7: 161–78.

Ruddock, A. (2007) *Investigating Audiences*. Los Angeles: Sage.

Ruppert, E., Law, J. and Savage, M. (2013) 'Reassembling social science methods: The challenge of digital devices', *Theory, Culture & Society* 30: 22–46.

Rushton, R. (2009) 'Deleuzian spectatorship', *Screen* 50: 45–53.

Ryan, J. (1997) *Visualising Empire: Geography, Empire and Photography*. London: IB Tauris.

Salah, A.A., Manovich, L., Salah, A.A. and Chow J. (2013) 'Combining cultural analytics and networks analysis: Studying a social network site with user-generated content', *Journal of Broadcasting & Electronic Media* 57: 409–26.

Savage, M. and Burrows, R. (2007) 'The coming crisis of empirical sociology', *Sociology* 41: 885–9.

Scarles, C. (2013) 'The ethics of tourist photography: Tourists' experiences of photographing locals in Peru', *Environment and Planning D: Society and Space* 31: 897–917.

Schrøder, K., Drotner, K., Kline, S. and Murray, C. (2003) *Researching Audiences: A Practical Guide to Methods in Media Audience Analysis*. London: Arnold.

Searle, A. (1999) 'Here's looking at me', *The Guardian*. Available from www.theguardian.com/culture/1999/jun/08/artsfeatures1 (accessed August 13, 2015).

Seidel, L. (1993) *Jan van Eyck's Arnolfini Portrait: Stories of an Icon*. Cambridge: Cambridge University Press.

Seko, Y. (2013) 'Picturesque wounds: A multimodal analysis of self-injury photographs on Flickr', *Forum Qualitative Sozialforschung / Forum: Qualitative Social Research* 14 (2). http://www.qualitative-research.net/index.php/fqs/article/view/1935 (accessed August 16, 2015)

Sekula, A. (1986) 'Reading an archive: Photography between labour and capital', in P. Holland, J. Spence and S. Watney (eds), *Photography/Politics: 2*. London: Comedia. pp. 153–61.

Sekula, A. (1989) 'The body and the archive', in R. Bolton (ed.), *The Contest of Meaning: Critical Histories of Photography*. London: MIT Press. pp. 342–88.

Seltzer, M. (2009) 'Parlor games: The aprioritization of the media', *Critical Inquiry* 36: 100–33.

Seppänen, J. (2006) *The Power of the Gaze: An Introduction to Visual Literacy*. New York: Lang.

Shaw, I. (2013) 'The "art object" as an epistemic process: Contesting difference in mounting an exhibition of paintings of the "Middle East"', *Journal of Material Culture* 18: 409–22.

Sheridan, J., Chamberlain, K. and Dupuis, A. (2011) 'Timelining: Visualizing experience', *Qualitative Research* 11: 552–69.

Sherman, D.J. and Rogoff, I. (1994) *Museum Culture: Histories, Discourses, Spectacles*. London: Routledge.

Sherratt. T. (2011) *The Real Face of White Australia*. http://invisibleaustralians.org/blog/2011/09/the-real-face-of-white-australia/ (accessed August 22, 2015).

Shildrick, M. (2005) 'Beyond the body of bioethics: Challenging the conventions', in M. Shildrick and R. Mykitiuk (eds), *Ethics of the Body: Postconventional Challenges*. London: MIT Press. pp. 1–18.

Shohat, E. and Stam, R. (1998) 'Narrativizing visual culture: Towards a polycentric aesthetic', in N. Mirzoeff (ed.), *The Visual Culture Reader*. London: Routledge. pp. 27–49.

Short, H. and Deegan, M. (2005) 'ICT as a research method', in G. Griffin (ed.), *Research Methods for English Studies*. Edinburgh: Edinburgh University Press. pp. 213–29.

Sicart, M. (2009) *The Ethics of Computer Games*. Cambridge, MA: MIT Press.

Signs (2002) 'Roundtable: Gender and September 11', *Signs* 28: 431–95.

Silverman, K. (1988) *The Acoustic Mirror: The Female Voice in Psychoanalysis and Cinema*. Bloomington, IN: Indiana University Press.

Silverman, K. (1992) *Male Subjectivity at the Margins*. London: Routledge.

Silverman, K. (1996) *The Threshold of the Visible World*. London: Routledge.

Silverstone, R. (1994) *Television and Everyday Life*. London: Routledge.

Silverstone, R. (2007) *Media and Morality: On the Rise of the Mediapolis*. Cambridge: Polity Press.

Silverstone, R., Hirsch, E. and Morley, D. (1991) 'Listening to a long conversation: An ethnographic approach to the study of information and communication technologies in the home', *Cultural Studies* 5: 204–27.

Simpson, P. (2012) 'Apprehending everyday rhythms: Rhythmanalysis, time-lapse photography, and the space-times of street performance', *Cultural Geographies* 19: 423–45.

Slater, D. (1983) 'Marketing mass photography', in H. Davis and P. Walton (eds), *Language, Image, Media*. Oxford: Blackwell. pp. 245–63.

Slater, D. (1995) 'Photography and modern vision: The spectacle of "natural magic"', in C. Jenks (ed.), *Visual Culture*. London: Routledge. pp. 218–37.

Slater, D. (1998) 'Analysing cultural objects: Content analysis and semiotics', in C. Seale (ed.), *Researching Society and Culture*. London: Sage. pp. 233–44.

Smith, L. (1998) *The Politics of Focus: Women, Children and Nineteenth-Century Photography*. Manchester: Manchester University Press.

Sontag, S. (1979) *On Photography*. Harmondsworth: Penguin.

Spencer, S. (2011) *Visual Research Methods in the Social Sciences: Awakening Visions*. London: Routledge.

Spurgeon, C. (2008) *Advertising and New Media*. London: Routledge.

Srinivas, L. (2002) 'The active audience: Spectatorship, social relations and the experience of cinema in India', *Media, Culture & Society* 24: 155–73.

Stafford, B.M. (1991) *Body Criticism: Imaging the Unseen in Enlightenment Art and Science*. London: MIT Press.

Staiger, J. (2005) *Media Reception Studies*. New York: New York University Press.

Stanczak, G.C. (2007) *Visual Research Methods: Image, Society, and Representation*. London: Sage.

Starn, R. (2005) 'A historian's brief guide to new museum studies', *American Historical Review* 110: 68–98.

Steedman, C. (2005) 'Archival methods', in G. Griffin (ed.), *Research Methods for English Studies*. Edinburgh: Edinburgh University Press. pp. 17–30.

Stenglin, M. (2014) 'Space and communication in exhibitions', in C. Jewitt (ed.), *The Routledge Handbook of Multimodal Analysis*, 2nd edition. London: Routledge. pp. 419–30.

Steyerl, H. (2012) *The Wretched of the Screen*. Berlin: Sternberg Press.

Strauss, A. and Corbin, J. (2008) *Basics of Qualitative Research: Techniques and Procedures for Developing Grounded Theory*, 3rd edition. London: Sage.

Stubblefield, T. (2015) *9/11 and the Visual Culture of Disaster*. Bloomington, IN: Indiana University Press.

Sturken, M. and Cartwright, L. (2009) *Practices of Looking: An Introduction to Visual Culture*, 2nd edition. Oxford: Oxford University Press.

Suchar, C. (1997) 'Grounding visual sociology in shooting scripts', *Qualitative Sociology* 20: 33–55.

Suchar, C. (2004) 'Amsterdam and Chicago: Seeing the macro-characteristics of gentrification', in C. Knowles and J. Sweetman (eds), *Picturing the Social Landscape: Visual Methods and the Sociological Imagination*. London: Routledge. pp. 147–65.

Suchar, C.S. (2006) 'The physical transformations of Metropolitan Chicago: Chicago's central area', in J.P. Koval, M. Bennet, M.I.J. Bennet, F. Demissie, R. Garner and K. Kim (eds), *The New Chicago: A Social and Cultural Analysis*. Philadelphia, PA: Temple University Press. pp. 56–76.

Sunderland, J. (2004) *Gendered Discourses*. Basingstoke: Palgrave Macmillan.

Sweetman, P. (2009) 'Revealing habitus, illuminating practice: Bourdieu, photography and visual methods', *Sociological Review* 57: 491–511.

Tagg, J. (1988) *The Burden of Representation: Essays on Photographies and Histories*. London: Macmillan.

Tagg, J. (2009) *The Disciplinary Frame: Photographic Truths and the Capture of Meaning*. Minneapolis, MN: University of Minnesota Press.

Taylor, J.C. (1957) *Learning to Look: A Handbook for the Visual Arts*. Chicago: University of Chicago Press.

Taylor, L. (2008) *A Taste for Gardening: Classed and Gendered Practices*. Aldershot: Ashgate.

Theron, L., Mitchell, C. and Smith, A. (eds) (2011) *Picturing Research: Drawing as Visual Methodology*. Rotterdam: Sense Publishers.

Thieme, S. (2012) '"Action": Publishing research results in film', *Forum Qualitative Sozialforschung / Forum: Qualitative Social Research*, 13. http://www.qualitative-research.net/index.php/fqs/article/view/1671 (accessed August 25, 2015).

Thomas, N. (1991) *Entangled Objects: Exchange, Material Culture and Colonialism in the Pacific*. London: Harvard University Press.

Thomas, N. (1999) *Possessions: Indigenous Art/Colonial Culture*. London: Thames and Hudson.

Thomson, P. (2008) *Doing Visual Research with Children and Young People*. London: Routledge.

Thomson, R. and Holland, J. (2005) '"Thanks for the memory": Memory books as a methodological resource in biographical research', *Qualitative Research* 5: 201–19.

Thornham, S. (1997) *Passionate Detachments: An Introduction to Feminist Film Theory*. London: Arnold.

Thornton, S. (2008) *Seven Days in the Art World*. London: Granta.

Thrift, N. (2008) *Non-Representational Theory: Space Politics Affect*. Abingdon: Routledge.

Thurlow, C. and Thurlow, M. (2013) *Making Short Films: The Complete Guide from Script to Screen*, 3rd edition London: Bloomsbury.

Tickner, J.A. (2002) 'Feminist perspectives on 9/11', *International Studies Perspectives* 3: 333–50.

Tilley, L. and Woodthorpe, K. (2011) 'Is it the end for anonymity as we know it? A critical examination of the ethical principle of anonymity in the context of 21st century demands on the qualitative researcher', *Qualitative Research* 11: 197–212.

Tinkler, P. (2012) *Using Photographs in Social and Historical Research*. London: Sage.

Tonkiss, F. (1998) 'Analysing discourse', in C. Seale (ed.), *Researching Society and Culture*. London: Sage. pp. 245–60.

Tufte, E.R. (1991) *Envisioning Information*, revised edition. Cheshire, CT: Graphics Press.

Tufte, E.R. (2001) *The Visual Display of Quantitative Information*, 2nd edition. Cheshire, CT: Graphics Press.

Tulloch, J. (2000) *Watching Television Audiences: Cultural Theories and Methods*. London: Arnold.

Uricchio, W. (2011) 'The algorithmic turn: Photosynth, augmented reality and the changing implications of the image', *Visual Studies* 26: 25–35.

Uricchio, W. (2014) 'History and its shadow: Thinking about the contours of absence in the construction of media history', *Screen* 55: 119–27.

Urry, J. (1990) *The Tourist Gaze: Leisure and Travel in Contemporary Societies*. London: Sage.

van Dijck, J. (2009) 'Users like you? Theorizing agency in user-generated content', *Media, Culture & Society* 31: 41–58.

van Dijck, J. (2010) 'Search engines and the production of academic knowledge', *International Journal of Cultural Studies* 13: 574–92.

van Eck, C. and Winters, E. (2005) 'Introduction', in C. van Eck and E. Winters (eds), *Dealing with the Visual: Art History, Aesthetics and Visual Culture*. Aldershot: Ashgate. pp. 1–13.

van Leeuwen, T. (2001) 'Semiotics and iconography', in T. van Leeuwen and C. Jewitt (eds), *Handbook of Visual Analysis*. London: Sage. pp. 92–118.

van Leeuwen, T. (2005) *Introducing Social Semiotics*. London: Routledge.

van Leeuwen, T. and C. Jewitt (eds) (2001) *The Handbook Of Visual Analysis*. London: Sage.

van Straten, R. (1994) *An Introduction to Iconography*, translated by P. de Man. Reading: Gordon and Breach.

Vergo, P. (ed.) (1989) *The New Museology*. London: Reaktion.

Verhoeff, N. (2012) *Mobile Screens: The Visual Regime of Navigation*. Amsterdam: Amsterdam University Press.

Vernallis, C. (2013) *Unruly Media: YouTube, Music Video, and the New Digital Cinema*. New York: Oxford University Press.

Virilio, P. (1994) *The Vision Machine*. London: British Film Institute.

Wagner, J. (2007) 'Observing culture and social life: Documentary photography, fieldwork, and social research', in G.C. Stanczak (ed.), *Visual Research Methods: Image, Society, and Representation*. London: Sage. pp. 23–60.

Walkerdine, V. (1990) *Schoolgirl Fictions*. London: Verso.

Walkowitz, J. (1992) *City of Dreadful Delight: Narratives of Sexual Danger in Late-Victorian London*. London: Virago.

Wallace, D. (2010) 'Words as key to the image bank', in C. Bailey and H. Gardiner (eds), *Revisualizing Visual Culture: Digital Research in the Arts and Humanities*. Farnham: Ashgate. pp. 83–96.

Wang, C. (1999) 'Photovoice: A participatory action research strategy applied to women's health', *Journal Of Women's Health* 8: 185–92.

Wang, C. and M. Burris (1997) 'Photovoice: Concept, methodology, and use for participatory needs assessment', *Health Education & Behavior* 24: 369–87.

Warren, S. (2002) 'Show me how it feels to work here', *Ephemera: Critical Dialogues on Organisation* 2: 224–65.

Warwick, A. and Willis, M. (eds) (2007) *Jack the Ripper: Media, Culture, History*. Manchester: Manchester University Press.

Washor, E., Mojkowski, C. and Newsom, L. (2009) 'At the core of the Apple store: Images of next generation learning', *Phi Delta Kappa* 91: 60–3.

Waterfield, G. (1991) *Palaces of Art: Art Galleries in Britain, 1790–1990*. London: Dulwich Picture Gallery.

Weber, R.P. (1990) *Basic Content Analysis*. London: Sage.

Weller, K., Bruns, A., Burgess, J., Mahrt, M. and Puschmann, C. (eds) (2013) *Twitter and Society*. New York: Peter Lang.

Wells, L. (1992) 'Judith Williamson, *Decoding Advertisements*', in M. Barker and A. Beezer (eds), *Reading into Cultural Studies*. London: Routledge. pp. 165–80.

Wells, L. (ed.) (2009) *Photography: A Critical Introduction*, 4th edition. London: Routledge.

Westerbeck, C. and Meyerowitz, J. (1994) *Bystander: A History of Street Photography*. London: Thames and Hudson.

White, A., Bushin, N., Carpena-Mendez, F. and Ni Laoire, C. (2010) 'Using visual methodologies to explore contemporary Irish childhoods', *Qualitative Research* 10: 143–58.

White, P. (1995) 'Governing lesbian desire: *Nocturne*'s Oedipal fantasy', in L. Pietropaulo and A. Testaferri (eds), *Feminisms in the Cinema*. Bloomington, IN: Indiana University Press. pp. 86–105.

Wiles, R., Clark, A. and Prosser, J. (2011) 'Visual research ethics at the crossroads', in E. Margolis and L. Pauwels (eds), *The Sage Handbook of Visual Research Methods*. London: Sage. pp. 685–706.

Wiles, R., Coffey, A., Robinson, J. and Heath, S. (2012) Anonymisation and visual images: Issues of respect, "voice" and protection', *International Journal of Social Research Methodology* 15: 41–53.

Willett, R. (2009) 'Always on: Cameraphones, video production and identity', in D. Buckingham and R. Willett (eds), *Video Cultures: Media Technology and Everyday Creativity*. Basingstoke: Palgrave Macmillan. pp. 210–29.

Williams, R. (1976) *Keywords: A Vocabulary of Culture and Society*. London: Croom Helm.

Williamson, J.E. (1978) *Decoding Advertisements: Ideology and Meaning in Advertising*. London: Marion Boyars.

Wollen, P. (1970) *Signs and Meaning in Cinema*. London: British Film Institute and Thames and Hudson.

Woodward, S. (2008) 'Digital photography and research relationships: Capturing the moment', *Sociology* 42: 857–72.

Wright, C.Y., Darko, N., Standen, P. and Patel, T.G. (2010) 'Visual research methods: Using cameras to empower socially excluded black youth', *Sociology* 44: 541–58.

Young, I.M. (2003) 'The logic of masculinist protection: Reflections on the current security state', *Signs* 29: 1–25.

Young, L. (1996) *Fear of the Dark: 'Race', Gender and Sexuality in the Cinema*. London: Routledge.

Young, L. and Barrett, H. (2001) 'Adapting visual methods: Action research with Kampala street children', *Area* 33: 141–52.

Žižek, S. (2002) *Welcome to the Desert of the Real! Five Essays on September 11*. London: Verso.

Žižek, S. (ed.) (2010) *Everything You Always Wanted to Know about Lacan (But Were Afraid to Ask Hitchcock)*, updated edition. London: Verso.

KEY TERMS

NAME INDEX

NOTE: page numbers in *italic type* refer to figures.

SUBJECT INDEX

NOTE: Page numbers in *italic type* refer to figures and tables.